Spectrum Guide to
ZIMBABWE

MPC

Spectrum Guide to Zimbabwe

First published 1991 by
Moorland Publishing Co. Ltd.,
Moor Farm Road,
Airfield Estate,
Ashbourne,
Derbyshire DE6 1HD,
England

© 1991 Camerapix

ISBN 0 86190 404 4

This book was designed and produced by
Camerapix Publishers International,
P.O. Box 45048,
Nairobi, Kenya

The **Spectrum Guides** series provide a comprehensive and detailed description of each country they cover together with all the essential data that tourists, business visitors, or potential investors are likely to require.

Publisher and Chief Executive:
Mohamed Amin
Editorial Director: Brian Tetley
Picture Editor: Duncan Willetts
International Projects Director:
Debbie Gaiger
Editor: Catie Lott
Associate Editor: Dick Pitman
Production Editors: Jennifer Trenholm and
Sally McFall
Editorial Assistant: Mary-Anne Muiruri
Typesetting: Kimberly Davis
Photographic research: Abdul Rehman
Design Consultant: Craig Dodd

Printed and bound in Hong Kong.

Editorial Board

Spectrum Guide to Zimbabwe is the latest in the acclaimed series of high-quality, lavishly and colourfully illustrated international *Spectrum Guides* to exotic and exciting countries, cultures, flora, and fauna.

One of the most spectacular tourist destinations in the world, Zimbabwe constantly invites superlatives. Yet until this book — the product of months of work by a dedicated team of writers and researchers in the *Spectrum Guides* editorial office and in the field in Zimbabwe — there were few, if any, comprehensive guides to its many attractions.

All the pictures are from the cameras of *Spectrum Guides* Publisher and Chief Executive **Mohamed Amin** and his colleague, **Duncan Willetts**, who is equally renowned for his superb photography. Zimbabwe, with its mountains, forests, lakes, rivers, and game-filled savannah plains, has long been one of their favourite countries, adding both inspiration and challenge to their outstanding photographic skills.

Amin led the drive to complete *Spectrum Guide to Zimbabwe* on schedule and with International Projects Director British-born **Debbie Gaiger** was responsible for the complex liaison and logistics.

Working closely together, *Spectrum Guides* Editorial Director **Brian Tetley**, Editor **Catie Lott**, and Associate Editor **Dick Pitman**, laboured long and hard to produce a fascinating, in-depth, and readable guide book.

Tetley, an English-born Kenyan, contributed most of the text by researching and writing Parts One to Three and specialist sections of Part Four, while Pitman, a Zimbabwean author and noted natural historian and conservationist, verified facts and distances, and provided much general information as well as authoritative contributions about wildlife, birds, and flora.

Catie Lott, who edited the text, also undertook responsibility along with American **Sally McFall** for maintaining *Spectrum Guides'* in-house style.

Working as Production Editor, **Jennifer Trenholm** organized and compiled volu-minous details and directories for Part Five, In Brief, and Listings, including the comprehensive Gazetteer. Design was by **Craig Dodd**, one of Europe's leading graphic designers, while Kenyan **Abdul Rehman** oversaw photographic research.

Editorial assistant Kenyan **Mary-Anne Muiruri** worked long hours coordinating the preparation of manuscripts for typesetting, which was carried out by another American, **Kimberly Davis.**

Above: One of the many colourful species of aloe found in Zimbabwe.

TABLE OF CONTENTS

Half-title: Soapstone sculpture of Zimbabwe Bird. Title: Hippo on sandbank at Mana Pools. Overleaf: Victoria Falls World Heritage Site. Pages 10–11: Harare skyline with Harare Gardens in right foreground. Page 12: Poinsettia in bloom.

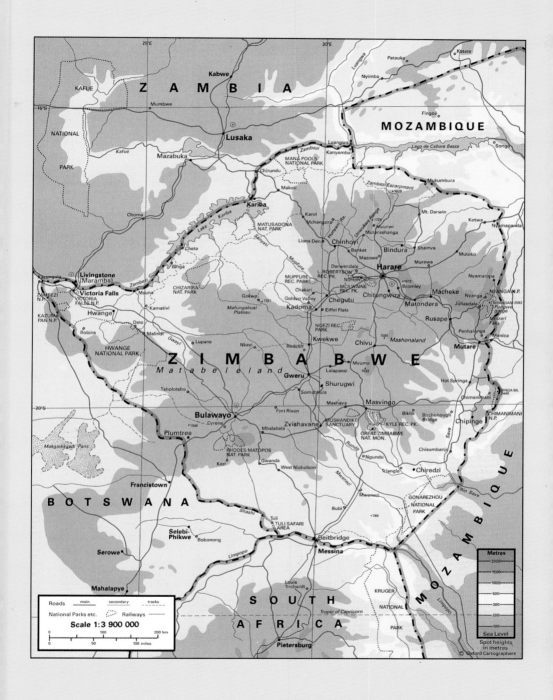

MOZAMBIQUE

ZAMBIA

Kabwe

Petauke
Katete

Luangwa

Nyimba

Fingoè

Songo

KAFUE

Mumbwa

16°S
25°E
30°E

NATIONAL

Lusaka
Kafue

Lago de Cabora Bassa

Luangwa

Mukumbura

Mazabuka

Zambezi
Kanyemba

Mt. Darwin

Kotwa
Nyamapanda

PARK

Chirundu

MAN & POOLS
NATIONAL PARK

Makuti

Zambezi Escarpment
•1628

Choma

Chete

Karoi

Mchangura

Hurngwe

Umniwkwe Range
•1729

Mvurwi
Muterashanga

Shamva
Mutoko

Kariba
MATUSADONA
NAT. PARK

Lions Den
Chinhoyi
Banket
Mazowe

Murewa

Karkba
Lake

Sinyati

Mhutire

Darwendale
L. ROBERTSON

Nyamaropa

Binga

Gokwe

Chakari

MUPFURE
REC. PK.
MCILWAINE
REC. PK.

Harare
•1613
Bromley

Macheke
Nyanga
NYANGA W.P.
•2592
Pungwe
gorge

CHIZARIRA
NAT. PARK

•1321

Golden Valley
Chegutu
Chitungwiza
Marondera

Juliasdale
Mtarazi
Falls

Livingstone
(Marambal)

Zambezi

Msuna

Mafungabusi
Plateau

Kadoma

Eiffel Flats

Rusape
Penhalonga
Manica

Victoria Falls
VICTORIA
FALLS N.P.

Kamativi

NGEZI REC.
PARK

•1580

Mashonaland

Mutare

ZAMBULA
N.P.

Hwange

Dete

Malindi

Gwayi

Nkayi

Redcliff
Kwekwe
Chivu

Hot Springs

KAZUMA
PAN N.P.

Robins

Lupane

ZIMBABWE

•1533

Chimanimani

Matabeleland

Mvuma

BINGA Mt.
•2440

HWANGE
NATIONAL PARK

Gweru
Shurugwi

Lalapansi

CHIMANIMANI
N.P.

20°S

Tsholotsho

Somabhula
Mashava

Masvingo

Bikita
Birchenough
Bridge

Chipinge

Bulawayo
Cyrene
Fort Rixon

Mbalabala
Zvishavane
MUSHANDIKE
SANCTUARY

KYLE REC. PK.

GREAT ZIMBABWE
NAT. MON.

Chisumbanje

Plumtree

•1346

RHODES MATOPOS
NAT. PARK

Kezi

Gwanda

West Nicholson

Ngundu

Runde

Mwenezi

Triangle
•Chiredzi

Makgadikgadi Pans

Francistown

Shashi

Tuli

TULI SAFARI
AREA

Bubi
•789

GONAREZHOU
NATIONAL
PARK

BOTSWANA

Selebi-
Phikwe
Bobonong

Limpopo

Beitbridge

Mwenezi

Messina

Rio Save

MOZAMBIQUE

Serowe

Louis
Trichardt

KRUGER

Mahalapye

SOUTH

NATIONAL

Limpopo

Tropic of Capricorn

AFRICA
PARK

Pietersburg

Roads   main   secondary   tracks
National Parks etc.   Railways
Scale 1:3 900 000

0   100   200 km
0   50   100 miles

Metres
2000
1500
1000
500
300
200
100
Sea Level
Spot heights
in metres

13

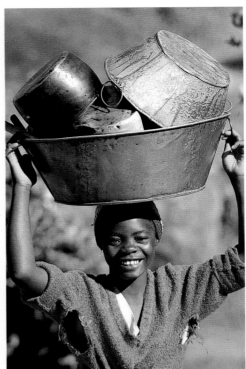

The Zimbabwe Experience

Sundown over the drowned forests of Lake Kariba fulfils the expectations that Zimbabwe has always promised to romantics and adventurers. The country's crimson sunset beauty reflects the shadows and images of those long-gone days when great civilizations held sway over this land — civilizations of such power, sophistication, and riches that they gave rise to legends that stirred imaginations around the world.

Born many millions of centuries ago, Zimbabwe wears its age gracefully. This ancient land, whose rocks are among Planet Earth's oldest, is also one of its youngest nations. It celebrated its tenth birthday in 1990 and continues to rejoice in its youth.

Despite Zimbabwe's immaturity as a nation, it offers many age-old attractions. The country's tawny deserts are filled with elephant and lion — and antelope, buffalo, rhino, and myriad other creatures continue to roam its savannah plains as they have done for thousands of years.

Among its craggy peaks and hidden valleys are thickly forested escarpments and rolling moorlands, cascading falls, and bright, capricious streams.

The sweltering, humid lowlands now yield rich harvests of sugarcane and fruit, and Zimbabwe's fertile highveld soils conceal a treasury of mineral wealth unequalled by all but two or three other countries.

But Zimbabwe's most important treasure lies in its great wilderness areas. Almost 50,000 square kilometres (20,000 square miles) — thirteen per cent of Zimbabwe's total land area — is preserved as a wildlife estate without equal.

These spectacular landscapes, teeming with a rich array of unique African wildlife and flora, dominate the country. It remains much the same as it did before the first Bantu migrations into the land of the "San" began at least a thousand years or more ago.

Man has added to the wonders of this natural paradise: magnificent Lake Kariba, the largest of its many man-made lakes, is an incredible inland sea raised from the waters of the mighty Zambezi that flow from the unforgettable Victoria Falls — one of the greatest physical spectacles in Africa.

Kariba Dam was built during the 1950s, upstream from a deep gorge only half a kilometre wide in the north-east corner of the Zambezi Valley. Now, where once there was only a narrow river gorge, the cool waters of a new African lake spread out over more than 5,000 square kilometres (2,000 square miles) of once parched earth.

Long and slender, stretching almost 300 kilometres (186 miles) from south-west to north-east, Lake Kariba is more than forty kilometres (25 miles) across at its widest.

If nature and man combined to transform the landscape, it is man alone who has endowed Zimbabwe with its enduring legacy of art and cultures. This rich heritage can be seen in rock paintings and engravings etched during the last 20,000 years on the walls of granite cliffs and caves; the cities and fortresses designed systematically a thousand years ago by the ancient civilization of Great Zimbabwe; and in a treasury of stone sculpture that belongs solely to the twentieth century.

It was also man who built the clean and spacious towns and cities, with their wide streets shaded by jacaranda and flamboyants and lined with bougainvillaea, which seem to belong exclusively to the twenty-first century.

Man once again was the driving force that ploughed and watered the highveld and the middleveld, then watched the land burgeon with prairies of wheat and maize, plantations of sugarcane and tobacco, meadows of fruit and flowers, and highland slopes of tea bushes and coffee trees.

Finally, it was man who tapped Zimbabwe's rivers for power to fuel his industries and dug from this remarkable country such mineral treasures as gold, silver, platinum, emeralds, diamonds, copper, iron, lead, and coal to develop his economy.

Opposite top left: Tonga woman smokes traditional pipe. Opposite top: Smiling Shona girl hurries washing-up to the river. Opposite left: Respected elder of the Shona people. Opposite: Tonga youngster.

Above: Elephants in Lake Kariba area

Yet never were nature and man more in harmony. All across Zimbabwe, interspersed between man's sturdy and sometimes scouring handiwork, are pristine wildernesses, botanical and bird reserves, forest sanctuaries, lakes that serve as fisheries and leisure playgrounds, and superb rock climbs in dramatic mountain ranges. Blue-water lakes, great savannah plains, forested hills, and vibrant modern cities make Zimbabwe a land of stunning contrasts and endless delights.

There, in the heart of Africa, this new nation clings to the fabric of a turbulent, romantic, and fabled history stretching back thousands of years, its cultures and landscapes melding into a timeless mosaic that is both ancient and modern.

Together the old and new of Zimbabwe proclaim their unity and celebrate their freedom with a joyful smile for all visitors.

Welcome.

Travel Brief and Social Advisory

Some do's and don'ts to make your visit more enjoyable.

Unspoilt splendour

Africa still has plenty of wildlife but the plains on which it flourishes are often inaccessible and inhospitable — two things you cannot say about modern Zimbabwe.

Its wildlife sanctuaries are easily reached and the abundant game is spectacularly visible. Together with Zimbabwe's botanical and nature reserves they are models of ecological management and conservation. The tourist infrastructure matches the promise of its magnificent landscapes and prolific wildlife.

Zimbabwe offers the widest range of accommodation found anywhere on the continent. From superb luxurious international hotels, complete with casinos, to self-service cottages and caravan parks, Zimbabwe provides comfort for every kind of visitor — be they a budget-conscious backpacker or a no-expense-spared executive.

Everywhere you go the amenities of western living are readily available: telecommunications, health services, and frequent road, rail, and air links.

All this makes Zimbabwe a tourist destination unmatched in southern and central Africa (and indeed most of Africa), for while ever close to creature comforts and modern civilization you are never far from the untamed wilderness in all its unspoilt and often ferocious splendour.

Getting There

Air Zimbabwe flies direct from London four times a week; direct from Frankfurt twice a week; direct from Athens and Larnaca, Cyprus, once a week. British Airways flies direct from London three times a week; Lufthansa direct from Frankfurt twice a week; Qantas from Sydney via Perth twice a week; Balkan (Bulgarian) Airlines direct from Sofia once a week; and TAP (Air Portugal) direct from Lisbon once a week.

Air Zimbabwe flies direct daily from Johannesburg; from Nairobi three times a week; from Lusaka, Zambia, three times a week; from Lilongwe, Malawi, three times a week; from Gaborone, Botswana, once a week; from Dar es Salaam, Tanzania, once a week; from Maputo once a week; and from Manzini, Swaziland, once a week.

South African Airways flies direct from Johannesburg daily; Air Malawi direct from Lilongwe four times a week; Ethiopian Airlines direct from Addis Ababa twice a week; Kenya Airways direct from Nairobi twice a week; Air Mauritius direct from Mauritius once a week; Air Tanzania direct from Dar es Salaam once a week; Ghana Airways direct from Accra once a week; and LAM (Mozambique Airlines) direct from Maputo once a week.

Landlocked Zimbabwe can also be reached on all sides by road and rail. There are border posts at Beitbridge, Plumtree, Chirundu, Victoria Falls, Kazungula, Mpadamatenga, Mutare, Nyamapanda, and Kariba. Only Beitbridge and Plumtree are open throughout the whole day. The others operate limited hours and some are closed during weekends.

Arrival formalities are kept to a minimum. Citizens of the USA, Britain and most Commonwealth countries are issued with visas on arrival. All that is required is a valid passport, a return ticket (or sufficient money to buy one), and sufficient funds to cover your stay.

Citizens of most other countries must obtain visas in advance of their visit.

If you have any doubts about your visa requirements, check with the nearest Zimbabwe consulate, travel office, or through your travel agent. Visas are issued on arrival and the usual duty-free allowances of liquor, tobacco, and perfume are observed. You cannot import firearms.

Getting Around

By Road

Zimbabwe's ordinance maps, obtainable from

the Department of the Surveyor-General in Harare, are excellent and kept constantly updated. You can obtain maps of the whole country, specific regions, and street maps of the major towns and cities.

The Automobile Association of Zimbabwe also produces an excellent map detailing all major roads and distances between major centres, so finding your way around the country should present no problem at all.

Driving in Zimbabwe is enjoyable. In 1990 more than 5,000 kilometres (3,000 miles) of superbly maintained trunk roads linked all the major centres with the main tourist resorts. Secondary roads are excellent, too, and signposting is frequent and includes clear, precise distances.

Along the main routes a distance marker is placed every kilometre on either side of the road, so whichever direction you travel you will know how far you have gone and how far you have to go.

This guide gives approximate distances in miles and kilometres, verified by the Automobile Association of Zimbabwe.

Wherever your destination may be, you are generally never far from contact with people or communication systems. The sense of isolation — and therefore sometimes despair — that you might experience in Africa's wilder destinations is something you never need to fear.

Driving is on the left. If you have a recognised and valid licence you can drive for up to ninety days without applying for an international or Zimbabwe licence.

Generally the standard of driving reflects the quality of the roads: well-disciplined with strict enforcement of traffic laws. Do remember, however, that for off-the-road driving on game sanctuary trails and in extremely remote areas, four-wheel drive is the most suitable, particularly during or just after the rains.

Most tour groups travel with experienced drivers in the privacy and comfort of well-maintained minibuses or in large, comfortable motorcoaches.

For the independent traveller major towns are linked by frequent and — by western standards—extremely cheap scheduled luxury coach and bus services. And, joy of joys, all licensed city and town taxis have meters. The rates are very reasonable.

By air

Zimbabwe has a well-developed domestic air network. The principal carrier is the national airline, Air Zimbabwe, which operates daily flights between Harare and the major commercial and tourist centres with its fleet of 737s. It also operates a daily "bus" service with a modern BAe 146 four-engine jet that links Harare with Hwange, Victoria Falls, and Kariba.

The biggest independent charter operator is the United Touring Company's subsidiary, United Air Charters, which operates a large fleet of small, modern single- and twin-engine aircraft out of Harare, Kariba, and Victoria Falls. Constant demand for the twenty-minute "Flight of Angels" over Victoria Falls keeps these flights operating virtually non-stop throughout the day.

By Train

Zimbabwe maintains more than 3,300 kilometres (2,000 miles) of railway track that is considered the core of the massive southern and central African rail network that links Zimbabwe to the countries of Botswana, South Africa, Mozambique, Zambia, and Zaire. Today the only regular passenger services that operate are between Botswana, South Africa, Mozambique, and Zambia.

Zimbabwe National Railways operates a large fleet of electric, diesel, and steam locomotives with frequent domestic passenger services to all major commercial centres and some tourist resorts, notably Victoria Falls.

Although electric locomotives haul freight between Gweru and Harare, and diesels operate over the rest of the system, Zimbabwe still has one of the largest surviving steam networks in the world.

The luxurious week-long steam safaris to places like Victoria Falls are a joy for railway enthusiasts. In their majesty, the giant veteran Garratt steam locomotives that roar along the edge of Hwange National Park match the elephant herds browsing by the line.

Opposite: Sunlit Tessa Falls in the Chimanimani Mountains.

Above: Air Zimbabwe Boeing 707 at Harare International Airport

Accommodation is excellent — on the Steam Safari excursions through Hwange National Park to Victoria Falls, run by a private operator in conjunction with the National Railways of Zimbabwe, opulent is the word — and the fares reasonable.

By Foot

There is little need to explore Zimbabwe on foot, although the walking safaris offered by many tour operators in Zimbabwe are a superb experience. The Eastern Highlands also offer some of the finest, most rewarding, and exhilarating trekking country in Africa.

The People

Zimbabweans are friendly and courteous and years "under the yoke" have done nothing to dispel their bubbling sense of good fun married to a strong streak of pragmatism.

A great many speak English — some much better than the native Anglo-Saxon — which is the official language. The two majority tongues are Shona and Sindebele.

Of Bantu stock, the Shona and Ndebele (whose martial history is that of the Zulu) share many cultural similarities, including their magnificent warrior dances and shining pride in their homesteads. The two cultures also possess an innate aesthetic instinct that has taken root and been given expression in the carving of the late twentieth-century's most prized stone sculptures.

Most noticeable to visitors from African or Asian countries will be the Zimbabwean commitment to civic pride and public well-being. There can be few more orderly communities than those you find in Zimbabwe, where queue-jumpers, jaywalkers, and litter-louts provoke glares of disgust and contempt. The people have a strong sense of civility and a marked respect for their fellow man (and woman) that might be considered old-fashioned anywhere else these days.

The police, modelled in the British mould, are smart, disciplined, courteous, and always helpful to visitors in need of direction or advice.

In recent years a number of beggars have begun to take up positions in the main shopping centres, but not to the extent found in most other African countries.

Although there is an air of cooperation and amicability (and the past if not forgotten is

Above: Zebra enjoys dust bath in a national park.

forgiven) the European and African communities tend to maintain the social barriers that divided them for so long. With a growing population Zimbabwe is short of jobs for school leavers. Despite this the quality of life for many is distinctly higher than almost any other country on the continent.

The more well-to-do generally practice a life style that has few, if any, equals. The roads leading out of towns and cities during weekends are crowded with modern cars almost inevitably towing a trailer mounted with a dinghy, yacht, or powerboat as everybody heads off for a few days in the sun.

As in most developing countries, the head of state commands a great deal more respect than leaders in the west; an attitude particularly inherent in African cultures.

Although strongly conservative in attitudes, social habits, and dress, there remains a remarkable air of freedom about this newly-independent society. Zimbabweans speak their mind easily on what they consider are the ills affecting their country. Remember, however, that they are proud of their homeland — and their hard-won independence. Provocative remarks and glib comparisons only serve to wound and alienate.

Whatever Zimbabwe's shortcomings, for a nation only ten years old it has a remarkable record of positive achievements in human relations and in social and economic development.

Safety

While Zimbabwe is a law-abiding nation, crime does exist. It is, however, much better policed than most other African countries and developing nations in Asia, and visitors observing sensible precautions will enjoy a trouble-free holiday.

Do not leave valuables in your car (if you do, at least lock them away out of sight in the boot or glove compartment).

Walking at night in all major centres is reasonably safe. There have been few instances of handbag and wristwatch snatching or muggings.

Weather

Nature has given Zimbabwe one of the most pleasant climates in the world: warm summers (October–February) that are rarely

21

Above: Tourist's eye-view of ostrich in a Zimbabwe game reserve.

oppressive, and sunny winters (May–August) that are rarely chilly.

Throughout the year sunshine ranges between four and ten hours a day, with the least amount during the rainy season. The seasons are more sharply pronounced in Zimbabwe than in countries nearer the Equator, with a distinct summer and winter.

During winter the generally dry and sunny days experience temperatures averaging between 15°–20° C (59°–68° F) though they can fall much lower. Nights are much cooler at this time, particularly in the highveld.

During summer, daytime temperatures range between 25°–30°C (77°–86° F). In October, the hottest month, temperatures often exceed 34°C (93°F). It is considerably warmer all year-round in the lowveld, which includes Victoria Falls.

Clothes

Medium-weight clothing is best for winter with woollens or other warm clothing for evenings. Lightweight clothes are ideal for summer, and casuals — T-shirts, shorts, etc. — are mandatory for resort areas like Victoria Falls, Kariba, and the Zambezi Valley. In higher areas, light woollens can be a blessing in the summer evenings.

Men should note that the conservatism inherent in Zimbabwe's colonial past still prevails. If you enjoy social evenings, pack at least one tailored jacket, shirt, and tie. For only with these will you be allowed into most restaurants and bars after sundown (fast-food diners excepted).

Health

Visitors from areas infected by yellow fever and cholera require certificates of inoculation against these diseases. Zimbabwe has excellent health services with fine hospitals in the major centres.

Malaria and bilharzia are endemic. All visitors should take an antimalarial prophylactic beginning two weeks before their arrival and continuing for six weeks after their departure and avoid bathing in streams, rivers, and lakes.

Doctors also recommend visitors to take sensible precautions against tetanus, polio, cholera, typhoid, and paratyphoid. A gamma globulin injection provides some protection against possible infection by hepatitis and is

Above: Jackal slinks through the bush.

well worth taking. That said, the incidence of these infections and diseases is not high.

There are first-class hospitals in Harare and Bulawayo with resident specialists and surgeons. There are also excellent dentists and opticians. Medical treatment, however, is expensive and visitors would be wise to take out medical insurance cover before their departure. This can be obtained in Zimbabwe, but usually at a higher premium than you would pay in Europe or North America.

There is no shortage of chemists or drugstores, all staffed by qualified pharmacists. If you are taking medication, however, it is recommended that you carry sufficient quantities to cover the duration of your stay.

Most drugs are available, but many will have unfamiliar brand names. If your specific prescription is unavailable, the pharmacist or doctor will often prescribe a suitable alternative.

Pharmacies are open during normal weekday shopping hours, 08.00 to 13.00 and 14.00 to 17.00, but few shops close for lunch. Selected pharmacies in main centres such as Harare and Bulawayo also offer a night service.

Rivers and dams are likely to contain bilharzia, so avoid swimming in them or drinking from them. All swimming pools are maintained to adequate health standards and are perfectly safe for swimming.

Tap water in all urban centres, whether from reservoirs or bore holes, is purified and completely safe to drink. Safari operators carry sufficient supplies for bush travel, but if you are travelling in such places alone it is advisable to carry water purification apparatus or pills.

There is a small measure of prostitution and only a fool would ignore the widespread existence of AIDS, but all blood donations are HIV-tested. There is little evidence of drug traffic or addiction.

Photography

There was a chronic shortage of film in Zimbabwe during the 1980s and visitors should carry all the film that they estimate will be needed. Remember also that this is one of the most photogenic countries in the world. Stock up with plenty in reserve so that you will not be disappointed.

Photo-processing is irregular when avail-

Above: Tsessebe at Lake Chiturikwi (formerly Lake Kyle).

able, and then only in major centres. Areas where photography is restricted or forbidden are clearly marked. Obey the injunction. It is also inadvisable to photograph government buildings and other installations.

Zimbabwe's position some degrees south of the Equator makes it a real photographer's paradise, particularly outside the summer months. For its day-long sunshine is not, as at the Equator, excessively harsh and there are seldom any vertical midday shadows, just even light and shade throughout most of the day.

When to go

With its distinctive seasons, Zimbabwe presents potential visitors with a range of choices for their vacation. If you intend to visit the lowveld — Victoria Falls, Mana Pools, Kariba, Gonarezhou National Park — you should be aware that the high summer temperatures are often uncomfortable, while in the middle of winter frosts have been recorded.

The most temperate times for this region are between winter and summer: March–April (the end of the rains) and August–September.

In the higher regions the summer weather is usually delightful. The rainy season occurs between December and April, and the Victoria Falls are at their most spectacular between February and May.

On Safari

Zimbabwe has one of the most highly developed tourist infrastructures in the African continent, including first-rate roads and communication facilities. Virtually everything you will need is close at hand.

If you are travelling alone in remote bush areas like Mana Pools you should carry plenty of small change and notes in case of emergencies, such as paying helpers to move you out of mud holes.

Always carry essential spares with you as well as a useful number of tools. For more detailed advice you should consult the excellent Automobile Association of Zimbabwe, which maintains offices in all major centres.

Zimbabwe's national and recreational parks are indeed the showpiece of Africa and their do's and don'ts — regarding off-the-road driving, game watching, etc. — are clearly stated at the entrance gates. Please observe these regulations. They are intended to help

Above: Pale blush of dawn breaks over a herd of sable antelope in Hwange National Park.

you enjoy Zimbabwe's superb natural attractions in complete safety.

Always remember that while some animals have become accustomed to the presence of people they are still wild animals. Keep your distance. Never feed monkeys, or other species, nor make excessive noise to attract their attention. Never deviate from designated trails for that closer camera shot and never get out of your vehicle except at designated areas. Close all windows and zippers when you leave your room or tent.

Many believe that their enjoyment is related to the number of species they can see within the shortest possible time. As an alternative, read up on wildlife to help you identify the different creatures and birds. Then, when they catch your eye, spend time observing them and learning their habits and characteristic behaviour. Chances are you will find this much more rewarding.

Always keep your camera loaded and ready for action. You never know when something may happen.

Where to stay

Zimbabwe's accommodation infrastructure is unequalled in Africa and ranges from truly five-star international hotels to homey guesthouses. There is a complete range of hotels, both in price and services; superb national parks' self-catering lodges; bungalows; chalets; and an incredible number of caravan parks and campsites, enviable both for their location and facilities.

National bird

The Zimbabwe Bird (species unknown) found carved from soapstone at Great Zimbabwe is incorporated into the national coat of arms. Originally, the only known seven birds were removed from the country by plunderers during the pre- and early-colonial period. All but one have been returned to their homeland. They can be seen in the site museum at the Great Zimbabwe World Heritage Site.

National flower

The national flower of Zimbabwe is the flame lily.

PART ONE: HISTORY, GEOGRAPHY, AND PEOPLE

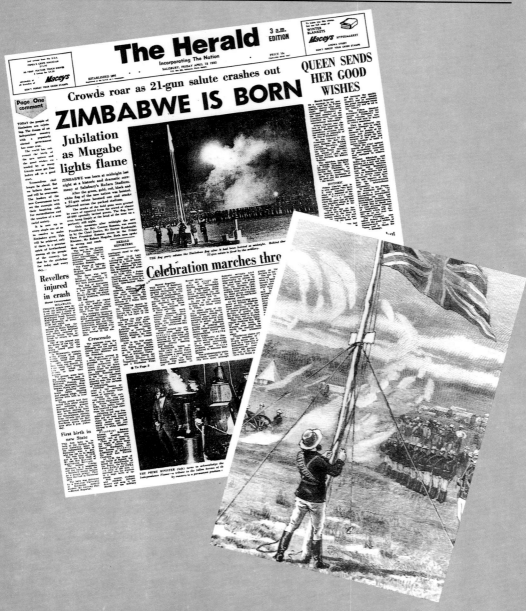

Above: Banner headline proclaims the birth of a free nation. Right: Colonel Edward Pennefather, leader of the Pioneer Column raises the Union flag of Britain at Salisbury on 13 September, 1890. Opposite: Paper moon in an ice-blue sky over Matobo Hills.

Land of Legend and Livingstone

Nature — and man — constantly reshape the glory that is Zimbabwe. Born many millions of centuries ago it wears its age as graciously as a bearded sage. Yet underneath the beard lies today's youth, celebrating the country's many new wonders, of which perhaps the Kariba sunset is the most magnificent.

Without a great body of water no land can claim true beauty. Yet there was neither great lake nor sea in this land — none in its tawny deserts filled with elephant and lion, nor any among its savannah plains where antelope, buffalo, and rhino roamed.

The sweltering, humid lowlands were also arid, along with the fertile highveld soils that cover the staggering mineral riches buried deep beneath.

Only among its craggy peaks and hidden valleys was water plentiful: thundering, cascading falls and bright streams singing at their sudden release from the thickly-forested escarpments and open, rolling moorlands.

Water was there in such plenitude that over the millenniums the currents of the mighty Zambezi probed the rock faults and fissures of its ancient bed to carve not one but eight successive gorges (and has now begun to carve a ninth) to form one of the greatest physical spectacles in Africa.

This wall of constantly falling water almost two kilometres wide plunges vertically more than ninety metres (300 feet) into a narrow gorge. Called locally "Mosi-oa-Tunya" ("the smoke that thunders"), this natural wonder is known around the world as Victoria Falls.

Thus high and landlocked, Zimbabwe needed only one thing to complete its beauty as a land of contrasts, one thing in which all life rejoices — an ocean or an inland sea.

Many millions of years ago there was such a sea, so large that none of its shores could be seen from the other. Sucked dry by the remorseless African sun, even the first Bantu migrants into the land of the "San" 1,000 years or more ago were too late to see its shimmering shores.

So, early this century man began to lay his hand upon the land. Streams were blocked and rivers dammed all across the country that was to become Zimbabwe. Small lakes began to form, springing up in the hollows and valleys around the towns and on the farms that the European colonists had begun to carve out.

Finally, during the 1950s, upstream from a deep gorge half a kilometre (one-third of a mile) wide, in the north-east corner of the Zambezi Valley, many hundreds toiled — and eighty-seven died — building the Kariba Dam.

The long and slender lake that formed behind its wall in the early 1960s was the final brush stroke that transformed Zimbabwe into a land of enduring beauty.

Prehistoric art

If nature and man combined to transform the landscape, it is man alone who has endowed Zimbabwe with its enduring legacy of art, cultures, and civilizations. Rock paintings and engravings etched on the walls of granite cliffs and caves, along with the impressive cities and fortresses built later, all point to a great heritage.

During the Stone Age the "San", small groups of hunter-gatherers, wandered over the country's massive central plateau. Much later these Khoisan-speaking communities were edged aside by waves of migrant Bantu agriculturalists and pastoralists.

Long before Christ, man had begun to domesticate the beasts and till the fields of what is now Zimbabwe. All across this sun-kissed land roamed herds of elephant and buffalo, prides of lion, families of leopard and cheetah, antelope and rhino.

Amid them, as their ancient ruins testify, cultures and civilizations rose and flourished at a time when the rest of the world, if they had heard of Africa at all, thought of the continent only as dark, mysterious — and unknown.

The most powerful of these dynastic kingdoms, ancestors of today's majority Shona communities, occupied much of southern and central Africa, from as far west as Botswana to the coast of Mozambique in the east.

Finally, early last century, the Shona dynasties came into confrontation with the Zulu ancestors of today's Ndebele communities. These were the *impi*, warriors, of the Nguni people who rebelled against the great warrior leader, Shaka Zulu, and marched northwards to invade Mashonaland in the 1820s.

The last of these Zulu warrior groups, the Khumalo, completed their conquests in the 1840s, establishing themselves in the southwest where their leader, King Mzilikazi, built a new capital, Mhlahlandlela. Gradually the Khumalo community assimilated and absorbed the people and cultures who had long lived there into their own to become the Ndebele.

This rich, mysterious history inspired romantic fiction by such authors as Rider Haggard, who wrote *King Solomon's Mines*. His imagination stirred by the letters he received from his brother, a colonial officer in Africa, he identified this fabulous land as Ophir, the location of the great treasure-troves that sustained Solomon and Sheba — legends brought to life in the 1980s through a range of movies filmed on location in Zimbabwe.

Among the first European visitors was Dr. David Livingstone, the Christian missionary whose name is irrevocably linked with that of Zimbabwe through the Victoria Falls.

The good missionary, whose heart lies buried in the continent to which he gave his life (under a tree on the shores of Lake Tanganyika) and whose body is buried at Westminster Abbey, named the majestic falls after his British queen.

Cecil Rhodes

Livingstone's was a compassionate mission. But that of the other European whose name is also irrevocably linked with Zimbabwe — whose name indeed preceded it — was driven by both financial lust and visions of imperial grandeur.

In fulfilling the first Cecil John Rhodes achieved the second and earned brief immortality as the "father of the British Empire".

It was all too brief for a man whose achievements in his short lifetime began a new epoch. Yet, a century after Rhodes landed in South Africa, and eighty-three years after the lands of the Ndebele and Shona were named Rhodesia by British royal decree, Zimbabwe was born and Rhodes's statue was removed from the streets of the capital he named Salisbury, now Harare.

From the moment Rhodes arrived at the southern tip of the continent, his heart was set on colonizing the length of Africa, from the Cape to Cairo, under the British flag. The first stage in his grand strategy was the annexation of the Zambezi basin and the great African lakes to the north. To begin this process he established the British South Africa Company — BSAC — under a royal charter signed by Queen Victoria on 29 October, 1889.

Subsequently Rhodes despatched mercenaries to Mashonaland in northern Zimbabwe, where they built Fort Salisbury, named after the incumbent British Prime Minister, Lord Salisbury. There the company flag, incorporating the Union flag of Great Britain, was raised on 13 September, 1890.

Emissaries were later sent to Bulawayo where — by ruses and deceit — Mzilikazi's heir and successor, King Lobengula, was duped into signing away Matabeleland (most of what is now southern Zimbabwe). Though later this great leader perceived the deceit and repudiated the agreement, both Matabeleland and Mashonaland had come under the British crown.

The British South Africa Company's newly-acquired Maxim guns, mowing down all those who resisted, sealed the fact almost before the ink on the contract was dry.

Lobengula retreated north-west towards the Zambezi, dying along the way in January 1894. In the aftermath, Rhodes took three of the ruler's sons into virtual slavery at his home on the Cape.

He then set about consolidating the power of the BSAC, and therefore the Crown, by expropriating all the arable and grazing land that he and his company claimed as their own. Indeed, a great many Zimbabweans today still live on the arid Tribal Trust Lands (now called communal lands) defined in 1894 by the Land Commission that Rhodes established.

Perhaps the greatest irony is that Rhodes, who died in March 1902 at the age of forty-eight, chose for his grave the natural grandeur of the Matobo Hills where Mzilikazi, the father of Lobengula, also lies buried.

As early as 1896 the Ndebele took up arms against colonial domination and, although

there were periods of acquiescence, the struggle for freedom never ceased. For ten brief years the two Rhodesias (southern and northern) and Nyasaland (now Malawi) formed a political and economic federation that ended when Northern Rhodesia attained independence.

With Ian Smith's illegal Unilateral Declaration of Independence in 1965, the stage for the final confrontation was set and Southern Rhodesia's war of liberation was joined. Though the battle was long and bloody, with retribution on both sides, the end of 1979 saw conciliation and the inauguration of a one-man, one-vote democratic society after years of oppression and suppression.

Final freedom

When the new green, gold, red, and black flag of Zimbabwe was raised at midnight on 17 April, 1980, bitterness was set aside in the joy of nationhood and Robert Mugabe, founding father, began the task of bringing together the many disparate groups as one people building one nation.

Set in south-central Africa between the Limpopo and Zambezi rivers, Zimbabwe's westernmost corner thrusts into the Caprivi Strip where it meets the borders of Namibia, Angola, Botswana, and Zambia.

Bounded by Zambia in the north and north-west, Mozambique in the east, South Africa in the south, and Botswana in the south-west, Zimbabwe's 390,245 square kilometres (150,674 square miles) — almost the size of California and three times the size of England — lie to the north of the Tropic of Capricorn.

Most of the country consists of a high plateau more than 6,000 metres (2,000 feet) above sea level. Apart from the Zambezi, Limpopo, and Lake Kariba, the country's most outstanding physical features are the 350-kilometre (218-mile) long mountain range in the east and the mineral-rich Great Dyke that runs like a backbone through the middle of the country, dividing it roughly into the highveld and middleveld.

Change in Zimbabwe since its independence in 1980 has been swift and stunning. More than 5,000 kilometres (3,100 miles) of smooth two-lane metalled highways, 20,000 kilometres (12,500 miles) of state-maintained gravel or dirt roads, and 60,000 kilometres (37,300 miles) of rural roads, maintained by local and district authorities, link virtually every area of the country.

Major cities and tourist centres are also joined by scheduled daily Air Zimbabwe jet services and frequent passenger trains. Zimbabwe has one of the most developed rail systems in Africa with more than 3,400 kilometres (2,100 miles) of track.

The largest of Zimbabwe's indigenous communities are the Shona and the Ndebele. Others are the Tonga people of the Zambezi Valley, most of whom were displaced and resettled when Lake Kariba was formed; the Hlengwe of the south; and the Vendao, a small group of hunter-gatherers from the lower Zambezi Valley. There are also minority European and Asian communities.

The most widely-spoken Bantu languages are Shona and Sindebele but English, which unites all the different people with one common tongue, is the official language.

Despite its population pressures, Zimbabwe has one of the finest conservation records in the world. Almost 50,000 square kilometres (19,300 square miles), virtually thirteen per cent of its total land area — is conserved as a protected wildlife and wilderness estate.

In 1990 there were eleven national parks, fourteen botanical reserves, three botanical gardens, seventeen designated safari areas, six sanctuaries, and fifteen recreational parks.

Joy of discovery

To travel through Zimbabwe is to experience the joy of discovery in one of Africa's — and the world's — great unspoilt tourist attractions. In the vastness of its national parks and game sanctuaries, the welcome and the wonder of that Africa which was felt more than a century ago by traders, missionaries, explorers, and adventurers, can be sensed again.

Proud of their magical land studded with granite hills, green and fertile plains, high moorlands, craggy mountains, rolling savannah, and flowing rivers, the Zimbabwean people are building a society where each man and woman, regardless of race, are equal and a better quality of life is sought for all.

In the process they have made their country one of the finest tourist destinations in the world.

History: The Gold and the Silver

Written in the rocks of Zimbabwe is a story older than that of humanity. These rocks, which are among the most ancient in the world, contain metals and fossils that tell of many things, including the lives and deaths of creatures and plants that rose, flourished, withered, and disappeared long before man was born.

Deep within them, even then, lay something that was destined to drive mankind to mayhem, murder, and mischief. For the chemical processes that formed these rocks created great seams of yellow and white metals for which mortals have lusted, and over which they have fought and destroyed for many millenniums.

The gold and the silver of Zimbabwe, and its many precious and semiprecious minerals and gemstones, have shaped the country's ancient past as well as its more recent history. It was largely for the wealth inherent in the soil that the region was invaded and its peoples subjected to alien dominion.

The parent rocks of Zimbabwe were formed about three billion years ago when molten masses far beneath the earth thrust upwards, cooling and solidifying several hundred metres beneath the surface.

Later, through millennium upon millennium of weathering and erosion, layers of soil and vegetation were stripped away by wind and rain leaving many of the granite rocks exposed, much as they were in their molten nascence.

Millions of years later life began to form and spread across this region of Africa. Strange footsteps in the fossil sands of the Zambezi Valley reveal that one species of dinosaur — a meat-eating, reptilian giant — walked on two legs in this region more than 150 million years ago.

Undoubtedly, many more prehistoric secrets were probably drowned by the deep waters of Lake Kariba. What remains must be scoured out along the course of the Zambezi, where explorations in hidden fossil beds on its banks have revealed a near-continuous record of human evolution. Preserved in the sands and gravels of its shores, a treasury of tools made by the early ancestors of modern mankind has been uncovered.

According to available evidence, Africa — in particular East Africa — is now considered the most likely cradle of mankind. Soon after our ancestral *Homo erectus* stood upright and took his first faltering footsteps in the savannah of the Great Rift Valley, which reaches as far as Zimbabwe, his new-found mobility inspired him to move much further afield in the search for food and water.

His subsistence wanderings eventually took him south down the African continent. Although little evidence of these intermediate millenniums spent roaming has been uncovered, it is known that the earliest settlers of southern Africa — hunter-gatherers of the bush and forest — shared the same cultural and language affinities as the earliest settlers of eastern Africa.

Even today remnant communities in Kenya and Tanzania have links with these click-speaking, Khoisan peoples, then thinly spread over vast areas, including the central plateau of present-day Zimbabwe.

During the course of a million years the early settlers developed tool-making skills. Extremely primitive at first, these life and death implements attained a level of surprising sophistication as far back as 10,000 years ago. One weapon was a throwing club with two or three round stone balls bound by thongs that wrapped themselves around the legs of a prey, bringing it down.

With these tools man became a skilled hunter and, later, a skilled agriculturalist. He learned to domesticate animals, and to plough the land, plant, and harvest crops as food. The Khoisan, however, remained simply hunter-gatherers.

They also discovered how to paint and draw images and began to bestow on the country its priceless legacy of rock-art. Rock paintings — found at more than 6,000 sites in Zimbabwe alone — indicate that the earliest were drawn, etched, or painted within the last 30,000 years. Most appear to have been completed between the last 5,000 to 2,000 years.

Towards the end of this period, about 2,500

Above: Great Zimbabwe's great enclosure with conical tower: shrine to both past and future.

years ago, the first ancestral influx of today's majority ethnic groups began when waves of the darker, physically larger Bantu farmers, warriors, and iron-makers started to spread out across the southern and eastern face of the continent.

During the 500 years between 200 BC and AD 300, Zimbabwe's original, Khoisan-speaking hunter-gatherer communities were overwhelmed, if not displaced, by these Shona-Bantu agriculturalists and herdsmen who used iron tools and lived on homesteads and in villages.

One thousand years later, the central plateau was dominated by the Shona but large areas, especially in the west, were occupied by non-Shona such as the Leya and the Tonga.

Great Zimbabwe

The earliest foundations of what would become the continent's greatest civic state — Great Zimbabwe — were laid when the Iron-Age Shona settled around some granite kopjes in the southern midlands of what is now Zimbabwe.

The area they chose was an island of green, even during the dry winter months, because of the unusually moderate climate. As the settlement grew in size and importance the granite rocks of the surrounding hills proved to be ideal for building.

Along with the development of an impressive architectural form, the settlers developed increasingly sophisticated forms of pottery and ironwork and, by the end of the first Christian millennium, cattle were grazing the land, crops were under cultivation, and trade with Arabia, through the East African coast, had begun.

Soon the pace of development accelerated. As Great Zimbabwe grew and prospered through the centuries, the cattle herds increased dramatically. The kingdom that first developed as part of the general migration from the north now grew prosperous on trade with Arabian, Indian, and Chinese traders who had established commercial links on the East African coast as early as the eighth century AD.

They exchanged gold and ivory for such commodities as cloth, beads, and ceramics, and sustained themselves by pastoral and agricultural activities.

Ruled by a succession of kings, Great

Zimbabwe's influence spread throughout what is now Zimbabwe. It was the capital of a great commercial empire with its own iron ore mines and smithies, a militant army that captured much plunder, tributary chiefs, and traders who dealt in gold, copper, iron, ivory, cotton, and cattle.

Radiocarbon dating and archaeological finds suggest that this royal capital reached its greatest eminence between the eleventh and fifteenth centuries AD.

As a result of their trading, wealth, and power the rulers of Great Zimbabwe established control over extensive regions, from Botswana in the west to the Mozambique coast in the east, and from the Limpopo River in the south to the Zambezi in the north.

During those three centuries, when Europe languished in its Dark Ages, the Karanga dynasty who ruled the kingdom built the magnificent citadels and walls that can be seen today; the stone houses known as "dzimbahwe". Great Zimbabwe, on the other side of the hemisphere from a stagnating Europe, was already a truly civic community with clear rankings of authority and concern for all citizens.

The dynasty's power structure served to emphasise the strength of the nation rather than its own hierarchy. Their architecture was conceived as a salute to the unity of the people and the dignity and glory of the ruling dynasty — not as defence.

Although the development and the extent of Great Zimbabwe's wealth and influence is well-documented, the reason for its sudden decline in the fifteenth century remains an enigma. Almost overnight it ceased to be of importance, although small groups continued to live there for three centuries or more.

This ancient city-state is also significant for other reasons. For 300 years or so, known to the outside world only by legend, it inspired stories of great wealth and was considered by many to be the Biblical kingdom of Ophir that Sheba visited; a myth that persisted even after its "discovery" in 1867.

The legend that it was the Biblical Ophir was based on the wild and wonderful speculations of sixteenth-century Portuguese travellers who heard many tales of its citadels and fortresses, its immense wealth and far-reaching power.

Such a legend was wonderfully romantic. For almost a century these mysterious ruins acted as a magnet, drawing adventurers and archaeologists from all parts of the world.

Most of these early "explorers", however, refused to believe that any African culture could be responsible for such sophistication and were only too happy to claim (or believe) that the ruins were connected to the Old Testament — to the Queen of Sheba, the Phoeniceans, the Sabeans, or Ophir.

Although there was no foundation for such fable, in reality Great Zimbabwe later became the touchstone that inspired the war of liberation, Chimurenga, and gave its name to the nation, a testimony to the centuries-old civilization that flourished there long before the arrival of the European.

The ruins and ancient works of art found there encompass a cultural and architectural heritage unsurpassed almost anywhere south of the Sahara. Not only does it contain all that is most sacred of the past, it also bequeaths to future generations the legacy for which so many gave their lives (See "Great Zimbabwe: The Kingdom of Ophir", Part Two).

As the influence of Great Zimbabwe spread, several scattered Shona groups began to emerge as independent or semi-independent dynasties.

The Mutapa State

One group, the Mutapa, for instance, became a separate state under its own dynasty as early as the 1420s.

Within a century, the Mutapa State could boast impressive power and wealth. Problems arose, however, with the arrival of the Portuguese early in the sixteenth century — and their subsequent attempts to conquer the state, combined with internal strife and civil wars, led to Mutapa's ultimate collapse.

By the early eighteenth century the dynasty had been driven off the plateau down into the Zambezi Valley. The last vestiges of the Mutapa State were finally destroyed by British and Portuguese colonialists in the late nineteenth century.

These events took place in the north and east, while in the south and west a group of Shona from Great Zimbabwe had colonized an area that came to be called Butwa. Ruled by a dynasty known as the Torwa, they estab-

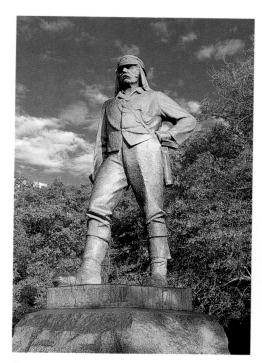

Above: Livingstone memorial, Victoria Falls.

Above: Empire-builder Cecil John Rhodes.

lished their sixteenth-century capital at Khame, south of what is now Bulawayo, in a virtual continuation of the Zimbabwe State (See "The Road to Botswana", Part Two).

Late in the seventeenth century, however, the Torwa dynasty was conquered by another Shona group, the Rozvi, which was ruled by the Changamire dynasty, and included migrants from the downfallen Mutapa in the north-east.

Despite their victory, the Changamire did nothing to destroy the Torwa state and culture. Instead, they adopted it and then proceeded to adapt it. Noted for their military prowess and strength, the Rozvi maintained their influence and power into the second half of the eighteenth century before falling victim to their own success.

Overextended by expansion, weakened by emigration and internal conflicts, and finally overcome by successive invasions from the south, the Rozvi State collapsed and was destroyed in the 1840s.

This demise coincided with the rise of several powerful, military kingdoms (or states) in southern Africa. The most prominent of

these was the Zulu State, which reached the height of its power under the rule of Shaka, whose reign was characterized between 1818 and 1828 by militarism and expansionism.

Annoyed by his persistent demands for tribute, however, some clans and subordinate groups rebelled and marched north, conquering other tribes along the way. These advances changed the social and political faces of much of southern and central Africa.

In the 1820s, one of these Zulu war chiefs, Soshangane, invaded Manyikaland (now Manicaland) and conquered the south-eastern Shona. The western part of the country was spared until the 1830s, when another dissident Zulu group, led by Zvangedaba, invaded the Changamire State on their way to Zambia, Malawi, and Tanganyika and killed the Rozvi ruler, Chirisamhuru. Yet, one final invasion was still destined to take place.

The Ndebele

Spread across more than 3,000 square kilometres (1,158 square miles), the rising serried ridges, granite hills, and cliffs of Matabeleland's Matobo Hills have been sculpted into spires and battlements, towers and turrets, by aeons of wind and rain, sun and erosion.

In the last century, the invincible grandeur of these crenellated citadels of rock made a profound impression on three men of absolute power: Mzilikazi, King of the Ndebele; his son and successor, Lobengula; and Cecil John Rhodes. (A fourth figure, a contemporary of Mzilikazi, stands in the wings at this time, a man whose name is indelibly etched on the history of Africa, but whose influence on the events that shaped Zimbabwe was less profound — David Livingstone.)

Mzilikazi and Lobengula played a significant part in the early events that led to the shaping of what, ultimately, was to become Zimbabwe, as did Rhodes. Driven by both greed and ambitions of imperial status, Rhodes made a great fortune in a remarkably short time and also earned brief eminence as the "father of the British Empire".

The destinies of Lobengula and Rhodes drew them into final confrontation in the last decade of the nineteenth century. The blood spilled in that outcome seeped into the soil and nourished the seedbed of nationalism that ninety years later gave birth to Zimbabwe.

Mzilikazi, who was born around 1795, was a scion of Matshobana, head of the Khumalo Zulu clan that was finally subordinated by Shaka Zulu. After Matshobana's death, Shaka confirmed Mzilikazi as clan chief, asking only for tribute as token of Mzilikazi's allegiance.

Later, Mzilikazi defied Shaka, and the Zulu king sent an army to bring him to heel. Mzilikazi and his warriors, *impi*, repulsed the first attack only to be cut down in a second raid during which Mzilikazi and a handful of supporters fled.

They regrouped themselves into a force of some strength and during the next few years slowly made their way north from the Vaal River, fighting all those they came across. Mzilikazi absorbed many of the warriors he conquered into his army, which came to be known as the Ndebele, and thus consolidated his power.

Eventually Mzilikazi settled at Kuruman in Botswana where the missionary Robert Moffat befriended him (Moffat's daughter Mary became the wife of Livingstone). Under constant threat from the Afrikaner Voortrekkers advancing across the country,

Mzilikazi later decided to move on from Kuruman.

After crossing the Limpopo, he and his men marched north towards the granite Matobo Hills that lie south of today's Bulawayo.

Mzilikazi was so overwhelmed by their grandeur that he decided to found a permanent kingdom there. Subduing the local tribes, "The Great Elephant, Great Mountain, Son of the Sun, God of Cattle and Men" established his capital, called Mhlahlandlela, at their southern base. He named the hills *Amatobo*, the Sindebele word for "baldheads".

The Ndebele ruler built upon and reinforced the Zulu tradition of kingship. Mzilikazi placed his wives and trusted *induna*, chiefs, in the villages and settlements that were scattered throughout the kingdom.

His authority was supreme. With a brief, dismissive wave of the hand he condemned those who unwittingly gave offence, or were suspected of disloyalty. Many died in this place, swept away by this omnipotent hand.

Yet his hospitality to the first European hunters, adventurers, and missionaries in search of game trophies, gold, diamonds, and souls, was as generous as his welcome was warm.

Indeed, when the German Edward Mohr travelled through Matabeleland he noted that a foreigner was "just as safe and his property just as secure as in the best-governed countries in Europe".

Livingstone

At this time Livingstone was shaking off the recurrent fevers caught in his God-driven search and crisscrossing the continent to open up Africa and end the slave trade. He was much encouraged in his mission by his equally devout father-in-law, Robert Moffat.

Eventually both Livingstone and his wife, Mary, succumbed to the pestilential fevers that were the great barrier to the continent's development (Mary died of fever in 1862 and was buried beside the Zambezi at Shupanga).

Livingstone first saw the Zambezi in 1851. One year after crossing the river's upper stretches, he pioneered a route to Africa's west coast and back, on a journey that took more than thirty months.

Above: Lobengula, King of the Ndebele.

taught artist from King's Lynn, England, who had accompanied Livingstone on one of the missionary's subsequent expeditions, to explore the Zambezi in 1857.

Dismissed on that occasion after an argument with the missionary, he set out again for the Zambezi with hunter and trader James Chapman in 1861. The following July the two men arrived at the falls, where Baines spent twelve days sketching and painting them from every angle. Many of these pictures, the first to portray the grandeur and the beauty of the Victoria Falls to the rest of the world, are now in the National Archives at Harare.

Lobengula

During this period of intensive exploration in the 1860s, Mzilikazi, burdened with gout and dropsy, sought more and more the peace and quiet of his beloved Matobo Hills to commune with the ancestral spirits that the Ndebele believed reposed among them. There he died, at his favourite sanctuary, Emanxiweni, on 5 September, 1868.

During the night, his body was taken back to the royal kraal at Mhlahlandlela in stealth, and his death was not announced until four days later. Guarded by his twelve senior wives, his body lay in state for two months before his burial on 2 November at Nthumbane in the Matobo Hills.

Because it was uncertain whether his first-born son, Nkulumane, was alive, the installation of his second son, Lobengula, was delayed for sixteen months. Even then the successor had to fight many fierce battles against other contenders to establish his supremacy. From the outset the new *inkosi* (king) accorded the Europeans an equal welcome (a number of them lived within the royal kraal or in the area).

Ten Europeans, including the Reverend Thomas Morgan Thomas, one of Moffat's colleagues, were guests at the prolonged coronation that began on 22 January, 1870. They watched as thousands of warriors who had travelled to Lobengula's home at Utjotjo escorted him into the royal kraal at Mhlahlandlela, where the ceremonies continued for several days. Lobengula was then thirty-four.

Many other Europeans who had entered

By September 1855 he was back on the upper reaches of the Zambezi, determined to trace its course to the east coast, and thus open "God's highway to the sea".

Travelling downstream by dugout canoe, the missionary hoped to pioneer a navigable route along which legitimate traffic would displace the slave trade.

Defeated by the rapids at Cabora Bassa in Mozambique, his mission to trace the Zambezi's course failed. But his discoveries, particularly that of the Victoria Falls in 1855, provoked even greater interest in Africa generally, and in the Zambezi Valley in particular.

Livingstone believed the falls had arisen because of a sudden and cataclysmic rifting of the earth's surface some time in Africa's ancient past. Edward Mohr, the German explorer who visited the falls in 1870, shared the same belief.

Although Livingstone made copious notes about the falls, no words or statistics could capture or convey the immensity and glory of this natural phenomenon.

This was left to Thomas Baines, a self-

this region, such as the hunter Frederick Courtney Selous, led a more transitory life, roaming the great wildernesses of Matabeleland and Mashonaland, seeking ivory, rhino horn, and other trophies.

Lobengula was particularly close to Selous until the two fell out in a dispute over the killing of hippos, which the Ndebele, who called them "sea cows", revered.

In the early part of his reign, Lobengula adopted a form of European dress, a sailor's striped shirt and cord trousers, and he commissioned Harry Grant, an old hunter, and his friend John Halyett (known to the Ndebele as Johnny Mubi), to build him a stone building in the style of a Flemish farmhouse.

Under its thatched roof, before a huge packing case that served as a table, seated on a leather "throne", its back decorated with a crown, Lobengula held court and entertained his European guests in good humour.

Lobengula's attitude underwent a profound change, however, with the arrival in 1877 of a British government expedition seeking free movement throughout Matabeleland. The king abandoned the European ways he had adopted and reverted to his own culture.

Colonial epoch

Ten years later, as European prospectors and adventurers continued to flood into his country, Lobengula — writing from his new capital of Gubulawayo (Sindebele for the "place of slaughter"), so named to commemorate his victorious battles — complained in a letter to British officials in South Africa that "the white people . . . come in here like wolves without my permission and make roads to my country. . . . Today is peace but I don't know what tomorrow may bring".

None of this escaped the attention of Cecil Rhodes who since landing in South Africa in the year of Lobengula's coronation eighteen years before had amassed one of the world's greatest fortunes. Matabeleland had long been the set piece of his grand design for a British empire in Africa.

The first stage of his strategy was to send a delegation to Bulawayo to negotiate a concession with Lobengula and the Ndebele that would allow him to operate in Matabeleland. The concession was cleverly worded.

In effect it constituted an abdication of Lobengula's powers and the annexation of the Ndebele lands.

Old friends contributed to Lobengula's betrayal, including Moffat's son, John. When the illiterate king asked him to explain the meaning of the words, Moffat lied. On the strength of Moffat's explanation, however, Lobengula put his seal (that of the elephant) to the proposed concession.

Though he later discovered the ruse and repudiated the contract, it was too late. On the back of this "agreement" Rhodes established the British South Africa Company.

Yet Lobengula still extended courtesy and protection to many Europeans. In August 1889, Harry Vaughan Williams, a nineteen-year-old medical student, dined with the king in his stone house on the site where Bulawayo State House now stands. Williams noted that the house was filled with treasure.

Two months later, on 29 October, 1889 — only days after Lobengula told Dr. Leander Starr Jameson, Rhodes's emissary to Bulawayo, "no more lies, I must see Rhodes himself" — Queen Victoria signed the company's charter and sealed the downfall of Lobengula and the Ndebele nation.

When news of the charter was carried to Lobengula by a detachment of the Royal Horse Guards, the king was still amiable enough to take part in the race meeting that was staged to celebrate the event. He entered his own horses in the Gubuluwayo Handicap and the Zambezi Plate.

But it was an end to happiness. The following year Rhodes despatched a mercenary army to annexe Mashonaland and so set in train the events that led to the overthrow of the Ndebele.

The army, known as the Pioneer Column, consisted of 200 police troopers and 500 mercenaries under the command of Colonel Edward Pennefather. Rhodes commissioned Lobengula's friend Selous to guide the column through Mashonaland.

Establishing three forts — Fort Tuli on the southernmost border; Fort Victoria, now Masvingo, at the edge of the central plateau; and Fort Charter in the north-east — during their long march north they finally reached the heart of Mashonaland and built a fourth, Fort Salisbury, on the spot where they raised

Above: British South Africa Company police and mercenaries fight off an attack by the Ndebele *impi* (warriors) of King Lobengula.

the Union flag of Britain on 13 September, 1890.

The land on which this fort stood was claimed for the BSAC and themselves. In fact it was originally occupied by the Harava people, a Shona group under Chief Mbare. When the pioneers arrived, however, it was in the possession of Chief Gutsa and his warriors who had conquered the Harava and killed Chief Mbare.

Refusing to acknowledge whoever claimed the land, Rhodes considered Fort Salisbury a major pivot in his masterplan for the annexation of Matabeleland and Mashonaland. Each civilian among the 500 pioneers in the column — the rest were BSAC police and regular troops — was given 1,250 hectares (3,750 acres) of land and the right to fifteen mining claims.

Like the Ndebele, the Shona bitterly resented this occupation. In response the BSAC built three forts on the slopes of the Kopje, the granite hill at the centre of the new settlement. The topmost one, Fort Leander, was fitted with a searchlight.

Three years later, in July 1893, without provocation, BSAC soldiers attacked a Ndebele attachment which Rhodes's aide and close intimate, Dr. Leander Starr Jameson, had summoned to Fort Victoria, massacring between thirty and fifty warriors. The *impi* predictably responded.

It was all the excuse that Rhodes and Jameson needed to launch their attack on Lobengula and his Bulawayo redoubt. Within fourteen weeks, on 4 November, the British flag fluttered from a tree over the smouldering ashes of the royal kraal in Bulawayo, and Lobengula was running north-west towards the Zambezi.

Although for many years afterwards the Ndebele clung to the belief that Lobengula was alive, the king died of smallpox near Kamativi in February 1894. His grave was proclaimed a national monument in 1943.

The Ndebele king left behind, unharmed, two Europeans who had settled in his capital some years before: his advisor and letter writer William Filmer Usher, a member of the Salvation Army who had been there for ten years; and James Fairbairn, who had arrived twenty-one years earlier and obtained a

Above: Cecil Rhodes raised this monument on top of World's View in the Matobo Hills in honour of Allan Wilson and the men who fell to the Ndebele at Shangani in 1893.

gold mining concession from the king.

Spurred by Rhodes's promises and his vision of a new El Dorado, hundreds more now poured in. The European settlement that rose swiftly from the ashes of the Ndebele capital was soon moved five kilometres (three miles) away. Most wanted land — land to settle and farm, or to prospect for the tantalizing riches that the BSAC and Rhodes promised lay beneath the surface.

To provide land, Rhodes appointed a commission that swiftly delineated 10,500 square kilometres (4,000 square miles) of arid, infertile land as the boundaries of a Matabele reserve and expropriated the rest to be sold or otherwise exploited.

Yet without people to work it, the newly confiscated land was worthless. So began the system of "forced labour". To coerce both Ndebele and Shona to work as farm hands and in other menial capacities, a hut tax was introduced.

Forced to labour on the new farms and in the new settlement through the introduction of the notorious hut tax, the Shona were crippled in 1895 by smallpox and their herds

wiped out by rinderpest, culminating in a locust plague the following year that decimated their crops.

Angered by the imposed European restrictions, the Shona took to arms in 1896 almost simultaneously with the Ndebele in the first of Zimbabwe's wars of liberation, *Chimurenga*. Surrounded by hostile warriors, the Salisbury pioneers sought refuge in the town gaol that they had fortified.

There they waited, prepared for siege. After six weeks, faced by superior arms and the arrival of troop reinforcements from South Africa, the Shona were forced to concede.

Their spiritual leaders, Mbuya Nehanda and Kaguvi, were taken prisoner, tried, and convicted. They were hanged in 1897, the year in which Salisbury attained municipal status under the leadership of its first mayor, W. E. Fairbridge.

The Ndebele war

Meanwhile the Ndebele, who had also refused to acquiesce to European coercion, had taken up arms against the pioneers in Bulawayo.

Usher — alone among the District Commissioners, missionaries, traders, hunters, and other Europeans living in Matabeleland — was convinced the Ndebele would rise up in anger after the razing of Lobengula's kraal at Bulawayo.

He was correct. Soon after the taxes and "forced labour" were introduced, a force of about 800 *impi*, led by Babyan, a relative of Lobengula and one of the senior Matabele *indunas*, made the Matobo Hills their stronghold, harassing the settlers with continual hit and run forays from their hidden caves and rocky lookouts.

In April 1896, between 12,000 and 15,000 Ndebele warriors laid siege to Bulawayo and its 1,500 or so citizens retreated into a laager that was encircled by the Ndebele on three sides. The Ndebele left the road south open — no doubt hoping to induce the settlers to leave. The settlers did not retreat. Nor did the Ndebele attack.

Instead, the beleaguered colonists dug a well and waited while the British Government hurriedly deployed troops along this route. By early June a force of more than 3,000 soldiers, BSAC police, and armed volunteers was camped within the laager.

The British reprisal was savage and the Ndebele retreated to their stronghold, among the ancestral spirits that reside in the Matobo Hills, to continue the fight.

Their resistance was so stern — and so effective — that Rhodes, under critical pressure in South Africa and abroad, sent the Zulu linguist and local administrator J. P. Richardson (at great risk) to arrange an *indaba* (meeting) to discuss peace.

Richardson's mission succeeded and on 21 August, 1896, accompanied by a friend, one interpreter, and a reporter for *The Times* of London, Rhodes rode out to talk to six of the Ndebele's senior *induna*, chiefs, at the place now known as Fort Usher. It was there, just a few kilometres to the east of the Matobo Hills, that William Usher had established a trading post. (Later, Lord Baden-Powell decided to build a fort on the spot and, inspired by his scouting expeditions into the hills, conceived the idea of the Boy Scout movement.)

Rhodes's journey was hailed as a great feat of bravery, but he confessed later that he had never been "in such a funk" in all his life.

During the *indaba,* Rhodes was shown Mzilikazi's tomb — a natural cave where the body had been placed in a sitting position looking out over the forbidding grandeur of the Matobo Hills. The grave had been desecrated and Rhodes gave orders for it to be restored (which perhaps started him thinking of his own burial place in these granite hills).

Rhodes held three more meetings, the last two with Lord Grey, who had replaced Jameson as the new administrator of "Southern Rhodesia". In the settlement reached on 21 October, 1896, Rhodes conceded much, restoring some of the lands and agreeing to a degree of Ndebele autonomy.

Though the city represented perhaps the pinnacle of all that he strove to achieve, Rhodes paid only a few visits to Bulawayo. Whenever he did he always made time to escape to Malindidzimu, the Ndebele's "place of spirits", to sit on top of that great granite outcrop and contemplate the grandeur that surrounds it.

No doubt the Matobo's Malindidzimu matched the mood of his melancholic megalomania and his often ill-conceived and ill-fated attempts to extend the British Empire. Maybe the immensity of this environment was something of an alter ego for Rhodes. There he found the empathy that enabled him to renew his faith and restore his vision.

Certainly Rhodes, who in his short lifetime wrote six wills and directed that he should be set inside a grave scooped out of Malindidzimu's granite when he died, had few if any doubts about his own greatness.

The man whose last words on his deathbed are reported to have been "so little done, so much to do" was confident enough that the world would remember him for the next 4,000 years by the inscription on the copper plate over his grave that simply read, "Here lie the remains of Cecil John Rhodes". At least the frenzy that attended his last wishes justified his conceit.

Barely able to breathe during his last fortnight of life on his Cape Town farm, Rhodes died at the age of forty-eight on 26 March, 1902, after a prolonged, debilitating, and painful illness. Vast crowds lined the Cape Town streets as his body was carried to the

Above: Granite boulders guard Cecil Rhodes's grave set on top of the kopje he named World's View.

station and placed in his Pullman car for the train journey to Bulawayo, where engineers led teams of navvies in a desperate race to complete a thirty-kilometre (19-mile) road to the foot of his chosen grave in the Matobo Hills.

Similar crowds gathered in Bulawayo to pay homage to the empire builder before the final leg of the journey on 9 April, when Rhodes's coffin was placed on a gun carriage. The route was long and arduous and the animals drawing the carriage rested overnight at his summer house.

The following day his coffin was lowered into the grave watched not only by a huge assembly of European mourners but by the disciplined ranks of the Ndebele chiefs and warriors who escorted the cortege to Malindidzimu.

The planned last salute — a volley of rifles — was cancelled. The Ndebele feared that it would disturb the benign spirits of this place that Rhodes had named "View of the World".

Instead, as his coffin was lowered into its granite grave, fifteen kilometres (nine miles) from Mzilikazi's tomb at Nthumbane,

the Ndebele spontaneously gave Rhodes the traditional salute normally accorded only to Zulu kings — "Bayete! Bayete! Bayete!" There he lies, surrounded by massive rounded granite boulders that serve as guardian "angels".

In his last will Rhodes directed that Malindidzimu should be reserved as the burial ground of those who had done special service to Rhodesia and the British Empire. Subsequently his intimate, Dr. Leander Starr Jameson, who served prison time for leading an 1895 raid against the Boers on Rhodes's instructions, was buried not far from Rhodes's grave.

Jameson died in London in 1917, but because of World War I his funeral was delayed. The coffin did not leave England until early 1920 and he was finally buried in the Matobo Hills in May. The inscription for this man who served as Prime Minister of the Cape between 1904–08, and became President of the BSAC in 1913, is even briefer than that on Rhodes's grave: "Here lies Leander Starr Jameson".

One obituary on Jameson noted: "On the summit of a bare granite hill Rhodes sleeps,

Above: Hunter Frederick Courtney Selous with men of the Bulawayo Field Force during the first *Chimurenga*.

side by side with Jameson, staunch liege-man, loyal coadjutor, unselfish, devoted friend, and more than brother, undivided even in death. Romance lights up the story of their lives, and lingers round their lonely graves."

The third grave on Malindidzimu is that of Sir Charles Patrick John Coghlan, a lawyer who became the first Prime Minister of Rhodesia from 1923 until his death in 1927. He was interred three years later, on 14 August, 1930, some distance from the others on the southern crest of the hill at a spot consecrated by Catholic rite.

Their simple, austere graves, with no headstones, counterpose the massive granite memorial that Rhodes raised before his death to Scottish-born Major Allan Wilson and the thirty-three men who went in pursuit of Lobengula after the king fled Bulawayo in November 1893.

The patrol crossed the Shangani River and made contact with the Ndebele ruler, but rains had swollen the river making return to Jameson's main force on the other bank impossible. On 4 December, 1893, the patrol

was surrounded by Lobengula's warriors and slaughtered.

Frederick Selous

The famous hunter Frederick Selous is not among those buried in the Matobo Hills. His last resting place lies several hundred kilo-metres to the north, in the lonely reaches of Tanzania's wilderness hinterland.

Born in London in 1851, Selous first went to South Africa when he was nineteen to become an elephant hunter. There he met Lobengula and, ultimately, Jameson and Rhodes. His return to England in 1875 was marked by the publication of his first book, *A Hunter's Wanderings in Africa* (since re-printed a number of times).

He returned to Africa intending to become an ostrich farmer, but the rewards were small and he soon resumed hunting, spending six years wandering the wildernesses of what are now Zimbabwe and Zambia, returning frequently to the banks of the Zambezi.

Despite the fact that he led the Pioneer Column into Mashonaland, his stock among the Ndebele and Shona remained high and he was welcomed wherever he went. Later he moved to East Africa where he hunted with Sir Northrup MacMillan, an American who was an early settler in Kenya.

Regarded by many as the greatest hunter of all, Selous was renowned for his bush lore and courage. He is said to have killed at least 100 lions, but by common consensus was said to contain no trace of cruelty or cunning in his make up.

He retired to Worplesdon, Surrey, England. There, close to sixty-three years of age when the 1914–18 war broke out, he immediately enlisted and was given a commission in the Royal Fusiliers.

Sent to the East African war theatre on the borders between British-administered Kenya and the German colony of Tanganyika, he was killed in action at Behobeho, in the Rufiji Valley, on January 4, 1916. He was buried there in what has since become the Selous Game Reserve, the largest in the world.

The reserve commemorates his name and courage, much as the Matobo Hills honour those great adversaries, Mzilikazi and the Ndebele; Rhodes and his compatriots.

After Rhodes

Following the formation of an all-white legislative council in 1899, the colony was officially renamed Southern Rhodesia under the administration of the BSAC.

Despite the introduction of punitive taxes and the exploitation of cheap labour, however, the BSAC never realised any real profit from their "colony" and, in 1923, Southern Rhodesia officially became a British crown colony.

Still clinging proudly to their title of "pioneers", the settlers were nonetheless determined to hold on to power despite the winds of change that were blowing through Africa as early as the 1920s.

With the advent of the 1930s came the first proposals for an "amalgamation" of Nyasaland (now Malawi) and Northern (now Zambia) and Southern Rhodesia (Zimbabwe) into one country. The colonists believed it would give them greater strength against Whitehall in their search for self-determination as a minority.

During this period, several African organizations and societies, such as the Southern Rhodesia Native Association and the Rhodesia Bantu Voters' Association, emerged in search of social justice and basic human rights.

The first attempt in Zimbabwe at organizing black workers was made by Masotsha Ndhlovu in 1928, as a branch of the ICU in South Africa. In 1934, Aaron Jacha, the Reverend Thompson Samkange, and other middle-class Africans formed the Southern Rhodesia African National Congress. The first general country-wide strike took place in 1948.

Petitioning the colonial governments whenever they had grievances, but otherwise doing little else, the approach of these early African organizations to their problems was naive and often lethargic, although some did demand the right to vote.

Nonetheless they signified the rise and growth of an African political consciousness, which manifested itself in the nationalist movements of the late 1950s. Among the first such organisations was the City Youth League — CYL — formed in Salisbury in 1955 by James Chikerema, George Nyandoro, and Edson Sithole.

Two years later, the CYL merged with the remnants of the old ANC to form the Southern Rhodesia African National Congress with Joshua Nkomo as President. In 1959 the organization was banned. To carry on the political work a new party, the National Democratic Party, headed by Michael Mawema, was formed in 1960.

Meanwhile Britain, which had consistently refused to consider the idea of the proposed federation, now accepted a plan put forward by Godfrey Huggins and Roy Welensky. Under the 1953 federation, the new parliament, which sat in Salisbury (now Harare), had thirty-six seats, of which only six were set aside for the African majority.

The first Federation prime minister, Garfield Todd, steered a liberal course considered too radical by the settlers. He was replaced in 1958 by Edgar Whitehead. Conservative though he was, his pace was much too slow for the white supremist Dominion Party, strong advocates of the apartheid system, which merged with other racist-inclined groups in 1962 to form the Rhodesian Front. Its leader, Winston Field, was prime minister.

Appalled by the independence of Nyasa-

Above: Grim memorials of the final struggle for Zimbabwe's freedom now held in Zimbabwe's National Military Museum, Gweru, and portraits of those who led the fighting.

land as Malawi and Northern Rhodesia as Zambia, the Rhodesian Front determined to make Southern Rhodesia an independent, white-ruled state.

Field, however, was unprepared to ride roughshod over the constitution and he was forced to resign in favour of the dogmatic Ian Smith who proclaimed a Unilateral Declaration of Independence — UDI — on 11 November, 1965.

Harold Wilson, the British Labour Prime Minister, equivocal and uncertain, vacillated too long. Compounding the crisis by refusing to put in troops to uphold the constitution (a measure he would almost certainly never have hesitated to take against an insubordinate black colony), Wilson's only option, and that a dubious one, was to apply sanctions.

A subsequent meeting aboard HMS *Tiger* between Wilson and Smith did nothing more than confirm Wilson's weakness and unwillingness to confront the rebels and Smith's belligerent intransigence.

Although the United Nations imposed sanctions in the same year, another futile meeting between Wilson and Smith on HMS

Fearless merely served to confirm the fanaticism of the European minority's determination to cling to illegal power at whatever cost. (Smith and his fellow rebels declared Rhodesia a republic in 1970.)

The die was cast for the bloody conflict to begin and many on both sides were condemned to die in the cauldron of hatred and recrimination that now boiled over.

The illegal Smith government moved swiftly, detaining many leaders without trial and holding them in remote areas for a decade or more. It was left to others who had fled the country to sustain the freedom fight, men like Jason Moyo and Herbert Chitepo.

Thousands of Africans, including school children, fled the country to join the independence struggle from abroad. As the liberation forces struck deep into Rhodesia, the whites emigrated in thousands, leaving behind a beleaguered European community. Encouraged by their success in the countryside, the guerillas began to attack economic and military targets in the urban centres.

This struggle, causing great loss of life and suffering on both sides, continued for almost

Above: Rebel Premier Ian Smith and his white cabinet colleagues defy Britain and the world and sign the 1965 Unilateral Declaration of Independence, leading Rhodesia into a bloody decade and a half of war.

two decades, despite attempts by the white minority to establish a constitutional settlement that would leave them in power.

Training camps were established in Tanzania and an important link was forged between freedom fighters operating in the north of what was then Portuguese-ruled Mozambique. In 1969, the exiled leaders of the Zimbabwe African National Union (ZANU) formed the *Dare re Chimurenga* as the high command of the liberation struggle.

A network of *mujibas* was created, young scouts who could pass on information by word of mouth; by war's end in 1979 they totalled 50,000.

As a countermeasure to the *mujibas*, the Rhodesians established a system of "protected villages" (concentration camps) where the African population was herded together to cut off all contacts with the guerillas.

Combined with the brutality of both the army and the police, this policy actually accelerated the recruitment of freedom fighters and by September 1975, about 1,000 volunteers a week were crossing into Mozambique for guerilla training.

As the war escalated, the Smith regime entered into a series of ultimately fruitless negotiations in a quest for peace. After extensive discussions involving Zambian leader Kenneth Kaunda, a "unity accord" was signed in the Zambian capital of Lusaka in December 1974. Under the terms of this "accord" nationalist leaders who had been detained by the Smith regime were to be released.

The cease-fire, however, failed to take effect and the struggle continued. More talks were held at Victoria Falls in August 1975 with South African Premier John Vorster, Kaunda, Smith, moderate black leader Bishop Abel Muzorewa, and Nkomo — but in vain.

At this juncture, US Secretary of State Henry Kissinger began to apply pressure on Smith to agree to some form of majority rule. This was to be worked out at a Geneva conference beginning in October 1976. In response, ZANU and the rival Zimbabwe African People's Union (ZAPU) merged to form the Patriotic Front (PF), which greatly strengthened their military and diplomatic positions. In Geneva they formed a formid-

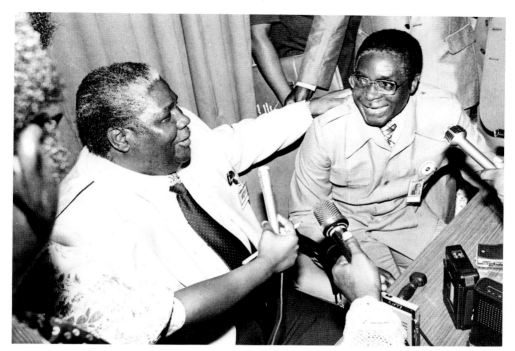

Above: Joshua Nkomo (left) and President Robert Mugabe, two of the leading figures in the bitter struggle for liberation, celebrate Zimbabwe's freedom.

able power and rejected the Kissinger package, while Smith stubbornly pressed on for an "internal settlement".

Smith's negotiations with the moderate black parties — Muzorewa's African National Congress (ANC), Sithole's faction of ZANU, and Jeremiah Chirau's party — and the following election in 1979 resulted in a transitional Muzorewa-led government.

Rhodesia's white minority approved the new "constitution" in a referendum, but international recognition was withheld. The Patriotic Front, regarded by the international community as the only authentic representative of the Zimbabwean people, had taken no part in the talks or the subsequent elections.

By now about 35,000 guerillas were active inside Rhodesia while 150,000 refugees had fled to Mozambique. On the verge of collapse, the Smith regime had become an international pariah — even South Africa had renounced its support.

After much diplomatic activity and some adept manoeuvring, especially by Kaunda

and Tanzanian President Julius Nyerere, the way was finally opened for an all-party constitutional conference at Lancaster House in London that ultimately led to independence.

Although the struggle had finally drawn to an end, the cost in human terms was horrifying. Smith's declaration of UDI had left a tragic legacy, scars which for many would never heal. In all, some 27,000 people on both sides had died in this second war of liberation.

Independent Zimbabwe

The Lancaster House Agreement, signed on 21 December, 1979 by the leaders of the Patriotic Front (Mugabe and Nkomo) and the Muzorewa and British governments, called for a cease-fire, the drafting of a new constitution, and free universal elections within six months.

The interim constitution provided for a multi-party state with free elections on the basis of one man, one vote, but on two different electoral rolls. Parliament was to have 100 seats, twenty of them reserved exclusively for the white minority during a ten-year transition period.

Elections were held in February 1980, and although the Patriotic Front's Robert Mugabe did not return home until 27 January, ZANU (PF) won a decisive victory and Mugabe became the first prime minister of Zimbabwe.

At the stroke of midnight on 18 April, 1980, virtually two decades after the country's Africans took up arms in the second *Chimurenga*, just over a century after Rhodes landed in South Africa, and only eighty-three years after the lands of the Ndebele and Shona were named Rhodesia by British royal decree, Zimbabwe was born and Rhodes's statue was removed from the streets of the capital he named Salisbury, now Harare.

The first decade

Zimbabwe — the name is taken from *zimba ramabwe*, the Shona words for "big house of stone" — became a democratic republic headed by a President who administers government policy through a ministerial cabinet. General elections are held every five years. The two-house parliament — a senate and a house of assembly — were merged into one chamber in 1990.

The green of the flag represents the land; gold its mineral wealth; red the blood shed for freedom; and black the country's people. To the left is a white triangle that stands for the final peace.

On the triangle is the Zimbabwe Bird, a representation of the seven carved soapstone birds found within the ritual enclosure in the ruins of Great Zimbabwe (and carried off by art collectors). All but one has since been returned. The red star behind the bird represents Zimbabwe's national hopes.

Similar themes are expressed in the national coat of arms. The colour green represents the fertility of the land; the wavy blue and white lines, the water that brings prosperity; the rifle and the hoe, the transition from war to peace; the gold and green wreath, the mining and agricultural industries; the star tinged with red, the hopes for the future and past bloodshed; the kudu's harmonious colours of black, brown, and white, the various ethnic origins of the Zimbabwe people; the earthen mound represents the plants and the clothing that give succour to the people; and finally the motto emphasises the need for unity and work to preserve the country's hard-won freedom.

The legacy that the freedom fighters, led by Mugabe, left on the landscape was not one of death and bloodshed, but of peace and hope.

Yet with an estimated population of 8.5 million in 1985, and growing yearly by more than 3.5 per cent, there is intense pressure on the government to meet the growing demands, and on demographic and development planners to create housing and employment.

To cope with the migration of rural people to the cities, planners built the satellite city of Chitungwiza, close to Harare. By 1989 it was the country's third-largest conurbation.

Among the most impressive achievements is the country's conservation record. Zimbabwe's national parks system is among the finest in the world, and farmers and other individuals have also established many private game ranches and wildlife parks. In some safari areas, the game is more than plentiful and hunting is allowed.

At an average cost of US$600 a day for each individual, plus heavy payments for trophy licences, hunting enables excess wildlife populations to be culled while earning income to meet the increasing overheads incurred by intensive wildlife management and conservation projects.

These wildlife sanctuaries sustain some of the last great concentrations of African wildlife: imperilled elephant and rhino, herds of buffalo, antelope such as the magnificent greater kudu, and Lake Kariba's 40,000 Nile crocodile which form the largest single population of the species in the world.

There have been equally dramatic improvements in social welfare and education, matched by impressive developments in the industrial, agricultural, and tourism sectors.

Indeed, as 1990 dawned, the old freedom fighters who led the country through its first ten years of independence had every reason to reflect with pride on the great good that has arisen out of the bitter struggle to create Zimbabwe.

The Land: Diamonds and Coal, Wheat and Tobacco

Zimbabwe lies between the Limpopo and Zambezi rivers in south central Africa. It is bounded by Zambia in the north and north-west, by South Africa in the south by Mozambique in the east and north-east; and by Botswana in the south-west.

The country, part of the great plateau that is a major feature of the geography of southern Africa, lies wholly to the north of the Tropic of Capricorn and covers a total area of 390,245 square kilometres (150,674 square miles).

Zimbabwe is roughly three times the size of England and almost the same size as California, with a population density of approximately sixteen people to every square kilometre.

Most of the country stands 300 metres (984 feet) or more above sea-level and at least four-fifths of it is 600 metres (1,967 feet) or more above sea-level. Slightly less than one-twentieth is higher than 1,500 metres (4,921 feet).

The most outstanding geographical feature is Zimbabwe's central plateau, known as the highveld. Running about 650 kilometres (400 miles) from north-east to south-west and eighty kilometres (50 miles) from east to west, it is bordered on either side by the middleveld.

The other outstanding feature of Zimbabwe is Africa's fourth-largest and least-spoilt river, the Zambezi, which marks the country's north-western border with Zambia and gave birth in the 1960s to what was then the world's largest man-made lake.

The Zambezi begins its 2,700-kilometre (1,678-mile) journey to the Indian Ocean on the slopes of a remote and little-known hill in north-west Zambia. At Kazungula it forms Zimbabwe's northern border with Zambia. Eighty kilometres (50 miles) downstream from this point the Zambezi plunges over the Victoria Falls.

Twice the height and one and a half times the width of North America's Niagara Falls, the ancestry of this great natural wonder of the world goes back 150 million years to the age of the dinosaurs when widespread volcanic activity changed the shape and form of southern Africa and — where the falls now thunder and rage — pushed up a huge slab of basalt.

Between eleven and ten million years ago, when the Zambezi is believed to have flowed southward into the Orange River, a gentle uplifting of the earth changed its course to the east and, much later, it began flowing over the basalt plateau.

About two million years ago, the river began to knife through the basalt to cut the Batoka Gorge. After cutting back 100 kilometres (60 miles) it reached the first of a series of transverse faults which formed the initial "Victoria Falls". Seven worn sets of falls preceded those of today. The first set of falls was formed some eight kilometres (five miles) downstream from the present one.

Nine falls

The Zambezi is now in the process of shaping the ninth set of falls. It is carving through Cataract Island. Eventually, many thousands of years from now, a new gorge will follow this line all the way across to Zambia, replacing the present falls.

Though undoubtedly this is the apogee of the river's long journey to the sea, it is by no means all that the Zambezi achieves.

Downstream from the falls, this great wall of water is captured between 300-metre-high (1,000-foot) cliffs, barely thirty metres (100 feet) apart, and for the next 100 kilometres (60 miles) funnels through the gorge over a series of foaming cataracts.

Where it enters the middle Zambezi Valley, its energy-spent waters trapped by the Kariba Dam, the river bellies out to form

Overleaf: Victoria Falls and the Zambezi upstream seen from the air over the Zambian shores.

Above: The spectacular Sanyati Gorge at Lake Kariba.
Opposite: Sightseers enjoy the awesome spectacle of the world's largest body of falling water.

one of the world's largest man-made lakes.

Tamed and under control, its flow regulated, the river passes out into the lower valley — transformed by the Kariba hydroelectric scheme into a wilderness without compare.

Leaving Zimbabwe behind as it enters Mozambique at Feira, the river, almost at once, forms a second man-made lake of great proportions. Lake Cabora Bassa is virtually as long and slender as Lake Kariba.

From there the Zambezi slowly makes its way downstream through Tete, entering the Indian Ocean through a many-fingered delta south of Quelimane and the coastal town of Chinde where, legend says, Solomon and Sheba's envoys began their journey upstream to carry away the treasures of Ophir.

Three levels

Massive granite outcrops occur in many parts of Zimbabwe, including the Eastern Highlands that form the border with Mozambique, a range of dramatic and beautiful mountains stretching some 350 kilometres (217 miles) from north to south. Within the chain stands Inyangani, which at 2,592 metres (8,504 feet) is the country's highest mountain.

Granite domes and rocky outcrops also dot much of the highveld landscape, particularly in the north. The highveld, the most fertile area of the country, contains the largest urban centres.

Rare, but thick, forests are also part of the highveld scenery in some sparsely populated areas largely reserved for wildlife. Kopjes — small granite hills severely weathered by the elements — formed along weak joints and cracks are striking features of the main plateau.

The natural vegetation of the highveld is mostly savannah woodland, with trees well spaced over wide expanses of grassland. Among the trees, *msasa* and *munhondo* dominate. Exotic species (pine, eucalyptus) have also been introduced.

The great dyke

Stretching more than 500 kilometres (310 miles) across the centre of Zimbabwe, from Guruve in the north-east to Mberengera in

Above: Coffee plantation in the Vumba Mountains.

the south-west, the mineral-rich Great Dyke is a ridge of 2,000-million-year-old hills ranging in width from three to eleven kilometres (two to seven miles).

The dyke is loaded with gold, gems, and precious minerals, a fabulously rich repository of all the fabled metals of legendary Ophir.

This ridge, which serves as the country's "backbone", is dominated in the north by the Mvurwi Range with Mount Mvurwi, 1,748 metres (5,735 feet) high and Mount Chikonyora, 1,731 metres (5,679 feet) high. The Mashava Hills constitute the centre and the Matobo Hills the backbone's southern extremity.

The middleveld

Riven by deep valleys, the middleveld, perched between 600 and 1,200 metres (2,000–4,000 feet) above sea-level, is split into many great blocks of fine plateau country.

The central plateau forms the main watershed and divides Zimbabwe's rivers into two drainage systems — one northbound into the Zambezi and the other south into the Save and Limpopo rivers. The north-ern edge of the plateau forms a rugged escarpment above the Zambezi Valley.

The middleveld (as its name suggests) is a transition area between the highveld and the lowveld. The vegetation found there varies considerably with altitude and rainfall and, although generally less fertile than the highveld, it is widely used for agriculture.

The lowveld

The lowveld, an area lying below 600 metres (2,000 feet), consists of a narrow strip along the Zambezi Valley where the Kariba Dam has created Lake Kariba, and a broader tract in the south-west of the country.

Tree species such as mopane often dominate the lowveld's peculiarly hot, dry, and flat environment, bordering on semi-desert in certain areas, along with occasional sparse dry savannah woodlands and scrub. Baobabs are also common in many lowveld areas.

Acacia species, such as mimosa thorn and whistling thorn, abound. Zimbabwe teak grows well in the Kalahari area. Gallery forests proliferate along streams where their roots can reach water.

Zimbabwe's lowest point is the junction of

Above: Aberfoyle tea plantation, Honde Valley.

the Save and Runde rivers — just 162 metres (530 feet) above sea-level.

The savannah

The savannah is biologically a very productive environment, supporting Zimbabwe's extremely rich and varied wildlife, with species often differing according to the type of vegetation. There are a great number of large mammals: elephant, rhino, buffalo, giraffe, antelope, and large predators such as lion, cheetah, and leopard. Bird life is varied, as are the reptiles and insects.

Many large species are threatened because of dwindling natural habitats and poaching. Rhinoceros, Lichtenstein's hartebeest, oryx, pangolin, and cheetah are among the species protected by law.

Railway route

Early railway development followed the line of the central plateau on which the main towns and cities — Harare, Bulawayo, Gweru, Mutare, Kwe Kwe, Kadoma, and Masvingo — now stand. Naturally, the greatest development has taken place in these areas. Recent years, however, have seen the emphasis shift to more remote regions, particularly the south-eastern lowveld — now often referred to as simply "the lowveld".

Linked with the South African railway system at Beitbridge, the National Railways of Zimbabwe also serve Botswana in the south-west. In the north, via Bulawayo and the coalfields of Hwange, the system joins the Zambian railway across the great road-rail bridge that spans the Zambezi within sight and sound of the Victoria Falls.

The climate

Nature has given Zimbabwe one of the finest climates in the world.

The altitude of the country eases the tropical temperatures that might be expected in this latitude, and its landlocked location maintains a comfortably low level of humidity.

Generally, most days are bright and sunny and most nights clear and cool. Breezes temper the heat of October, while the remainder of the summer months are cooled by seasonal rains. June and July are cooler and, while the nights may be downright cold, the days are comparable to those of the most delightful English spring.

Above: Rugged granite grandeur of the Chimanimani Mountains in Zimbabwe's Eastern Highlands.
Opposite: Nyanga Mountains viewpoint overlooks Honde Valley.

There are four distinct seasons: winter from May to August, when night temperatures can drop below freezing point and there is little or no rain; a warm and normally dry spring between August and November; a summer rainy season between November and April; and a transitional autumn during April and May. Both temperature and rainfall are directly influenced by altitude. The high-veld and the Eastern Highlands have lower temperatures both in winter and in summer than the middleveld and especially the low-veld areas in the south and in the Zambezi Basin. The highveld enjoys a very equable climate with maximum summer temperatures hovering just below 30°C (86°F).

Rainfall is more abundant in the Eastern Highlands than on the plateau, which usually receive more than 1,000 millimetres (39 inches) a year, while annual rainfall in the lowveld is often below 400 millimetres (16 inches).

Natural Resources

Zimbabwe is a geological mosaic, richly endowed with natural resources both above and below ground. Minerals from the deep interior of the earth, bearing the ores of the Gold Belt, iron, nonferrous metals such as chrome and nickel and several others in the Great Dyke, have created intrusions in the ancient granitic plateau.

Lower basins in the north-west and south-west are partially covered with sedimentary rocks, of which the Karoo formations at Hwange contain coal. Additionally, a number of minerals with industrial applications, such as asbestos, are also mined.

As long ago as the twelfth century, and perhaps earlier, gold was mined in Zimbabwe, and alluvial gold has been sieved from river sediment since time immemorial.

In the Middle Ages gold was bartered for goods with Arab, Asian, and European traders through East African coastal ports like Sofala, which was first controlled by the Arabs and later the Portuguese.

But as the mines became exhausted, or more difficult to work with the limited technology available, the trade began to diminish.

The introduction of modern technology

revived the industry and today mining plays a major role in the country's economy, contributing some eight per cent to the country's Gross Domestic Product — GDP — and creating six per cent of the jobs. It is the second-largest foreign exchange earner after agriculture.

Zimbabwe has known deposits of more than forty different minerals but, with the exception of chromite and asbestos, most of these deposits are meagre by world standards. This has contributed to the development of small-scale mining as the most viable means of exploiting the country's mineral wealth.

About ninety-six per cent of Zimbabwe's total mineral output derives from ten major minerals — gold, asbestos, nickel, coal, copper, chromite, tin, iron ore, phosphate, and silver. Other minerals, such as bauxite, graphite, cyanite, emerald, cobalt, magnesite, lithium, limestone, mica, pyrites, ornamental stones, and barytes, make up the remaining four per cent. Production of copper, tin, and nickel has declined with falling world prices.

Mineral exploration is undertaken by the Zimbabwe Government and the Zimbabwe Mining Development Corporation (ZMDC). Most notable was the Airborne Magnetic Survey conducted over a sizable area of the country.

The more fertile areas produce food for both local and regional consumption and cash crops such as cotton. The most important cash crop is tobacco, which is Zimbabwe's third-largest foreign exchange earner followed by coffee and tea. With varying climates and soil the country is roughly divided into five distinct zones, each with its own particular form of agriculture.

Energy

Most of Zimbabwe's hydroelectric power comes from the Kariba Dam. The power supply is operated jointly by Zimbabwe and Zambia. Zimbabwe utilizes the entire output of the southern bank station and imports a third of the output from the northern bank station.

The two thermal power stations at Hwange colliery are the other main sources of electricity. Zimbabwe's coal reserves have been estimated at 30,000 million tonnes. With three million tonnes mined annually, the deposits should last for at least another 10,000 years at the present rate of domestic consumption.

In the cities many African households have electricity, but it is available to only a small percentage of rural people who remain heavily dependent on wood fuel as their sole source of energy. Deforestation and soil erosion, always serious problems, are now critical.

Water Supplies

There are no natural lakes in Zimbabwe and surface water is limited and scarcely investigated. Most water supplies come from rainfall, collected for use in dams during the long season of annual drought when many rivers dry up.

With more than 7,000 dams, Zimbabwe leads the Third World countries in the scope and scale of its water conservation. The Kariba Dam on the Zambezi is the largest — more than 100 times the size of the third-largest, Lake Mutirikwi, which is an integral part of the large irrigation scheme in the south-eastern lowveld. Several new major dams were either under construction in the 1990s or on the drawing board.

Agriculture uses a large percentage of the total water supply. Thousands of small dams on farms and in villages also provide water for crop irrigation, livestock, and fish breeding.

The growth of population, industry, and mining, coupled with the rapid rise in demand from agriculture for water, have all contributed to a great increase in the demand for water throughout the country.

All the major urban centres take their water for domestic and industrial use from dams in the neighbourhood. Water utilization is closely monitored, and there is a constant search for new groundwater sources and programmes to improve river yields by building dams.

Previous pages: Buffalo herd on the shores of Lake Kariba.
Opposite: The haunting beauty of Lake Kariba's drowned forests.
Following page: Spectacular balancing rocks in Harare's Epworth suburb.

The People: A Culture Rooted in the Soil

Intense and carefree, cosmopolitan and parochial, the vast majority of Zimbabwe's people stem from the great family of Bantu-speaking migrants who first ventured east and south across Africa some 2,000 years ago.

Iron makers and agriculturalists, they settled on the highveld, middleveld, and around the Eastern Highlands and began the long process of establishing the distinctive Shona culture that is so much a part of Zimbabwe.

Their Bantu kin — the Zulu warriors of King Mzilikazi — did not arrive until the first half of the nineteenth century. They form the Ndebele, Zimbabwe's largest minority. Despite their late arrival, there are many cultural similarities between the two Bantu-speaking communities, which together form an overwhelming majority.

Made up of many ethnic constituents, the Shona language comes to life in a number of diverse dialects. Apart from the western-based Karanga, one of the largest Shona groups, the Shona communities occupy most of central and eastern Zimbabwe. Other large Shona groups include the Zezuru, Manyika, Ndau, and Korekore.

The Karanga speak a strange vernacular drawn from both Shona and Sindebele, the Nguni Zulu language of the Ndebele who dominate Matabeleland Province in the south-west.

Sindebele came with the invader Mzilikazi, who founded the Ndebele nation when he migrated north to escape Shaka the Zulu's warriors (See "The Gold and the Silver").

Other minority ethnic groups with their own indigenous cultures are the Tonga in the north-west, and the Vendao and Hlengwe communities living along the country's south-western and eastern borders. There are also small European and Asian minorities, but Zimbabwe no longer defines its people by individual tribe, colour, or culture, choosing to categorize all as Zimbabweans.

Zimbabwe's native cultures are firmly rooted in the soil. No more than one in four indigenous people make their homes in urban areas. Of those that do move to the city, few rarely forget their rural roots.

If you want to understand these sturdy but gentle folk, you must travel to their homelands. There, in the heart of the country, you will be able to see their individual and community persona.

Nowhere is it more instantly recognizable than in the traditional homestead — inevitably a mud and thatch rondavel with baked earth floors constantly swept and washed by houseproud womenfolk, and often decorated with beautiful, abstract colour designs using earth dyes.

The home usually consists of a separate kitchen hut, sleeping huts, and a granary. When a house is built the circular walls, reinforced with wood, are made first. Traditionally, the entrance faces west to shield it from the prevailing easterly winds. The walls are given a smooth finish from a plaster-like material of fine-grained soil taken from a termite mound, pounded into dust, and mixed with water.

Religion

Like many African communities, traditional Zimbabwean cultures have a firm mono-theistic faith rooted in the belief in one supreme creator. Today this has been melded with the Christian message into the syncretic faith — part Christian, part tradition — that is followed by at least fifty per cent of the people.

The traditional aspect of this dual-sided faith is rooted in the custom of channelling all prayers to the supreme creator, *Mwari* (God), through family ancestors. In times of trouble and misfortune worshippers consult a spirit medium for advice, for they are believed to have direct contact with the ancestors.

The mystical atmosphere of the caves used by the first inhabitants of Zimbabwe, the "San", thousands of years ago for their unique and extraordinary art, profoundly influenced later communities.

One such group, the Mbire Shoko community (a Bantu-Shona group), migrated south from East Africa's Lake Tanganyika during the last 1,000 years, taking with them

Above: Boaters and blazers in the British tradition for top echelon schoolboys in Harare, capital of Zimbabwe.

Top left: Young tea picker with child in Honde Valley.

Left: Smiling youngster of the Honde Valley.

their belief in one supreme creator.

This faith found its greatest expression in Great Zimbabwe, where it became the centralizing religious authority, and in the Matobo Hills. The caves that inspired the "San" artists became the spiritual shrines of the Mbire.

During the fifteenth century, at the height of the Mbire-ruled Rozvi Empire which was finally overthrown by Mzilikazi, the Shona frequently visited these shrines each of which had an oracle — the voice of the *Mwari*. So powerful was this faith that it spread across the Limpopo and was taken up by the Vendao community.

This spirituality attained its greatest strength in the Matobo Hills area. Indeed it eventually became known as *Mwari ve-Matonjeni*, God of the Matobo, and was adopted by the Ndebele whose reverence for the Matobo is sacred.

They called the creator *Mulimu*, provider of rain and guardian of nature, and sought divine intercession whenever calamity threatened. It was after such consultation with the priests, priestesses, and oracles of "the place of the benevolent spirits" (Matobo Hills) that the Ndebele took up arms against the Europeans in 1896.

Early Christian missionaries like the Moffat family recognised the purity of the Shona and Ndebele belief in the unknowable High God, the one creator, and adopted the local concept into their scriptural teachings, making it synonymous with the Christian faith.

Mwari shrines are still held in reverential awe by local communities and ceremonies to appease the ancestral spirits, overcome ill-fortune, and particularly to make rain, are still held in the Matobo Hills caves and at other sacred places throughout Zimbabwe.

At least a quarter of the population, however, has accepted Christianity outright — mainly Roman Catholic — although there are strong congregations of Anglican, Apostolic, Methodist, Baptist, Seventh Day Adventist, Presbyterian, and Salvation Army devotees.

The first Christian mission stations were opened in 1859 at Inyati, near Bulawayo and in 1870 at Hope Fountain, Bulawayo. Both were operated by the London Missionary Society and led by Reverend Robert Moffat.

Soon to follow were black evangelists sent out by the Dutch Reformed Church of South Africa, and the Jesuit Fathers opened a mission near Lobengula's kraal in 1880. The Anglican Church opened missions in the 1890s, as did the Methodists and a number of other denominations.

The missionaries erected schools, offered agricultural training, and provided medical help. Yet it took a considerable time before the Africans themselves could become priests and eventually take over most of the social and educational activities of the missionary institutions.

Today many new religions originating in Africa are gaining ground. The most important is the Zionist or Apostolic Church, a kind of revival movement dependent on charismatic leaders. It is characterised by social practices such as polygamy, dancing, and open-air sermons. Zimbabwe also has a minority of Muslims, Jews, and Hindus.

Traditional Crafts

Long ago in Zimbabwe, the Njanja, in the south-west along the Save River, were considered specialists in metallurgy, as well as performing the more functional tasks of iron smith and blacksmith.

Iron mining and smelting were introduced by the original Bantu immigrants several thousand years ago, and weapons and tools were fashioned from iron that had been repeatedly heated in the furnace and hammered until it was pure and malleable.

Along with knives and spears for war and defence, hoes for preparing the land were the most commonly manufactured items. The hoe or the *badza* was — and still is — the universal farming tool. It consists of an iron blade, usually oval in shape, set into a wooden handle.

Axes were made for many different purposes, both as weapons and tools for domestic use. Spears were either short *assegais*, the type that was introduced by the Ndebele as a stabbing weapon, or the long throwing spears used by the Shona.

Shields were made of selected ox hide, treated to become supple and strong, then applied to a wooden frame. The patterns on the Ndebele shield indicated the bearer's regiment and rank.

Above: Traditional dancers at folk village, Victoria Falls.

A wide range of daggers, their iron blades beaten from a central ridge into two sharp edges, was also produced. The wooden handle, as well as the sheath, was beautifully decorated.

Faced with industrial competition, this form of craftsmanship died out and few original items remain. Simpler versions, however, are still crafted for tourists. And carved wood still distinguishes many household and domestic items used in traditional society.

The family patriarch often had his own stool and a well-carved headrest was a treasured possession, handed down from father to son.

Walking sticks have religious significance as well as practical uses, as does the *hakata* — a divining implement made from bone or ivory — of the *nganga*, society's traditional healer. These implements traditionally come in sets of four, with individual symbols representing various omens.

The penis sheath (*umnecwado*) was widely used by Ndebele men. Encasing the penis, the sheath hung under an apron made from cloth and was tied around the waist by a bark fibre.

Weaving

Wild cotton was used for making cloth on wooden looms as early as the thirteenth century. The practice ended because of cloth imports brought by Arab and Portuguese traders from India and Europe.

Bark from certain species of trees, softened and twisted into thread or rope, was another raw material from which cloth was woven. The finished cloth was dyed and used to make mats, dresses (especially aprons for young unmarried women), containers in which to store cereals and dried provisions and hang from trees away from pests; and for fashioning beehives and arrow quivers. This handicraft still flourishes.

Baskets

Cane, reed, grass, palm fronds, sisal, and

similiar materials are still used to weave wickerwork into a variety of products including storage containers for cereals or scoops for winnowing grain. Other wickerwork is also fashioned into chairs, fish traps, carpets, and sleeping mats. Certain groups specialize in this craft, making it a full-time occupation.

Pottery

Pottery, made in Zimbabwe for thousands of years, is a traditional craft handed down from mother to daughter.

The clay is dried and ground into powder, then rinsed and mixed with water. The pots, shaped with various tools, are fashioned on a flat base and often inscribed with decorations. The finished surface is polished with a smooth pebble.

After drying in the sun, the pots are fired in a pit covered with burning grass, twigs, or cow dung. Some hours later the pots are removed and sealed with a mixture of liquid maize or cow dung to make them watertight.

The decorations, including some geometrical designs used for centuries, are painted later. The sizes and forms of these pots have remained virtually the same through hundreds of years, for rural needs have changed little. The basic uses are for fetching water, storing grain, brewing beer, cooking meals, and curdling milk.

Music, Dance, and Drama

Most communities use traditional instruments for their religious music and festival dances. Major celebrations involve a wide range of drums, such as *mbira* and *marimba*, combined with modern instruments, like the guitar and saxophone.

The *Mbira* is a "thumb piano" with metal keys fixed to a square wooden block. The number of keys varies from eight to twelve in a single row and up to fifty or more arranged in several rows. The *mbira* is sometimes played inside a gourd that serves as an amplifier.

The *marimba* is a xylophone type of instrument made of thin wooden keys on a frame, sometimes placed over a line of gourds to amplify and deepen the resonance.

The most common drum is cylindrical, narrow at the bottom, and covered at the top by cow, zebra, or elephant hide. There are also small hand drums, drums on legs, and friction drums played with a stick from inside.

Tambourines and rattleboxes are made from the dried seedpods of leguminous plants, which are sometimes strung and tied around the ankles of dancers. The unique Zimbabwe reed rattle is traditionally played by women, especially at weddings and in church.

Above: Salute to the Zulu warrior traditions of the Zimbabwe people.

PART TWO: PLACES AND TRAVEL

Above: The "Flight of Angels" over Victoria Falls.
Opposite: Bumi Hills Safari Lodge overlooking the shores of Lake Kariba.

The Zambezi: Dr. Livingstone and A Pride of Angels

Africa's fourth-largest and least-spoilt river, the Zambezi, rises on the slopes of a small, remote, and little-known hill — little more than 300 kilometres (186 miles) from the source of the Zaire (Congo) River — in the Mwinilunga District of north-western Zambia, where the Zaire border meets Zambia and the easternmost boundary of Angola.

Although the two rivers originate so close together, they soon travel their separate ways; the Zaire flowing north and then west, the Zambezi flowing south and then east. Indeed, almost as soon as this nascent, sunbright stream leaps and bounds down the hill, it enters Angola.

Never Zaire's and not quite Angola's, even though it flows through that country for 300 kilometres (186 miles), the Zambezi belongs exclusively in the world's mind to Zambia, Zimbabwe, and Mozambique.

From Angola the river continues its cross-country wanderings, re-entering Zambia at Angola's Caripande border post, then raging downstream over the Chovuma Falls and through the rapids of the Nyamboma Gorge before slowing down to meander across the Luena Flats, on past Senange to Kazungula. There, where rich riverine forests spring to life along its banks, it forms Zimbabwe's northern border with Zambia.

Some eighty kilometres (50 miles) downstream from this point the Zambezi reaches what for many explorers and millions of later visitors is perhaps the summation of a visit to Zimbabwe — Victoria Falls, also known as "Mosi-oa-Tunya" ("the smoke that thunders").

It is there almost exactly halfway along the river's 2,700-kilometre (1,678-mile) journey to the Indian Ocean that the Zambezi plunges headlong into a vertical chasm that spans the river's full one-and-a-half-kilometre (one-mile) width.

Now a solid curtain of water, fragmented only briefly by four small islands of startling green, the Zambezi thunders over the edge of a sheer, 100-metre (328-foot) precipice.

The power of the falls is awesome. On one occasion in 1958, when the flow reached more than 700,000 cubic metres (14.3 million cubic feet) a minute, the water in the gorge rose eighteen metres (60 feet) above its normal flood level, double the depth of the seasonal variation in the water levels.

This constant pounding by the currents of the mighty Zambezi has, over the millenniums, cut through the rock faults and fissures of its ancient bed and carved not one but eight successive precipices (and has now begun to carve a ninth) to form one of the greatest physical spectacles in Africa (See "Diamonds and Coal, Wheat and Tobacco", Part One).

Graceful palms

It was around sundown on 15 November, 1855, shafts of gold reflecting off the rippling waters, when the Makololo crew, glistening backs moving back and forth in rhythm, beached the canoe carrying Scottish missionary Dr. David Livingstone on Kalai Island, midstream in the Zambezi.

Livingstone camped there overnight and set off for the falls, some kilometres downstream, at sunup next morning, as elephant and other game paraded down to the mainland banks.

Along with the number and variety of wild animals, Livingstone was also impressed by the plants and wildflowers, including the ancient baobab trees: "There, towering over all, stands the great and burly baobab, each of whose arms would form the trunk of a large tree, beside groups of graceful palms which with their feathery-shaped leaves depicted on the sky lend their beauty to the scene." (See "Flora: A Land of Flaming Colour", Part Four).

Not far from the edge of the great falls, he noted: "After 20 minutes we viewed for the first time vapour or, as it is appropriately called, 'smoke'. . . ."

Negotiating the rapids a little upstream from the falls, his crew landed on the western

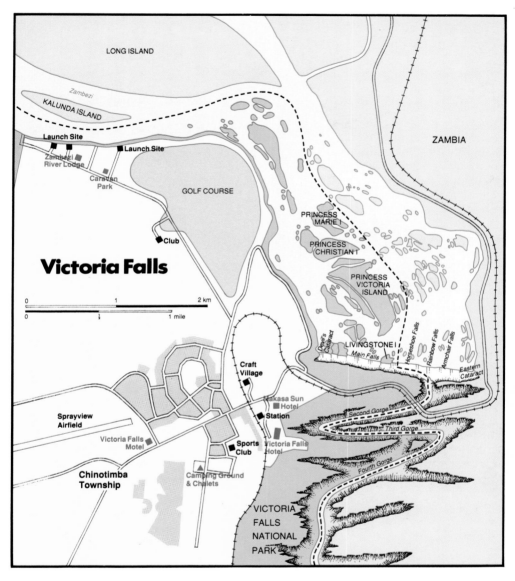

Victoria Falls

side of an island that stands in the centre of the river at the top of the precipice.

Though he had seen "five columns of vapour rising 250 feet [76 metres] to mingle with the clouds", he was unprepared for the spectacle that greeted him after he stepped ashore on the island that now bears his name and marks the Zambian border.

Reaching the edge of the precipice, he looked down in awe and humility. On either side of him a solid sheet of water launched itself over the brink.

To measure the depth of the falls, the missionary-explorer tied some bullets and a length of calico to a line and lowered it over the edge of the cliff. But it snagged on some rocks about ninety-one metres (300 feet) below.

"They were coloured white below and higher up became dark, probably as the vapour condensed and turned into showers," Livingstone noted in his journal.

Overleaf: Rainbow arches across Devil's Cataract on the western bank of Victoria Falls.

Above: Sundown's lengthening shadows fall over the Zambezi River.

"The falls are singularly formed. They are simply the whole mass of the Zambezi waters rushing into a fissure or rent made right across the bed of the river."

The prosaic but sensitive Scotsman was so overwhelmed by his first sight of the great falls on the Zambezi that he momentarily abandoned his pragmatic scientific observations to wax — not without justification — rhapsodic.

"It had never been seen before by European eyes," he wrote as the spray from the falls soaked him and his notebook, "but scenes so lovely must have been gazed upon by angels in their flight."

Loyally, the good missionary, whose heart lies buried in the continent to which he gave his life, named this great wonder of the world after Victoria, his British queen.

National park

The falls and the surrounding rainforest are preserved as a 23.4-square-kilometre (nine-square-mile) national park and one of Zimbabwe's four World Heritage sites.

Next to the falls and its forest is the Zambezi National Park, covering 573 square kilometres (221 square miles) with its elephant and buffalo herds; magnificent roan, sable, impala, and kudu antelope; and myriad other game.

To help visitors observe this seemingly endless variety of game, Zimbabwe's national parks and wildlife management authority maintains 125 kilometres (78 miles) of game-viewing roads in Victoria Falls National Park and adjacent Zambezi National Park, including a fifty-kilometre (30-mile) trail along the bank of the Zambezi.

The potential of the untapped power of the falls was all too obvious to the early Europeans. But although the Victoria Falls Power Company was formed to exploit it, less than a third of the shares were taken and the project never started.

It was planned to channel the Zambezi's waters to a generating station in the gorge below the bridge, ninety-one metres (300 feet) below the falls and three metres (10 feet) above the flood level. It provoked such feeling that a protest meeting in Salisbury (now Harare) demanded that the beauty of the falls should never be disturbed.

In fact, all that does mar the natural beauty

of this setting — though many will argue that its engineering attributes match the grandeur around it — is the bridge that spans the narrowest point of the gorge below the falls. It was placed there at the wish of Cecil Rhodes, who envisaged a Cape to Cairo railway as one of the main linchpins in his grand design to colonize Africa.

He said that the bridge should be built close enough for passengers to see the falls and feel the spray in their carriages. But Rhodes died in March 1902, a year before the preliminary work began and two years before the railway reached Victoria Falls in June 1904.

Almost 2,000 tonnes of steel were used to build the bridge, which was first assembled at the factory in England before being shipped in pieces to Rhodesia.

For the next fourteen months, men, equipment, and supplies were moved from one side of the gorge to the other on a trolley suspended from a cable slung more than 107 metres (350 feet) above the water raging through the gorge below.

The breaking point of the cable was fifteen tonnes, but when heavy rolling stock was being moved it sagged as much as 7.5 metres (25 feet).

Construction of the main girder work, which started on both sides early in 1905, took only nine weeks. So accurate was this great feat of engineering that on 2 April, 1905, the final 152-metre (500-foot) centre section slotted into place exactly. Legend says that the first living creature to cross it was a leopard.

Tollmaster

The bridge was opened on 12 September, 1905, by Professor Frances Darwin, President of the British Association and son of Charles Darwin, the English naturalist and author of *On the Origin of Species* and *The Descent of Man.*

Contractor George Pauling's daughter was given the honour of driving the first train across. Pauling, an indefatigable engineer, not only built most of the country's railway lines, but also walked 890 kilometres (553 miles) from Victoria Falls to the Congo border, tracing the route of Rhodes's proposed Cape to Cairo line.

Those who crossed the bridge paid a ten cent toll to Jack Soper who gave up crocodile hunting to become tollmaster, one of the first of many colourful eccentrics whose names stud the early European history of Africa.

Another was Pierre Gavuzzi, the first manager of the iron and timber Victoria Falls Hotel. Opened in June 1904, the hotel was raised on stilts to avoid damp and termites.

It consisted of twelve single rooms, four doubles, and a dining room and bar. In fact, it was so basic that many preferred to sleep aboard the train parked at the station.

Soon, however, a stream of visitors — mainly the wealthy, aristocratic, famous, and adventurous, as well as traders and hunters — all made the long pilgrimage to see this natural marvel and within eight years, overlooking the second gorge and the bridge, a new hotel had taken the place of the first.

Now much enlarged and frequently refurbished, the wide, terraced gardens, spacious guest rooms, banqueting hall, and original public rooms remain nostalgic reminders of the elegance and grandeur of those early days.

The hotel was given a royal accolade when Britain's King George VI, Queen Elizabeth, Princess Elizabeth, and Princess Margaret stayed there during their visit to Southern Africa in 1947.

In 1910, the original railway line that ran between the hotel and the gorge was realigned. The old track was taken up and relaid as a tramline for the old and infirm to travel the one and a half kilometres (one mile) to the falls in trolleys pushed by Africans.

Tragic bride

The falls have lured many to their deaths — either accidentally or suicidally. An eighty-four-year-old American widower, unable to bear the loss of his wife, made the long journey by road, sea, and rail to leap to his death from the bridge.

Overleaf: Century-old road-rail bridge spans the Batoka Gorge downstream from Victoria Falls to link Zimbabwe and Zambia. Victoria Falls Hotel, opened in 1904, overlooks the gorge.

A similar tragedy occurred in October 1912. After reporting the theft of Z$240 from his office, the local postmaster leapt into the gorge. And one unhappy bride ran from her honeymoon suite in the hotel after a tiff with her husband and jumped over the edge.

In 1932 another young woman, fleeing from a rapist in the rainforest, ran over the precipice in her panic — and her assailant, attempting to escape arrest, fell off the bridge.

Since the turn of the century the falls have claimed at least fifty lives. Others have only been saved by the daring and ingenuity of the rescue teams.

One team member, Ted Spencer, often performed breathtaking aerobatics over the falls in a light aircraft — which he once flew under the bridge. He always denied this for fear of losing his licence.

His charter flights gave visitors a unique view of Victoria Falls and the Zambezi, but on occasions the plane ran out of fuel and had to make a forced landing.

Spencer's night landings were a notable event. Flying low over the town he would cut his engines, lean his head out of the cockpit, and shout "Cars".

When his friends heard this, they drove quickly to the airstrip and lined their cars up on either side of the runway with their headlights on. After his death in an air crash at Croydon, London, just after the Second World War, his ashes were scattered over the falls.

Getting there

Victoria Falls, sixty-nine kilometres (43 miles) from Kazungula, 484 kilometres (300 miles) from Lusaka, 439 kilometres (273 miles) from Bulawayo, 878 kilometres (545 miles) from Harare, and 758 kilometres (471 miles) from Beitbridge, is linked to the rest of Zimbabwe by air, road, and rail. Air Zimbabwe operates a daily flight from Harare and a "bus" service from Hwange and Kariba. There is a regular passenger train service to Victoria Falls from Bulawayo and daily buses.

When to go

The Zambezi and Victoria Falls are at their most impressive between February and May when the river is in spate. But the weather is most pleasant between May and September.

Where to stay

Makasa Sun Hotel (4-star), Victoria Falls Hotel (4-star), Rainbow Hotel (3-star), A'Zambezi River Lodge (3-star), Sprayview Hotel (2-star). There are other hotels with varying standards of service and quality at Victoria Falls and luxurious fishing lodges along the banks of the Zambezi between Kazungula and Victoria Falls. See Listings for "Hotels". There is an excellent caravan park and campsite in Victoria Falls town. See Listings.

Sightseeing

Today most visitors fly into the airport twenty-one kilometres (13 miles) from **Victoria Falls town**, although some still arrive by rail while others journey by road from **Zambia** and **Botswana**'s nearby **Chobe National Park**.

Visitors from Chobe travel by road to the **border post** at **Kazungula** on the **Caprivi strip** in the extreme north-west of the country, where the boundaries of Zimbabwe, Botswana, Zambia, and **Namibia** meet. A **pontoon ferry** operates across the **Zambezi** between Zambia and Botswana at this point.

At some places in its eighty-kilometre (50-mile) journey from the border to Victoria Falls the Zambezi is more than two kilometres (1.2 miles) wide. Those who wish to discover more of the Zambezi's magic can explore the river by canoe safari — shooting a series of rapids at **Katombora**, **Sansimba**, and finally **Kandahar** during three days and nights of adventure in raw and totally unspoilt Africa.

Until recently only a handful of people, including Livingstone, had ever undertaken this journey, which combines long, idyllic stretches of calm water and palm-covered white sand islands with the nerve-tingling thrill of white-water canoeing.

For those who prefer something less strenuous and more relaxing, upstream fishing and wildlife lodges offer a touch of adventure with serenity and luxury in uncrowded intimacy. None cater to more than eighteen guests at a time and there is one that only accommodates six guests at a time.

Those short on time might simply choose the cruise upstream to **Kandahar Island** in the pale blush of dawn for a champagne breakfast and the crisp promise of newborn day as the rising sun strikes through the tall palms.

They say that only vervet monkeys live on Kandahar and **Palm Island** where giant palms flourish, but elephant periodically swim across to seek out the palm fruit. Both these islands are near **Kalai Island** where Livingstone camped the night before his discovery.

At this point the great river seems almost motionless. Indeed, the wind on its surface sometimes makes it appear to flow upstream. But out in the mainstream there is a brisk chop, and here and there the deceptively gentle eddies of treacherous whirlpools and hidden sandbanks.

It was at one of these mid-river points, just after the Second World War, that the Solent flying boats of the British Overseas Airways Corporation (BOAC) landed on their leisurely five-day journey from Southampton, across the Mediterranean, via Cairo and Khartoum on the Nile, Lake Victoria, to the Zambezi, and then on to Vaal Dam in South Africa.

In December 1982, British Airways placed a **memorial** on the former **landing stage** along the river banks where their "jungle junction" operated and the small airline buildings are now a **fishing camp**.

In a deep pool nearby, a sounder of hippos break surface, indistinguishable from the rocks that surround them save for the endless fidget of their ears and the swivelling intensity of their periscope stare.

Cormorants stand in frozen silhouette, wings extended like a taxidermist's window display, on the stump of a dead tree against the red orb of the setting sun.

Along the banks flutter egrets, alternating between piggy-back rides on their symbiotic hosts, the buffalo, and a final sundown display of formation flying.

Almost imperceptibly, the surface close to the bank is silently broken by the swirl of a Nile crocodile taking to the water. At one stage the river's crocodile population was seriously threatened but it is now being carefully managed. Within Zimbabwe these great saurians are being reintroduced to large stretches of the Zambezi.

For many visitors all this is a magical experience — the hypnotic spell of unchanging Africa and the wonder of its river banks crowded with elephant, buffalo, and antelope come down to water and its bottom-trotting hippo and lurking crocodile, all revealed against the late afternoon or early morning skies.

In the nearby **Zambezi** and **Victoria Falls National Park Rainforest** there is a wide variety of animal and bird life, and the sanctuary is renowned for its large herds of stately sable antelope.

Sadly, some of the physical scars of the 1965-79 liberation war — including the ruins of the **Elephant Hills Country Club**, with its panoramic view over the Zambezi, and a fenced section of the Zambezi National Park that warns of mines where today elephant roam — still remained in 1990.

Still, nothing mars the glory of the Zambezi upstream glistening in the late afternoon or early morning light. And, in 1990, plans to rehabilitate the club and its championship **golf course** were announced.

The Smoke That Thunders

Just a few paces from the stunted scrub bush of the scorched, dry Kalahari sands that stretch from Botswana to the banks of the Zambezi in north-west Zimbabwe, an ancient miracle continues to slake its thirst from the unceasing benediction that has sustained it for thousands of years.

Night and day the solid veil of mist that rises from the chasm of the Victoria Falls pours down on the thick canopy of tangled trees and lianas that cloaks the top of the facing cliffs.

The rainforest and Livingstone's larger-than-life bronze likeness, cast in 1954, have endured Africa better than he did. Jet travel has placed the continent within reach of the world. Modern medicine, smooth roads, and luxury hotels have rendered its excitements as safe and enjoyable as they are enthralling.

Much the same as it was in Livingstone's day, this pristine area allows visitors to enjoy the river landscapes, the many animals that come to water, and the incredible bird life, from well-marked footpaths or the comfort and safety of their boat or car.

Above: Elephant takes a cooling dip in Hwange National Park.

Conscious of the heritage it holds in trust for the world, Zimbabwe's national parks management has maintained the falls and the rainforest virtually as they were when Livingstone first saw them almost 150 years ago.

The same timber giants of mahogany, ebony, and fig, together with their symbiotic and parasitic attendants, including rare ferns and mosses, continue to refresh themselves from its soft and nourishing caress.

In the flood season, the force of the falling water sends clouds of spray spinning high into the air to "rain" down again sustaining the luxuriant rainforest that flourishes only on the Zimbabwe side of the gorge.

As you step inside the cathedral-like gloom, with its drenched forest floor and rotting underbrush, the sharp African sunlight is suddenly dimmed.

As bushbuck and other small game dart suddenly in and out of view, there is none of the still silence usually associated with rainforests, only the continuous thunder of the falls and the perpetual patter of falling rain, ranging in intensity from gentle drizzle to torrential downpour.

Sightseeing

In spate, between February and May, the **Victoria Falls** resounds with a deafening anthem of rage as the waters of the **Zambezi River**, pulverized to vapour, rise 457 metres (1,500 feet) into the sky.

Bank to bank the total width of the falls is more than one and a half kilometres (one mile). **Four island** account for 400 metres (1,312 feet) out of a total width of 1,708 metres (5,604 feet). The height of the various falls ranges between 100 and 116 metres (327 and 380 feet). The width of the **gorge** at its narrowest point is sixty metres (197 feet).

The volume of water that flows over the falls varies considerably. At its lowest, between late October and early November, as little as 20,000 cubic metres (410,400 cubic feet) of water a minute flow into the **gorge** below.

But when the rains are heavy, the flow increases swiftly and dramatically. Between February and May, when the falls are at their most spectacular, more than 500,000 cubic metres (10 million cubic feet) of water a minute cascade over the edge.

Above: Elephants in a national park mud bath.

In April and May, the peak of the flood season, the six falls — **Devil's Cataract, Main Falls, Horseshoe Falls, Rainbow Falls, Armchair Falls**, and the **Eastern Cataract** — form the largest curtain of falling water in the world.

But in the dry season, between September and November, almost no water plunges over the Rainbow and Armchair Falls or the Eastern Cataract on the Zambian side.

More and more, the Zambezi funnels itself into the narrow Devil's Cataract on the west bank, already worn down more than ten metres (33 feet) below the level of the other falls.

Though small in size, the unique nature sanctuary that overlooks the falls is rich with wildlife, birdlife, and botanical glories. One of the marvels of Zimbabwe is its butterflies and yellow pansies, diadem, orange-tips, and many others flit through the forest there.

In the trees, soaring above the falls, and silhouetted against the blue Zimbabwean sky, bird lovers are able to see the tawny-flanked prinia with its long, slender upstanding tail, blue waxbills, firefinches, mannikins, tchagaras, black-eyed bulbuls, bateleur eagles, Heuglin's robin, the exquisite paradise flycatcher, collared and scarlet-chested sunbirds, and many others.

They feast on the forest's abundant insects, including dragonflies, which constantly hover over the perpetual pools, particularly in December when they come out in swarms.

One of the most outstanding birds is a rarely seen turaco — the remarkable Livingstone's lourie. If lucky you may see it in distant flight between the treetops or over the gorge.

In the shimmering mist its plumage glimmers metallic blue-black against its vivid red flight feathers, but closer inspection reveals that the upper parts in fact are bright green. With its tapering crest, eyes set within a red, white, and black triangle, this turaco is unmistakable.

Disappearing through the sopping undergrowth of leaf litter and rotting twigs at the first footfall of an approaching visitor are skinks and snakes. Less likely to bolt is the dung beetle, which you may come across in a clearing, assiduously rolling a ball of manure back to its nest.

81

Above: Long-maned patriarch of the lion world at water.

The spoor of bigger denizens is frequently seen: bushbuck, waterbuck, leopard, wart hog, mongoose, and baboon. At night, hippo emerge from their pools to wander the open crest of the cliffs, foraging for the lush grasses sustained by the perpetual rain.

The real glory of the forest, however, is its plant life — creepers, vines, and giant trees, including the parasitical strangler fig that soon embraces and smothers its host.

Among the tangled mass of interwoven trees and lianas are the African mangosteen, an unusual climbing acacia, and the potato creeper, which sends out clusters of mauve and yellow flowers remarkably similar to those that bloom on nightshade.

Curious tree

You will also find the curious spreading Cape fig, a large leafy tree whose fruit sprouts only from leafless branches or straight from the main trunk. Elsewhere small trees and shrubs are festooned with the brown and green flowers of the creeping flame lily and aloes maintain a tenacious toehold in small crevices along the cliffs of the falls.

Where the forest becomes more luxuriant,

the trees are embraced by many creepers and the undergrowth is rich in ferns. Between October and December the large vivid-red flowers of the blood lily seem to set the undergrowth on fire.

And everywhere, among the mahoganies and the ebonies, false date palms, cape figs, waterberries, the creepers, and the lianas, a profusion of orchids flourish.

Most visitors view the falls for the first time on foot, walking through the forest from **Livingstone's statue** overlooking the Devil's Cataract. As you follow the **path** winding in and out of the forest, perhaps descending the steps to the **lower viewpoint**, you see the falls from many perspectives — and the more you look and listen, the more the sound and the fury mesmerises.

The statue, "erected to the memory of their distinguished countrymen through the united efforts of the Caledonian Society", was unveiled on 6 August, 1954, by Livingstone's nephew, Howard Unwin Moffat, who served as Prime Minister of Rhodesia from 1927 to 1935.

The impressive likeness, commemorating Livingstone's life from 19 March, 1815, until

Above: Rare daytime glimpse of leopard, the most elusive of the big cats.

1 May, 1873, was raised through the efforts of William Lowe, Chairman of the Livingstone Memorial Committee from its inception in 1926 until his death in 1935.

On 16 November, 1955, fifteen months later, another ceremony took place when a **plaque** commemorating Livingstone's discovery was unveiled by Lord Llewellin, Governor-General of the Federation of Rhodesia and Nyasaland, and dedicated by the Archbishop of Central Africa, Edward Francis Paget.

The inscription reads: "On the occasion of the centenary of David Livingstone's discovery of the Victoria Falls men and women of all races in, and from all parts of, the federation of Rhodesia and Nyasaland assembled solemnly to dedicate themselves to carry on the high Christian aims and ideals which inspired David Livingstone in his mission here."

It is from this point that the visitor first sees the great plunge of the Devil's Cataract, a seventy-metre (230-foot) fall that is thirty metres (98 feet) wide. Beneath it, a **rainforest path** known as **Chain Walk** leads down into the gorge. The name derives from the chain

that was strung to support visitors during their descent. All that remains today are the old posts on some of the trees.

A **viewpoint** near the statue and the plaque offers a stunning vista of the gorge with an unobstructed view of the ninety-three-metre (305-foot) Main Falls. To the east of it is **Livingstone Island** and the grassy edge of the precipice from which the explorer first saw the falls. The island now marks the **border** with Zambia.

Beyond this are the slim, crescent-shaped Horseshoe Falls; followed by the tallest of all the cataracts, the 108-metre (354-foot) Rainbow Falls; and at the extreme eastern end, the 101-metre (331-foot) Eastern Cataract.

As you travel along the path, clifftop glades overlook their own particular spectacle: Cataract Island, the Main Falls, Livingstone Island, Horseshoe Falls, Rainbow, and Armchair Falls — some no more than sixty metres (197 feet) distant. Views into the bottom of the gorge, however, are rare. The pounding rapids and vast plumes of spray obscure the final part of the water's descent.

Maelstrom

Finally you reach the precipice overlooking the magnificent spectacle of the Eastern Cataract, Rainbow Falls, and the Main Falls. The great sheet of water seems almost to pause as it gathers itself together and then, in a stunning increase of tempo as if scenting liberation, hurls itself into the abyss — only to be as suddenly captured, choked, and constrained in the narrow neck of the **Boiling Pot.**

On the Zambian side, you can take the path that winds down to the raging cauldron of the Boiling Pot. Nothing, you may think, could survive this seething maelstrom of malevolent energy as wave after pounding wave is stirred into incredible eddies and whirlpools before breaking free from their rocky prison to begin the 100-kilometre (60-mile) race down the **Batoka Gorge** to **Lake Kariba.**

Yet, amazingly, this is now the locale for one of the most perilous river-running enterprises in the world. It makes a Hollywood production of the same thing seem like a peaceful river cruise.

Early mornings on most days between May and December those in search of heart-stopping adventure make their way down the cliffs to launch their rubber dinghy into the maniacal waters of the Zambezi.

For twenty-three kilometres (14 miles) the adrenalin never stops pumping as the dinghy plunges in and out of thirteen of the Zambezi's most formidable grade eight to ten rapids, with their uncharted potholes and whirlpools, hidden rocks, and boulders.

Enthusiasts, admittedly sometimes a little pale under their tan, rate it the world's ultimate white-water rafting adventure.

When the sport was pioneered in this section of the Zambezi in the 1980s, it was thought that crocodiles — something that river-runners do not have to contend with in other parts of the world — could not survive in such turbulent water. Not true. These prehistoric reptiles have been added to the list of uncounted perils.

And the challenges do not end even when the run is over and you step ashore, still breathlessly alive. You then have to find your way up the 304-metre (1,000-foot) cliffs of the Batoka Gorge.

Many prefer, and who can blame them, to take the twenty-minute "Flight of Angels" which provides a memorable panorama of the upstream river and its many islands, and the fearful constriction of the downstream gorge.

Apart from the gorges and mountains of the Himalaya, nothing so well evokes an awareness of nature's infinite majesty — nor emphasizes so sharply the insignificance of mankind.

Victoria Falls Town

The development of the small and once remote town above the falls as a major tourist destination did not begin in earnest until the 1960s. Before that, there was only a trader or two selling curios and souvenirs.

In the last thirty years new **hotels**, an **international airport**, and a rapidly-growing **shopping centre** have replaced the curio stalls. Lining the **main street** today are **banks**, **fast food restaurants**, an **information bureau**, and the **immigration office**.

The pretty little **railway station** at the northern end of the street, near the Victoria Falls Hotel, draws steam buffs from around the world. The **destination board** noting the 2,651 kilometres (1,647 miles) to **Cape Town** and the 1,534 kilometres (953 miles) to **Beira** is a monument to the vast distances that the old steam mammoths of the track used to cover.

Modern hotels and casinos entertain tourists during the evening, and the all too brief days are spent exploring the wonders of the falls and the scenic beauty of the Zambezi River.

Apart from the falls and the river, there is much to see in the Victoria Falls area. The **border post**, where you clear customs and immigration if you want to walk across **the bridge** to Zambia, is a few metres from the **entrance** to the **national park**. The formalities are made easy enough and the view from the bridge is impressive.

Built by the Cleveland Bridge and Engineering Company of Darlington, England, it has a main arch of 150 metres (492 feet) and two approach spans of 18.6 and 24.3 metres (61 and 80 feet).

On the scenic **Zambezi Drive**, which circles the rainforest, there is another reminder of the omnipotent power of nature: a giant, 1,500-year-old **baobab tree** with a trunk that has a girth of sixty metres (197 feet) — large enough to park a car within.

In the evening, in the *boma* of an indigenous **craft village**, entertainers demonstrate the vigour and spirit of Zimbabwean cultures through dance, mime, and comedy. The living quarters, grain storage bins, and other structures of traditional village life have been faithfully copied. All the country's major tribes are represented in the building styles, decorations, and implements.

Under the pin-bright stars of the southern skies, the drums pound out the pulsating rhythm of the Zulu war dances and circumcision rituals. The accompaniment of reedy soprano salutes by young maidens echo with the soul of timeless Africa.

Expressed in the stirring rallying call of a high-pitched fanfare from a kudu horn trumpet is the joy of a people exulting in the triumph of their warriors.

The light catches in the eyes of a pretty young African dancing girl, white diamonds set in ebony, and their hidden depths sparkle with fires that were lit long before Livingstone made his way downstream on the river that murmurs in the dark just beyond the village.

Perhaps, too, the display is not something pulled from the past merely for the tourist audience, but a celebration of the heritage and freedom so recently reclaimed.

At the **Crocodile Ranch** you can see more than 2,000 of these long-snouted reptiles, ranging in length from fifty centimetres (20 inches) to four and a half metres (15 feet).

There are daily cruises by riverboats along the wide expanses of the river above the falls. Keep your eyes open for the elephant, buffalo, and other animals that come down to the river to drink, particularly near the national parks cottages, where hippo can also be seen.

For the fisherman, the river abounds with combative tigerfish, succulent tilapia, giant vundu, and many other species. Licences are not required.

Vast land

Victoria Falls is the north-western extremity of a vast land dominated by the sands of the Kalahari and empty of all but the great herds of wild animals that roam this vast semi-arid terrain bordered in the west by Botswana.

Forty-seven kilometres (29 miles) from Victoria Falls along the main Bulawayo road, there is a right turn onto a **gravel road** that leads south some kilometres to **Matetsi**, 855 metres (2,805 feet) above sea-level.

Little more than a railway **siding**, the small settlement's **graveyard** contains the remains of many missionaries and early settlers. The town takes its name from the Matetsi, a **tributary** of the Zambezi that joins the river halfway between the falls and Lake Kariba, after flowing through a land of stark rock outcrops covered with extensive ancient mine workings.

Shortly after leaving Matetsi the road enters one of Zimbabwe's major wildlife **hunting preserves**, the 2,995 square kilometres (1,156 square miles) of **Matetsi Safari Area**.

For most of the century this bleached and stark land was used for game ranching, but it was taken over by the government in 1969 and divided into units that were leased to safari operators for game viewing and photographic or hunting expeditions.

The magnificent sable, elephant, and buffalo trophies taken by wealthy clients in this area are an important source of foreign exchange.

Border town

More forgotten graves, their occupants victims of malaria and other tropical diseases, lie scattered on either side of the road that leads beyond Matetsi to Mpandamatenga, which is sixty-five kilometres (40 miles) from the Victoria Falls–Bulawayo road.

It lies 1,060 metres (3,480 feet) above sea-level on the border of Zimbabwe and Botswana. During the 1970s, Mpandamatenga was a strategic crossing point for the nationalist freedom fighters who operated out of secret camps in Botswana.

It was established in 1870 by trader George Westbeech at the side of a small stream. Mpandamatenga means "the place of trade" and it soon became a significant staging post for the European settlers who swept across the country.

Westbeech, who frequently travelled between this base and the Zambezi by ox-wagon, was an ivory trader and he soon became wealthy after making friends with Lewanika, King of the Barotse.

One of the first Europeans to visit Westbeech was the naturalist Frank Oates, author of *Through Matabeleland*, who made many attempts to reach Victoria Falls, failing on one occasion because his companion had to return to have a finger amputated. During another attempt the local chief refused to let him pass because the tribe's cattle were suffering from a plague of red-water fever.

Planning what turned out to be his final attempt, Oates refused to heed the advice of his friend, a seasoned hunter named van Rooyen, who urged him to wait until after the rains because malaria was prevalent. Van Rooyen's sound wisdom was ignored and Oates, with a companion, finally reached the falls on New Year's Eve, 1874. But it was too late. Burning away with fever, Oates died on 5 February during the return journey and was buried near the Deka River, southeast of Mpandamatenga.

He is remembered for his ornithological and entomological discoveries, which included several new species of birds and insects.

The first mission station was established at Mpandamatenga in the late 1870s by a French Huguenot, François Coillard of the Paris Missionary Society, after a nightmarish two-year trek from South Africa with his wife.

During this journey he narrowly escaped death at the hands of the Shona, only to fall prisoner to Lobengula before finally arriving at Mpandamatenga. There he quickly became influential among the Barotse, although it was a long time before he could persuade them to abandon their war parties.

That he eventually did so can be attributed to his remarkable personality, gift for the local languages, and deep insight into Barotse character.

His influence was so powerful that when a Jesuit priest attempted to establish a mission at Mpandamatenga, Coillard used his sway to thwart him. As a result, the priest and his companions suffered untold hardship and four Jesuits died within a year from fever and malnutrition. (Coillard had also lost his wife to malaria, just four years after opening the mission.)

Eventually, however, the Barotse ruler agreed to let the Catholics set up their evangelistic shop. But they found life hard. Food was in short supply and malaria virulent.

These early missionaries eked out a frugal existence from the few vegetables they could coax from the infertile soils, supplementing them with an occasional antelope or gazelle.

It was such a difficult life that in the end they abandoned the mission and settled themselves at Empandeni, near Plumtree, and Chishawasha, near Harare (then Salisbury), where the land was more productive, the climate more benign, and the people more receptive. Coillard too became a victim of the plagues and fevers that flourished around Mpandamatenga. He contracted blackwater fever and died, at seventy years of age, early in 1904, the year that a new road and the railway to Victoria Falls, via Hwange, were completed.

Sightseeing

Now all that remains of the old road to Mpandamatenga are a few ruts in the hardpacked earth, the **derelict foundations** of the **old mission**, and the ghosts of long ago that roam the banks where Westbeech first made camp. These are overlooked by the modern **police station** on the hill above.

In the old **Huguenot cemetery** at the foot of the hill, near a **grove** of small trees, eleven graves are laid out in two rows. A short distance from these are twelve more. And even more in the land that the Jesuits tilled — all reminders of the difficult life and sacrifices of those committed early missionaries.

Today Mpandamatenga is more noted as one of the leaping off points to remote **Kazuma Pan National Park** which lies some forty-two kilometres (26 miles) to the northwest.

One of Zimbabwe's least-spoilt wildlife sanctuaries, the park's 313 square kilometres (121 square miles), and many seasonal flood pans draw great flocks of waterfowl.

First proclaimed a national park in 1949, it was removed from the list in 1965 for lack of development, but regained its status under the Parks and Wild Life Act of 1975.

Getting there

No roads link this remote and enchanting

Above: White rhino and young calf.

wilderness with the rest of the country and the only way in is by four-wheel-drive, preferably with the tour organisation that runs a luxury camp based at one of the permanent waterholes.

Where to stay

There is no accommodation. Camping, however, is allowed, with permission from the Department of National Parks and Wild Life Management.

Sightseeing

Surrounded by dense teak forests, the park is alive with many prides of lion; rare antelope such as the gemsbok, tsessebe, and oribi; buffalo; and endangered species like black rhino, the Disney-like bat-eared fox, and Cape hunting dog. It is also an ideal habitat for the fleet-footed cheetah, fastest land animal in the world.

Nights spent there talking quietly around the camp fire to the sounds of the African night induce euphoria — unless the spell is broken by the roar of lion close by or the sawing grunt of leopard.

Halfway between Mpandamatenga and Matetsi a **road** leads sixteen kilometres (10 miles) south-east to **Nantwich Camp**, one of the gateways into **Hwange National Park**. Five kilometres (three miles) inside the park the road arrives at **Robins Camp** (See "Hwange National Park: Wildlife Wonderland").

From the point where the Mpandamatenga road rejoins the Victoria Falls–Bulawayo road it is another fifty-three kilometres (32 miles) **south-east** through a featureless flatland of mopane to **Thomson Junction**.

The impression is that of travelling through a single, infinite avenue of trees where the beautiful colours of fall and spring meld in a sonnet of red, russet, ochre, and green. Some green foliage, in particular, is startling in its intensity, almost phosphorescent.

Briefly glimpsed through breaks in the bush are fascinating kopjes and inselbergs that rise out of the semi-arid landscape.

To Deka Drum

Thomson Junction marks the **turn north** — for forty-eight kilometres (30 miles) — to the small settlement of **Deka Drum** about thirty-five kilometres (22 miles) from **Lake Kariba**. Set at the confluence of the Zambezi and Deka rivers 500 metres (1,640 feet) above sea-level, the settlement serves as a popular base for fishermen and little else.

Continuing from Thomson Junction, the main road climbs gently over a low pass for another six kilometres (four miles) to the incongruous sight of **Hwange**, a vast area of opencast and underground collieries with all the attendant scars of industrial development — cooling towers, slag heaps, a land stained black, a countryside eroded by mankind's exploitation.

If the land carries scars, so do the hearts of many townspeople. In 1972 an underground explosion rocked Hwange's Number Two colliery and killed 427 miners. It was one of the worst disasters in mining history. Despite this tragedy the industry has grown considerably. Many new mines have been developed not only for coal, but also for copper and tin.

The early Europeans learned of Hwange's coal reserves from a group which had fled far west to escape Mzilikazi's marauding Ndebele. The delegation that brought gifts of ivory to greet the new settlers told stories of the "black stone that burns".

These tales fired the imagination of Albert Giese, a trader in Botswana who had served with the Natal Mounted Rifles and the Bechuanaland Border Police. He walked ninety-six kilometres (59 miles) from his store in 1894 to stake the first claim to Hwange's rich coal deposits.

Five years later, the forerunner of the modern colliery company — Wankie (Rhodesia) Coal Railway and Exploration Company, founded by Australian Edmund Davis — acquired exclusive mining rights to the area surrounding Hwange.

The coal-mining boom took off in 1904 with the arrival of the railway, and within a few years it was producing more than a million tonnes a year. The colliery had swiftly become a linchpin in the economy of the newly colonized region.

Getting there

Hwange, 104 kilometres (65 miles) from Victoria Falls and 335 kilometres (208 miles) from Bulawayo, is served by road and rail.

There is also a daily domestic service to and from Hwange Airport seventy kilometres (44 miles) to the south.

Where to stay

Baobab Hotel (2-star). There are also lodges, self-service cottages, caravan parks, and campsites at various sites in Hwange National Park. See Listings.

Sightseeing

An estimated four billion tonnes of coal lie buried in a 46-square-kilometre (184-square-mile) area around Hwange — enough to produce two million tonnes a year for the next 2,000 years. But the mining company no longer maintains exclusive rights.

The reserves that they do own are estimated at 350 million tonnes. The current production from the two large **opencast quarries** and **underground collieries** is more than six million tonnes a year.

The first colliery, which opened in 1901, produced 9,000 tonnes a day during the 1930s–40s before it closed down. When **Number 2 colliery** came into production in 1930 its output was much higher until that fateful day — 6 June, 1972 — when an explosion ripped through the galleries killing 427 miners almost instantaneously.

With the opening of **Number 4 colliery**, the mine was able to meet the demand for coal in Zimbabwe and neighbouring Zambia, and further development was stopped.

One of the most important by-products is the asphalt used to seal and carpet Zimbabwe's trunk and metropolitan roads.

Hwange coal still powers the fleet of ninety-five steam locomotives run by the National Railways of Zimbabwe — NRZ — and the town is a Mecca for steam enthusiasts from around the world. Most gather on top of a hill to the west of the town where there is a comfortable English-style **pub**.

The **Baobab Hotel** — famous for its bacon sandwiches — takes its name from the massive old giant that sits on the brow of the hill from which there are incredible views to the south-east. The hotel also serves as an impressive **viewpoint** from which to take pictures of the giant Beyer-Garratt steam locomotives rolling their way to the Hwange colliery yards and north-west to Victoria Falls.

Today, trains ferry the fuel that drives the furnaces of the national steel mills, gold processors, tobacco curing plants, and the turbines of the power stations.

Zimbabwe is still dependent on thermal generating stations throughout the country, including those at Hwange which supply the west, despite the hydroelectric output from Kariba.

Many African *aficionados* will find the images of Hwange schizophrenic, out of tune with their cherished images of a Utopian wilderness land, for despite its well-planned streets and smart suburbs, nothing can disguise the town's purpose.

But if a necessary blot on the landscape — and necessary it must be, since it is also the dynamo that drives economic development — the despoliation is visible only briefly, before the main road curves on through Hwange's residential area.

To Kamativi

Within minutes of leaving Hwange, the main road crosses communal lands with many neatly thatched homesteads — each dominated by a main hut circled by several smaller huts in a fenced compound where the livestock is penned at night — and Africa stretches ahead again in all its arid, untouched infinity.

The western civilization laid on Eastern Africa is only a veneer. In Zimbabwe it is thicker, more visible and durable, especially in such places as Hwange. But the cultures and landscapes outside the European influence remain wholly African.

This land, where the termite hills grow to massive mounds and conical peaks, is too dry to be of any value except to those who have survived centuries in Africa; a land that looks too mean to be cherished and too harsh to be exploited (See "The Gold and the Silver", Part One).

Yet, though its owners may be several rungs down the economic ladder, the neatness of their homes shows the level of pride they feel, even though theirs is a subsistence existence.

The **old road** to Bulawayo — two tyre-tread-wide strips of asphalt — constantly crisscrosses the new road until fifty kilometres (30 miles) beyond Hwange. There you find a **crossroad** leading **north** to **Kamativi** or **south** to **Dete**.

The road north runs twenty-nine kilometres (18 miles) through communal lands to Kamativi, where a prospector called R. H. Aldworth staked a claim to large deposits of tin in 1936. The mine was taken over by a Dutch firm in 1952.

One of the hills overlooking the mine — **Hojokwe** — is believed to be the place where Hwange, the Rozvi tribal chief, replenished his pigeon flocks by sending young men (one at a time) to climb the mountain by ladder.

Legend says that when enough birds had been handed down to the people below, the ladder was removed leaving the young man to die, thus ensuring, it was believed, that the pigeons would never return.

To the south, Dete — meaning "narrow passage" — serves as a station on the main railway line and most villagers are railway workers. The area is also a mining centre and the main commercial and tourist communication point for nearby **Hwange National Park** and **Deka Safari Area**, adjoining the park's northern boundary. Together the two form part of the wildlife complex that extends from the Zambezi River.

Deka's 510 square kilometres (197 square miles) contain a great number of indigenous mammals and are used for sport hunting by professional safari operators.

The **turn off** to Hwange National Park lies at another **crossroad** seventeen kilometres (10 miles) beyond the Dete crossroads

One road leads **north** to the abandoned **Gwaai River Copper Mine**, which lasted briefly for about one decade between the 1960s and the mid-1970s; the other heads twenty-three kilometres (14 miles) **south** to Hwange National Park along a road lined with stands of sap-green trees.

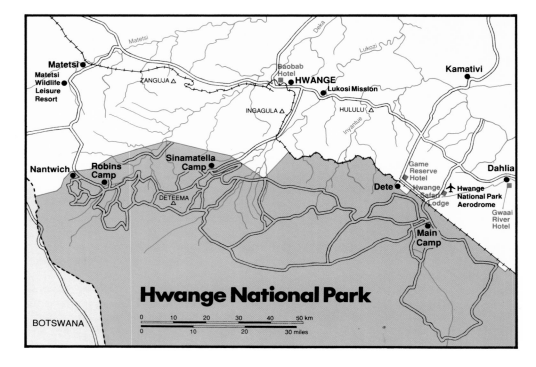

Hwange National Park

Hwange National Park: Wildlife Wonderland

Hwange National Park, one of the world's last great elephant sanctuaries, is the largest national park in Zimbabwe. Covering more than 14,600 square kilometres (5,863 square miles), it has more animals and a greater variety of species — 107 — than any other park in the country, and more than 400 species of bird.

There are two distinct geographic zones, neither able to support viable agriculture. The flora of the well-drained northern area, part of the Zambezi watershed, is dominated by mopane and mixed terminalia, which is distinctly different from the rest.

Elsewhere the Kalahari scrublands, covered with stunted, scattered woodlands of teak and *umtshibi* trees, drain into Botswana's Makgadkadi Depression. This habitat is characterised by many marshy depressions, vleis, and fragile open grasslands on shallow soils.

In the nineteenth century this land was the royal hunting reserve of Mzilikazi and his successor Lobengula. But the arrival of the first white hunters and settlers signalled the slaughter of its wildlife by the thousands. As their blood soaked deep into the sparse soils, it left an empty, useless wasteland, denuded of wildlife, unfit for farming.

It was declared a game reserve in 1928 and, with neighbouring Robins Game Sanctuary, became a national park under the National Parks Act of 1949. Originally, Robins Game Sanctuary belonged to H. G. Robins, a cattle rancher.

Because his herds were constantly attacked by lion and leopard, Robins turned the ranch into a wildlife preserve. Later, in exchange for a new house and a water supply, he gave the sanctuary to the government.

When founding warden Ted Davison walked across virtually every single square kilometre in 1928–29 he discovered wildlife was almost nonexistent. The once-teeming herds of elephant numbered fewer than 1,000 and the rhinoceros, black and white, had been exterminated.

Anyway, the poorly-drained Kalahari sands, with their relatively low rainfall, were unable to support permanent large wildlife populations. The seasonal pans and fossil

90

Above: Sable in flight at Hwange Safari Estate.

river lines held water all too briefly after the rains, and only occasionally did any large numbers migrate into the region.

Davison perceived that water was the critical key and, in the years that followed, he drilled boreholes to create sixty new pans, linked to the seasonal pans that already existed. Slowly, the animals, particularly elephant and buffalo, began to move back.

Growing numbers

Close to half a century later, Hwange faced another, different crisis — too many elephants. Their numbers had risen to more than 20,000 and in their wake the massive beasts left fallen woods and fragile, over-grazed grasslands. Hwange's existence was threatened.

Wildlife authorities intervened, culling at least 5,000 to bring the population down to between 12,000 and 15,000, the maximum that Hwange can support without damage.

Thus Hwange, with its great wildlife populations, remains one of the most unspoilt wildlife sanctuaries in the world where the varied geography encourages a meeting of two distinct faunal groups. The animals of the arid Kalahari intermingle in great concentrations with species suited to less-harsh, less-arid habitats.

The animals that roam the park today include a growing number of rhino, 15,000 buffalo, 3,000 zebra, 3,000 giraffe, and sixteen of the thirty-three species of southern African antelope — among them 6,000 impala, 5,000 kudu, 2,000 sable, wildebeest, hartebeest, tsessebe, roan, and gemsbok. Such numbers attract many predators: lion and leopard, an occasional cheetah, abundant spotted hyena, and now and then a rare brown hyena.

Water remains the single most important management factor in Hwange's continued existence — absolutely vital to the survival of what is perhaps Africa's largest single concentration of elephant.

The constant maintenance of the artificial but natural-looking water pans, complete with resident hippo and predatory crocodiles, has been the major factor in sustaining this ecological treasury. Without them, Hwange would return to the empty wasteland it once was.

Above: Male greater kudu, Hwange National Park.

Getting there

Hwange National Park Main Camp, 174 kilometres (108 miles) from Victoria Falls and 275 kilometres (170 miles) from Bulawayo, is served by road, rail, and air services. Hwange National Park airport is a few kilometres from Main Camp. There is a daily air "bus" service between Hwange National Park, Victoria Falls, Kariba, and Harare.

When to go

Hwange National Park is open all year. Even in summer the nights can be extremely cold.

Where to stay

Hwange Safari Lodge (3-star), Dete; Gwaai River Hotel (1-star), Gwaai. See Listings for "Hotels". Bush camps managed by commercial photo-safari operators provide facilities for groups of up to twelve in remote areas far from the normal routes. Guests at these tented camps can explore the surrounding area and see game on walking expeditions. See Listings.

Above: Tree house for overnight tourists in Hwange's Sable Valley game resort.

Above: Wart hog and young in Hwange National Park.

At the three national park camps — Main Camp, Sinamatella, and Robins Camp — there are chalets, cottages, and lodges. Chalets have basic furniture, bedding, external cooking facilities, and neighbouring toilet block with hot and cold baths and showers.

Cottages are self-contained with their own cooking facilities and individual toilet and bathroom. The lodges are also self-contained, with refrigerators, cutlery, crockery, cooking utensils, and house servants.

Each camp provides caravan parks and campsites, and Main Camp contains a licensed restaurant, filling station, and supermarket.

The two-bedroom luxury cottages at Sinamatella Camp stand on a small plateau near the park's northern border overlooking the waterhole and plains fifty-five metres (180 feet) below.

Robins Camp, with its two- and four-bed chalets, is named after the rancher who created the private game sanctuary that now forms the north-west area of the park. Eight kilometres (five miles) to the west is Nantwich — with three double-bedroom lodges overlooking a large waterhole. See Listings.

Sightseeing

For those travelling by car, the **Bulawayo-Victoria Falls road** runs near the park's **northern boundary**, with access roads to each of the three camps. The **Bulawayo-Victoria Falls railway line** forms the park's northern boundary and trains serve **Dete**, the nearest station to **Hwange National Park**.

Experienced tour operators offer game-viewing drives. At **Hwange Safari Lodge**, for instance, the United Touring Company maintains a fleet of minibuses, specially adapted for game viewing.

Viewing platforms overlooking the waterholes at **Nyamandhlovu Pan** and **Guvalala Pan**, near **Main Camp**, allow visitors to watch herds of different animals coming to drink from an ideal vantage point. Moonlight viewing from these platforms is unforgettable.

But none of these amenities, catering for thousands of visitors each year, has been allowed to mar the natural beauty of the sanctuary. The size of each camp and number of vehicles is limited.

Much of the park is inaccessible simply because the number of roads has been

Above: Zebras frolic in lush grasslands.

deliberately restricted and off-road driving prohibited. Consequently Hwange's wildlife lives an existence untrammelled by intrusive mankind.

Where you can travel, however — in the west, centre, and to the east — three well-developed safari circuits, served by more than 450 kilometres (280 miles) of well-maintained roads, richly reward the visitor.

The species you are most likely to see around Main Camp are zebra, giraffe, kudu, elephant, steenbok, impala, wart hog, buffalo, wildebeest, sable, lion, black-backed jackal, hyena, and bat-eared fox.

The major species at **Sinamatella** are impala, kudu, elephant, wart hog, giraffe, hippo, klipspringer, hyena, lion, and leopard.

And **Robins Camp** is noted for its congregations of impala, waterbuck, buffalo, kudu, elephant, giraffe, sable roan, reed-buck, lion, hyena, side-striped jackal, cheetah, and tsessebe.

From these camps, roads take you through a wilderness filled with large herds of wild-life to many of the waterholes where the creatures, great and small, come to drink at sundown.

Perhaps you will see a mother elephant guiding her calf gently to water or a large-eyed steenbok peering through the grass at the roadside. Maybe you will enjoy the see-saw canter of giraffe crossing the veld or even a pride of lion on a kill.

An afternoon spent on a viewing platform at one of the waterholes, strong cool winds alternating with moments of fiery stillness, is unforgettable. Friendly hornbills, unused to mankind and unsuspecting, cocking their heads, left, then right, with beady-eyed curiosity, perch within hand's reach.

Aerobatic bird

Above the waterhole, where two inert forms lie half-submerged on the sandy bank, a bateleur eagle circles on a Kalahari thermal, its wings a model of futuristic aerodynamics.

The bird takes its name from the French word for "tumbler" because of its erratic, jerky flight and the many side-stalls that it performs. The French connection is apt: with its ruff fluffed up it looks exactly like a seventeenth-century Parisian courtier.

All the world stands still. Only the lyrical sounds of silence — the soughing of the wind,

Above: Giraffe in woodlands.

the rustle of the sand, and the whirr of a hovering dragonfly—move the clock forward.

Tails erect, a family of unheeding wart hog trots with brisk military gait towards the waterhole, only for the leading patriarch to suddenly skitter and brake on his rear legs as, now nervous, he scents the presence of the two crocodiles.

The wart hogs skirt the recumbent forms. Now a magnificent sable bull strolls gracefully in, suddenly freezing as it comes within two metres of the crocodiles whose positions have changed imperceptibly.

As the afternoon wears on, one of the crocodiles, restlessly hungry, moves with sudden sluggishness into the water. There, through the rest of the long hot day, it drifts first to one point and then another. But it is destined to stay hungry. Today there will be no privileged witness to the great life and death pageant of the wilderness.

Outside the park, on the road from Main Camp to **Hwange Airport** (where lion sometimes block the runway), the land is still filled with game; an elephant in a waterhole by the roadside, giraffe crossing unconcerned by the traffic. All seem blessed

by the benevolence of this environment where the birds are uncannily tame and only natural predators spook the game.

To the north, the 148 square kilometres (60 square miles) of **Hwange Safari Estate**, a private game reserve, offer a similar wildlife spectacle.

The three-star Hwange Safari Lodge, with its own waterhole and viewing platform with bar, also runs a safari camp of three comfortable **tree houses** in the bush.

Pampered guests at the luxurious lodge do not have to move farther than the bar or their bedroom for close-up encounters with herds of elephant that sometimes number 100 or more, buffalo, sable, impala, and the creatures, wild and wonderful, that make Hwange a wildlife destination unmatched in southern Africa.

There are three luxury retreats in the reserve run by Touch the Wild. These "secret valley" **lodges**, with their own **waterholes**, offer a unique way to experience raw Africa in comfort.

On a still and breathless late afternoon, as the sun's shadows lengthen over **Sable Valley**, a tusker trumpets herald of its approach to water where a group of white-chested marabou stork, black shrouds on their back, stand motionless like pallbearers drawn to attention for a funeral.

At sundown, minutes after the scorching daytime heat, the temperature drops dramatically, often to well below freezing, chilling evidence that despite the thick woodlands this land is held in bondage by the sands of the Kalahari.

Top: Lilac-breasted roller.
Above: Yellow-billed hornbill.

To Gwaai River

Back on the main road to Bulawayo it is another seventeen kilometres (10 miles) from the Hwange National Park crossroads to **Gwaai River**, also known as **Dahlia** — little more than a bottle store that flashes by in the blink of an eye. For many years it was a prosperous farming area, but in the 1940s the farms were incorporated into Hwange National Park and the **Sikumi Safari Area**. All but one — owned by a widow, a Mrs Frick.

She stubbornly refused to leave despite being laid to siege by elephants and other wildlife (as well as bureaucracy) that constantly damaged her borehole and pump in search of water. She eked out a living selling vegetables to the Kamativi Tin Mine and held out on her farm until she died.

In earlier days, when they were isolated by floods, the farmers hauled themselves and their supplies and mail over the river in a cage suspended from a steel hawser fixed to the trees on either bank.

Once, when the hawser snapped and the postman fell into the river, Mrs Frick braved the raging torrent to carry a new hawser to the cage, thus saving man and mail.

Twenty-six kilometres (16 miles) beyond, past **Halfway House**, is the **turn north** to **Jotjolo**, just another dot on the map. From Jotjolo it is fifty kilometres (30 miles) to **Lupane**, the small administrative centre that grew up around an early mission station.

Another five kilometres (three miles) brings you to a **gravel road** that leads **south** to **Gwaai**, a **railway station** on the Bulawayo – Victoria Falls line named for the river that rises near Figtree and flows through it to enter the Zambezi 146 kilometres (90 miles) north of Victoria Falls. Gwaai is a Sindebele word for tobacco.

To Kenmaur

From Gwaai, via another **dirt road**, it is thirty-seven kilometres (23 miles) back to the main Bulawayo road and **Kenmaur**, a village close to the old **St. Luke's mission**.

Alternatively, you can continue **south-east** from Gwaai to **Tsholotsho**, in the land that Mzilikazi trekked through on his way to establish his capital at Bulawayo (See

Above: Young lion cubs.
Previous page: Top: Mature Nile crocodile at a game park water hole. Below: Elephants bathing.

"The Gold and the Silver", Part One).

Tsholotsho is linked by an asphalt road that runs sixty-five kilometres (40 miles) to **Nyamandhlovu**; another forty-three kilometres (27 miles) to Bulawayo; and by **gravel road** through the cloying sands of the Kalahari to Figtree.

Early prospectors, hoping that they might find gold and other precious minerals, searched the alluvial belt that runs along the Gwaai River intensively, but they came away empty-handed.

More recently Tsholotsho has become a ranching centre with an experimental **research station** that concentrates on the breeding of indigenous cattle, notable for their lyre-shaped horns and massive heads, first introduced from Swaziland by the Ndebele during their trek north in the first half of the nineteenth century.

On the railway line **north** of Tsholotsho — lying halfway between Nyamandhlovu and Gwaai — is **Sawmills**, centre of a massive timber industry founded on the wealth of the Gwaai **teak forest** that covers 140 square kilometres (56 square miles).

The forest represents the only economic resource in this infertile land of infernal sand, devoid of all water save for the seasonal pans that fill with the rains and empty with the drought.

The teak and other hardwoods felled in the forest are used mainly for parquet flooring, mine props, and railway sleepers. Herbalists use teak bark as a cure for eye ailments — and a pick-me-up for patients recovering from debilitating illnesses.

It was near Nyamandhlovu, where the **railway station** and **District Commissioner's headquarters** now stand, that Gundwane, one of Mzilikazi's loyal *indunas*, escorted his king to the top of a hill to show him the land that lay beneath.

Impressed by the teeming elephant herds that thronged these arid Kalahari grasslands, and later drew ivory hunters like Selous, Mzilikazi named the region Nyamandhlovu, the Sindebele word for elephant head.

Today the area is an important ranching and dairy farming centre, where cattle fatten up for the abattoir on the grasslands that the elephant once grazed.

Matobo Hills: A World In Tortured Disarray

From the top of the Matobo Hills, south of Zimbabwe's second-largest city, Bulawayo, the eye scans across a world in tortured disarray.

Granite masses — split, seamed, sculpted, and shaped by time and weather — form an array of whalebacks and castle kopjes that dominate 3,000 square kilometres (1,200 square miles) of Matabeleland South Province.

There, Mzilikazi, scion of Matshobana, head of the Khumalo Zulu clan, first set his mark upon them after crossing the Limpopo on his march north (See "The Gold and the Silver", Part One).

Much of the country's history has been written within the confines of the Matobo Hills — from the time thousands of years ago when ancient Bushmen used the granite faces as a canvas for their unique and extraordinary art, to more modern times when black and white met in war and peace.

Thousands of years after the San, the monotheistic Mbire were so moved by the spirituality of this art and the ambience of these hills that they made many of them into religious shrines (See "The People: A Culture Rooted in the Soil", Part One).

This holy area is still held in reverential awe by local communities, and ceremonies to appease the ancestral spirits, overcome ill-fortune, and in particular to make rain, are still held in the shrines in the Matobo Hills.

Standing 1,547 metres (5,000 feet) above sea-level, the hills made a profound impression on two men of absolute power whose destinies drew them into final confrontation in the last decade of the nineteenth century.

One of them, Cecil Rhodes, lies buried in the hills, quite close to the grave of Mzilikazi, the father of his adversary, Lobengula. The Matobo Hills became the last stronghold of Lobengula's *indunas* and *impis* in the war against Rhodes's colonizing "pioneers".

Now all is tranquil within these rugged rocky hills stretching eighty kilometres (50 miles) from east to west. The stronghold of the Ndebele warriors during the first *Chimurenga*, "war of liberation", has become a place of peace.

Forty thousand years ago the caves and crevices formed out of these rocks became home to Zimbabwe's earliest inhabitants, the "San". Twenty thousand years later, "San" artists began painting on the walls of the caves and cliff faces, using pigments and natural minerals that have survived the ravages of climate and time.

Many caves contain superb galleries of Bushman paintings. Especially notable are the caves named Silozwane, Bambata, Gulubahwe, Pomongwe, and the rock known as White Rhino Shelter. All are accessible and well worth visiting, not only for their prehistoric art, but also for their singular beauty (See "Rock Art: The Priceless Legacy", Part Four).

The region's wooded valleys and hills have a handsome diversity of trees, including brilliantly coloured msasas and the erythrinas with their blood-red blossoms. Ground orchids and other flowering plants make the Matobo Hills a garden of infinite variety. It has been nominated by Zimbabwe for inclusion as a World Heritage Site for both its natural and cultural treasures.

Getting there

From Bulawayo's International Trade Fair showground, the Matobo Road leads twenty-four kilometres (15 miles) to the outliers of the Matobo Hills. There is a passenger bus service.

When to go

Visits to the Matobo Hills National Park can be enjoyed at any time of the year, but during the rains four-wheel drive vehicles provide better traction on the dirt roads.

Where to stay

Bulawayo Sun (3-star), Cresta Churchill (3-star), Bulawayo Holiday Inn (3-star), New Royal Hotel (2-star), Rio Hotel (2-star), Selborne Hotel. There are many more hotels with varying standards of comfort and service. See Listings for "Hotels". In the

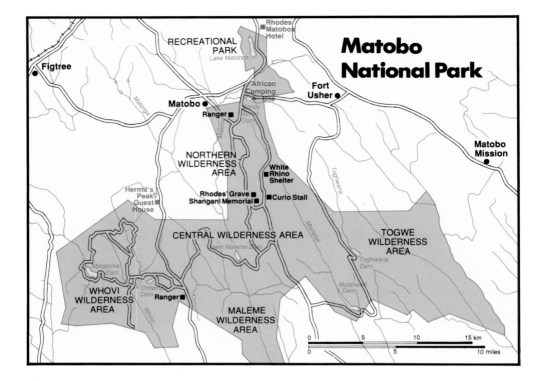

Matobo National Park

RECREATIONAL PARK
Lake Matobos
Rhodes Matobos Hotel
Figtree
African Camping Site
Matobo
Fort Usher
Sandy Spruit Dam
Ranger
Matobo Mission
NORTHERN WILDERNESS AREA
Matopos
White Rhino Shelter
Toghwana
Hermit's Peak Guest House
Rhodes' Grave
Shangani Memorial
Curio Stall
Mtsheleli
CENTRAL WILDERNESS AREA
Lower Maleme Dam
TOGWE WILDERNESS AREA
Toghwana Dam
Mpopoma Dam
Mutshelel Dam
WHOVI WILDERNESS AREA
Chitan Dam
Ranger
Whovi
MALEME WILDERNESS AREA
0   5   10   15 km
0   5   10 miles

national park there are self-service chalets, caravan park, and campsite at Maleme Dam, and caravan parks and campsites at Matobo Gate, Mtsheleli Dam, Togwana Dam, and Mwizilume Dam. See Listings.

Sightseeing

The road from Bulawayo touches the northernmost extremity of Matobo Hills National Park where it snakes above **Matobo Dam**, headquarters of the **Matopos Sailing Club**. It then skirts the eastern boundary of the school located in Rhodes **summer house**, easily recognisable by its distinctive Cape architecture so reminiscent of Holland. The farmlands that Rhodes developed on this estate now serve as the **Matopos Research Station**.

Just before the **park entrance**, but still inside the park, is **Sandy Spruit Dam**. Also near the entrance, set in a group of **rocks**, is the **grave** of Lobengula's sister, Nini, who was executed on his orders for her illicit affair with a commoner. The king loved his sister deeply, but was forced by public outrage to condemn her. She asked her executioners to strangle her with her own girdle.

If you follow the **loop road** south and then north around the **obelisk**, soon after the entrance, you arrive at the other northern **park entrance** where there is an **arboretum** and **campsite and caravan park**. Admission to the park is free.

Rhodes also bequeathed money to build a railway from Bulawayo so that its citizens might enjoy the glory of the Matobo Hills. From the main line at **Westacre Junction**, between Khame and Figtree, it ran for fifteen kilometres (nine miles) to the old **terminus** located just outside the northern gate.

The ninety-minute service opened in November 1903, with one train from Bulawayo on Saturday afternoon and Sunday morning, and a return train on Sunday evening.

It remained popular for many years but when a motor road was built it began to lose money, although the railways continued to operate a passenger service until 1948 when the track was taken up.

Following the **Circular Drive** south from the main gate, the road soon passes **Steadfast Park**. There the road plunges into strange and eerie hills where, at every twist and turn, pantheons of granite gods and headless or caricatured rock deities rise up in such profusion, that the mind is unable to assimilate them.

War memorial

One large granite whaleback stands to the **east** of the drive near the **gates** of **Rowallan Park**, which was set aside for the Girl Guide movement in memory of Baden-Powell, who conceived the inspiration for the scouting movement in these dramatic hills.

Continuing along this road you then pass **Imadzi**, rising directly above the **eastern side** of the road, which contains some famous **rock paintings** in its **Njelele Cave**. There is also a **shrine** at its base dedicated to the men of the Memorable Order of Tin Hats — MOTH — who fell in the two World Wars.

Endangered but docile white rhino pause as they forage in the grasslands by the roadside against the unique backdrop of the hills. Stately sable, graceful impala, agile klipspringer, wildebeest, zebra, buffalo, giraffe, leopard, baboon, vervet monkey, squirrels, and the rock hyrax (known as the "dassie" or rock rabbit), are also found in abundance within these hills and valleys.

Guinea fowl quarter the ground constantly in idle search for pickings, while eagles and other raptors soar on the constant daytime thermals looking for carrion.

Behind the looming mass of the **Tandale Range** to the **east** of the circular road, outside the park but very much within these granite hills, is the little-known settlement of **Fort Usher**, named after William Filmer Usher, one of the two Europeans left behind in the ashes of Bulawayo when Lobengula fled.

Usher, a member of the Salvation Army who had been living with the Ndebele for ten years, was Lobengula's advisor and letter writer. (The other European was James Fairbairn, who had arrived twenty-one years before and obtained a gold mining concession from the king).

The village, founded on a site chosen by Baden-Powell, is where Rhodes held his famous *Indaba* on 21 August, 1896. It was after this meeting that Rhodes went to see Mzilikazi's tomb (See "The Gold and the Silver", Part One).

Today Fort Usher is a sleepy little village with a few trading stores. In 1941, under the shade of an *umgugutu* tree that has since died, Rotarians raised a memorial to the Ndebele king on the site of his **royal kraal** in the hills. The inscription reads:

"Mzilikazi, son of Shobana, King of the Amandebele. All the mountain fell down on 5th September, 1868. All nations acclaim the son of Shobana! Bayete!"

Soon after Imadzi, again to the **east**, the road passes another rock painting site, **Mtsheleli**, before leading **south-west** around **Gordon Park** past one of Zimbabwe's most famous rock painting sites, the **White Rhino Shelter**, which is reached by scrambling up and over massive boulders.

Grafted onto its granite wall — with remarkable delicacy considering the coarse surface — are stunning examples of prehistoric art. A line of dark red hunters is superimposed over a herd of wildebeest and there are caricatures of people with a small flock of guinea fowl in the lower panel (See "Rock Art: The Priceless Legacy", Part Four).

Rhodes's grave

Some two kilometres (just over a mile) beyond the White Rhino Shelter, a **curio stall** marks the **west turn** to **Rhodes's grave** at **World's View**. There is a **car park** at the foot of the hill, a helpful national museum attendant, and a brief biography and outline of Rhodes's work in words and pictures.

In his last will Rhodes directed that World's View — the Ndebele's *Malindidzimu* — should be reserved as the burial ground for those who had performed special service to Rhodesia and the British Empire.

Subsequently, his intimate, Dr. Leander Starr Jameson, was buried not far from Rhodes's grave. The third grave on *Malindidzimu* is that of Sir Charles Patrick John Coghlan (See "The Gold and the Silver", Part One).

Their simple, austere graves, with no headstones, counterpose the massive **granite memorial** that Rhodes raised before his death to Scottish-born Major Allan Wilson and the thirty-three men who went in pursuit of Lobengula after the king fled Bulawayo in November, 1893.

They were buried where they fell, but when Rhodes first saw *Malindidzimu* he decided at once to build a memorial there in their honour.

Above: Zimbabwe is one of the last strongholds of steam, with a fleet of more than 90 locomotives.

The bodies were reinterred in a Grecian-style **mausoleum** that has four **bronze relief panels** by John Tweed, depicting their last stand.

The names are all inscribed and the main dedication to the "enduring memory of Allan Wilson and his men" states simply: "There was no survivor."

Fifteen kilometres (nine miles) **north-east** of *Malindidzimu*, just across the Tandale Range at **Nthumbane** outside the park, is the hilltop cave in which Mzilikazi is buried.

The circular road loops around the southern base of *Malindidzimu* to return through the **northern wilderness area** to the obelisk, and the choice of leaving the park by two gates.

However, just a few metres after the turn to *Malindidzimu,* another **surfaced road** continues **south** and then, after some three and a half kilometres (two miles), veers **south-west** to **Lower Maleme Dam.**

More ancient art

Where it veers south-west a **dirt road** continues four kilometres (two and a half miles) to the **southern boundary** of the park and another eight kilometres (five miles) through the harsh and arid **Khumalo Communal Lands.**

The winding, dusty road links tiny villages of mud and thatch houses, each one decorated with colourful designs painted on the exterior walls with earth pigments (See "The People: A Culture Rooted in the Soil", Part One). Eventually, the twisting trail leads to **Silozwane**, considered among the most outstanding of Zimbabwe's rock painting sites.

Once there, you make your way to the foot of a massive **whaleback** and follow **painted arrows** up the precipitous ninety-metre (300-foot) **trail**, then risk an airy scramble across the exposed lower face of the domed hill to a huge **cave**; not for those who suffer vertigo.

The **back wall** of the cave served the prehistoric painters as an enormous canvas. The **centrepiece** is a two-metre-high (six-and-a-half-foot) **picture** of a giraffe, and an even larger antelope-headed snake.

Other animals depicted on the wall are lion, rhinoceros, kudu, tsessebe, impala, zebra, elephant, birds in flight, hunters armed with bows and arrows, and an incredibly detailed flying termite. Even the veins in its wings are shown.

Those visiting the Matobo Hills for the first time will not be surprised that they are a bastion of invincible faith. Described, rightly, as among the most majestic granite scenery on earth, they emanate an overwhelming sense of power, a power far greater than that of mankind.

They certainly affected Rhodes profoundly. Undoubtedly, he sensed in their majesty an even greater will than he could ever hope to exert — they were perhaps the one place where even he felt a degree of humility.

But the impression of an alien world is softened by its beauty. Despite its gaunt and rocky profile, none of this land is barren. Among the trees that have taken root on the most unlikely ledges, and in the floors of the many valleys, are mountain acacia, vividly-coloured *msasas*, and blood-red erythrinas, while many ground orchids and flowering plants carpet the grasslands with pastel colours.

Lower Maleme Dam

The hills are cut by diamond-bright streams and waterfalls, some of which have been dammed to form small lakes and reservoirs, creating a geological, botanical, and wildlife wonderland.

Back on the winding, surfaced road, temples of doom, towers of stone, surrealistic images of Buddha, grinning gargoyles, giant dwarfs, reptilian monsters, rock pyramids, and sublime sphinxes flash by in an endless blur on the five-kilometre (three-mile) journey to Lower Maleme Dam.

The **notice** at the dam prohibits swimming and warns: "Beware of bilharzia, crocs, and humps". It goes unheeded. In this bizarre landscape caution is a banal consideration.

On the lake **shores**, the national park's comfortable thatched **lodges**, **caravan parks**, and **campsites** allow visitors to enjoy the magnificent beauty of these surroundings where a silver paper moon, pasted on an ice-blue sky, rises in the cleft of a cliff washed in orange by the sun's dying rays, and bream, barbel, and black bass chasing midges break the still surface of the water.

In such a place at such a time, *Mwari*, the supreme creator, seems supremely close.

Above: Ndebele woodcarver fashions the traditional masks of his warrior ancestors.

103

There are many other dams in this superb national park, which takes days to explore in full, including **Mpopoma Dam** located in the game-rich westernmost extremity where wildlife can be observed from several **viewing platforms**.

To Kezi

A **dirt road** that runs roughly halfway between Lower Maleme and Mpopoma dams cuts **south** for eighty kilometres (50 miles) to **Kezi**, a small trading and administrative centre for the large cattle ranches in the surrounding area that was once rich in wildlife.

Although there is little of interest in the village, just beyond it, fourteen kilometres (nine miles) away to the **south** along a **dirt trail**, is **Antelope Mine**, where hundreds of years ago the ancients toiled to dig up the treasure of Ophir.

These old workings were discovered in 1894 by A. M. Wright, one of the many prospectors searching the area. Although he pegged a claim on 8 October, 1894, the owner of the claim was the Rhodesian Exploration and Development Company, which waited more than a year before investigating the gold-bearing reefs beneath the shallow but extensive ancient workings.

The teeming wildlife that thronged the area inspired the mine's name, but actual mining did not begin until 1913. No fabled treasure was found and after five years the mine closed down never to reopen. Some forty-four kilometres (27 miles) **south** beyond the old mine, the trading centre of **Legion Mine** takes its name from another abandoned gold mine.

The **gravel road east** from Antelope Mine, however, leads to **Gwanda**, an administrative centre 148 kilometres (92 miles) from Bulawayo on the main Bulawayo–Beitbridge road. The town was founded in 1899 on land that was once the pastoral and hunting reserve of the Ndebele royal family. It was linked to Bulawayo and Tuli by the railway line on 25 August, 1903.

At the end of the last century it was the scene of a minor gold rush, with many mines being established including **Sabiwa, Antenior, Eagle Vulture, Jessie** — and **Geelong**.

This flurry of mining activity led Rhodes to hope that his dream of finding a second Witwatersrand in the north would at last be realised. Geelong produced some spectacular results, although it never proved as rich as the South African discovery.

The reef was so large that when the mine came on line in 1898, it yielded more than 125 kilos (276 lbs) from 8,890 tonnes of ore — an output of pure gold that more than trebled by 1903 when the mine produced 397 kilos (875 lbs). Geelong, taken over by the London Rhodesia — Lonrho — Company in 1905, ceased production in 1931.

Antenior, twenty-nine kilometres (18 miles) north-west of Geelong, was one of the first mines to operate in Rhodesia. The high hopes for its success were based on the fact that it was on the site of some ancient workings. But it experienced a setback almost at once.

Above: Rock hyrax, a distant and tiny relative of the elephant.

Opposite: Nature's fascinating rock sculptures adorn the 3,000 square kilometres of the Matobo Hills.

On its way from Britain aboard the *Clan Drummond*, a boiler essential to the success of the mining operation was lost at sea. The mine ceased operations years ago and the **siding** on the **Heany–West Nicholson railway line** is the only reminder of the golden dreams that first began to founder on the Indian Ocean.

Daytime service

The first trains along these lines only ran during daytime because the woodcutters left the fuel to fire their furnaces by the side of the track. The trains, which stopped whenever the drivers saw a woodstack, carried two or three labourers to load the wood onto the engine.

Today a well-travelled **road** has usurped the tracks from Gwanda. The road leads **north** for sixty kilometres (37 miles) to **Mbalabala**, close to **Mzingwane Dam**, built in 1958 and now a **watersports centre** for Bulawayo citizens. Its name derives from the Sindebele word for kudu. Gold and farming are the main industries.

Twenty-two kilometres (14 miles) **northwest**, between Mbalabala and Bulawayo, is the tungsten and gold-mining centre of **Esigodini**, which once rejoiced in the nostalgic name of Essexvale, no doubt the result of homesickness in one of the early settlers.

Founded in 1894, F. C. Selous made his home there the following year. Importing a woven wire house from the UK, his intention was to develop a large eucalyptus plantation. In 1896 — when he was away putting down the Ndebele uprising — the house was burnt down by one of the rebel leaders. Soon after, Selous retired to the UK where he wrote an autobiographical book, *Sunshine and Storm in Rhodesia*.

There are two gold belts around Esigodini, which lies thirty-seven kilometres (23 miles) from Bulawayo, and during the early days there were many profitable gold mines. The largest of these was **Bushtick** — once managed by Sir Digby Burnett who went on to become Managing Director of Lonrho. It ceased production in 1935.

The old mine buildings became a private school for boys three years later. The cottages were transformed into dormitories and classrooms, the dance hall became the assembly hall — and the gold vault was used as a darkroom by the photographic club.

Wildlife orphanage

Halfway between Esigodini and Bulawayo is **Chipangali Wildlife Orphanage**, a haven for sick and unwanted animals and birds, founded in 1973 by Viv Wilson, former Director of the Bulawayo Natural History Museum. Now run by a trust, the orphanage is also the centre of a major duiker conservation project.

Many animals — either through disability or because they were reared from birth as pets — will never leave this sanctuary. Some birds in the handsome **aviary** have lost wings or legs and left to fend for themselves would simply die.

But whenever possible Chipangali's lame and laggard are rehabilitated to the wild. Its greatest success story so far is that of a troop of vervet monkeys. Led by a former house pet, the troop was settled on an island in Lake Kariba where its numbers have flourished and multiplied. The orphanage is entirely dependent on public donations and sponsorship.

The Road to Botswana

Bulawayo's Main Street leads south to become Mafeking Road, which runs for 100 kilometres (62 miles) to Plumtree, just ten kilometres (six miles) from the Botswana border.

Some sixteen kilometres (10 miles) from Bulawayo, it passes one of the nation's four World Heritage Sites, the imposing fifteenth- to sixteenth-century ruins of Khame, the old capital of the Torwa State, the second-largest known stone ruins in Zimbabwe, dating from around the same time as Great Zimbabwe (See "Great Zimbabwe: The Kingdom of Ophir", Part Two). The ruins lie close to the west of the road on the banks of the Khame River (See "The Gold and the Silver", Part One).

Although nothing at Khame rivals the size of Great Zimbabwe's conical tower or hill complex, there is clear evidence of common links. Like Great Zimbabwe, Khame was the source of myth and legend — a place of no known certainty — until the discovery of its ruins in 1893, and then only after the death of Lobengula, who guarded its secrets jealously.

Spread over an area of a few square kilometres, Khame was the place where the Rozvi's Mambo dynasty held court. Later the place became an important spiritual shrine for the Ndebele. Indeed, the first settlers knew only of these ruins by word of mouth — the earliest maps mark them as "The King's Preserve".

Evidence of 40,000 years of continuous occupation has been uncovered at Khame, which flourished until the 1830s when the Zulu's Nguni warriors, retreating from Mzilikazi's advance, destroyed it.

Later, Lobengula and his *induna* used the ruins for the Ndebele's sacred rainmaking ceremonies. No doubt, they acquired some of the ritual from the Shona, for whom rainmaking is one of the most important ceremonies.

Every year, between September and January, the Shona still practice these rainmaking rites in their sacred shrines, with petitions to the tribe's ancestral spirits. All are involved — providing music, food, drink, and dancers. Honey and millet beer is an essential ingredient, and the songs and dances are offered as an appeasement to the spirits that control the clouds.

Zimbabwe's rainfall is often erratic and in 1971 the country's meteorologists introduced another form of rainmaking ceremony that also takes place each year. Between November and March planes are deployed to measure the raindrop spectrum of the cumulus clouds and, where necessary, seed them with silver iodide crystals. On some occasions this technique has yielded as much as 120 tonnes of rain for each cloud treated.

The first investigation of the Khame Ruins was disastrous. It was carried out by the Rhodesia Ancient Ruins Company which had a franchise to explore old gold mines and other places for treasure. As at Great Zimbabwe, and other archaeological sites, they did untold damage and found precious little in the way of gold or treasure — only the priceless relics the searchers destroyed, thinking they were worthless.

It was 1947 before the first serious excavations and studies were undertaken at Khame

when K. R. Robinson, the Chief Inspector of Historical Monuments, uncovered significant late Stone Age artefacts.

Sightseeing

The **central complex** is made up of twelve ruins. On the **Hill Ruin** many of the hut floors are still visible and the charred timbers of the passageways tell of a terrible conflagration.

A **cross** in one of the ruins is an enigma: some postulate that it was left behind by Portuguese missionaries who may have visited the capital in the seventeenth or eighteenth centuries.

But many **implements** found on the site, now contained in the nearby **museum**, are more than 1,000 years old. Much has yet to be learned from these ancient stones — and from other ancient ruins close to Bulawayo.

Mission

Halfway between the Khame ruins and **Figtree** stands the Anglican **Cyrene Mission**, founded in 1939 as an **educational centre** for African children by the Reverend Edward Patterson, who had served with Bishop Paget, Archbishop of central Africa.

He had an instinctive talent for art and a unique gift for encouraging his pupils to develop their artistic talents and highly individualistic African style. His inspiration was so great that the mission soon established its own art form, so distinctive that it is known today throughout the art world as the Cyrene School.

Under his benign guidance, great and original talent in the arts and the crafts won quick recognition, particularly the innate carving and sculptural skills of the African students.

So successful were teacher and pupils that by 1949 their work received acclaim when an exhibition of Cyrene art was held in London, and again in 1954.

When the Reverend Edward Patterson retired in 1953, the Cyrene interpretation of traditional scenes and religious depictions in colours and oils had become established as a unique art form. Today, still run as a secondary school, the Cyrene Mission continues to enhance its reputation as a pioneering school of art.

Above: Decorative wall at Khame Ruins, one of Zimbabwe's four World Heritage Sites.

The House of Usher

The American Salvation Army's **Usher Institute** at **Leighwood**, near Figtree, is another worthy educational institute that has earned fame for the quality of its academic work. It is named in honour of Lobengula's friend and advisor, William Filmer Usher.

Some ten kilometres (six miles) beyond the mission, the borders of Mzilikazi's and Lobengula's territory were marked by a large fig tree where visitors waited for royal permission to enter the kingdom. The custom is commemorated today by **Figtree**, the **village** that now stands there.

Renowned for the herds of Hereford heifers established in the area by two brothers, Joe and Redmund Connelly, Figtree was first surveyed in 1896 by Maxwell Edwards. In fact, he was lining up his theodolite when a group of Ndebele *impi*, up in arms over forced labour, attacked him. Edwards evaded the hostile warriors to reach the shelter of besieged Bulawayo.

Early Figtree consisted of no more than six settlers and a store, post office, and police station, all built of mud and wattle with a canvas awning over the front to make it "cool" in summer and "cosy" in winter. Calico, stretched across wooden frames, formed the improvised windows, and bath water was heated outside in paraffin tins. The only light was provided by hurricane lamps, and the furniture was fashioned from old packing boxes.

Lee's House

Thirty-one kilometres (19 miles) beyond Figtree, a **south-east fork** off the main road leads twenty-seven kilometres (17 miles) along a **gravel road** to **Mangwe**, an insignificant **mission town** on the **loop road** to **Kezi**.

However, twelve kilometres (seven and a half miles) beyond this turning, another road leads in the same direction — to **Mangwe Pass**. There you find the **memorial** to Robert Moffat, Dr. Livingstone's father-in-law, and the fellow missionaries who travelled this road with him in 1854. It is also the site of a **fort** built by the Pioneer Column in their attempt to conquer Matabeleland.

Little known today, the fort, once an essential communications centre on the.

Above: Rock art at Nswatugi Cave, Matobo Hills, has weathered many milleniums.

route from Tuli to Bulawayo, is a **national monument**.

Some seventeen kilometres (11 miles) along the road you come to **the monument** built to mark the centennial of missionary Robert Moffat's march through the pass. Although he was sixty-one, he travelled more than 1,100 kilometres (700 miles) to Mzilikazi's kraal on the Bembesi River, near Inyati, for permission to build a mission on behalf of the London Missionary Society.

The inscription on the memorial reads: "Through the Mangwe pass the first missionaries, hunters, and traders passed slowly and resolutely into the interior. They revealed to those who followed the bounties of a country they themselves might not enjoy."

Before Rhodes began his imperial mission, the pass was a well-known camping spot for many of Mzilikazi's European intimates and confidants. The Ndebele King gave one of them, an ex-Royal Naval officer named John Lee, as much land as he could cover by riding a horse for one hour in each direction of the compass.

Lee rode furiously — east and west, south and north — and ended up with 500 square kilometres (200 square miles), which Mzilikazi endowed to him in perpetuity.

Soon after, Lee opened a store and built other buildings. By 1870 Mangwe was well established — enough to boast its own **cemetery**. Life at Mangwe was dangerous and exciting. When Lee's son Hans found a lion attacking cattle in the kraal next to their house, he shot it. He was just twelve.

Inevitably Hans became famous in his own right, and when Lord Randolph Churchill trekked through Mashonaland from Tuli, via Fort Victoria, to Salisbury in 1891, he was appointed as guide. Lord Randolph recounted his experiences with Lee in his book *Men, Mines and Animals in South Africa*.

Hans Lee's father was a loyal friend to both Mzilikazi and his successor, Lobengula. After he refused to take sides with the BSAC during the 1893 suppression of the Ndebele, Cecil Rhodes annexed his land — some distance beyond Moffat's memorial — and the **house** which Lee built on it. Today the building is a **national monument**.

Above: Distinctive frescos adorn the round walls of the famous Cyrene Chapel at the edge of the Matobo Hills.

St. Andrew's Fort

In between the house and the memorial is the fort that was built, during the Ndebele uprising, by the reinforcements on their march north. It was to guard the coach road that led through the hills to Bulawayo.

Known as **St. Andrew's**, the circular fort, fourteen metres (46 feet) in diameter, is built of stone. Set underground, it was roofed with hardwood poles covered with sandbags and earth. From the centre of the circular underground chamber rose a solid earthen pillar four metres (13 feet) high that supported the roof.

During the uprising many families — more than 150 people, of whom forty-two were children — crowded into the fort using their wagons to form a defensive circle about the fortification, the boom of each resting under the wagon in front so that the gap between was minimal.

Together they lived in this overcrowded and vermin-infested stronghold, and there were frequent clashes between the British and the Afrikaner inmates, who were still smouldering over the Jameson raid that had taken place only a few months before.

In between these brawls, a constant stream of soldiers, arms, and ammunition made its way north to help bring about the final defeat of the outnumbered Ndebele.

One heroine to emerge from all this was a Mrs. Prescott, the mother of a large family, who acted as the local midwife. She delivered many babies — six of them inside the fort itself — often in the worst possible circumstances.

On one occasion she had to cross a flooded river. When the horse refused, Mrs Prescott dismounted and swam the raging, crocodile-infested torrent to lead the horse across.

Yet never once was the fort attacked. For when the rebellion broke out a Ndebele soothsayer and visionary, who lived in a cave in the Matobo Hills, had ordered that the road south should be left open so that the Europeans could leave the country in peace.

Following the Ndebele defeat at the end of 1893, the fort was used as a granary. Three years later, when the Ndebele rose up again, it was infested by rats, bats, and weevils.

These in turn attracted hundreds of snakes, many of them lethal puff adders.

One telegraphist tapping out an urgent message felt one crawling across his feet but did not stop. Only when he had transmitted the cable did he pause to pick up a Zulu *assegai* and spear it to death.

The puff adders were so replete with their continuous banquet that, barely able to move, they lay in stupor on the paths around the fort. They were so lethargic that many soldiers would grab them by their tails and swing them around their shoulders like a whirligig — the half-digested rats popping out of their mouths like shot from a sling.

To Plumtree

Plumtree, 100 kilometres (62 miles) **southwest** of Bulawayo, was founded in 1897 when the **railway** to Bulawayo was built. Today it is a ranching centre, the **border post** between Zimbabwe and Botswana, and the **district headquarters** of an area covering 1,360 square kilometres (526 square miles).

One major problem for the early European railway staff at such remote stations was educating their children. The first school to be established along the line in 1902 was at Plumtree — because one official stationed there had nine children.

Initially classes were held under a Bishop Gaul in the refreshment room, then moved to the Customs House while permanent buildings were built on land donated by the BSAC. The school's first headmaster, R.W. Hammond, a young Cambridge graduate, served the school for thirty years until his retirement in 1936. Modelling the curriculum after those of English public schools, he founded a lasting academic tradition.

Although Plumtree never developed to any great extent, it was home to many eccentric and famous characters, including the hunter Cornelius van Rooyen, an adventurer who roamed the wilds of Matabeleland long before the first settlers arrived.

Van Rooyen spent his last days at Plumtree with his son-in-law, a Mr. Wilde, a noted taxidermist who preserved many specimens shot by his father-in-law. Some can be seen at the national museums in Harare and Bulawayo.

Another character was W. E. Thomas, son of the Reverend Thomas Morgan Thomas, the missionary who attended Lobengula's coronation (See "The Gold and the Silver", Part One). W. E. Thomas, who was born at Inyati in 1865 and grew up among the Ndebele, was five when Lobengula was crowned. He became the only white man ever to serve in Lobengula's bodyguard.

When Lobengula burnt down his royal kraal near the present Sauerdale in September 1881 and moved to Bulawayo, he refused to let the missionaries accompany him.

Instead, he gave one of them permission to go and teach at **Empandeni**, thirty kilometres (18 miles) from Plumtree. The Ndebele king thought his citizens there to be the worst in the country.

The **mission** was built on **Msasa Hill** in 1885. When Empandeni township was founded ten years later, the mission moved to a new site some six and a half kilometres (four miles) to the north where it, and the many educational institutions it has developed since, still stand.

Two other **mission stations** — one Methodist, the other Anglican — were established to the **north** and **west** of Plumtree much later.

Inyati: Missions and Mines

Running out of Bulawayo city centre, **Robert Mugabe Way** (formerly Grey Street) leads past the **international airport** and forty-five kilometres (28 miles) later reaches what was once the richest gold mine in the region.

Queen's Mine was pegged in 1893, on the site of some ancient workings, by Sir John Willoughby, who accompanied the Pioneer Column as Chief Staff Officer to Lieutenant-Colonel Pennefather. The mine earned its name because of its closeness to the kraal of a Ndebele queen.

By 1896, a 140-metre (460-foot) shaft had been sunk, but development was slow and the mine was no deeper by 1904 and still short of capital to install a mill. To counter the losses, it was leased out for three and a half years to an operator who was able to put up a mill. He worked the mine until 1908.

Two years later, when the Matabeleland Queen's Company was floated on the stock market, the mine had four levels and was prospering. Values improved continuously as it went down through the fifth and sixth levels, reaching the seventh level in 1913.

All seemed well, but in 1919, following an influenza epidemic and a wave of desertion, the company ran into crisis. The mine, which was liquidated, was bought by Bembezi District Gold Mines, but only worked on a small scale.

In 1930 it changed hands again and in 1935 it was bought by Thomas Meikle. Finally, the mine was worked out and it was abandoned in 1946.

Eleven kilometres (seven miles) beyond Queen's Mine, to the **east** of the road, stands **Turk Mine**, which Meikle acquired in 1924 after a disagreement between the owners. The mine had been prospected and pegged at the turn of the century, but was never mined. In 1918, however, the **Angel Mine**, which today forms part of the Turk, yielded a small amount of gold.

Serious development of the Turk began in 1921 when two partners, G. F. Hickey and C. Findley, pegged the claims that they sold three years later to Meikle. In turn he gave shares to P. J. Phillips, who at one time had been connected with the fabulously rich Globe and Phoenix mine at Kwe Kwe, and other mines at Bindura.

Moffat's mission

Just a few kilometres beyond the turning to Turk Mine stands the **mission** founded at **Inyati** by Dr. David Livingstone's father-in-law, Robert Moffat, who with fellow missionary William Sykes was shown the spot by Mzilikazi.

Although Mzilikazi had welcomed his old friend with great warmth, he was in no hurry for the missionaries to start work among his people. Leaving Sykes and his colleague, Thomas Morgan Thomas, to work out their own salvation at Inyati, Moffat returned to his base in Botswana.

After Mzilikazi's death in 1868, his son Lobengula allowed the missionaries to establish a second station at **Hope Fountain**, close to his capital of Bulawayo. But Sykes never left Inyati. He died there in 1887 — without having produced a single convert to the Christian faith.

Twenty-six kilometres (16 miles) **north** of Inyati stands **Lonely Mine**, which was discovered at the end of 1906 by an African prospector who carried specimens of the ore to his European bosses in Bulawayo for assaying. He then led them to an extremely dense cluster of thorn bush that hid a small ancient working ten metres (33 feet) long and about a metre (three feet) wide.

In its first year of operation in 1907, 950 tonnes of crushed ore yielded forty-eight kilos (105 lbs) of gold and Lonely Mine, once the deepest mine on a quartz reef in Africa, developed rapidly.

During its first twenty-one years the mine produced almost twenty-three tonnes of gold, worth nearly Z$8 million, as well as moderate quantities of silver. The Lonely Mine Gold Mining Company, formed at the end of 1909, bought the mine for Z$400,000, the largest sum ever paid for any mineral deposits in the country.

But not all was wealth — the 1918 influenza epidemic left 142 workers dead, while more than 300 survivors fled into the bush never to return. Among the victims was the manager, C. Bright.

Now, although gold is still mined, the nearby copper mine opened by Lonrho in the 1960s is the lodestone of the region's wealth.

More than 100 kilometres (60 miles) northwest, the old ro d to the Ndebele **Queen's kraal** leads through **Gwampa valley** to the **drift** on the **Shangani River** where a **memorial** marks the spot on which Major Allan Wilson and his men were killed in 1893.

Lobengula's former envoy, Dawson, who volunteered to lead the search, found the bodies and buried them near an ant hill beneath a large mopane tree on the trunk of which he carved the words: "To Brave Men". The **tree trunk** is now in Bulawayo's National Museum.

The Lowveld: Sugar and Citrus, Heat and Hazard

Sere and scorched, its arid floor cut by the wide reaches of the meandering Save, Runde, and Mwenezi rivers, the sweltering, once pestilential lowveld stretches from Zimbabwe's western border with Botswana at Mphoengs, across to the east, ending in a salient thrust deep between the highveld and the wall of the Eastern Highlands, the massive granite buttress that forms much of the country's border with Mozambique.

The Save, of all Zimbabwe's rivers second only in size to the mighty Zambezi, rises in the highveld some 100 kilometres (60 miles) south-west of Harare, then drops swiftly about 600 metres (2,000 feet) during the first 100 kilometres (60 miles) or so of its journey to the Indian Ocean.

By the time it reaches the lowveld, it becomes broad and sluggish. It is joined by the Runde at the far corner of Gonarezhou National Park on the Mozambique border, to the north-east of the Limpopo River which forms the lowveld's southern borders.

Another of Zimbabwe's main rivers, the Runde, has long featured in the country's history. Often impassable in the rainy season, it became a major obstacle for the Pioneer Column during its 1890 trek to Mashonaland.

The river's rocky, uneven bed and depth — and the force of its swift-flowing currents when in spate — threatened to capsize the wagons. Undeterred, the pioneers felled some trees, tied them together, anchored them to either bank, then laid the logs across the river bed. After a protracted struggle — pulling on both sides with ropes and chains — the pioneers saw the last of the ox wagons across.

The Runde, which derives its name from the Bantu word *warunda*, meaning "flooded river", rises near Gweru. During the summer months, the plentiful rains collected by the Shurugwi Hills flow into the river, which in spate often floods the surrounding countryside as it meanders through the lowveld.

For most of the year, however, stunted patches of withered grass, rock, and sand characterize this unproductive land of almost perpetual famine. The only solace that the leached soil of the communal lands can offer to the people who attempt to eke out a living from it is the flood bounty and dry season trickles of the Save, Runde, and their tributaries.

Theirs is the harshest of existences. Villagers walk long distances to collect sacks of grain from the relief centres organized by the Government. For those who only pass through it, however, the ravaged scenery holds a certain gaunt and barren beauty.

Getting there

Beitbridge, 321 kilometres (200 miles) from Bulawayo, 580 kilometres (360 miles) from Harare, and 288 kilometres (179 miles) from Masvingo, is served by road and rail. There are regular bus and passenger train services.

When to go

The summer heat, November–March, is often unbearable. The best time to visit is during the cooler winter months, May–September.

Where to stay

In Beitbridge, the Beitbridge Hotel (2-star), Peter's Motel. See Listings for "Hotels". There is a caravan park and campsite. See Listings. At Bubi River, the Lion and Elephant Motel. See Listings.

Sightseeing

The first stop on the **Bulawayo–Beitbridge road** to the **lowveld** is the town beyond **Gwanda — Colleen Bawn**, an odd name to find on a map of Africa.

The town rose up around a claim pegged in 1895 by Sam Daly, an Irish gold prospector who named his find for the sweetheart he left behind in Dublin. Romantic he might have been, but wealth he did not find.

Today Colleen Bawn is noted for its unromantic cement industry. It is also an important ranching and mining area.

Seventeen kilometres (11 miles) **south-**

Above: Granite sentinels guard the Masvingo-Johannesburg road.

east lies **West Nicholson**, named after prospector Andy Nicholson who was living there when it was founded in 1903. It marks the **terminus** of the railway **branch line** from Bulawayo.

Set on the **west bank** of the **Mzingwani River**, at the foot of **Mount Olympus**, a copper mine was opened nearby in 1906, but was soon abandoned as it was unviable.

Soon after, however, in 1910, one of the country's largest ranching operations was established by Liebig's, the multinational meat canners, on 3,087 square kilometres (1,249 square miles) of land. The ranch factory processes various extracts, cans meat, and also processes fruit and vegetables.

Fort Tuli

Some fifty-eight kilometres (36 miles) out of West Nicholson, a **dirt road** leads 100 kilometres (62 miles) **south-west** off the main highway to **Fort Tuli** built by the BSAC's mercenary Pioneer Column in 1890 on the spot where the hunter F. C. Selous established a base.

Lying on Zimbabwe's **southern border** with Botswana, 765 metres (2,500 feet) above

sea-level, Tuli's name derives from the Bantu word for dust, *utuhli*. When the Pioneer Column reached the wide, sandy **Shashi River**, which then marked the borders of Matabeleland, on 1 July, 1890, they built a strong defensive **fort** atop a small kopje.

Soon after this, police and pioneers experienced a bruising struggle on the dry river bed in what is reputed to have been the first rugby match played in Rhodesia (See "Sporting Zimbabwe", Part Four).

The telegraph line from the south, an essential communications link in Rhodes's dream of colonizing Africa from the Cape to Cairo, reached Tuli on its way to Fort Victoria on 28 May, 1891.

Not long after the fort was completed, the commander, Colonel Frank Johnson, received an advance guard of Lobengula's 20,000-strong army led by *indunas*. Johnson laid on a demonstration of firepower, complete with searchlights, machine guns, and nine-pound artillery cannons to impress — and discourage — them.

For three years Fort Tuli was the main point of entry from South Africa. Wagons from the Transvaal crossed the **Limpopo** at

Rhodes Drift, where the Transvaal authorities had established a customs post.

In August 1902, C. H. Zeederberg began a passenger coach service between Bulawayo and Pietersburg via Tuli, crossing the Limpopo through the drift. When it was flooded during the rains, however, the company had to use a pontoon ferry — cumbersome and often dangerous.

Even though a new drift was established just north of Messina, the problems still remained and two years after it started, the service was suspended. The problems were just too many and the profits too small.

During the Boer War, Fort Tuli served as a British depot and by 1891 a small town with a hotel and post office had grown up around the fort, which had become a training depot for new recruits. The same year — on 1 April — Mother Patrick and her nursing sisters established the first hospital in Rhodesia at Tuli.

The sisters were no fools, but their choice of location for the new hospital was as ill-fated as Fort Tuli itself. After the railway reached Bulawayo in 1897, Fort Tuli was completely bypassed and by 1904 the town and fort were virtually abandoned. A force of no more than nine troopers under a sergeant patrolled the border and only two stores remained open.

When the route through Beitbridge was opened in the middle of the first decade of this century, Tuli ceased to be of any importance.

Sightseeing

Tuli today is derelict. All that marks the former **border crossroads** is the **flag** that flutters over the **Pioneer Memorial** and the scars of that early occupation — the old fort, the outlines of roads, discarded tins, and the **cemetery** where so many hopeful adventurers and carpetbaggers lie buried.

Most died of malaria, some through fatal misfortune. The inscription on one **headstone** — in memory of Theodore C. Fenton — reads simply: "Mauled by a lion, and died."

You may notice, looking at a map of Botswana and Zimbabwe, the strange semi-circle that marks the border between the two countries, known as the "**Tuli Circle**". It came about in June 1891 when magisterial districts in Mashonaland were defined. The magistrate at Tuli was given jurisdiction over the area that fell within a sixteen-kilometre (ten-mile) radius of Tuli between the Shashi and another river.

This odd and distinctive crescent on the map of southern Africa now embraces the **Tuli Safari Area**. Established in 1963, it lies 695 metres (2,280 feet) above sea-level and covers 416 square kilometres (160 square miles) of relatively flat, basalt country bordered in the east by the eroded valley of the **Shashi River**.

It contains three Botanical Reserves — **Tolo River**, more than four square kilometres (1.6 square miles); **Pioneer**, almost four square kilometres; and **South Camp**, 2.6 square kilometres (one square mile) — where hunting is prohibited.

Species in the botanical reserves include fuchsia, monkey thorn, and nyala tree. The area is dominated by mopane woodland with open to fairly dense scrub, small trees, and a well-developed riverine **gallery forest** along the Shashi River.

Among the wildlife that serve as game trophies for the hunting parties are duiker, eland, impala, zebra, grysbok, steenbok, and wildebeest. Elephant also move in and out of the area, but sable and roan antelope disappeared long ago, apparently as a result of habitat deterioration.

There is some poaching and trespass by pastoralists bringing their cattle to graze, but all the hunting allocations are fully taken up each season. There are few other visitors in this wild and remote area.

Those rare visitors, however, are likely to see some distinctive and magnificent cattle grazing around the ruins of the old town. They belong to the indigenous breed to which Tuli lent its name. Light fawn in colour, the breed has been developed since the end of the Second World War by the Tuli Breeding Society, formed in 1945. The stud herd is held at the **Tuli Breeding Station** under the Ministry of Internal Affairs.

To Beitbridge

From Tuli it is another 120 kilometres (75 miles) along the **gravel road east** through the sun-scorched thornbush wilderness to **Beitbridge**, the main **border post** with **South Africa**. The post is marked by the kilometre-

Above: Young chicks on a Chiredzi ostrich farm.

and-a-half (one-mile) length of **road-rail bridge** across the Limpopo, just 456 metres (1,500 feet) above sea-level.

The fourteen-span bridge designed by Sir Ralph Freeman is ten metres (33 feet) wide and was built between 1927 and 1929 with money from the Beit Trust — a £1.2 million fund established at the bequest of Alfred Beit, Cecil Rhodes's closest associate, who died in 1906. A **tower** on the **centre pier** carries a bronze **memorial plaque** to Beit.

The bridge was built under appalling conditions: oppressive heat, malaria, and fevers. Nonetheless, despite these hardships, the speed at which the bridge was constructed in the midst of an arid, undeveloped thorn scrub wilderness was remarkable.

But only just in time. The foundations for the piers — sunk into the river bed to a depth of nine metres (30 feet) — had just been completed (the men were still concreting the piers) when the first of the Limpopo's seasonal flash floods surged down the river.

The engineer in charge described them as a "roaring sea" but, despite the pounding waves and the battering of uprooted trees, the freshly set pillars stood the strain.

Completed at a cost of Z$260,000, the bridge was formally opened on 31 August, 1929, when the Earl of Athlone, Governor-General of South Africa, and Sir Cecil Rodwell, Governor of Rhodesia, boarded the train that moved slowly across the bridge breaking the ribbon stretched across the track above the **central pillar** that marks the **border** between the two countries.

Yet another forty-five years passed before — in October 1974 — the South African railway line that crosses Beitbridge was finally linked to the Rhodesia Railway system at Rutenga, more than 130 kilometres (80 miles) inside Zimbabwe. Today the small town by the bridge has a **post office, customs post**, and **immigration post**.

To Chiredzi

Just a few kilometres outside Beitbridge, along the **Masvingo road**, a **gravel road** leads 195 kilometres (121 miles) **east** to the **Mabalauta Gate** of **Gonarezhou National Park**. The easiest approach to the park, however, is the thirty-four-kilometre (21-mile) gravel road south from **Chiredzi** in the north of the lowveld.

Seventy-five kilometres (47 miles) **north** of Beitbridge, the Masvingo road crosses the **Bubi River** at the village of the same name and then rolls on another forty-two kilometres (26 miles) to **Mwenezi**, headquarters of one of the biggest **ranches** in Zimbabwe. The area is also well-known for its abundant wildlife.

Another eighteen kilometres (twelve miles) beyond Mwenezi the road cuts through **Rutenga**, the **junction town** where the line to Mozambique joins the line from South Africa.

And forty-one kilometres (25 miles) beyond the junction, the Masvingo road crosses the Runde River at the village of **Lundi**, 561 metres (1,840 feet) above sea-level.

When the Pioneer Column camped at Lundi in 1890, its officers discovered a small **ruin**, splendidly preserved, which was associated with the city-state of Great Zimbabwe.

During the early part of this century, the Runde often became impassable in the rainy season and travellers were delayed for long periods. The mail riders, however, braved the dangers by swimming their horses across the swollen waters of the crocodile-infested river.

Occasionally, the risk proved too great but there were few applicants for the vacancies created when the crocodiles snapped up one of the mail riders.

Even when a low-level bridge was built, the floods were so fierce the river often remained impassable. Today's high-level **bridge** has ended these dangers.

The **east turn** to Chiredzi lies twelve kilometres (seven and a half miles) beyond Lundi at **Ngundu Halt**, a small insignificant village ninety-five kilometres (59 miles) **south** of Masvingo. From there the road runs **east**, virtually arrow-straight for eighty-two kilometres (51 miles) through the sweltering lowlands to the small centre called **Triangle**.

After the first rains, night drivers face a blizzard of "sausage flies", termites, and myriad other winged insects that take the downpours as their cue to hatch, often in such large numbers that they eventually block the windscreen.

The giant Triangle **sugar mill**, built close to the branch railway line that ends at **Nandi**, is the first indication of the metamorphosis that has transformed this region from a monotonously flat, bush-tangled, tsetse fly-infested wilderness, dotted with baobab trees and choked with scrub, into one of Zimbabwe's most prosperous and productive areas.

Nearby **Buffalo Range** with its **airfield**, seven kilometres (four miles) **east** of Triangle, is the second indicator and thirteen kilometres (eight miles) further east is the third, the town of **Chiredzi** and neighbouring **Hippo Valley sugar plantation**.

The Making of a Town

The first feasibility study to explore the potential for developing the lowveld through irrigation was carried out by the consulting engineers, Sir Alexander Gibb and Partners in 1947. The survey included engineering and economic studies based on agricultural and mineral production.

The survey concluded that some 2,850 square kilometres (1,100 square miles) were irrigable and that the area was suitable for settlement. Thus, some years later, Chiredzi came into being.

It was not until 1965, however, with the establishment of the African township of Towani, named after a local chief, that it was given any form of municipal administration.

Three agricultural research stations, each established on one of the major soil types of the lowveld, were established to study the problems of irrigation agronomy and define the cropping practices most suited to the prevailing soil and climatic conditions. The sugar industry was also instrumental in providing a sugar research station.

During the 1950s, intensive tsetse control programmes instituted over an extensive area, reaching beyond the Mozambique border, eradicated the fly, and farm developers noted that the climate was ideal for citrus production — if only there was enough water.

In 1956, after tapping the waters of the Runde River, Hippo Valley established its first citrus plantation. Three years later, water was diverted from Lake Mutirikwi, near Masvingo, and the plantation expanded. But, lacking sufficient domestic or export markets, the company reduced the land devoted to citrus growing and turned to large-scale sugar growing.

Getting there

Chiredzi, 483 kilometres (300 miles) from Bulawayo, 495 kilometres (307 miles) from Harare, 203 kilometres (126 miles) from Masvingo, and 301 kilometres (187 miles) from Beitbridge, is linked to Harare and Masvingo by air from the Buffalo Range Airport; by road from Bulawayo, Harare, Gweru, Masvingo, Beitbridge, and Birchenough Bridge; and by rail from Gweru and Zvishavane. There are regular bus and passenger train services.

When to go

The summer season is often uncomfortably hot, but the winter climate is ideal.

Where to stay

Tambuti Lodge (2-star), Planter's Inn. Game ranches around Chiredzi operate comfortable and attractive game lodges and there are hotels in major centres. See Listings for "Hotels". There is an excellent caravan park and campsite. See Listings.

Sightseeing

The **rail link** between **Chiredzi** and **Mbizi Station**, on the Maputo line, was opened in October 1964. The **bridge** that carries it across the Runde River is the longest railway bridge in Zimbabwe, with a length of 418 metres (457 yards) made up of nineteen spans, each measuring twenty-two metres (72 feet).

This line, and the surrounding agricultural developments, have made Chiredzi what is perhaps Zimbabwe's fastest-growing town. With a modern **shopping centre**, **restaurants**, **chain stores**, **schools**, **health clinics**, and many amenities, the town has made great strides in only three decades of existence.

Chiredzi is located at the threshold of the 160-square-kilometre (65-square-mile) **Hippo Valley plantation** of which, in 1990, more than 100 square kilometres (40 square miles) were covered by sugarcane.

Neat roads slice through the plantation where the company has built more than twenty model workers' **estates**, as well as **schools** and **health clinics**. The **mill** is capable of producing more than 10,000 tonnes of sugar a day.

The cane is burnt before harvesting to make cutting and handling easier. During the cutting season, great tongues of flame climb dozens of feet into the sky all across the plantation as the fires rage through each chosen block.

Many small outgrowers in the area, who supply cane on contract, depend on the sugar company for their livelihood, and cane from the sister **Mkwasine Estate**, some thirty kilometres (19 miles) to the northeast, is also processed at the Hippo Valley mill.

The amount of land under cultivation in Zimbabwe is governed by water levels and in 1990 it had yet to recover from the severe droughts which reduced **Lake Mutirikwi** to less than a fifth of its usual size.

Some private **game ranches**, a few with their own **motels**, flourish in this arid region. Game ranching has become a major growth industry — particularly ostrich and crocodile farming.

Chiredzi Wildlife Investments, ten kilometres (six miles) **east** of Chiredzi on the main road to **Birchenough Bridge**, has established itself as a major **ostrich ranch** and **crocodile farm** and plans to farm other wild game species. The ostriches are reared under extremely hygienic conditions, while the crocodiles are kept in large ponds close by.

Demand for ostrich meat is experiencing a boom in the west, particularly the United States of America, because of its low cholesterol content — each bird produces between five and seven kilos (11–15 lbs) of meat fit for human consumption — and the leather industry's insatiable demand for ostrich skin. Exports of ostrich feathers also bring valuable foreign exchange earnings.

The chicks, which are hatched in sterile conditions in giant incubators, grow like weeds. But they are not as hardy. These giant, flightless birds are prone to many blights and diseases.

There is a similar demand for crocodile products with the soft belly skin fetching around US$7 dollars a centimetre. Culled while still young, the belly pelt averages around thirty centimetres (one foot), bringing between US$200–250 each.

Meat and other by-products make crocodile farming extremely lucrative. As part of their agreement with the conservation authorities, the farm also restocks rivers and lakes.

There is plenty of room for expansion. The ranch covers ninety-six square kilometres (37 square miles) of land and the crocodile and ostrich farm occupies only a small area.

The ranch also trains safari guides, hunters, and conservationists, and quotes as its philosophy, "If you don't put a price tag on a species, it's dead".

Gonarezhou National Park: A Natural Disneyland

Some thirty-five kilometres (22 miles) south from Chiredzi, off the Tanganda Road, lies the entrance to one of Zimbabwe's great wilderness retreats, the 5,000 square kilometres (1,950 square miles), that represent Gonarezhou National Park, its south-east boundary drawn along the Mozambique border.

Established as a National Park in 1975, its existence also highlights the perennial dilemma between wildlife conservation and economic development.

One of Zimbabwe's major foreign exchange earners is the ranching industry, and in this region beef and buffalo are in virtual confrontation. The European Economic Commission's regulations demand that exporting countries be free of foot-and-mouth disease, and wild bovines rapidly infect domestic stock.

To ensure control of the disease, many buffalo were killed and fences, vaccination zones, and buffer zones were built around Hwange and Gonarezhou national parks.

Many experts believe that, ultimately, the land will have to be left to the buffalo — if any survive that long — for despite these precautions the ranching industry still suffers outbreaks of the disease.

For administration purposes, the park has been divided into two sections: Chipinda Pools in the north and Mabalauta in the south.

Getting there

By road from Beitbridge or Chiredzi to Mabalauta; by road from Chiredzi to Chipinda Pools.

When to go

The park is only open during the May to October dry season.

Where to stay

There are many campsites throughout the park and a comfortable rest camp at Chinguli. There are caravan parks at Chipinda Pools Camp and at Swimuwini Camp in the Mabalauta area, but to enter this part of the reserve you need written permission. See Listings.

Sightseeing

Although game walks are allowed, visitors are cautioned to behave with discretion, particularly when close to elephant, buffalo, or rhino.

Gonarezhou National Park is mainly flat or undulating country, broken by scattered ranges of isolated hills including the **Chikunja Range**, reaching altitudes between 162 and 578 metres (532 to 1,897 feet) above sea-level. The park is cut by the river valleys of the **Mwenezi**, **Runde**, and **Save**.

The wide variety of vegetation includes mixed woodland on the hills, with steeper slopes dominated by *Kirkia*, *Commiphora*, and *Adansonia digitata*. Mopane is dominant in scattered areas; there are some croton and acacia; one small, dry, evergreen forest with thicket patches of an endemic tree; and Zimbabwe's only stands of ironwood, or *musimbiti*.

The sandy soils of the Runde Valley support a mixed community of deciduous woody species, and one patch of relict riverine forest containing several threatened species. Gonarezhou is also the only location in Zimbabwe for several species of aloe.

The rivers abound with crocodile and many freshwater species, including freshwater turtle, lung fish, tigerfish, and bream. Amazingly, marine species — tarpon and

Above: Birchenough Bridge spans the wide meandering reaches of the Save River.

swordfish — have also been caught in the Runde, hundreds of kilometres from the saltwater of the Indian Ocean.

For almost half its journey through the park, the river's south bank is marked by the spectacular red sandstone **Chilojo Cliffs**, riven by many gullies that the animals follow down to the water.

The **Chipinda Pools** attract large numbers of migratory game from **Kruger National Park** in South Africa and a neighbouring **game area** in Mozambique. Hundreds of eland and elephant regularly cross between Gonarezhou and Kruger.

Gonarezhou's resident species include black rhino and hippo. The park is also a major stronghold for nyala, suni, and Lichtenstein's hartebeest. Colonies of steenbok, grysbok, grey duiker, Livingstone's suni, oribi, and klipspringer, all live together: such a combination of so many different small antelope in close proximity to each other is perhaps unique in Africa.

Much of the vegetation suffered grievous harm from the burning and bush-clearing that was carried out during the tsetse control programme. The flora continues to suffer

damage from grazing elephants, which are quite capable of transforming their habitat from woodlands into grasslands.

Dams and irrigation schemes have also affected the flow and water quality of the Runde and Save rivers. As a result **Manjinji Pan** on the south bank of the Mwenezi River, which used to be a haven for thousands of birds, is silting up.

Nonetheless Gonarezhou remains one of Zimbabwe's most pristine wildernesses. Magnificent to behold, memorable to experience, only one cloud darkens this natural Disneyland — the constant threat of poachers crossing the border from Mozambique.

To Birchenough Bridge

Ten kilometres (six miles) **east** of Chiredzi, a **gravel road** leads **north** to **Ndanga** and **Masvingo**. Sixty kilometres (37 miles) along this road there is a **turn east** that runs twenty kilometres (12 miles) to the unspoilt beauty of thirty-five-square-kilometre (fourteen-square-mile) **Manjirenji Recreational Park**, a little-visited haven encompassing **Lake Manjirenji**, formerly Lake McDougall, and its foreshores. Famous for its boating, fishing, and unspoiled scenic surroundings, the fish are said to be uncommonly canny.

A similar distance to the **south-west**, off the same gravel road, lies the neighbouring **Bangala Recreational Park**, formed around the **Bangala Dam**, whose waters help to irrigate the sugar plantations in the south.

Thirty kilometres (19 miles) from the Manjirenji turning, the road passes through **Zaka**, an administrative centre founded in 1923. Eighty-six kilometres (53 miles) **east** of Masvingo, it is the headquarters of the District Commissioner for **Ndanga district**.

Lying 774 metres (2,540 feet) above sea-level the village is at the northernmost edge of the lowveld. Its name, in fact, derives from the Bantu Kwo-ka-Zaka — meaning "where it goes down".

At Zaka, a dirt road leads thirty kilometres (18 miles) **north-east** to **Bikita**, notable as the centre of the region that has a greater variety of **mineral deposits** than any other place on earth — including the largest single deposit of lithium ore yet discovered. Other ores contain beryllium, lepidolite, petalite, and potassium rubidium.

These deposits were first mined in 1931 by George Nolan, the son of the man who discovered the mineral-rich veins beneath the arid, sun-bleached soil. But after a few years he was virtually penniless.

To protect his claims — as required by mining law — he had to continue digging with pick and shovel to show that they were under development. He lived on maize porridge and an occasional antelope that he shot; and eked out a sparse living by writing random features for overseas magazines.

Nolan's patience paid off. At the end of the Second World War, his beryllium and lithium production was snapped up by the USA. The sale of these strategic materials, essential to America's nuclear development, soon made him a millionaire.

The once dirt-poor prospector responded in true rags to riches style. He hired two Italian stonemasons to build him a unique **mansion**. Nolan filled "Lithium Lodge" — which took seven years to complete and is constructed entirely of lithium rock — with elegant antique furniture and precious items from around the world. He claimed it was the only house of its kind in the world.

Bikita is also renowned for an unusual entomological phenomenon — the annual migration of millions of stinkbugs. It is believed that these foul-smelling insects gather there to mate.

Whatever the reason, it is the undoing of countless stinkbug numbers for, despite the repulsive odour they emit, they are regarded as a delicacy by the local people who sweep them off the branches of the trees each morning while the insects are still drowsy.

Some twelve kilometres (seven miles) **north** of Bikita, the dirt road joins up with the main Masvingo–Birchenough Bridge road.

Visitors who do not want to make the diversion to these remote areas can simply continue along the fine new road from Chiredzi that leads 200 kilometres (124 miles) to **Birchenough Bridge**.

Stark and scorched, there is a desolate beauty about the arid landscape through which the road cuts, even more pronounced by contrast to the first upthrust of the highland wall that shadows the eastern horizon some fifty kilometres (30 miles) out of Chiredzi.

Cool promise

The promise of **Tanganda Junction**, and the cool relief that lies in the highlands beyond, is made when the junction is 100 kilometres (62 miles) distant. The promise continues to draw visitors through this haunting heat-ridden wilderness — bordered in the immediate **east** by the 261 square kilometres (100 square miles) of **Chipinga Safari Area**, where hunters stalk small and medium-sized antelope for the walls of their trophy rooms.

The large signs that renew the promise every forty kilometres (25 miles) suggest that Tanganda Junction is an important centre. With only twenty kilometres (12 miles) to go, the road begins to climb a **pass** between two massive, forested **whalebacks** and there it is — a promise unfulfilled, no more than what the signposts say: a **junction** where two roads meet. There is not even a shack to justify the pledge.

The **turn north** at Tanganda Junction leads twenty-four kilometres (15 miles) to Birchenough Bridge, 455 metres (1,500 feet) above sea-level. It is a small enough village, but its large enough bridge is more than enough to ensure it prominence.

It spans the **Save River**, not far from where Thomas Moodie guided his pioneer settlers across its treacherous quicksands in 1891 on their way to the Chimanimani Mountains (See "Chimanimani Mountains: High Peaks and Magic Valleys").

In spate, the Save rises as much as seven metres (23 feet) or more. For this reason and the shifting, silting sandbed of the river, piers were reckoned unsuitable. The bridge, therefore, was designed with a single-arch span.

Built in two sections from each bank of the Save, the gap was closed on 17 June, 1935, becoming the first bridge of such size to be built from high-tensile steel. At that time the highest of its type in Africa, it was the third-largest suspension bridge in the world. It is named after Sir Henry Birchenough, President of the BSAC from 1925 to 1937.

Birchenough Bridge was opened on 20 December, 1935, by Sir Herbert Stanley, Governor of Southern Rhodesia. **Bronze plaques** recording the Trust's gifts and commemorating Sir Henry Birchenough — later his ashes and those of his wife were buried in the bridge foundations on the east bank of the river — were fixed to the bridge.

Designed by Ralph Freeman, in all but size the bridge is an exact replica of Sydney Harbour Bridge, Australia, which Sir Ralph also designed. Indeed, from the Sydney bridge came the cable backstays that had been used to hold the main arch ribs as they were placed in position. They were deployed at Birchenough as the permanent hangars for the main deck.

Rising 76.8 metres (252 feet), the ribs support a seven-and-a-half-metre-wide (25-foot) main span more than 330 metres (1,000 feet) long that hangs some eighteen metres (60 feet) above the river.

But even the broadest dreams outlive their reality and in 1984 the bridge's dimensions increased when it was widened and strengthened through a World Bank project.

Birchenough Bridge marks the end of the lowveld. From there the road rises steadily as its runs along the base of the eastern escarpment to **Mutare**.

In the rugged river valleys to the **north-**west, however, where the Save cuts its way down through granite hills and arid sandveld to the lowveld, stands **Dorowa,** notable for its phosphate deposits.

These deposits form a remarkable ring complex, thought to be volcanic in origin, that allows the phosphate to be recovered without blasting and treated without crushing — in a similar way to the high-grade phosphate deposits found in Florida.

Above: Copper plaque in concrete pier of Birchenough Bridge commemorates Sir Henry, President of the British South Africa Company from 1925 to 1937. The bridge was opened in 1935.

Great Zimbabwe: The Kingdom of Ophir

Great Zimbabwe and Lake Mutirikwi (former-ly Kyle), a mix of architectural marvel and natural beauty, are both located in one of Zimbabwe's most convenient tourist re-gions. Together they offer magnificent historical grandeur, an impressive array of wildlife, and some exceptional landscapes.

Great Zimbabwe is the site of the most spectacular ruins in Africa south of the Sahara, the largest and most intact of over 150 examples of such walled remains found in the country.

First occupied in the eighth century AD, Great Zimbabwe evolved from a small settlement into an immensely powerful state, ruled by a succession of kings whose influence spread throughout what is now Zimbabwe.

For many years, however, the full extent and significance of these ruins was not read-ily appreciated. Indeed, from the time that renegade American sailor Adam Renders (the first known white man to see them) set eyes on the ruins in about 1867, they were despoliated and plundered for almost four decades. Priceless treasures and relics were uprooted and hauled away with impunity.

Renders never made his discovery known, for he married the daughter of an African chief and remained in the area until his death in 1881. It was left to Carl Mauch, a German adventurer who arrived at the site on 5 September, 1871, to confirm to the world the existence of the ruins.

Despite his firm and erroneous belief that this was Ophir, the credit for much of what is known today must rest with the diligent Mauch who was the first to describe them accurately (indeed, the only one to describe them in their pristine state, for the subse-quent looting destroyed much of what he saw).

But the ruins have no link with the Bible, Sheba, or Solomon. Sheba's Axuma is the ancient city of Axum in Ethiopia's Tigray Province. Great Zimbabwe — the ancient city that the Portuguese declared was Axuma — was the powerhouse, however, of a unique southern African economy.

In fact, the truth about these ruins, where the spirit of the national persona seeps from every granite stone, is far more incredible than any fantasy (See "The Gold and the Silver", Part One).

Never a plunderer, Mauch's one concern was the preservation of the ruins and he recorded much essential data in great detail, including descriptions of the religious cere-monies (both past and present) that took place.

Evidence of the scope and size of this ancient nation's trade is dramatic. Over the years, excavations have uncovered articles from China, India, and Asia.

Of all the finds, however, the most intrigu-ing — eight delicately carved soapstone birds, which have since been adopted as the national symbol of independent Zimbabwe — had nothing to do with trade, wealth, or foreign countries. About thirty-three centi-metres (13 inches) high, the birds adorned the tops of one-metre (three-foot) columns.

Carved from a soft green-grey soapstone common to central and northern Zimbabwe, they have been described as the "only sculp-tures of any size or complexity, or displaying any attempt at representation, from Great Zimbabwe or any south-central African pre-historic site". Although the carvings follow essentially the same pattern, the ring and chevron markings vary, making it possible to identify each bird.

Within years of their discovery all were plundered, some irrevocably. The first was taken by Transvaal hunter Willie Posselt, who visited the ruins in 1889.

Uncaringly, Posselt simply hacked one bird from its pillar and carried it back to the Transvaal where he offered it to President Kruger. He showed no interest, but Rhodes did. He paid fifty dollars and mounted it on a pedestal in the library of his Groote Schuur home. Later, cement replicas were placed on the gateposts of Dalham Hall, his English home.

Seven other birds were looted after Posselt's discovery. Five went to Cape Town, one to Bulawayo, and the head of the seventh to Harare while the body went to Berlin in Germany.

The bird in Bulawayo, unweathered and fresh from the sculptor's chisel, was apparently never erected. It is believed to have been the "tombstone" intended for the king who died shortly before the 1831 invasion of the Zwabgendaba, which finally destroyed Great Zimbabwe.

The carved birds represented the zenith of this great civilization which, like many great civilizations, went into swift and traumatic decline. By the beginning of the sixteenth century it had lost all power and importance.

Getting there

Great Zimbabwe and Lake Mutirikwi are both located close to Masvingo, formerly Fort Victoria. Masvingo, 288 kilometres (179 miles) from Beitbridge, 280 kilometres (174 miles) from Bulawayo, 183 kilometres (114 miles) from Gweru, and 292 kilometres (181 miles) from Harare, is served by road, rail, and air services.

When to go

The climate is pleasant all year-round.

Sightseeing

From **Bulawayo**, the road to **Masvingo** and **Great Zimbabwe** begins along the Bulawayo to **Beitbridge road**, which soon branches **east** at **Mbalabala**. After twenty-five kilometres (16 miles) the road arrives at **Filabusi**, which was founded as a mining settlement in 1899.

The town's main claim to fame, however, arose not from any mining riches that came to town but from the mining riches that were taken from town — in true Wild West style — during one of the country's earliest bullion robberies.

The gold was being shipped on the mail stagecoach run by C. H. Zeederberg when it was held up by a gun-toting outlaw on horseback. Although the coach was escorted by a mine executive, he had no chance to draw his pistol and was forced to watch as the outlaw gunned down the two leading horses.

The gunman then ordered the gold to be loaded onto his mount. But it was so heavy the horse could barely move. Still keeping a wary eye on the coach driver and the exe-

cutive, the robber buried his haul in an ant-bear hole by the road.

Before he could return to collect it, however, the driver and guard rode pell-mell into Bulawayo, raised the alarm, and returned to recover the precious metal. The gunman was never captured.

Seven kilometres (four miles) beyond Filabusi is the village of **Fred Mine**, established around a claim pegged in 1907. The mine was a lucrative gold producer for many decades, despite the 1918 influenza epidemic that killed three of its European managers and a large number of the work force.

A **south-east turn**, fifty-four kilometres (34 miles) from Fred Mine, leads seventeen kilometres (11 miles) to **Mberengwa**, centre of an important mining area where large deposits of chrome, asbestos, and emeralds are exploited.

In the old days it was also an important gold-mining area, best remembered for the nostalgically Anglo-Saxon names of its major mines — Agincourt C, Suffolk, Clifton, Wanderer's Rest, and Belmont.

There are many ancient **ruins** in the surrounding countryside. The largest — at **Mundie** — extend for about thirty kilometres (19 miles). When they were first explored they yielded a king's ransom in golden ornaments. It was also a royal hunting preserve of the Ndebele. Mzilikazi and his successor, Lobengula, both hunted lion and antelope, buffalo and elephant in these parts.

To the **north-west** of the main Bulawayo–Masvingo road, just a few kilometres before **Zvishavane**, stands the little-known **mission** of **Dadaya** run by the Church of Christ. Its most famous preacher was Garfield Todd, who gave up evangelism to lead the federation of Rhodesia and Nyasaland.

The smart town of **Zvishavane**, 184 kilometres (114 miles) **east** of Bulawayo, is founded on the fortunes of the large **asbestos mine** that provides employment to thousands and prosperity to the region.

The asbestos deposits were discovered in 1907, but nobody established any claim to them until 1916 when the Bechuanaland Exploration Company opened the Zvishavane Mine.

Within five years, a constant convoy of

oxen and waggons were hauling more than 1,000 tonnes of asbestos (from five producers) a month, as well as trade goods, along the only road. Under pressure, the government agreed to build a branch **railway line** that opened in May 1928.

When the original holdings were amalgamated some years later, Zvishavane Mine became the largest producer of asbestos in the southern hemisphere.

The town's first bank opened in 1925 in a hut in the grounds of the only hotel — just a few metres from the bar. The arrangement seemed to work well. Neither bartender nor teller was ever short of potential (slightly or well-inebriated) customers.

Forty-five kilometres (28 miles) **north-east** of Zvishavane a **turn** runs thirty kilometres (19 miles) **south-east** along a **gravel road** to **Chibi**. The name is derived from the seventy-year-old Bantu chief whom Rhodes and Lord Randolph Churchill visited in November 1891, in an attempt to persuade him to repudiate a land deal he had struck with the South African Boers.

Chibi's influence in that region, however, was short-lived. When the chief's brother failed to pay tribute to Lobengula, the Ndebele king had him clubbed to death. Soon after, Chibi also met a similarly grisly death when he was skinned alive on Lobengula's orders.

Not much remains at Chibi's old kraal, high on a **granite hill** overlooking the route the Pioneer Column followed to Mashonaland, only the old **graves** of some missionaries, including those of a German and his children who died there in 1902. So unhealthy was the climate, in fact, that the mission was abandoned.

The missionaries lie close to the **grave** of another victim of malaria — a young policeman who was found at his last gasp in the 1890s by a passing European. He buried the officer beneath some trees with a cross made from a packing case, inscribed with the epitaph: "Somebody's boy".

Mashava, a few kilometres beyond the Chibi turn and fifty kilometres (30 miles) from Zvishavane, has a concentration of no fewer than seven mines, of which the most important are **Gaths** and **Temeraire**.

Production of chrysolite asbestos from these and the mines at Zvishavane is the highest in the world and the quality of the fibre unequalled. The shorter ones are woven into fire-resistant fabrics.

From Mashava it is another thirty-eight kilometres (24 miles) to **Masvingo**, the oldest town in the country, where the Bulawayo road links with the one from Beitbridge.

The Way of the Pioneers

The way north that Rhodes's mercenary Pioneer Column followed a century ago is marked by the chain of forts — four in all — that they built along their route.

The first of these was Fort Tuli. The second, Fort Victoria, stands on Clipsham Farm on the perimeter of what is now Masvingo, the oldest town in the country, where Rhodes's white conquistadores arrived on 17 August, 1890.

Masvingo lies close to a winding twelve-kilometre (seven-mile) pass through which the column marched, although they feared it was a dead end and that they might be ambushed. Such was their relief at finding their way safely through that they named it Providential Pass.

Within months, the fortress and the small settlement that sprang up around it — known as Fort Victoria until independence — became an important staging post on the road to Fort Salisbury (now Harare) and a major mining centre.

After only two years the town was moved to a new site some five kilometres (three miles) from what is now Clipsham Farm, and a permanent fort, with narrow embrasures, was built at the new centre.

Bricks for the fort were fashioned and baked on the banks of the Mucheke River, then carried to the site in ox wagons operated by a trio of transport riders from the Transvaal, Tom Meikle and his brothers John and Stewart, who went on to found one of the country's wealthiest dynasties.

But when Matabeleland was opened to Rhodes's mercenaries and settlers, the town fell into swift decline. Even ten years later its European population numbered only slightly more than 300, mainly settlers and prospectors (of which less than a third were women), who were often so strapped for cash that the town's first postmaster, George Bowen, who also doubled as the mining commissioner, let them have their postage stamps on credit.

For all that, however, Fort Victoria had the style and stamina of a gold rush town with grizzled, bush-hardened veterans of the African heat drifting into town to slake their thirst at the "Thatched House".

Among the most colourful of these characters, as many a man discovered to his cost, was "French Marie" who, dressed in breeches and boots and carrying a *sjambok* (a heavy whip made from rhino or hippo hide), was built like the proverbial brick privy and swore like a trooper. French Marie, who started the Green Rose Mine, developed several other claims before retiring to farm at Borrowdale, near Harare.

Above: Fruit vendor in Masvingo's street market.

Opposite: Old bell tower of the second Fort Victoria in Masvingo built by settlers in the early 1890s.

Overleaf: Luminous murals painted by Italian prisoners of war adorn the ceilings and walls of St. Francis Church, Masvingo, which was built during their internment in the first half of the 1940s.

Fort Victoria was also the place where the Meikle brothers opened a crude store built out of whisky cases and roofed with tarpaulin, the first of what became a chain of hotels and stores throughout the country, and founded the family's fortune.

Fort Victoria was elevated to town status in 1926, and became a municipality in 1953. Today it is the capital of Masvingo Province and still an important farm and mining centre.

Where to stay

Chevron Hotel (2-star), Flamboyant Motel (2-star, Great Zimbabwe Hotel (2-star). There are others. See Listings for "Hotels". There are caravan parks and campsites at Masvingo, Great Zimbabwe, and Lake Mutirikwi. See Listings.

Sightseeing

When Tom Meikle bought the "Thatched House" in 1914, he knocked it down and replaced it with the **Victoria Hotel** which still occupies the site. The present-day successor to Meikle's original **store** now covers almost one hectare (two and a half acres) of ground and dominates Masvingo's **main street.**

The second of the two forts built by the pioneers at Masvingo is the building that you see in the centre of the town on the road to **Great Zimbabwe**. Two **towers** still stand and one of them contains a small **museum**, well worth visiting. Masvingo also has an attractive and challenging **golf course**, just over a kilometre away.

Great Zimbabwe National Monument

The reason for Great Zimbabwe's sudden decline in the fifteenth century remains an enigma. Almost overnight it ceased to be of any importance, although small groups continued to live there for three centuries or more.

When the kopje and the valley were first settled, the area was an island of green, even during the dry winter months, because of the unusually moderate climate. Moreover, as the kingdom grew in size and importance, the granite rocks of the surrounding hills proved to be ideal for building.

Above: Civic Centre sign marks downtown Masvingo.

Some experts believe that most of the people were forced to move elsewhere after destroying the forest and wood cover and overgrazing the surrounding grasslands.

What they left behind, however, after occupying what is now Zimbabwe's premier national monument for seven centuries, is stunning testament to the wealth, sophistication, and stability of the *dzimbahwe* civilization.

Getting there

Great Zimbabwe, twenty-eight kilometres (17 miles) from Masvingo, is connected to the town by a good road that becomes a single lane.

When to go

The Great Zimbabwe National Monument is open from 08.00 to 17.00 every day of the year. The museum, however, closes at 16.30 to enable visitors to leave the area before the main gate is locked. There is a nominal entrance fee to both the monument and museum, although organised educational groups may be admitted free by prior arrangement.

Where to stay

Great Zimbabwe Hotel (2-star). See Listings for "Hotels". There is a caravan park and campsite. See Listings.

Sightseeing

Now a **World Heritage Site**, **Great Zimbabwe National Monument** sprawls across seven and a half square kilometres (two and a half square miles) of **valley** and **hilltop** and is made up of three main groups of stone structures: the **hill complex; great enclosure;** or great house (Imba Huru); and the **valley complex**.

A huge elliptical **wall**, nine metres (30 feet) high and more than five metres (16 feet) thick — with a circumference of more than 250 metres (820 feet) — encircled this impressive capital's great enclosure. At its peak the city, the largest of any in southern and eastern Africa at that time, boasted about 20,000 citizens.

Perhaps most fascinating of all is the fact that the intricate complex has endured 700 years without mortar, as all the walls were built using the dry-stone technique.

Above: Fishermen enjoy the serene waters of Lake Mutirikwi, formerly Lake Kyle.

Since independence, the natural vegetation of the vleis and hills around the ruins has been restored and exotics, such as the Australian eucalyptus introduced by the Europeans, removed. Nearby are four hectares (10 acres) of **aloe gardens**.

Perhaps the only thing that remains unchanged is the natural fauna. The ruins abound with wildlife such as the greater kudu, bushbuck, duiker, steenbok, klipspringer, leopard, and baboon. Among the many birds that live among the ruins and the trees are hornbills, freckled nightjars, green pigeons, and purple-crested herons.

There are many trails from the **car park** and **gate**. Two lead **north** up the hill complex, and one leads **south** to the **museum**, then beyond to the **ruined walls** on **the ridge** and the great enclosure. For the best perspective visitors normally go directly to the hill complex, the oldest part of Great Zimbabwe, which was built on the edge of a sheer 100-metre (330-foot) **granite cliff**.

Seen from a distance, bathed in the gentle sunlight of early afternoon, the ruined walls curving so gracefully along the contour of the great whaleback kopje seem almost sensuous, as if moulding and flexing themselves to each rise and fall of the ridge.

During the heyday of Great Zimbabwe, this was the royal residence. Close by on the same ridge stand many smaller enclosures of ritualistic and historic significance — one a **recess**; another an **ironstone cave**; a third for **smelting**; and a fourth site, where most of the eight Zimbabwe Birds were discovered, the **ritual enclosure**.

The great enclosure, the largest and best preserved of the remains, lies in the valley at the southern foot of the hill. It was the residence and the court of the king's wives.

Stretching across the valley floor, the **ruins** of the dry-stone enclosures that made up the valley complex were home to the lesser dignitaries of the king's court and other important people.

The **National Museum**, close to the ruins, contains many splendid **exhibits** including displays relating to history and prehistory of Great Zimbabwe as well as many artefacts recovered from the area. Among these treasures are some of the **Zimbabwe Birds**, finally returned to their place of origin.

For a closer look, follow the **trail** from

Above: Giraffe, the world's tallest animal, reaches speeds of more than 50 k.p.h.

the **gate**, which is at the **car park**, over lush **meadow lands** to the foot of the **kopje** and the **Ancient Ascent**, originally the only access path to the hill complex.

Watch your step. The staircase is made of narrow stone steps carved between enormous boulders. Toward the **summit** it becomes so narrow that many are forced to turn sideways to continue.

Today, however, there is an alternative, less strenuous climb to the summit around the **eastern side** of the hill, with a wider and much more gentle incline.

Breathless now, the solid masonry of the **wall** stands in front of you with a slim **portcullis** for entry. Step through this and the walls surrounding you still seem to breathe of all those yesterdays. Despite the deserted enclosures, it's easy enough to imagine yourself back in the twelfth century.

The silence is filled with the echoes of forgotten sounds and movements that murmur on the gentle breeze. Dragonflies hover over the rocks, and skinks and lizards dart among the cracks and crannies of the ancient walls causing images of those long ago days to playback constantly in the mind. The ambience is mesmeric.

In style and content there is no other architecture like this. Rooted in the land that gave it life, it's a startling osmosis growing with splendid spontaneity from the rocks on which the edifices stand.

Through time the ruins have drawn the ancient granite, split by the hot sun and freezing nights of the middleveld, into the soul of their existence, so that rock and structure become as one.

In their flowing, harmonious curves and contours, inspired by the hills around them, these walls impart a feeling of liberation. For, perhaps unique in the world all those years ago, these walls were never built for defence. This was where, splendidly aloof from their citizenry, gazing down from on high at the greatest city-state of its time and place, the ruling kings lived; and where it all began.

The great enclosure below the hill complex was built later. The massive **outer wall**, which in places stands as high as ten metres (33 feet), is a quarter of a kilometre in circumference. Shaped roughly like an ellipse, the enclosure's widest point is more than 100 metres (330 feet) across.

Above: Great Zimbabwe ruins seen from the hill complex, protected as a World Heritage Site.
Opposite: Stone tower inside Great Zimbabwe's great enclosure remains an unsolved riddle.

The wall contains more than 15,000 tonnes of granite blocks, making it the largest single ancient structure in sub-Saharan Africa. The scale of achievement this represented should not be measured by the proportions of the work alone, but also for the extreme level of skill that the masons displayed in shaping and laying the stones.

This is especially notable in the sixty-centimetre-wide (two-foot), eighty-eight-metre-long (228-foot) decorative **chevron band** that runs along the top of the massive exterior wall.

The pattern, seen elsewhere in Africa on walls and doors or clothing (though never on this scale), pays homage to "the snake of fertility". It is a votive symbol designed, in this instance, to ensure a continuous line of dynastic Karanga rulers in the royal palace above.

Through the centuries, the quality of the masonry constantly improved. The first walls, built of uneven stone, look irregular. But those built 200 years later have great symmetry.

The stone is matched and laid in straight, even lines, each level set fractionally back from the one below so that the wall slants, providing equilibrium and stability.

Along with the increasing sophistication of the stonework, other innovations also took place: drainage systems were developed; stairways became sinuous, expressive works of grace as well as functional steps; and doorways were given rounded jambs.

Such impressive creativity was used to emphasise the power of the nation — a salute to the unity of the people and the dignity and glory of the ruling dynasty — not to defend the city-state.

The great enclosure was such an expression, built to house the women of the royal family. It is dominated by a magnificent **conical tower,** a solid stone structure rising more than eleven metres (36 feet) with a base circumference of five metres (16 feet). The top of the tower is decorated with **two rows** carved in a **dog-tooth pattern**, but since the rulers and citizens left no known written records — neither inscriptions nor documents — the tower's purpose remains a mystery.

Beyond the great enclosure stretches the remains of the dry-stone structures that make up the valley complex. Despite the early plunder, this site has yielded many valuable relics and artefacts.

Most of the clay-and-gravel thatched huts in these enclosures were joined by stone walls, each with its own platform where the wealth of the individual family — pots and precious metal (gold and copper in particular) — were displayed. The peasantry lived outside the walled enclosures in similar huts.

Almost every entrance to and within the valley complex is marked by an empty slot. These slots held the city's totems — pillars of wood or stone carved with abstract images of reptiles, animals, and birds. The best of the wood carvings were enclosed in sheaths of beaten copper and gold, but tragically this wealth of sculpture has vanished, now lost to all but the imagination.

Mission station

Six kilometres (three and a half miles) away, in the **southern shadows** of these ruins, stands the **mission post** of **Morgenster** founded on **Mugabe's Mountain** by the Dutch Reformed Church.

The founding missionary, Andrew Louw, married the sister of the Reverend Daniel Malan, who later became Prime Minister of South Africa. Among those who accompanied Louw on his journey to Morgenster was an African evangelist, Isak Kumalo, a grandson of Mzilikazi.

Louw, when still a young man, fell sick, and Mugabe, the local chief, asked him why his God had sent him to die so far from home. The young missionary bowed his head in answer and in prayer — and soon recovered. He died in 1956, aged ninety-three.

Lake Kyle Recreational Park

Eight kilometres (five miles) north-east of Great Zimbabwe's hill complex is Lake Mutirikwi (formerly Lake Kyle). Though a minnow by comparison to Lake Kariba, Lake Mutirikwi is the country's third largest.

It was formed at the confluence of the Mshagashe and Mutirikwi rivers when they were dammed in 1960 to feed the vast irrigation schemes needed to develop the Triangle and Hippo Valley sugar and citrus estates in the humid lowveld to the south (See "The Lowveld: Sugar and Citrus, Heat and Hazard").

More than 300 metres (984 feet) long, the dam rises sixty-three metres (207 feet) from the bed of a narrow granite gorge. It caused the river to flood the valleys until the lake spread over ninety square kilometres (35 square miles).

Mutirikwi features one of the most varied shorelines of any of Zimbabwe's inland waters, ranging from granite cliffs to tree-lined rocky beaches. The lake's many islands provide a secure refuge for a rapidly growing bird population, and even hippo have discovered a good home there.

Getting there

Lake Mutirikwi is twenty-five kilometres (16 miles) from Masvingo, connected by a good asphalt, and then gravel, road.

When to go

Lake Kyle Recreational Park is open all year-round.

Where to stay

There is a rest camp, caravan park, and campsite at Sikato Point near the dam wall. See Listings.

Sightseeing

To reach **Lake Mutirikwi,** follow the **Birch-enough Road** out of **Masvingo**. Some ten kilometres (six miles) from town you pass the stunning **chapel** built during World War II by Italian prisoners of war, complete with golden **frescos** and **murals** reminiscent of the Sistine chapel. Most of these works were done by one man, a peacetime civil engineer. The chapel is also a **mausoleum** for seventy-one prisoners who died during their captivity.

Five kilometres (three miles) after the chapel, the first **road** to the **lake shore** is a **turn south**. Another **turn south**, fifteen kilometres (nine miles) beyond this one, also leads to the **park**. The **park entrance** is about ten kilometres (six miles) from the main road.

The luxurious **rest camp** on a hill overlooking the lake is built under the shade of large *msasa* trees upon a series of terraces. The chalets are fully equipped with stoves, cooking utensils, and bed linen. The **caravan**

park and **campsite** on a nearby hill also provide a beautiful view of the lake. **Boat clubs** occupy part of the lake's **southern shore**.

Much of the land around the lake forms the 169 square kilometres (65 square miles) of **Lake Kyle Recreational Park**. Sixty-four kilometres (40 miles) of winding roads enable the visitor to see a variety of game.

In 1990, however, years of drought had reduced the lake to about one-fifth of its original size. But whether swollen or shrunken, nothing can diminish the beauty of its setting.

The park lies in a landscape broken by ranges of weathered granite hills and deep ravines. To the west the **boundary** is formed by the sensual outline of the **Beza Range**. In the east rise the spectacular, thickly-wooded **Nyuni Mountains**.

When full, the lake is an ideal **water resort** with fishing, yachting, powerboating, and water-skiing. It also offers some of the finest black bass fishing in the country. Other species include bottlenose, yellowfish, and tilapia. Licences can be obtained from the national park's office.

The eighty-nine-square-kilometre (34-square-mile) **game reserve**, located along the lake's **northern shores**, supports the greatest number of antelope species found in any national park or game sanctuary in the country, including wildebeest, greater kudu, nyala, bushbuck, eland, reedbuck, impala, sable, oribi, duiker, Lichtenstein's hartebeest, and steenbok.

The wildlife also includes zebra, wart hog, ostrich, white rhino, buffalo, and giraffe. The white rhino were imported into the reserve from Natal, South Africa, to replenish the Zimbabwean species that was wiped out in this area during the last century. The first calf was born to the rhino immigrants in 1967. The park's nyala and Lichtenstein's hartebeest were also introduced.

Lake Mutirikwi supports abundant hippopotamus, crocodile, and nesting colonies of cormorants and herons that thrive on the lake's many islands. Game-viewing on foot is permitted in special areas, but a particularly exciting way to see the animals is by pony trek under the guidance of one of the park rangers.

Overleaf: Sundown over Lake Mutirikwi.

The Midlands: Prairies, Ranches, Gold and Diamonds

Stretching more than 500 kilometres (310 miles) across the centre of Zimbabwe, from Guruve in the north-east to Mberengwa in the south-west, runs a ridge of two-billion-year-old hills ranging in width from three to eleven kilometres (two to seven miles).

This is the Great Dyke, Zimbabwe's backbone with a vertebrae of gold, gems, and precious minerals, a fabulously rich repository of all the fabled metals of legendary Ophir.

Few nations in the world possess the mineral wealth that lies in the seams and veins that run all through the Great Dyke and in the plateaux that stretch away on either side (See "The Land: Diamonds and Coal, Wheat and Tobacco", Part One).

Buried deep in the plutonic rocks of its upper layers are gold and silver, platinum and tungsten, copper and chrome, iron and tin, magnesite and asbestos, emeralds and diamonds.

For hundreds of years, from at least the seventh century AD, alluvial gold has been recovered from the sediment of rivers and streams. As far back as the twelfth century people dug primitive mines to recover the precious metal.

European exploitation of these ancient mines began just under 100 years ago, when many of these sites were pegged and claimed by the prospectors who flocked to this new El Dorado. Although some were soon exhausted, gold today remains one of Zimbabwe's largest sources of foreign currency.

Precious stones combine with industrial minerals — asbestos, nickel, coal, copper, chrome, and iron — to sustain this economy. In 1990, a joint Zimbabwean-Australian project began mining the country's rich lodes of platinum.

These minerals, which form a geological mosaic in the deep interior of the earth, were the central core of the country's early economy. Gold was bartered for goods and exported to Asia and Europe through such Indian

Ocean ports as Sofala, controlled by the Arabs and, later, the Portuguese. Iron too was exploited, but the mining and smelting processes were equally primitive.

Modern technology in mining, smelting, and refining makes today's mineral extraction much more sophisticated and diverse, resulting in the production of more than forty minerals and metals that account for almost half the country's exports and seven per cent of the Gross Domestic Product — GDP.

The great majority of this mineral wealth, especially gold, lies in and alongside the Great Dyke. Throughout the well-developed farmlands, large-scale mining and processing operations have transformed the Zimbabwe midlands into the nation's industrial heartland.

So important is this region to the nation's economic wellbeing that in 1983 the railway line between the capital and Gweru became the first to be electrified.

Any intensive industrial activity, particularly smelting, refining, and steel making, leaves deep and permanent scars across the land, but in Zimbabwe these are scarcely seen, apart from an occasional intrusive cooling tower or giant chimney stack. The rest remains hidden from the passing eye and there is little of the squalor and pollution found in the industrialised nations of the north.

Indeed, wherever you travel in Zimbabwe's industrial midlands, cattle ranches and arable farms turn a fresh and verdant face to the African sun. There, among the ranches and farms, mines and steelworks, are wildlife sanctuaries, lakes, forested hills, and scenic waterfalls. All the midlands' cities are adorned with handsome, tree-lined avenues, and flower-filled parks and gardens.

Where else in the world can a day's organised sightseeing combine visits to a gold mine, gold processing plant, and steelworks with a nature walk in a wildlife park, bird sanctuary, and botanical gardens?

Where man's industry dominates the

horizon, Zimbabwe clearly still cherishes its natural heritage.

Getting there

Gweru, 469 kilometres (291 miles) from Beitbridge, 277 kilometres (172 miles) from Harare, and 164 kilometres (102 miles) from Bulawayo, is centrally situated and served by road and rail. There are regular air services between Bulawayo and Harare and regular train and bus services between the main Midlands towns and cities.

When to go

Any time of the year.

Where to stay

In Bulawayo, the Bulawayo Sun (3-star), Cresta Churchill (3-star), Bulawayo Holiday Inn (3-star), Grey's Inn (2-star). There are others. See Listings for "Hotels". Bulawayo has one of the finest caravan parks and campsites in southern Africa. See Listings.

In Gweru, Midlands Hotel (3-star), Fairmile Motel (3-star). There are others. See Listings for "Hotels". Gweru has an excellent caravan park and campsite. See Listings.

In Chivhu, Chivhu Hotel (1-star), Enkeldoorn Hotel. See Listings for "Hotels". There is a caravan park and campsite.

In Kwe Kwe, Golden Mile Motel (3-star), Shamwari Hotel (1-star). See Listings for "Hotels". There is a caravan park and campsite. See Listings.

In Kadoma, Kadoma Ranch Motel (2-star), located on its own game ranch, offers a fine wildlife spectacle. See Listings for "Hotels". There is a caravan park and campsite.

In the nature reserves and recreational parks there are caravan parks and campsites. See Listings.

Sightseeing

For most, the country's industrial belt starts at **Bulawayo** on the 164-kilometre (102-mile) road to **Gweru**. Another road runs through the Midlands between Gweru–**Mvuma**–**Chivhu**–Harare.

Twenty-eight kilometres (17 miles) **northeast** of Bulawayo, **Heany Junction** marks the point where the **branch line** to **West Nicholson** leaves the **main line.**

The junction was named in 1904 in honour of Major Maurice Heany, who played a prominent role in the early settlement of Mashonaland and took part in the 1893 war against Lobengula's Ndebele *impi* as commander of a troop of the Salisbury Horse.

During the Second World War the junction became a major air training school. It closed in January 1954, but subsequently reopened as a teachers' training college. Eventually the college was moved to Bulawayo and the old air station was occupied by the military and renamed Llewellin Barracks, in honour of the first Governor-General of the Federation of Rhodesia and Nyasaland. It was renamed Imbizo Barracks in 1990.

Twenty-two kilometres (14 miles) beyond Heany Junction is the small **railway station** of **Bembezi**, on the banks of the **Bembezi River** near a hill known as **Ntaba Konjwa**. It was at this site that Mzilikazi made his kraal when he first arrived in Matabeleland.

It is perhaps better known, however, as the **battlefield** in the second major engagement of the 1893 Ndebele War when the Ndebele ambushed a 750-strong British column advancing on Bulawayo. Withering machine gun fire decimated the Ndebele ranks and the column marched on to Bulawayo and ultimate victory.

Just a few kilometres beyond Bembezi a **gravel road** leads thirty-two kilometres (20 miles) **east** to **Fort Rixon**, named after a settler who built a **fort** on his land during the Ndebele rebellion of the 1890s. The **graves** of the settlers and soldiers killed during the uprising lie in the small **cemetery** below the **fort.**

There are some notable **ruins** (similar in style and execution to those at Great Zimbabwe) along the road past "**Cumming's Store**", scene of a fierce 1896 battle between the British and the Ndebele. The **grave** of Sergeant J. O'Leary, who was killed by the Ndebele, is at this spot.

Regina Ruins

The first of three notable ruined settlements, **Regina Ruins**, comprising an old fortification made up of three large **terraces** built around a granite **kopje**, lies close to Fort Rixon.

The Bantu name of this settlement was Zinjanja and huts were built on the top two

Above: Glowing sun warms intricate chevron pattern of Nalatale's ruins.

terraces. There the ruling mambo, king, levied tributes of grain from his subjects, which were delivered to the **chambers** below through a series of **holes** in the ruins, some of which are still intact.

Other **smaller ruins** surround this complex, which suffered much damage during the 1890s from the Ancient Ruins Company and other treasure seekers who regarded the site as a gold mine. They pilfered a small fortune in gold beads, gold wire, and unrefined gold. Now all that exists are the ruins and the splendid and unusual **euphorbia** trees that have taken root there.

Beyond Fort Rixon are the **Daragombe Ruins** — still known as the **Dhlo Dhlo** — which are contemporaneous to the Khame Ruins and the place where the ruling mambo held sixteenth-century Portuguese visitors and missionaries captive.

Excavations amongst the ruins, which are just over one hectare (five acres) in size, have uncovered the religious icons of their prisoners: a **silver chalice**, **candlestick**, **ring**, **bell**, **priest's private seal**, and three feet of **golden medallion chain** were found among the objects of European origin, together with **bronze bowl**, **bronze censer**, and **bronze oil lamps**.

Gold bangles and beads were also discovered on the original floor, which was made of a raised cemented platform about sixteen metres (52 feet) in diameter. The **walls** that still stand are well decorated, but a great deal of damage was done by early European treasure hunters.

Twenty-six kilometres (16 miles) from these ruins stands a high, mound-shaped **kopje** with what is undoubtedly the most magnificent ancient **stone wall** in southern Africa. The beauty of the **Nalatale** ruins is in the intricate herringbone, chevron, and chequer patterns of stones of contrasting colour woven into the main wall.

Architecturally they are perhaps the most satisfying of all Zimbabwe's stone ruins. Although the structure is not large — about fifty metres (164 feet) in diameter — without doubt the wall is the most impressive of its kind in the country. But the fortifications were never finished. The builders were overwhelmed by Swazi *impi* raiding far from the south.

From the Nalatale Ruins it is another

twenty-eight kilometres (17 miles) back to the main road at **Insezi**, named after a tributary of the **Mzingwane River**, and the **railway station** serving **Inyati**, Fort Rixon, and Filabusi districts.

The railway, which opened in October 1902, was for many years a well-known port of call for passengers on the Bulawayo–Salisbury (now Harare) express. Trains stopped there so that passengers could walk across to the local hotel for afternoon tea or beer.

Nine kilometres (five and a half miles) further along the road is **Shangani**, scene of an epic battle against the Ndebele in October 1893, when hundreds of *impi* were scythed down by the BSAC's Gatling guns.

A cement **obelisk** on the **west bank** of the **Shangani River** is known as the **Pongo memorial**. It bears the names of some of the settlers killed during the 1896 Ndebele war when the *impi* attacked the mail coach from Salisbury (now Harare) and the store where the settlers had taken refuge.

Today Shangani is the centre of a farming and mining area where gold and large deposits of nickel have been discovered.

Some thirty kilometres (19 miles) or so beyond Shangani, a **road** veers **east** to follow the railway line for ten kilometres (six miles) to **Somabhula**, an important **railway junction** where the line from Maputo, Mozambique, and Pretoria meets the main Harare–Bulawayo line. The junction has one of the largest **marshalling yards** in southern Africa.

Somabhula is named after Shamaburu, a famous African elephant hunter of old who lived in the area. It became a boom town in 1903 when a European prospector, R. H. Mois, discovered diamonds, sapphires, and chrysoberyl in the local forest. The boom was short-lived, however, and the bust soon followed. The deposits were so small they did not justify commercial exploitation and by 1908 Somabhula was virtually deserted.

Resort centre

A **dirt road** leads twenty kilometres (12 miles) **east** of the junction to one of Gweru's major **resort centres**, the leafy shores of

Gwenoro Lake, formed by the **dam** built on the **Runde River** in 1958 to create a major **reservoir** for Gweru's water needs. The five-square-kilometre (two-square-mile) lake that formed behind the dam is now a boating and fishing resort.

The road loops around the **northern shore** continuing another twenty-one kilometres (13 miles) to the chrome-rich **Shurugwi Hills**, their highest point rising 1,500 metres (5,000 feet) above sea-level to form another wooded **weekend resort** for Gweru citizens.

Founded in the 1890s as Sebanga Poort, seat of one of the world's largest chrome deposits, it changed its name to Selukwe in January 1896, and became Shurugwi after independence.

Along with chrome Shurugwi was once rich in gold. In less than two decades one mine alone produced more than eight and a half tonnes from two million tonnes of ore.

The town's first banker, Alfred Ellenberger, once helped to rescue one gold mine from liquidation — not as a financial expert but as a diviner. When the head of the **Glen Rosa Mine** told him it would have to close down because it did not have enough gold to justify continuing, Ellenberger offered his divining services.

Inspecting the mine workings with his divining rod, the bank manager told the mine manager that all he had to do was dig down another two metres (six–seven feet) to find the yellow metal. Within days, more than Z$8,000 in gold had been recovered — a considerable sum in the second decade of the century, and the Glen Rosa Mine prospered for many years.

Despite the nearby mine workings, Shurugwi was long a noted beauty spot. The 1990s, however, reveal the doors and windows of the massive **Grand Hotel** barred and shuttered, the "For Sale" signs long faded, and the town — birthplace of Sir Roy Welensky, first prime minister of the Federation of the Rhodesias and Nyasaland (now Malawi) — returned to the limbo of its long ago past, a pleasant but forgotten mining backwater nestled in a tree-shrouded valley.

Years ago, **Ferny Creek**, a small valley

Opposite: Workers tend a Midlands tobacco plantation.

Above: Extensive irrigation on a Midlands wheat farm.

beyond the town's immaculate hillside **golf course**, was a well-developed day resort with rest huts, camping site, caravan park, many picnic spots, and a swimming pool.

But now the trail is overgrown and the swimming pool empty save for the rainwater that fills the bottom of the deep end.

Today the gold mines are also abandoned, but the **chrome deposits** worked by the giant multinational Union Carbide continue to contribute to this sleepy hill capital's prosperity.

A modern **scenic highway** winds **south**, through the forested hills over **Wolfshall Pass** to the sweltering plains below. Hidden deep in the valley beside the road are the beautiful **Dunraven** and **Camperdown falls**, found by following a steep downhill **path** through the **forest**.

Several **lay-bys** along the road offer exceptional views of the surrounding countryside. The mining company's **light railway** — the only one still left in the country — runs through spectacular scenery, and was taken over by the Lions Club of Shurugwi which operates passenger trains to raise funds for the needy.

To Chivhu

From Shurugwi it is thirty-seven kilometres (23 miles) to Zimbabwe's third-largest city, **Gweru** (See "Gweru: Zimbabwe's Industrial Heart", Part Three). Twenty kilometres (12 miles) to the **north-east** of the city, the road to **Mvuma** and Harare passes the **southern shores** of another delightful **resort** for Gweru's city dwellers — **Whitewaters Dam**, built on the **Kwe Kwe River** in 1948 to form the first of the city's major **reservoirs**.

Twenty-three kilometres (14 miles) beyond is **Lalapanzi**, a **railway siding** on the **Masvingo line** and another important chrome mining area. Apart from the mining activity, the district contains a number of large farms and cattle ranches.

During the 1896 *Chimurenga*, the settlers built the nearby **Fort Gibbs**, named after the commanding officer Captain J. Gibbs of the Salisbury Horse. It stands atop a small granite **kopje** to the **east** of the road to Mvuma and Harare.

To the **north**, another eleven kilometres (seven miles) further on, **Iron Mine Hill**, a **siding** on the Masvingo line takes its name from the hill that the Ndebele named the "iron mountain", where the scars of ancient ironworkings can still be seen.

Ndebele blacksmiths also smelted iron ore there and, with their goat and buckskin bellows forging *assegais*, spears, and hoes, did a brisk trade with the neighbouring tribes.

Lining the old **coach road** to Masvingo, three kilometres (two miles) to the **south**, are the **graves** of travellers who died from malaria during their journeys, including that of a Captain Campbell, wounded in a skirmish with some Ndebele herdsmen. Although Dr. Leander Starr Jameson amputated his leg, he died the next day.

From Iron Mine Hill it is twenty-eight kilometres (17 miles) to Mvuma, a once prosperous gold town and the junction of the Harare–Masvingo road. You know you are approaching the town by the landmark **chimney stack** of the old **Falcon Gold** and **Copper Mine**, visible for many kilometres around. Gold was first discovered there in 1903, but it was another eleven years before mining began. Once production started, Mvuma's population exploded overnight.

For at least a decade the Falcon mine produced more gold and copper than any other in the country, but when the veins ran dry in 1925, the mine was closed. Now this small town slumbers on, undisturbed by dreams of wealth, content with its place in Zimbabwe's gold rush history.

The area today is famous for its Texas-size **ranches**, one as large as 1,470 square kilometres (567 square miles), while another covers more than 2,000 square kilometres (772 square miles).

During his 1925 royal visit to South Africa, Britain's Prince of Wales went hunting on one ranch, sleeping in a Ndebele-style grass hut. The Prince claimed a record wildebeest trophy as well as "bagging" eland, tsessebe, and sable antelope. He donated the meat to hospitals in Gweru, while his resident taxidermist prepared the skins and trophies to take back to England.

The sixty-five-square-kilometre (25-square-mile) **Mtao forest reserve** near Mvuma was established in 1925 to protect its indigenous softwoods and hardwoods.

Leaving the woods of Mtao behind, the main road travels fifty-one kilometres (30 miles) **north-east** to **Chivhu**, known until independence as Enkledoorn — Single Thorn — because when the Dutch Reformed Church decided to build a **mission centre** at this place only a single tree grew there.

To Beatrice

From Chivhu, the road to Harare runs thirty-seven kilometres (23 miles) through pleasant farmlands to **Featherstone**. Twenty kilometres (12 miles) **north** of Featherstone, a **minor road** leads twenty kilometres (12 miles) or so **east** to the vicinity of **Fort Charter**, the third **fort** in the chain that the BSAC's Pioneer Column built on their march north.

Built on a site chosen by Frederick Selous, the hunter who was the column's chief scout, the fort was named after the Chartered Company and manned by a force of sixty men.

Crudely built, the structure surrounded an enclosure of about twenty square metres (50 square feet) with outer walls about two metres (six–seven feet) high, supported by timber poles cut from the nearby bush.

Maxim machine guns poked their deadly muzzles through the embrasures that were reinforced by sandbags. The men slept in four simple log huts and another one was used as a storeroom. In later years the place was renamed Marshbrook, although the district still retained the name of Charter.

Twenty-nine kilometres (18 miles) beyond the turning to Fort Charter, the road arrives at the gold mining town of **Beatrice**, named after the sister of Pioneer Corps officer Henry Borrow. It stands on the banks of the **Mupfure River**.

Fifty-five kilometres (34 miles) **north** of Beatrice is the capital city of Harare. It is also possible to arrive at the country's seat of government via a **parallel** western route through industrial Zimbabwe.

The Rich Heart of Zimbabwe

At the heart of the country's industrial belt is Gweru, Zimbabwe's third-largest city with more than 80,000 people (See "Gweru: Zimbabwe's Industrial Heart", Part Three).

Thirty kilometres (19 miles) **north** of Gweru, road and rail meet at a **station** named after the **Connemara Mine**, once a major producer of gold. When it closed, the mine was turned into a lacklustre **prison**.

Five kilometres (three miles) beyond the station, **Hunters Road**, centre of a mining and farming area, was built on the old "Hunters Road" that Selous and others followed on their way into Mashonaland. Aerial photographs taken just after the Second World War clearly show the line of the old trail.

Fifteen kilometres (nine miles) further on, a broad **highway** sweeps three kilometres (two miles) **west** to the steel city of **Redcliff**, founded in 1942 during the Second World War when it was deemed necessary to establish a national steel industry.

Redcliff, with abundant supplies of high-grade iron ore and substantial limestone deposits, was an ideal site for the steelworks and Hwange collieries could supply ample coking coal. The first **blast furnace** was tapped by Sir Godfrey Huggins — Lord Malvern — in April 1948.

The government-owned company was privatised in 1957 when a consortium of the Lancashire Steel Corporation, Stewart and Lloyd, Anglo American Corporation, British South Africa Company, Rhodesian Selection Trust, Messina (Transvaal) Development Company, and Tanganyika Concessions took over the company's Z$8.6 million assets. After independence it again became a parastatal.

Most of the iron ore is quarried from deposits in the adjacent **Kwe Kwe river valley** and a sixty-metre-high (200-foot) range of **ironstone hills**. In the 1960s, excavating machines at this **quarry** unearthed significant **fossil bones** and **Stone Age implements**, leading to the biggest archaeological "dig" in Zimbabwe's history.

It was thought that the fossils might provide a link between the Kwe Kwe area and the famous Broken Hill man *Homo rhodesiensis*, identified from a fossil skull found in 1921 at Kabwe in Northern Rhodesia (now Zambia), that aroused worldwide interest.

Although an exceptionally large number of stone implements and animal fossils were unearthed, no humanoid fossils were found. Nonetheless, what was uncovered has helped unravel some of the mystery surrounding the successive cultures that have settled in the area during the past 40,000 years.

Today, neat **housing estates**, a **town centre**, and the **offices** of The Zimbabwe Iron and Steel Company — ZISCO — stand on one side of the pleasant, tree-clad hills; **ironworkings** and a **steel making plant** — close to a seemingly bottomless **hole in the ground** — on the other. The plant is capable of producing a million tonnes of liquid steel a year.

These days, however, most of the ore comes from **Buchwa**, 190 kilometres (118 miles) south-east of Kwe Kwe on the main railway line to Rutenga. Buchma is a **mountain** of iron ore which is mined simply by slicing it away from the summit downwards.

Even though Redcliff and its twin, **Kwe Kwe**, fourteen kilometres (eight and a half miles) to the north, make the same claim as Gweru to be the industrial heart of Zimbabwe, Kwe Kwe is also the centre of a substantial wildlife hunting and photographic safari industry approximately **halfway** — 220 kilometres (138 miles) — between **Bulawayo** and **Harare**.

Within sight of belching chimney stacks and opencast workings, predators like leopard stalk antelope, and rhino roam the countryside.

Despite the abundance of wildlife, Kwe Kwe's genesis and continued existence are tied to the excoriating fires of its steel furnaces and thermal power stations. Yet with its wide boulevards lined by immaculate lawns and flowering trees, smart **town centre**, and the elegant Cape-style architecture of its **post office**, Kwe Kwe would pass anywhere in the world as a genteel country market town.

Originally called Sebakwe, the town, which began its life as a BSAC fort, changed its name in 1905 to Que Que, after the croaking sound of the frogs in the Que Que River.

Above: Paper house imported a century ago as residence for the manager of Kwe Kwe's Globe and Phoenix Mine is now Zimbabwe's National Gold Mining Museum.

The spelling of this phonetic name was Africanised to Kwe Kwe after independence.

Rich in both minerals and farmlands, major crops like maize, soya beans, cotton, sorghum, coffee, and citrus fruits make this region one of the granaries of Zimbabwe and an important centre for cash crops. There are also extensive cattle ranches and dairy farms. In fact, Kwe Kwe's farmers produce ten per cent of the winter cereals grown in Zimbabwe.

Zimbabwe's largest and only beer producer, National Breweries — Natbrew — located their **malting plant** in Kwe Kwe because of the high-quality barley grown in the region. Producing more than 21,000 tonnes of malt a year, Natbrew exports some fifty per cent of this output to neighbouring African countries.

Gold-mining Museum

The most fascinating part of a visit to Kwe Kwe is the **National Museum of Gold Mining** — and the parastatal **roasting plant** for the gold industry, which processes around 500 kilos (1,102 lbs) of gold a year for eight gold mines in the region on a "no profit, no loss"

basis. It also refines silver.

Roasting is necessary when gold-bearing ore contains other metals such as antimony, arsenic, bismuth, copper, lead, and nickel, making direct cyanidation either impossible or extremely costly.

During the process the unwanted minerals come together by gravity or flotation. These concentrates are then roasted to remove them — or change them through oxidisation — so that the gold can be recovered.

The museum, next to the **head office** of the **Globe and Phoenix Mine**, is located in one of Africa's most unusual buildings — a prefabricated **paper house** imported from Britain in 1894. The papier-mâche outer panels are reinforced with wire, the inner panels are cardboard. Together, these were mounted on a wooden framework.

The paper house was originally the residence of the mine's general manager for two years before being turned into offices, and finally a store room.

Altogether three of these buildings were imported into Zimbabwe in the last decade of the last century. The other two were sent to

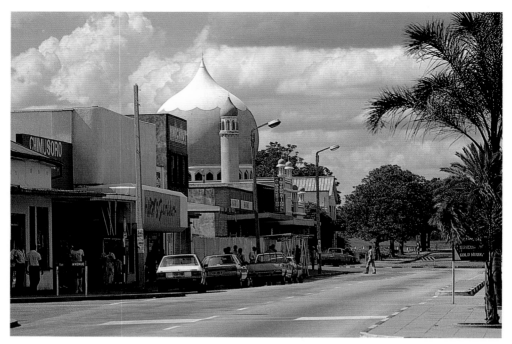

Above: Mosque in Kwe Kwe's main street

Bulawayo and Harare (then Salisbury), but ceased to exist long ago. The creosote-treated wooden piles on which the house was built at Kwe Kwe ensured its continued life. Next to it stands a **thatched rondavel** built of corrugated iron that dates from the same era.

Because of their historical significance, these two buildings house the **National Museum of Gold Mining**. Within their round and paper walls, **specimens** of gold-bearing **quartz rock** are on display as well as a **working model** of a gold mine, complete with **ore-crushing machinery**. Outside are many other **machines** used in gold-mining and processing.

The Globe and Phoenix Mine began operations as two separate mines, but in 1894 the two prospectors who pegged the original claims sold them to a syndicate. The result was the creation in London of the Globe and Phoenix Gold Mining Company in October 1895. Within three decades the mine produced more than Z$20 million of gold.

Up until 1905 the **Globe reef** was the company's principal asset but declining values led to its 1907 closure. Work, however, continued at the **Phoenix reef** and its

many branches until it reached a depth of some 1,300 metres (4,000 feet) with about eighty kilometres (50 miles) of drives, crosscuts, and winzes.

After almost a century of continuous production the Globe and Phoenix Mine, once one of the country's richest mines, ceased mining operations in 1988 with the loss of more than 1,000 jobs.

In 1990, however, work was going ahead on a short-term project of between three and five years to recover gold from the **waste ore** that had piled up over the last ninety years.

Rich not only in gold, the industrial heartland of the country also supports the Zimbabwe mining and smelting plant at Kwe Kwe. One of the largest in the world, it produces more than 150,000 tonnes of high-grade carbon ferrochrome a year.

Another gold mine, **Gaika**, lies just **south** of the town in an area where extensive **ancient workings** have thrown up some interesting archaeological finds — **stone hammers, iron gads, chisels, rings, stone mortars**, and many other Stone Age **implements**.

As well as mines and industrial plants,

Kwe Kwe also boasts the Dominican **Loretto mission school**, one of the few missions directed entirely by women. Founded in 1944, the Dominican Sisters have transformed the complex into an oasis of pleasant green lands, gardens of beautiful flowers and trees, and fine buildings. The school, which is entirely self-supporting, grows its own food. In 1947 a **school for the deaf** was added to the institution.

Sebakwe Recreational Park

Thirty-nine kilometres (24 miles) **south-east** of Kwe Kwe is **Sebakwe Recreational Park**. Renowned for its beautiful surroundings, the park's **freshwater lake** was formed when the **Sebakwe River** was dammed in 1957. The park was closed for some time in 1982 while the **dam wall** was raised another seven metres (23 feet), substantially increasing the surface area of the lake. The main attraction of this small, twenty-seven-square-kilometre (10-square-mile) park, which is open all year-round, is its coarse fishing. **Nature walks** through wildlife areas are also popular. There are **overnight cottages**, **caravan park**, and **campsites**.

Sixty kilometres (37 miles) **west** of Kwe Kwe along a **dirt road** is **Silobela**, the main **trading centre** for the small-scale peasant farmers in the **Silobela Communal Lands**. There is also limited gold mining.

Following another **dirt road** 145 kilometres (90 miles) **north-west** from Kwe Kwe, you will come to the edge of the **Mafungabusi Plateau** in the remote settlement of **Gokwe** at the heart of the forested **Gokwe Communal Lands**. Peasants tend smallholdings far from the hectic pace and bustle of twentieth-century Zimbabwe.

One of Gokwe's more colourful European characters was Frikkie Marr, an administration officer. Each year he set off from Gokwe to collect taxes and arbitrate disputes in the remotest reaches of the **Zambezi Valley**, accompanied by a number of carriers with large loads of salt to serve as currency.

Marr and his party travelled down the **Zambezi River** as far as **Chirundu** by raft, returning on foot, from village to village, constantly alert for wild animals, particularly elephant, which abounded in the valley.

To the **north**, thirty-two kilometres (20 miles) beyond Kwe Kwe, is **Umniati**, home to one of Zimbabwe's first thermal **power stations**, built in 1938 and considerably enlarged in 1974. The power station lies close to **Battlefields**, established in 1902. This peaceful enough stop was so named because a number of mines in the area, such as **Waterloo** and **Trafalgar**, were named after famous English battles.

At one time the area boasted more than twenty mines, of which eighteen were for gold. Cattle ranching and cotton growing are the principal agricultural activities.

Battlefields is also the **junction** of the **gravel road** that leads **south** to **Ngezi Recreational Park**, a sixty-three-square-kilometre (24-square-mile) **nature reserve** formed around the **lake** that was created by damming the **Ngezi River** (northernmost of three rivers with the same name) in 1945.

Along with fishing and boating, there are also **nature trails** in the wilderness areas, enabling wildlife such as antelope to be seen at close quarters. The sanctuary's birdlife is prolific and varied. There are many **campsites**, comfortable **cottages**, and **caravan parks** scattered along the lake **shoreline**.

Eighteen kilometres (11 miles) along the **road north** from Battlefields is **Umsweswe**. In the early days of European settlement, the land around the village was noted for its many illicit mines.

A **dirt road** leads forty-five kilometres (28 miles) **west** from Umsweswe to the **Empress** and **Commoner mines**, one producing gold, the other copper. To the **east** of Umsweswe, not far from the main road, is **John Mack Lake**, named after an early gold prospector who became one of the country's outstanding mining personalities.

Mack went to Rhodesia in 1893 to take part in the war against the Ndebele and first prospected around Umsweswe before founding the **Golden Valley Mine**, north-west of Kadoma.

The Klondike of Africa

If any town can claim to be Zimbabwe's El Dorado, it must be Kadoma, born as a mining village in 1906, when an enterprising trader named Godwin opened a small canteen and started a forwarding agency along the railway to serve the needs of the prospectors and small workers seeking their fortunes.

There were so many mines, in fact, that Kadoma became known as the "Klondike" of Africa and, as more and more prospectors arrived, the canteen flourished.

It was John Mack who persuaded the railways to open a **station** at Kadoma. The original "station" and office took the form of a railway truck equipped with telegraph, furniture, a wood-burning stove, and accommodation for the new stationmaster. A wood and iron building followed later.

On the **northern outskirts** of Kadoma, an attractive **motel** is marked by the old **steam engines** that stand at its **entrance**.

Although mining has declined in recent years, some of the country's largest and most profitable gold mines are still found in this area. But Kadoma does not depend on gold alone for its continued and increasing prosperity. It is a major collection centre for local cotton farmers and supports a large textiles manufacturing industry.

Gold still reigns supreme, however, at the small village of **Eiffel Flats**, seven kilometres (four miles) **east** of Kadoma. There gold smelting continues on the spot where Dr. Starr Jameson pegged out claims to gold mines. They formed the nucleus of what became the largest gold mine in Rhodesia and one of the largest in the world, the Cam and Motor, made up of 755 claims, including Jameson's and those pegged by a syndicate headed by Selous.

Above: Venerable tortoise enjoys sunshine.

Yet it was not until the 1920s, after their 1909 acquisition by Lonrho, that these claims revealed their real worth. They yielded more than Z$72 million in gold for the company.

Not all was sunshine and riches, however. On the grimmer side, arsenic from the mine killed large numbers of cattle and farmers were warned not to grow vegetables anywhere near the mine.

Duchess Hill Mine, eighteen kilometres (11 miles) **north-east** of Eiffel Flats, was named in honour of the Duchess of Connaught after she toured Rhodesia in 1910 with her husband, the Duke. Never as wealthy as the Cam and Motor, the mine closed down at the end of the 1920s.

The valley of gold

While many of these mines still produce gold, the real heart of Zimbabwe's gold belt beats in **Golden Valley**, north-west of Kadoma, along the **loop road** that takes you into the heart of this golden bonanza.

Miners there still hew the quartz and rocks in which the precious metal is found, maintaining Zimbabwe's status as one of the world's major gold producers.

When John Mack took over the mine its future was uncertain but he was convinced of its prospects and poured all his wealth into its development. It brought him to the edge of bankruptcy. Broke but still convinced, however, he contacted his old friend Colonel Frank Johnson, commander of the Pioneer Column, who had once had an interest in the area.

With Johnson's help he formed J. Mack and Company, a syndicate that consisted of Johnson, financier Herbert Latilla, and himself. Within a short time, Golden Valley became one of the richest gold mines in Rhodesia and Mack one of its most famous millionaires.

He also owned the nearby **Kruger Mine**. When his favourite cow, which he called Patch, fell to its death down the shaft, he renamed it the **Patchway Mine** — still marked on the map of Zimbabwe — in memory of the animal.

Chakari, located on the loop road thirty-nine kilometres (24 miles) from Kadoma, was known as **Turkois Mine** when it was founded in 1907. The name was changed to

Above: Old steam engines mark the entrance to a Kadoma motel.

Shagari in 1911, but Europeans still found it a tongue-twister and in July 1923 it was renamed Chakari.

The area produces maize, tobacco, and cotton, but mining remains king. The largest mines, the **Dalny** and Turkois, have been important gold producers for many years. (A **rough road** leads some sixteen kilometres [ten miles] from Chakari, past the Dalny Mine, to the entrance of the little-known **Umfuli Recreational Park**).

From Chakari, the loop road leads another thirty-four kilometres (21 miles) back to the **main road** and **Chegutu**, another mining and farm town, and the last major centre before Harare, 106 kilometres (66 miles) to the **north-east**.

North-east of Chegutu, about halfway between Harare and Kadoma, lies **Selous**, known as Chingford until 1965. The **Halfway Hotel**, located at the **junction** of the road leading to **Seigneury Mine** and **Makwiro railway station**, provided the nucleus of the settlement. Later, the Farmers' Association built a **country club.** A **store** and **police station** soon followed.

Pamuzinda, one of Zimbabwe's finest wildlife lodges, is situated there on its own game sanctuary. **Old Hartley**, a few kilometres **south** of the Gweru–Harare road, was named after Yorkshire-born hunter-explorer Henry Hartley, the first European to discover gold in Rhodesia on a joint expedition to the Mazowe Valley with Dr. Carl Mauch.

Their belief that the hills around Hartley contained rich gold deposits drove Rhodes to obtain mining concessions from Lobengula, who at that time dominated Mashonaland.

The **hills** where Hartley made his camp (and also the terminus of the old hunter's road) were named on an **1869 map** drawn by the artist Thomas Baines. The only other English place name at that time was Victoria Falls.

The first claims were pegged at Hartley by Colonel Frank Johnson, who doubted their legality because he pegged them before the country was annexed by the BSAC — and were therefore not recognisable either by the Ndebele and Shona rulers or by the BSAC (not that a little technicality like that ever seemed to bother Rhodes and his intimates).

Johnson also bought an option on another claim, known as the Salamander, for Z$2,000.

When Lord Randolph Churchill visited the site in 1891 and said he wanted to buy the option, Rhodes ordered that Johnson should sell it for no more than Z$10,000, far below the option's value.

Along with mining, much of this area is devoted to tobacco growing. The crop is the country's largest single foreign currency earner — realising around US$150 million a year in the second half of the 1980s. Grown long before the European settlers arrived, it was developed as a commercial crop in the first decade of this century.

Until Smith's illegal Unilateral Declaration of Independence — UDI — in 1965, Zimbabwe was the world's second-largest producer of tobacco, yielding more than 105,000 tonnes a year from about 1,500 farms and plantations. Since independence, production has constantly increased and the country now produces well above 110,000 tonnes a year. The main species is Virginia but production of Burley has been increasing in recent years. Some oriental — Turkish — tobacco is also cultivated.

Norton, thirty-five kilometres (22 miles) beyond Selous, is named after a family that was killed during the 1896 *Chimurenga*. Originally it was a **railway siding**, but by 1914 it had developed into a village. In April 1969, Norton was the venue of the World Ploughing contest.

Darwendale Recreation Park

Three kilometres (two miles) to the **west** lie the **eastern shores** of **Lake Manyame** and one of Zimbabwe's finest man-made nature sanctuaries: **Lake Robertson Recreational Park**, established in 1976 after damming the **Manyame River** thirty kilometres (19 miles) downstream from **Lake Chivero**.

The dam created eighty-one-square-kilometre (31-square-mile) Lake Manyame (formerly Robertson) — named after a former director of the Department of Irrigation — and is now a major **weekend resort** for Harare citizens who go there to enjoy watersports, fishing, and boating in natural, unspoilt surroundings. Large mammals, particularly greater kudu, roam the lake's **woodland shores** and the **dam basin** draws many species of water birds.

The dam also led to the boring of

Zimbabwe's longest **tunnel**; a large water intake more than fifteen kilometres (nine miles) long which took four years to complete. It funnels water to a station where it is pumped to Harare.

To the **east** of the road, some five kilometres (three miles) beyond Norton, is sixteen-kilometre (10-mile) long Lake Chivero (formerly McIlwaine), formed in 1952 when the **Manyame Poort Dam** staunched the waters of the **Manyame River**.

The lake was named after Sir Robert McIlwaine, an Irish-born lawyer who served in Zimbabwe as a High Court Judge and former chairman of the Natural Resources Board during colonial times. The twenty-five square kilometres (10 square miles) of **foreshore** and the thirty square kilometres (11 square miles) of water were originally established as a national park, then later changed to **recreational park** status.

Sixteen square kilometres (six square miles) of the **thickly-wooded shores** are **sanctuary** to buffalo, kudu, reedbuck, baboon, leopard, and many species of monkey. Introduced species include white rhino, giraffe, eland, and wildebeest. There are more than 250 species of bird (including ostrich) and more than twenty species of fish.

Every Saturday and Sunday dozens of water-skiiers churn the lake's waters behind their powerboats. Within an hour's reach of the capital, Chivero is a remarkable and popular weekend playground for Harare residents, an asset that any capital would envy.

It is at its best during midmorning, when the bleached white sails of 100 yachts or more dot the sparkling blue waters. Private yachting and powerboat **clubs** line the **northern shore** together with **swimming pools** and **play areas** for children.

A **hotel**, **tea garden**, **marina** with lush lawns, and **caravan parks** and **campsites** are located around the lake.

On the **southern shore**, inside the **game park** where game walks take place within a specified area, there is a delightful **rest camp**. The lake's tigerfish and bream offer good sport for anglers, and licences are available from national parks' staff or lake-shore establishments.

The Eastern Highlands: Mountain and Moor, Forest and Waterfall

Whichever way you approach them the Eastern Highlands of Zimbabwe hold an irrevocable promise — a promise of the cool and temperate climate to come, manifested when you see the first faint upthrust of the highland wall on the horizon fifty kilometres (30 miles) distant.

And soon those refreshing images cascading through the mind — images of coffee and tea plantations, thick forests, cloud-crested peaks, rolling moorland, and glistening waterfalls — become reality.

From their northernmost point in the Nyanga Mountains, the massive granite bluffs stretch more than 300 kilometres (186 miles) to Mount Selinda — host to the tree-crowded tropical Chirinda Forest — in the extreme south.

Centuries ago these mountains were a place of refuge for communities under pressure from invading peoples and many ruined settlements and crop terraces remain witness to their long occupation.

Today, the magnificent mountains and invigorating air make the highlands a refuge for jaded city dwellers and tourists seeking peace and quiet away from the hectic pressures of late twentieth-century civilization. They have become one of Zimbabwe's major holiday resorts.

With colourful Mutare, the country's third-largest city at their centre, visitors have many choices of recreation and leisure: they can fish for trout in the many cold, clear streams and lakes; ramble through dark, quiet forests; climb impressive peaks; visit spectacular waterfalls; go golfing on some of the loveliest courses in Africa; or simply enjoy the crisp, refreshing mountain air.

Much of the highlands area consists of well-cared-for national parks offering a diversity of attractions, ranging from the rainforest flora of the Vumba to the high, stark peaks of the Chimanimani Mountains.

Everywhere, spectacular scenery and welcoming people, combined with first-class roads and superb tourist hotels and amenities, serve to make each visit memorable.

Getting there

Mutare, 263 kilometres (163 miles) from Harare, 577 kilometres (359 miles) from Bulawayo, and 585 kilometres (363 miles) from Beitbridge, is served by road and rail services. There is a daily night train between Mutare and Harare and a luxury coach service five days a week. It does not operate on Tuesdays and Thursdays.

When to go

The highlands are pleasant all year-round, although the streets of Mutare are at their most colourful from November to December. For trout fishermen the latter part of the rainy season, from January to April, provides the best fishing. For other visitors, Nyanga provides cool relief during the hot summer months.

Where to stay

In Mutare, Manica Hotel (3-star), Christmas Pass Motel (2-star). See Listings for "Hotels". There is an excellent caravan park and campsite. See Listings.

In Juliasdale, Brondesbury Park Hotel (3-star); Montclair (with casino) (3-star); Pine Tree Inn. See Listings for "Hotels".

In Nyanga, Troutbeck Inn (3-star); Rhodes Hotel; and Nyanga Holiday Hotel (1-star). All are excellent. See Listings for "Hotels". There are superb, fully-equipped, self-service twin- and single-bedroom national park lodges at Nyangwe Dam; Nyanga Dam; and Udu Dam. There are caravan parks at Nyangwe and Inyangombe, which also has a campsite. See Listings.

Sightseeing

Marondera, the first major centre on the road to the **Eastern Highlands**, is seventy-four kilometres (46 miles) from **Harare**. The town is named after the headman who ruled in the last decade of the last century.

When the pioneers arrived, his kraal lay

atop a **kopje** called **Nyameni**, about three kilometres (two miles) **west of the Ruzawi River**. The settlers formed their outspan about six kilometres (four miles) **south** of the present town and it soon became the nucleus of the first European settlement.

The first administration camp was organized on a piece of land given by Rhodes to anyone willing to offer accommodation to travellers between Salisbury (known today as Harare) and Umtali. The offer was taken up by three ex-BSAC policemen who ran the Ruzawi Inn for three years, then sold it to a stagecoach company that ran services from Salisbury to Umtali (known today as Mutare).

Within years, the junction with the road to Fort Charter had become a vital supply depot for both the fort and Umtali. During the 1896 *Chimurenga*, the fledgling town's post office and inn were used as places of refuge from the fierce *impis*. When the settlers finally abandoned the place, however, the inn was razed. The town was rebuilt on its present site after the *Chimurenga*.

During the Boer War the Rhodesia Field Force, an army of more than 5,000 men, was garrisoned at Marondera. The troops never saw service and the only reminder of their presence is the small **cemetery** known as "Paradise". It contains the **graves** of two Australians and seven Englishmen who died while based there.

Now an important farming area, particularly for tobacco, Marondera has one of the oldest turf clubs in Zimbabwe. The tree-lined **racecourse** is in a lovely setting. The first race meeting took place in 1923, but until 1936 all competition was restricted to amateur riders.

Now the town is the centre of traditional farming, such as cattle ranching and grain and tobacco production, as well as the hub of the nation's expanding wine industry.

Forty-eight kilometres (30 miles) **south**, at the end of the **asphalt branch road**, lies **Wedza**, established in 1910, on a site thirteen kilometres (eight miles) from the slopes of **Mount Wedza**, which is noted for its remnant **tropical forest**.

Today Wedza is the centre of a prosperous farming community, noted for its privately owned **Imire Game Park** which is a popular day out from Harare. You can also book in at the park's luxurious **Sable Lodge** for a longer stay.

Thirty-four kilometres (21 miles) beyond Marondera, on the main Mutare road stands the small town of **Macheke**, centre of an important tobacco growing area set amid attractive countryside.

The town stands on the banks of a small river of the same name that marked the borders of Mashona power and influence. Lobengula's raiding *impi* never dared to pursue their Mashona adversaries beyond this barrier.

From Macheke, it is another twenty-eight kilometres (17 miles) east to **Headlands**, originally called Laurencedale after Laurence van der Byl, an early pioneer who led a group of twenty-five settlers to this spot in 1891 on a trek sponsored by Cecil Rhodes.

Within a year, three of the settlers, including their leader, were dead and fifteen of the survivors had fled. Ultimately, only three of the original twenty-five remained.

Rusape, a major commercial and farm centre, some thirty-four kilometres (21 miles) beyond Headlands, at the **road junction** to the **Nyanga Mountains**, was established in 1894 as a BSAC administrative post.

Makoni, the paramount chief of the area, however, rallied his people to rise up against the Europeans who had come to seize the tribal lands and join forces with the Mashona during the 1896 *Chimurenga*.

Making his headquarters in a cave in the surrounding hills, Makoni was duped into surrender by three Africans loyal to the BSAC after he had bravely defied the might and firepower of the BSAC's artillery and dynamite.

Tried by a military court, he was sentenced to death and shot by a firing squad in his own kraal, on the same spot where he sent his own people to their death when they transgressed tribal law or disputed his authority.

From Rusape, it is ninety-three kilometres (58 miles) to **Mutare**. Many, however, prefer to **turn north-east** there, along the road that

Opposite: Hazy horizons seen from the summit of 2,160-metre World's View Nyanga Mountains.

climbs steadily through the granite highland foothills for eighty-six kilometres (53 miles) to **Juliasdale**, located at the threshold of **Nyanga Mountains National Park** in the northern extremity of the Eastern Highlands.

Nyanga: Mountain Majesty

The north-eastern highlands form some of Zimbabwe's most breathtaking scenery, contain many of the country's oldest historical sites, and provide the largest range of outdoor pursuits.

They are dominated by the craggy magnificence of the country's highest mountain, 2,592-metre-high (8,504-foot) Inyangani, with its trout-filled lakes, sparkling rivers, spectacular waterfalls, glorious forests, rolling moorlands, and dramatic gorges.

These highlands, standing on a giant plateau of uplifted doleritic intrusions 1,970–2,575 metres (6,500–8,500 feet) above sea-level, have been a favourite holiday retreat for most of this century.

Rhodes paid his first visit to Nyanga in 1897, when he travelled by coach from Umtali. He was so taken by the beauty of the area that he established an estate of 820 square kilometres (316 square miles) and stocked it with cattle imported from Mozambique.

He also experimented with growing fruit. The first apples on his estate were cultivated by his farm manager, Dunbar Moodie. Since then, fruit production has become a thriving industry and there is a fruit research station near Nyanga. When Rhodes died he bequeathed much of his estate, which now forms the national park, to the nation.

Earlier cultures also found fruit cultivation worthwhile. Stone ruins established by an agricultural people of remarkable sophistication, dating back many centuries, cover hundreds of square kilometres. They built irrigation channels, fed by the mountain streams, and planted their crops in terraced fields. Their outlines are still clearly visible on the mountain slopes.

Most of the settlements have a number of pits which archaeologists and sociologists postulate were used as cattle pens. The walls and floors were covered with stone and fitted with drains so that they could be washed down.

The level of sophistication found among this early group of settlers has led some to suggest that they had ties with Great Zimbabwe. Many experts, however, reject this idea. They hold that these communities arrived there about the fourteenth century from an entirely different, far north-east culture as part of the cultural migration that swept across Africa for more than 2,000 years and continued well into this century.

Rich in forests and rolling downs, Nyanga also contains many important rivers — Pungwe, Odzi, and Gairezi — which are born in the park to tumble over the escarpment in a series of magnificent waterfalls, including the 762-metre (2,500-foot) Mtarazi Falls that plunge sheer into the Honde Valley.

The indigenous vegetation, including a stand of Malange cedar (the country's only native conifer), stunted woodlands, patches of lowland forest, and high-altitude heath, has strong affinities with South Africa's southern Cape Province.

Though there are relatively few animals, Nyanga is an important mountain wildlife and bird sanctuary with a range of species unique in Zimbabwe. On the mountain slopes, nyala and duiker drift like phantoms through the clouds that frequently roll across them. Cisticolas, waxbills, mannikins, widowbirds, buzzards, and eagles, all flourish at these heady heights.

But frequent fires and the rapid disappearance of the natural forest on unprotected lands threaten many of the birds and animals that migrate seasonally to the park.

Essentially scenic, the area inspires a range of outdoor recreational activities, including angling for exotic rainbow, brown, and brook trout. Many rivers have been dammed to form small lakes and provide a challenge for the fly-fisherman during a season extending from October to April. Visitors can also enjoy golf, tennis, and boating.

Well-served by hotels, caravan parks, and campsites, the rustic but modern "capital" of the region, just outside the northern perimeter of the park, is Nyanga, 1,878 metres (6,162 feet) above sea-level. The name derives from *Inyanga*, the place of the witch doctors.

Above: Riders trek through the heather moorlands and pine forests of Nyanga's Troutbeck.

Standing some hundreds of metres above Nyanga to the north-east is the alpine resort of Troutbeck, established in 1951 by Colonel A. H. MacIlwaine.

Getting there

Nyanga, 105 kilometres (66 miles) from Mutare, 268 kilometres (166 miles) from Harare, and 682 kilometres (423 miles) from Bulawayo, is served by first-class roads.

Sightseeing

From **Juliasdale** it is twenty-three kilometres **north** (14 miles) to the administrative centre of **Nyanga** with its **country club**, **hospital**, **church**, **library**, **post office**, and **shopping centre**. The **cemetery** in the "old" village bears testimony to the hazards faced by those early settlers. It contains the **graves** of a number of police troopers who died of fever and other illnesses, including that of Lord Baden-Powell's grandson.

One kilometre **south** of Nyanga, a **gravel road** off the main road leads twenty-one kilometres (13 miles) **west** to the ancient **ruins** discovered by Major P. H. Van Niekerk in 1905. This staggering, single complex dwarfs that of Great Zimbabwe in extent if not in majesty, spreading across more than eighty square kilometres (30 square miles) and containing many mysteries that have yet to be resolved.

Five kilometres (three miles) before you reach these ruins, another **gravel road** leads **east** for seven kilometres (four miles) to **Nyahokwe**, where there are some similar but smaller **ruins**. The adjacent **field museum** displays evidence of human activity in the area dating back to the Stone Age. You can return to Nyanga by continuing another five kilometres (three miles) **east** to a **south turn** that leads eleven kilometres (seven miles) back into the town.

Five kilometres (three miles) **south** of Nyanga, a fork leads onto a **scenic road** that climbs fifteen kilometres (nine miles) **north-east** to **Troutbeck**, where mist billows and boils over the canopy of the **pine forests**.

Half a century ago this region was composed of empty, barren but magnificent moorland. Between the late 1940s and 1950s, however, the area was transformed by the energies of one man into a leisure and retirement resort, where thick forest, landscaped

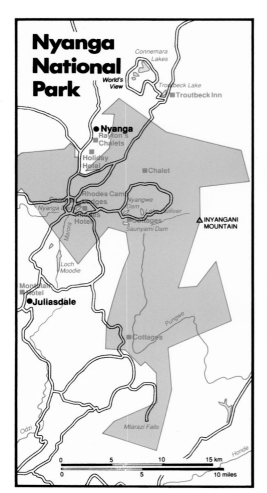

Nyanga National Park

Connemara Lakes
World's View
Troutbeck Lake
Troutbeck Inn
Nyanga
Rayton's Chalets
Holiday Hotel
Chalet
Rhodes Camp Lodges
Nyanga
Nyangwe Dam
Lake Gulliver
Rhodes Hotel
Cottages
Saunyami Dam
△ INYANGANI MOUNTAIN
Marora
Loch Moodie
Montclair Hotel
Juliasdale
Pungwe
Cottages
Odzi
Mtarazi Falls
Honde

0   5   10   15 km
0   5   10 miles

Below: *Msasa* tree, Nyanga Mountains National Park.

golf course, and delightful man-made **tarns** now counterpose the undulating **downs**.

Many people have built retirement homes in the forest overlooking the three delightful little **Connemara tarns** created by Colonel MacIlwaine, mastermind behind the Troutbeck estate and Zimbabwe's most exclusive hotel.

Graciously luxurious, yet always rustic, the **Troutbeck Inn**, which boasts its own sparkling trout-filled **lake** and superb nine-hole **golf course**, has given birth to a tiny English-style **village** complete with **bakery**. Pony and **motor trails** lead around the resort, culminating at the daunting **north-west escarpment** of the Nyanga Mountains.

On a clear day, hundreds of metres above the northern plains, you can look out from the aptly-named **"World's View"**, 2,160 metres (7,086 feet) above sea-level, over the infinity of Zimbabwe's **middleveld**.

A **stone monument** indicates the direction of major centres and their distances, including Harare, located directly **north-west** more than 200 kilometres (124 miles) away.

Tiny church

Just a few hundred metres outside Troutbeck **village**, a **forest trail** leads **north** two kilometres (just over a mile) to the tiny **church** of **St. Catherine's-on-the-Downs**. Built in the 1950s, it has no resident preacher, but serves faithfully the community that so evidently faithfully serves it. Both chapel and the tiny **graveyard** are immaculately maintained.

When Colonel MacIlwaine died in 1983, at the age of ninety-four, he was buried there beneath an **inscription** that gives credit to

Above: Gorse lines the shores of one of the three man-made Connemara lakes at Troutbeck.

his "vision and achievement" in creating Troutbeck and Connemara.

Among the few — there are no more than **twelve graves** — who rest there in eternal sleep are MacIlwaine's contemporary, Charles Gordon Hanmer, who died two years later at ninety-one. His **tombstone** immortalizes him as the man "whose valiant spirit built roads and planted trees opening Inyanga Downs to all who entered".

Along with MacIlwaine and Hanmer there is also the **grave** of Second Lieutenant John Charles Innes, only eighteen years of age, one of the last victims of the final *Chimurenga*. He was killed in action on 29 October, 1978.

Three kilometres (two miles) **south** of Troutbeck on the Nyanga road, an **east turn** along a **gravel road** leads four kilometres (two and a half miles) to the rocky wilderness retreat of 289-square-kilometre (111-square-mile) **Nyanga Mountains National Park** (you can also enter from the **south** and from the main road to the **west**).

Nyanga Mountains National Park: Stream and Waterfall, Down and Forest

The park ranges in height from 880 metres (2,540 feet) to around 2,300 metres (7,550 feet), reaching its pinnacle in Inyangani. These splendid uplands, rich in natural beauty and wildlife, have long been a favourite holiday area. The park is also an important mountain wildlife sanctuary containing montane fauna unique to Zimbabwe.

Conservationists are worried, however, by the persistent inroads of the wild exotic vegetation that is destroying the natural low-altitude forest outside the park boundaries.

The destruction of this habitat poses a threat to the birds and animals that migrate seasonally between the park and the forest. Many would like to see the whole of Mount Inyangani, particularly the sub-montane rainforest to its south-east, protected.

Along with scenic vistas and wildlife retreats, the park is also the national centre

Above: Centuries old cattle pit and village houses of the Manyika people in the Nyanga Mountains.

for trout propagation and research, and an important horticultural research centre.

A warden, five rangers, and support staff run the park; the trout centre is manned by a fishery ecologist, technicians, and support staff.

Sightseeing

The **gravel road** from the **Troutbeck turn off** follows the contours of **Mount Inyangani's western slopes** where, along eleven and a half kilometres (seven miles) of the route, sheer drops unveil fabulous **views** of secret **valleys** and rolling **downs**.

The road then reaches the **shelter** that marks the start of the most frequently used **climb** to the **summit** of this rugged mountain. Although of no great height, Inyangani is victim to sudden storms and mist, endowing the slopes with their own latent menace. Many have been lost and died trying to scale its heights.

If, however, conquering Inyangani can wait until another day, continue another eight kilometres (five miles) **west**, past deep valleys where antelope stand frozen in the moment of discovery, to **Lake Gulliver**, then two kilometres (just over a mile) beyond that to **Nyangwe Dam**, a man-made resort that reflects the tranquillity of nature.

Neat **lodges** welcome the visitor, as does the **trout hatchery** and **research centre** where millions of fish are reared to stock Nyanga's dams and rivers throughout the fishing season. The fish are raised in large ponds, grouped by varying stages of maturity.

The work is fascinating and the hatchery is open to the public between 14.00–15.00 and 16.30–17.00 Mondays to Fridays and on Sundays from 09.00 to 12.00 in addition to the afternoon hours.

A **dirt road** branches **west** off the gravel scenic road at Nyangwe Dam to climb half a kilometre or so to the **ruins** of **Fort Nyangwe**. Built by the sophisticated farming communities that inhabited this area centuries ago, the fort is one in a chain of ancient fortifications that leads across the lower slopes of Inyangani, each building clearly in line with the next for easy communication by signals.

From the **fort junction** it is five kilometres (three miles) **west** to the Nyanga Mountains **park headquarters**, where the pretty little **lake** formed by the **Nyanga Dam** (overgrown tees indicate its shores were once a golf course) is overlooked by the **Rhodes Hotel**.

Although only a one-star hotel by Zimbabwean standards, it is elegant enough to deserve the accolade luxurious. It reeks of nostalgia, a genteel throwback to the days of colonial glory which *Time* magazine's John Borrell described in a January 1990 essay on Zimbabwe ten years after independence.

Borrell ate a six-course meal in the dining room of Cecil Rhodes's former Nyanga farmhouse, served in such style by the hotel's blue-liveried retainers that he concluded the old rascal, whose **portrait** still gazes upon diners, would have approved.

Rhodes's old **stables**, adjoining the hotel, have been converted by the Zimbabwe National Trust into a **museum** filled with memorabilia of the region and the great imperialist's life.

From the park headquarters it is a kilometre or so to the main **Nyanga–Mutare road**. **Turn north** and then **west** onto a **gravel road**, following it for five kilometres (three miles) to the delightful **Udu Dam**, another popular trout **fishing centre** with smart, modern **lodges**, and a fairly easy clamber down the hillside to the spectacular **Nyangombe Falls**.

Sparkling in the sun, these glistening waters cascade down twenty-seven metres (89 feet) in two steps — the first is broad and

Overleaf: Nyangombe Falls near Udu Dam, Nyanga.

Below: Protea blooms in the Nyanga highlands.

Above: Alpine flowers in Nyanga Mountains National Park.

wide, the second is narrow and deep.

To Mtarazi Falls

From the Udu Dam junction on the main road you can return to the park headquarters and follow the scenic road twenty-one kilometres (13 miles) to the **viewpoint** overlooking **Pungwe Falls**. A second option is to return fourteen kilometres (nine miles) **south** along the main road, past the lush **groves** of fruit trees and **trout ponds** of **Claremont Orchards**, then turn **east** onto another leg of the Nyanga Mountains **scenic road**. Within half a kilometre of the turning this latter route leads to the **Montclair golf course**. Five kilometres (three miles) further along, there is a **turn south** that arrives, after twelve kilometres (seven and a half miles), at Pungwe Falls viewpoint.

The falls can be seen from below, at the point where the hills roll away from the long spine of the high peaks and the **Pungwe River** drops 244 metres (800 feet) into the deep gorge of the **Pungwe Valley**.

From there the river winds eastwards to take a final 800-metre (2,625-foot) leap down the escarpment where, levelled out, the waters flow lazily on towards the Indian Ocean.

The spectacle is immense. Seen far below, the falls are postcard perfect against the vast panorama of moorland and mountain. There is a four-wheel drive track that leads to a **path** that you can walk along to reach the top of the falls, but the turning is some distance from the viewpoint.

From this point the moorland road switchbacks up and down for four kilometres (two and a half miles) through moorland valleys and **forest** to an **east turn** off the scenic road to **Honde Valley Viewpoint**, a mesmeric place to park your car and walk to the brink of the **escarpment precipice**.

Although all instinct forbids those who suffer vertigo from doing so, the view entices many to stand on the giddying edge, 1,500 sheer metres (5,000 feet) above the valley floor, and gaze upon the panorama in all its sun-dappled beauty.

From this viewpoint, follow the single-lane track for a kilometre through **misty forest** to a small **glade** with a **picnic bench**. This is at the heart of Nyanga's neighbouring **Mtarazi Falls National Park**, which covers a total of twenty-five square kilometres (10 square miles).

Situated at the southernmost tip of Nyanga Mountains National Park, the Mtarazi Falls area is built around the dramatic beauty of Zimbabwe's highest **waterfall**, which drops over a vertical **cliff** and falls 762 metres (2,500 feet) in two stages.

An ill-marked **footpath** leads out of the glade onto the rock-strewn approach to the escarpment's edge, then down to the **Mtarazi River** and a precarious **foothold** just above the point where the waters disappear over the lip into the Honde Valley.

Lizards scuttle over the granite rocks. Late afternoon sunlight strikes through the billowing clouds like a celestial ray to stalk the shadows where the river falls.

To Honde Valley

From Mtarazi Falls, return eight kilometres (five miles) along the **single-lane road** to the scenic road, then **turn south** and travel fifteen kilometres (nine miles) through thick **pine plantations** to the **asphalt road** that leads down to the majestic **Honde Valley**.

At **Chipururi** on the edge of the **escarpment**, where the road plunges down in a series of tortured hairpin bends, you can see below, tin roofs glinting in the sun, farms and settlements, and the **communal lands** of the Honde Valley.

Hugging each contour of the almost sheer slopes, the precipitous road drops 1,300 metres (4,250 feet) in no more than thirty kilometres (19 miles). Seven kilometres (four miles) after Chipururi, the road winds through **Gatsi**, one-third of the way down the escarpment.

On one side, high above the road, **waterfalls** weep down the dark and sombre face of the massive cliffs — ribbons of white lace on a black granite shroud — while on the other side, far below, the hills and plains of Mozambique stretch away into the azure infinity of the **eastern horizon**.

The road levels out on **Holdenby communal land**, at first glance a mean and arid area, studded with **small villages**, **schools**, and a lonely — and closed — **petrol station** at the second-largest village, **Mparatsu**, thirty-five kilometres (28 miles) from the Nyanga–Mutare road.

Above: Tea pickers harvest the crowns of the tea bushes all year-round in the Honde Valley.
Overleaf: Emerald hills of the Aberfoyle tea plantation.

The **District Administrator's Camp**, seven kilometres (four miles) beyond, is the valley's main settlement with a **church**, **school**, **store**, **government office**, and an **airstrip**.

Two **dirt roads** lead from this point: one eleven kilometres (seven miles) **south** to **Mutumbadaka** and the **Loretto Mission School**; the other thirteen kilometres (eight miles) **east** to **Sanyatsuro** and the **Sacred Heart School**. Both villages are flush along the **Mozambique border** and the communities suffer terribly from raiding rebels and plain bandits.

After the DA's Camp the landscape changes, becoming green and fertile as the road begins to climb. Another series of tortuous bends around the base of Inyangani — its summit far above — takes you into what arguably are among the loveliest plantation landscapes in the world.

Tea and coffee are two crops that grace the countryside with an especial beauty and there, growing side by side upon the rolling hills, they clothe the Honde Valley with a mantle of arborescent perfection.

The bright early afternoon sun gives way to brooding and distended rain clouds. Thunder echoes around the hills and lightning cleaves the sky. Sudden torrential downpours flood the roads and steaming mist rises over **the plantations**, caressing the emerald crown of the tea bushes and the dark verdure of the coffee trees.

The road comes to an end in the tea-clad hills of the **Aberfoyle Plantation**. Estate security guards wave you through **the gate** with a smile. The plantation roads are well-maintained and near the company **offices** there is a small estate **village** complete with a well-stocked **store**.

The plantation also has its own members' club. The **Aberfoyle Club** is open to non-members and boasts a golf course as verdant as the surrounding tea fields.

This is the end of the line. The only way out is to backtrack the seventy kilometres (44 miles) along the valley and up the escarpment to the great pine and wattle plantations that skirt the edge of the Nyanga escarpment.

The Honde Valley is no place to visit at

night. Set flush alongside the **Mozambique border**, rebels, insurgents, and bandits were still taking advantage in 1990 of the prevailing conditions in Mozambique — and making raiding forays across the border to steal food and valuables and sometimes murder peasant families.

To Old Umtali

Nonetheless, there is an undeniable peace found almost everywhere you travel in this region — whether it be the Nyangombe Falls or the heights of the Vumba and Chimanimani Mountains south of Mutare.

Nineteen kilometres (12 miles) **south** of the Honde Valley and the **Nyanga–Mutare road junction** is **Watsomba**, where a **south-east turn** leads along eleven kilometres (seven miles) of **gravel road** and nineteen kilometres (12 miles) of **asphalt** to **Penhalonga**, one of the country's major gold-producing areas, some ten kilometres (six miles) from Mutare.

Forestry and timber also contribute to the area's wealth. John Meikle planted the first forests in the mountains of Penhalonga in 1905, and by 1930 the government had established extensive pine plantations around Stapleford, some thirty-one kilometres (19 miles) **north-east** of the valley. The road passes delightful **Lake Alexander**, as well as the attractive **Odzani Falls** and the National Trust's **Fort Goma Kadzoma**.

Penhalonga is encircled by a ring of verdant hills that form a natural bastion and it was from the ridge on one of the hills that Rhodes first saw the country which came to bear his name. A **plaque** was placed on the spot, marked on the map as **beacon 19**, where Rhodes crossed the **Mozambican border**, less than five kilometres (three miles) to the **east**.

Penhalonga's **Anglican Church of St. Michael's and All Angels**, built of corrugated iron on stilts in 1906, is said to be the second-oldest church in Zimbabwe. Its minister and congregation have organised a fund for its preservation.

The name of the Penhalonga Mine, which also gave the town its title, derives from the Portuguese *pena*, "rocky mountain", and *longa*, "large". By the 1920s, Penhalonga was producing more gold than any other area of comparable size in the country.

As operating costs increased, however, the mines became worked out and production began to fall. By the early 1960s, it looked as if Penhalonga's boom days were over. The discovery of a **new reef** during exploration work in 1968, however, brought renewed prosperity to the town, which has an excellent **caravan park** and **campsite**.

Just south of Penhalonga, where a small **trail** branches **east**, is a delightful, well-kept **flower garden** and the **Pioneer Nurses Memorial** commemorating three nursing sisters — Rose Blennerhassett, Lucy Sleeman, and Beryl Welby.

In 1891, these three women walked more than 200 kilometres (124 miles) through the fever-ridden Mozambican lowlands, after first sailing up the **Pungwe River** from the Mozambique coast, to open a **camp hospital** in Penhalonga and thus inaugurate the first nursing service in the country. They built their little mud "hospital" on top of **Sabi-Ophir Hill**.

The memorial is close to a huge **fig tree** which, legend says, was the place where the Manica chief's war leader prepared his medical potions before the advent of the white man. There is also a **sundial**, mounted on a stone pedestal, and a **plaque** inscribed with the names of fifteen European prospectors who mined this valley before the 1890s.

When A. R. Colquhoun led an advance party of the Pioneer Column to Penhalonga, they built a fort — ostensibly to protect Chief Mutasa and the Manica people from the Portuguese; strategically to establish a stranglehold. This settlement, which became the first Umtali, was manned by a police contingent under Captain H. M. Heyman. They were soon followed by the first settlers, but the settlement did not last long.

Driven by gold fever, prospectors staked claims everywhere, even in the fort, and then proceeded to undercut the entire area until it was a treacherous honeycomb. The **ruins** of the **old fort** still stand, close to the nurses' memorial, testimony to Rhodes's imperial obsession and the lust for wealth that drove the "pioneers".

A **dirt road south** of Penhalonga leads **east** into the beautiful **Imbeza Valley** where Sir Stephen and Lady Courtauld made their

Above: Golden gardens of La Rochelle, home of the late Sir Stephen and Lady Courtauld.

home in **La Rochelle**, thirteen kilometres (eight miles) from Mutare.

They bequeathed their gracious home, and its fourteen-hectare (35-acre) **gardens**, including **rare orchids**, unusual **trees**, and **ornamental shrubs**, to the nation and it is now managed by the National Trust.

The second Umtali was established near the Mutare River in 1891. Now known as **Old Umtali**, it lies to the **west** of the main Nyanga–Mutare road some kilometres **south** of the Penhalonga junction.

Promising prospect

The second attempt at making a settlement was more successful than the first and the new township flourished. From 1893 it was administered by a sanitary board governed by a committee of six under the civil commissioner. By March 1895, it had a population of almost 100: seventy-eight men, thirteen women, and nine children, with a crude hospital, post office, bakery, butchery, church, and cemetery.

It was indeed a promising prospect. Close to the Mozambique border, Umtali assumed strategic importance as the proposed head-quarters of the railway from Beira on the Indian Ocean. The plans for the new railway arose from the 1891 Anglo-Portuguese treaty, after which the BSAC formed the Beira Railway Company.

Contractor George Pauling began construction at Fontesvilla in September 1892. For more than five years his labour force of 1,200 men struggled through the tsetse fly-infested scrub of lowland Mozambique, battling not only heat but fatal malaria, blackwater fever, and sleeping sickness.

It was then that Pauling suggested to Rhodes that Old Umtali, by now a flourishing gold rush town with four hotels, one weekly newspaper (the handset *Umtali Advertiser*) a library, two banks, and the trading store established by Thomas Meikle and his brothers, would have to be moved.

The sanitary board held its last meeting in Old Umtali on 11 August, 1887, and its first in the new Umtali on 29 September. Old Umtali was left to the missionaries of the American Methodist Church. The **mission** and **training school** they built are still in operation.

Above: Thick forests enhance the glories of the Mountains of Mist — Vumba.

Vumba: The Mountains of Mist

Although the olive-green slopes of the Vumba Mountains — the "Mountains of Mist" — rise no more than 1,920 metres (6,300 feet), every metre, from the forested crests to the deep-cut valleys, proclaims their alpine majesty.

The sight of the mountain peaks shrouded by billowing morning clouds makes an unforgettable picture of ephemeral splendour. Hidden deep within these mountains are many secret and magic valleys.

Lying just a few kilometres from Mutare, the tree-shrouded bastions that guard Mutare's south-east flanks have been endowed with a splendid circular scenic route that climbs a winding course through steep mountains and rolling farmland. Along the way, viewpoints offer a succession of spectacular panoramas, each one revealing some new magnificence of the mountains or the Mozambique plains far below.

The mountains contain two marvellous sanctuaries — the dense Bunga Forest Reserve and the colourful Vumba Botanical Garden — that illustrate the incredible range of Zimbabwe's highland flora. Indigenous and exotic plants provide year-round colour; and the hydrangeas, azaleas, and fuchsias number in their thousands.

Getting there

Cloudlands, located in the heights of the Vumba —the "Mountains of Mist" — is eighteen kilometres (11 miles) from Mutare on a first-class road.

When to go

The Vumba Mountains are open all year-round and are delightful during any season.

Where to stay

In Mutare, the Manica Hotel (3-star), Wise Owl Motel (2-star). See Listings for "Hotels". There is a first-class caravan park and campsite, complete with laundry and electricity. See Listings.

In Vumba, Impala Arms (2-star), White Horse Inn (1-star), impeccable English-style country inn with magnificent gardens. There

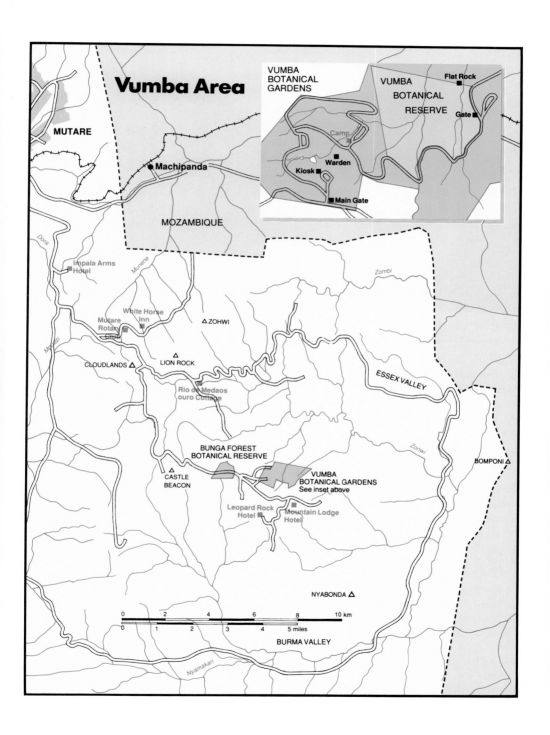

Vumba Area

Above: Landscaped beauty of Vumba Botanical Garden.

are other hotels with varying degrees of service and standards. See Listings for "Hotels". There is a caravan park in Vumba Botanical Garden with a swimming pool, and one campsite. Chalets and cottages can be rented in the Vumba Mountains. See Listings.

Sightseeing

The **Vumba Road**, the second **turn east** out of **Mutare** off the **southbound road** to **Birchenough Bridge**, is surprisingly poorly signposted for meticulous Zimbabwe. But the **view north** over the city on the first section of the drive is more than adequate compensation for any confusion experienced.

As you round each curve you may think the scenery can hardly be equalled — until it disappears along the next hairpin and you catch another glimpse of the unfolding panorama of the "Mountains of Mist" rolling away, each ridge ascending higher to the **east**, south-east, and south.

Some seven kilometres (four miles) out of the city is the **Prince of Wales Viewpoint** where, dozens of metres far below, you can take in **Machipanda** and the **Beira Corridor** of **Mozambique**.

A few kilometres beyond this, **a road** leads **east** one-third of a kilometre to the **Impala Arms Hotel**. Twelve kilometres (seven and a half miles) out of the city and several hundred metres higher the road reaches the **junction** of the circular **scenic route** which you can follow either to the **south-east** or **south-west**.

Continuing **south-east** beyond this junction for five kilometres (three miles), the road arrives at another **turn east**, into winding **Laurenceville Road**. The road, lined with palatial houses, is what passes for Mutare's "stockbroker belt". Lying in an almost enchanted glen, the elegantly rustic **White Horse Inn**'s architecture and service bespeak an impeccable pedigree. Eight-kilometre (five-mile) long Laurenceville Road is a *cul-de-sac* that ends flush against the Mozambique border.

Following the Vumba Road from Laurenceville Road it is another six kilometres (three and a half miles) to the **Cloudlands junction** at 1,584 metres (5,200 feet). There the scenic route around these marvellous mountains, **Essex Road**, branches east to **Essex Valley** and Vumba Road continues to **Bunga Forest Reserve** and **Vumba Botanical**

Above: Sheaves of tobacco turn to gold in a Burma Valley drying barn.

Garden, an eighteen-square-kilometre (seven-square-mile) national park.

The thirty-nine-hectare (96-acre) Bunga Forest Reserve, twenty-seven kilometres (17 miles) from Mutare, casts its shade on either side of the road. The sturdy forest, an area of dense indigenous trees, is nourished by the abundant rain trapped by the "Mountains of Mist". Rambling, well-kept **footpaths** guide the visitor through the shadows of this luxuriant and unspoilt wonderland. It deserves at least a day's outing.

A few kilometres beyond Bunga, in the **eastern lee** of 1,911-metre-high (6,270-foot) **Castle Beacon**, is the **entrance** to **Vumba Botanical Garden** which, by contrast, is a landscaped garden created around a series of small streams where flowering plants from all over the world flourish.

The garden is the gift of Fred Taylor, a settler from the north of England, who so delighted in the splendour of his adopted home that he moulded this wild forest into the sublime proportions that he prosaically named Manchester Park.

Now man and nature combine to create enduring beauty. Motes of sun strike through the forest canopy and glisten in the streams. Fish flicker in the crystal-clear ponds and lakes.

Clinging to the stone footpaths, moss and ferns intertwine in the humid forest groves. Fuchsias, hydrangeas, protea, begonias, lilies, azaleas, cycads, orchids, and aloes paint the lawns and forest glades in brilliant colours.

Many of the trees and shrubs at Vumba can be found nowhere else in Zimbabwe. Rising 1,828 metres (6,000 feet) at its highest point, the garden also offers a resplendent panorama of the **Mozambique plain** more than 1,000 metres (3,200 feet) below.

Fred Taylor's gift, however, is not just a repository of floral and botanical glory. The reserve is rich in wildlife as ornithological and botanical studies at the splendidly-named **Seldomseen Naturalist Centre** have revealed.

Graceful antelope — blue duiker and bushbuck — bushpig, baboon, and Samango monkey haunt the glades, cliffs, and forest. Look upward and discover, soaring in the thermals above the cliffs and darting through the upper storeys of the forest, an outstanding display of birds. Or look downward and spy flitting on the forest floor, the orange ground thrush.

Vumba's bird species include the wood owl, red-winged starling, bronze sunbird, augur buzzard, forest weaver, Nyasa crimson-wing, Swynnerton's robin, and two species endemic to Zimbabwe, Chirinda apalis and Roberts' prinia.

From the botanical garden gate the road hairpins **east** and **south-east** for a kilometre or so beneath the magnificent granite bluff of **Leopard Rock**. Then the road **forks south** through a manicured landscape of rolling **coffee** and **tea plantations** and the waters of Mozambique's **Chicamba Real**, a large and impressive man-made **lake**, appear in the hazy distance far below.

Four centuries ago, after a long trek west under Chief Zimunyo, the Mbire people arrived at these mountains and found them welcoming. Its forests and caves were a natural fortress against marauding enemies and animals, and the Mbire reinforced them with their own defences. You can still see the **ruins**.

Leopard Rock, aptly named as it was once the haunt of leopard, is known to the local communities as *Chinyakwaremba* — the "hill that sat down". Their folklore tells how the spirits were angered by the villagers that lived at its base and so caused the mountain to fall upon them.

Beneath the rock bluff sits Mutare's own version of the Palace of Versailles. **Leopard Rock Hotel** was closed down after liberation forces attacked it in the 1970s, but in 1990 it was being refurbished for its reopening.

Seymour Smith built the hotel after the Second World War and it was given the royal accolade in the 1950s when Queen Elizabeth, the Queen Mother, and Princess Margaret stayed there.

The Vumba Road is a dead end, and it involves a backtrack of some kilometres to return to the Cloudlands junction and the start of the circular scenic route that switchbacks more than sixty-seven kilometres (42 miles) through and around the Vumba Mountains to the Prince of Wales Viewpoint.

Winding its way beneath the heights of 1,871-metre-high (6,139-foot) **Lion Rock**, it soon becomes a **gravel road** climbing up and down through cool, lofty **eucalyptus**

forests into the neat **coffee plantations** of the Essex Valley.

After another twenty-five kilometres (15 miles) the road snakes down along the **Mozambique border** and rejoins the asphalt in the scorching heat of the twelve-kilometre-long (seven-and-a-half-mile) **Burma Valley**, nestled between the mountains. There rainbows glitter from the cascading drench of hundreds of sprinklers irrigating the **banana plantations**, tea pickers perspire in the midday heat, and **tobacco plantation** workers seek shade in the **drying barns** by the graceful brick Cape **farmhouses**, flush alongside the Mozambique border.

Finally, the road cuts through the **Zimunya communal lands** and **Chitakatira town** back to the Prince of Wales Viewpoint.

Above: Lychees ripen in the Burma Valley sun.

Opposite: Granite splendour of the Chimanimani Mountains.

Chimanimani Mountains: A Grand Array of Peaks

The rugged **Chimanimani Mountain Range** forms the southern bastion of the Eastern Highlands. More than fifty kilometres (30 miles) across, the Chimanimani stretch almost 100 kilometres (60 miles) from north to south in a grand array of peaks, the highest reaching 2,440 metres (8,000 feet).

The range was formed when violent earth movements forced the quartzite massif against an immovable plateau, folding it over to create the dauntingly beautiful landscape that you see today. No roads enter this alpine zone, although you can explore some of the foothills by four-wheel drive vehicle along rough tracks. Even on the scenic route to Cashel, skirting 2,144-metre-high (7,034-foot) Musapi, the going is rugged.

The only way into the high mountains is on foot along a single pathway, as ancient as the peaks themselves, that follows a section of the old slave trail that led from the interior to the Indian Ocean coast.

The eastern boundary of the 171-square-kilometre (66-square-mile) national park, established in 1953, forms the border with Mozambique and embraces all the major peaks, including the highest point, 2,440-metre (8,005-foot) Binga. The major river in the marsh of this range is the Bundi.

One major problem confronting the park's staff is the frequent forest and grass fires that spread into the park from pastures and farmlands with uncontrollable speed. Because there are so few trails, they are extremely difficult to extinguish.

Another problem that confronts mountain enthusiasts are the storms that blow up in minutes, frequently draping the slopes in impenetrable mist. But walkers, hikers, and climbers will revel in the sense of discovery and adventure that comes from exploring the steep, forest-clad slopes, ravines, and valleys making this nature sanctuary such a delight.

Though Zimbabwe's mountains claim no great heights, the views that greet you at every turn in this region are proclamation enough of their magnificence.

Gathering the rain from the south-east monsoon winds sweeping inland from the Indian Ocean, the mountains receive an average rainfall varying between 1,000 and 1,270 millimetres (25–30 inches) a year. No surprise, then, that the harvest these mountains yield is timber.

Once blessed with an abundance of timber — from teak to mahogany — demand for fuelwood has had a rapacious effect on Zimbabwe's natural forests. Even trees held sacred by local communities now fall to the axe and the Government has launched a major conservation and reafforestation programme to halt the damage and restore the woodlands.

Few trees provide as much wood as quickly as the fast-growing eucalyptus — gum tree — which forms the basis of the programme. Critics claim, however, that the tree draws too much water from the ground table and affects the water cycle balance. It also depletes the nutrients in the soil too quickly, and its leaves and bark provide poor fodder.

On the other hand, say eucalyptus supporters, no other tree can do more to stop the rape of the woodlands and the tree yields other benefits. One species, *Eucalyptus mellodara*, is considered the best honey tree in the world and Zimbabwe's rapidly-growing honey industry is heavily dependent on this variety. Other eucalyptus trees produce oils essential for pharmaceutical and industrial applications as well as essences for perfumes.

Experiments with slower growing indigenous acacias have shown real promise, and forestry experts believe their growth rate can be accelerated through selective seed and breeding programmes.

One of these trees, the *Acacia albida*, thrives in alien habitats and loses its nitrogen-rich leaves at the start of summer when the soil is most in need. As a result, livestock grow fat and glossy on its pods and leaves. Moreover, field crops can be grown right up to its trunk without affecting either crop or tree.

Delightful contrast

The Chimanimani District covers 3,100 square kilometres (1,196 square miles). In the extreme south, 300 metres (1,000 feet) above sea-level at the junction of the Save and Runde rivers, it is hot, humid, and uncomfortable.

By contrast Chimanimani, 152 kilometres (94 miles) from Mutare and 1,585 metres

(5,200 feet) above sea-level, is delightfully temperate.

The Chimanimani District is home to the Vendao people, whose Tshindao language is widely-spoken across a large area, from the lowlands of Mozambique as far north as Mutare.

The area has many ancient ruins similar in style, but not scale, to Great Zimbabwe and, more ancient still, bushmen rock paintings near the old drift across the Save River.

This land took away the breath of the first white man to reach it in the last decade of the last century. After weeks of slogging through the highveld and then the lowveld, Thomas Moodie strode up these hills in 1893, saw how good the land was, and strode no further. He had done more than enough to deserve his place in the sun, but he paid the supreme price for his effort.

His nine-month trek from South Africa was a vital part of Rhodes's plan to occupy the eastern region for, despite the 1891 Anglo-Portuguese treaty that settled the borders of the disputed territories, the Portuguese still felt that Manicaland and Gazaland fell within their sphere of influence.

To establish a European settlement George Benjamin Dunbar Moodie was commissioned by Rhodes to recruit settlers from the Orange Free State — offering large farms in Gazaland to every man and boy who trekked there.

In turn, Moodie invited his uncle, Thomas Moodie, a grain farmer of Scottish descent from the Bethlehem district of South Africa's Free State, to lead the twenty-nine settler families who took up the offer, most of whom were Afrikaners. The thirty-seven men and thirty-one women set off in May 1892, with seventeen wagons and 350 horses and cattle.

Hit by foot-and-mouth disease, attacked by lion, and short of water, the weary wagon train eventually reached Fort Victoria where most of the families promptly quit, choosing instead to make their way northwards to Enkeldoorn (now Chivhu) and Salisbury (now Harare).

On the second leg of his trek to an unknown land, Moodie set off with only fourteen men, four women, three small children, and seven wagons. At the wide sandy reaches of the Save River, treacherous with quicksand, Moodie crossed the river from island to island on horseback, marking out a safe passage for the wagons.

Worst was yet to come. Horse sickness attacked the horses and malaria the men. Soon after crossing the Save, the weakened party found their way barred by the massive granite barrier of Areman Hill.

For more than a week they chopped, hewed, dug, and finally blasted their way through this forbidding gate — the route now followed by the main Birchenough Bridge–Masvingo road — chaining three teams of oxen to each wagon to finally reach the mountain summit.

When they gathered at the top four days later, they named the mountain "Threespansberg". Finally, on 3 January, 1893, nine months after leaving Bethlehem, they reached the green rolling hills of Chimanimani.

Mountains aside, there are many other attractions including sparkling waterfalls, the most graceful being Bridal Veil Falls, and the Eland Sanctuary, where a protected herd of the largest species of antelope survive in benign peace.

In these unspoilt, lightly populated regions, visitors can frequently observe many different wildlife species, especially duiker, bushbuck, eland, sable, and the rare samango monkey. Bird life is especially prolific, since the forests and open heathlands provide habitats for a great number of species.

Getting there

Chimanimani, 150 kilometres (93 miles) from Mutare, 413 kilometres (257 miles) from Harare, 560 kilometres (348 miles) from Bulawayo, and 106 kilometres (66 miles) from Birchenough Bridge, is served by a first-class road. There are few bus services.

When to go

The Chimanimani Mountains are delightful all year-round, but best enjoyed in the dry summer season.

Where to stay

Chimanimani Hotel (1-star), extremely comfortable with swimming pool, snooker room, and other indoor recreations. Chipinge Hotel (1-star). See Listings for

"Hotels". There is a caravan park and camp-site at Chimanimani and Chipinge and a campsite at Mutekeswane Camp, the head-quarters of the national park. Camping is allowed anywhere in the park, provided you obtain the consent of the warden. See Listings.

Sightseeing

Wengezi Junction stands on the **lowveld** sixty-seven kilometres (42 miles) from Mutare along the main **Mutare–Masvingo road**. It marks the **east turn** onto the **scenic** drive to **Chimanimani**.

Follow the road to **Cashel**. After fifteen kilometres (nine miles) a **turn south** offers the direct route to **Chipinge** over the **Vumbere Mountains**, the western outliers of the Chimanimani.

The road runs beneath peaks that rise as high as 1,940 meters (6,400 feet), covered with thick cloaks of commercial plantations where giant, exotic Australian eucalyptus sway in the wind, and rejoins the Chimanimani sce-nic drive at **Skyline Junction**.

However, if you ignore this diversion the scenic route to Chimanimani continues three kilometres (two miles) **east** to **Mutambara**, perhaps best known for its **mission** and **mission school** founded in 1893 by the **American Episcopal Mission**. In the dis-tance, remote and isolated, lies the northern-most outlier of the Chimanimani Moun-tains, 2,211-metre-high (7,255-foot) **Himalaya**.

Seven kilometres (four miles) beyond Mutambara, the village of Cashel became famous through a series of radio and tele-vision commercials extolling the quality of its farm produce — peas, beans, and other crops grown in its fertile soil, then picked and canned all in the selfsame sunny day.

Cashel was originally known as Melsetter north, one of three villages Thomas Moodie named after his ancestral homelands in the Scottish Orkneys. Because of its constant con-fusion with Melsetter (now Chimanimani), it changed its name several times in the first sixty years of its existence, finally be-coming Cashel in 1957.

Mainly a **tourist centre**, the village lies in the shadow of the **"Black Mountains"** (a range that forms part of the Chimanimani Mountains), namesake to the popular **hos-telry** and **holiday resort** in the village.

The asphalt ends at Cashel and the scenic drive winds ten kilometres (six miles) **south** along a **gravel road** to **Tandai**, revealing tantalizing glimpses of the Chimanimani's majestic peaks and great panoramas of the Mozambique plains hundreds of metres below.

From there the scenic road continues forty-five kilometres (28 miles) **south**. Wind-ing beneath glistening **waterfalls** around the contours and deep-cut ravines of the **east-ern escarpment** of the Chimanimani, and through the leafy secret valleys of the **Martin Forest Reserve**, it finally arrives at the **district headquarters**, one of the earli-est European settlements in Zimbabwe and the village "capital" of this stunningly beau-tiful mountain region. It, too, was originally named Melsetter by Thomas Moodie. Today known as **Chimanimani**, it is a major tourist, forestry, and farming centre.

Chimanimani Village is the base from which to visit the scenic **Bridal Veil Falls**, **Chimanimani National Park**, **Chimanimani Eland Sanctuary**, and the many other attrac-tions of this unspoilt region. The village boasts a **country club**, **golf course**, **police station**, and **two-star hotel**, set in beautiful gardens with panoramic views of the moun-tains. There is a **caravan park** and **camp-site** near the village.

Some fourteen kilometres (nine miles) **north-east** of Chimanimani Village, high up on the flanks of the mountain at the **northern corner** of the national park, Zimbabwe's **Outward Bound Mountain School** provides outdoor adventure training to shape young characters into independent and resourceful individuals.

Four and a half kilometres **north-west** of the village, the fifty-metre (164-foot) Bridal Veil Falls emerges from its forest shroud to cascade down a series of steps in a delicate tracery like the nuptial mask that inspires their name.

Beyond the falls lie the 120 square kilo-metres (46 square miles) of Chimanimani Eland Sanctuary, established in 1975 with funds from the small Chimanimani com-munity and the Conservation Trust of Zimbabwe. The sanctuary was specifically created to protect the area's resident herd of eland, the largest of all antelope species.

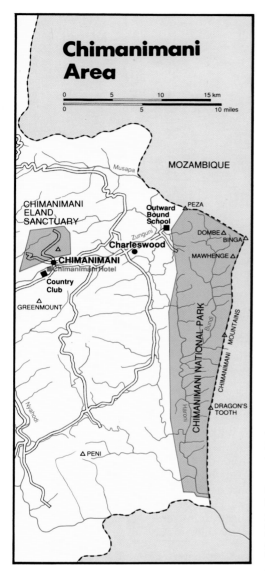

Chimanimani Area

0   5   10   15 km
0   5   10 miles

MOZAMBIQUE

CHIMANIMANI ELAND SANCTUARY

Musapa

Outward Bound School

△ PEZA

DOMBE △

BINGA △

Zunguni

Charleswood

MAWHENGE △

■ CHIMANIMANI
Chimanimani Hotel

Country Club

△ GREENMOUNT

Nyahodi

Bundi

Haroni

CHIMANIMANI NATIONAL PARK

CHIMANIMANI MOUNTAINS

DRAGON'S TOOTH

△ PENI

Chimanimani National Park: Land of Adventure

The **Chimanimani National Park** includes virtually all of the **Chimanimani Mountain Range** that lies within Zimbabwe. **Mutekeswane Camp**, the **park headquarters** and **gateway** to the **main trail** into the mountains, lies along a **gravel road** at the base of the main range, some eighteen kilometres (11 miles) **east** of Chimanimani Village.

It has a **campsite**, but nothing else. Beyond this point trekkers are very much on their own. It is no place for the comfort-seeker or the timid, but an adventure for the ardent hiker and climber, for access is by foot only, and all provisions must be carried.

For botanists, a walk in the Chimanimani is a special joy because of the diversity and loveliness of the flora. The rocks have eroded into a fine, sandy soil, white as salt, yet cedar and yellowwood trees, *erica* and *leucospermum*, along with ferns, orchids, and aloes, all flourish in this unlikely loam.

Only **one trail** leads from Mutekeswane into the mountains. After passing through a **grassy plateau** dotted with **odd-shaped rocks**, the path tops a rise and offers a superb view of the **main inner valley**.

There in the deep, thick grass of an extensive upland **marsh**, the **Bundi River**, with its many **crystal pools**, springs free of this great natural sponge to flow east over **Martin's Falls** on the lip of the **eastern escarpment** overlooking Mozambique, directly below. You can follow the **east trail** to the edge of this spectacular cascade.

Several other **trails** strike off the inner valley and ascend the main peaks and ridges — one leads a few kilometres north to the impressive **peak** of **Peza**, 2,179 metres (7,150 feet) high.

Another **trail** takes you south-east to the summit of 2,215-metre-high (7,267-foot) **Dombe**, and on a few more kilometres to the **circular trail** around **Binga**, at 2,440 metres (8,005 feet) the summit of the Chimanimani.

Two or three kilometres **south** of this stands glorious **Mawhenge**, 2,399 metres (7,871 feet) high but the only **trail** in this

Long present in Chimanimani's ancient forests, wild eland is the only species of all the large antelopes to have adopted the artificial habitat of the more recent pine plantations as its own. Indeed, they flourish in this supposedly unnatural environment. There are also some waterbuck and zebra.

Twenty-three kilometres (14 miles) south into the mountains stands **Rusitu Forest Botanical Reserve**, 150 hectares (370 acres) of dense, low-altitude, forest. There are no facilities for visitors and the area is primarily of interest to botanists.

Above: Spring sunshine bathes a coffee plantation near Chipinge in the Eastern Highlands.

direction leads **south**, constantly crisscrossing the ridge until it reaches the unmistakable **Dragon's Tooth** peak.

Among the impressive features of the remote, almost inaccessible **southern region** of these mountains are the **Haroni** and **Tarka forests** and the forbidding but beautiful **Haroni Gorge**.

Early morning finds the folds of the grasslands and the gaunt cliffs bathed in a soft, fine mist, but soon the sun rises, flushing out the last clinging shadows lurking in the deepest rills.

The white rocks sparkle with the promise of warmth to come, and on the banks of the trout-filled streams a riot of colourful ferns and orchids stretch their petals to the morning light.

Fringing the moorlands that host these rare flowers and semi-tropical plants are the last remnants of the great native forests of giant cedars and yellowwoods. Unusual, too, in Zimbabwe, the lower slopes of the mountains host some low-altitude rainforest.

Throughout the national park, the flash of wild animals in startled flight — sable, eland, blue duiker, klipspringer — darting in and out of thicket and forest cover will delight the walker and climber (who may also find an occasional leopard).

While the wildlife is special, the Chimanimani range is best known for its stunning bird life, some of it unique to Zimbabwe. Species include violet-crested turaco, malachite sunbird, laughing dove, lark, visiting swifts and swallows, trumpeter hornbill, secretary bird, francolins, and many kinds of eagle.

To Chipinge

The **asphalt** resumes at Chimanimani and climbs seventeen kilometres (11 miles) **south-west** through groves of pine and other major forest exotics to rejoin the **main road** from Mutambara at the aptly-named **Skyline Junction**.

Nothing stands there, but it is worth pausing to take in the view of Chimanimani Valley. Lying in a natural bowl surrounded by magnificent mountains, Chimanimani Village reflects the rugged beauty of its setting.

South of Skyline Junction, the road switchbacks through twenty-three winding

Above: Country bus carries plantation workers home through the gentle, rolling beauty of Chipinge Hills.

kilometres (14 miles) of superb mountain forest scenery to a **hairpin gorge** blasted through the cliff — **gateway** to the valley that Thomas Moodie found so alluring after his long trek from South Africa.

He is remembered by a **memorial** that was raised in his honour on his **Waterfall farm**. **Moodie's Grave**, marked by a **sign**, lies on the **east side** of the road just a few kilometres before the **junction** of the **Chipinge–Birchenough Bridge** road.

At the junction, you can either take the **west turn** to Birchenough Bridge or continue directly **south** for another thirteen kilometres (eight miles) to delightfully sleepy **Chipinge town**, heart of the prettiest postcard countryside anyone could ever wish to see.

Thomas Moodie named the settlement he founded as **Melsetter**, but it was changed in 1907 to Chipinga, after a local chief whose name was spelt Chipinge. It became Chipinge after independence.

There is a distinct, and these days delightful, sense of isolation in the area around Chipinge and the town itself, but in days of yore the early settlers felt lost in limbo, particularly during the rainy season. They campaigned for the construction of a railway link with the Umtali–Beira line — going so far as to lay out the route and begin their own construction. Part of the cutting can still be seen.

Complete with **rustic pub** and Tudor-style **library**, Chipinge marks the southernmost extremity of the dramatic Chimanimani Mountains, there cast down into gentle, flowing hills; their contours moulded into unsurpassing beauty flushed with the emerald- and olive-green squares, oblongs, and rhomboids of **tea** and **coffee estates**.

Bathed in the gentle warmth of a late afternoon sun, the hills roll away to distant horizons. Their undulating slopes, rising and falling between 1,120 and 1,370 metres (3,700–4,500 feet), are blessed with enough sun and rain to ensure that the quality of Zimbabwe's two major farm export commodities, after tobacco, command top world market prices.

The first tea bush was planted in 1924, but it was another twenty-six years before coffee took root. Dairy farming also flourishes and Chipinge boasts three **cheese factories**.

Other major crops are **pine**, **wattle**, and

179

macadamia nuts and, in 1989, **tobacco plantations** were also beginning to burgeon in these fertile hills, where the panorama changes round every bend in the road.

Between the plantations and forests, smallholdings of bananas and vegetables serve as lush contrast to the arid lowveld below.

Chirinda Botanical Reserve

Twenty-eight kilometres (17 miles) south of Chipinge, on the western slopes of 1,234-metre-high (4,049-foot) **Mount Silinda**, a **dirt trail** leads seven kilometres (four miles) **south-west** to the ten square kilometres (four square miles) of **Chirinda Forest Botanical Reserve**, an ancient legacy and one of Zimbabwe's few remaining primaeval rainforests.

Rare and ancient indigenous red mahoganies climb sixty metres (200 feet) through the tangled lianas to pierce the thick green canopy above the dappled, cathedral-like gloom of the forest glades.

Although the largest trees in the forest, only about 300 remain, most of them concentrated in the **"Valley of the Giants"**. The **oldest**, which took root six centuries ago, rises sixty-six metres (216 feet) and is five metres (16 feet) in circumference.

One useful tree, Chitonga (*Strychnos mellodara*), seldom more than forty centimetres (15 inches) in circumference and rarely more than thirty metres (100 feet) high, is easily recognised by its dark green, leathery leaves.

Its tiny white flowers bloom in September and its yellow berries cover the forest floor in February. Although the hard, close-grained wood warps and cracks during drying, it is good for making cabinets.

This garden of nature is also noted for a rare blue ground orchid (*Callianthus natalensis*). More rare orchids and ferns add to the variety of its jungle undergrowth and the forest is rich in many other unique species of trees, plants, and flowers.

Charles Francis Swynnerton, the naturalist who lived in the forest for two decades at the turn of the century, kept immaculate records and most of what is known of the reserve's flora and fauna stems from his impeccable observations.

Golf courses

The Eastern Highlands have some of the finest golf courses in Africa, well forested and with many challenging hazards.

Brondesbury Park Hotel, Nyanga — 2,734 metres (2,990 yards) 9–36. Hilly, undulating, good views, caddies, licensed hotel.

Claremont Golf Club, Juliasdale — 2,865 metres (3,133 yards) 9–36. Scenic course, pulpit tees, clubhouse, caddies, near hotel and casino.

Troutbeck Inn, Nyanga — 2,602 metres (2,845 yards) 9–34. Pulpit tees, water hazards, caddies, licensed hotel.

Hillside, Mutare — 6,207 metres (6,788 yards) 18–73. Three kilometres (two miles) from Mutare, sloping water hazards, clubhouse, caddies.

Mutare Golf Club — 5,973 metres (6,532 yards) 18–72. Two kilometres (just over a mile) from Mutare, undulating, well wooded, clubhouse, caddies.

Leopard Rock, Vumba — 5,486 metres (6,000 yards) 9–69. Thirty-two kilometres (20 miles) from Mutare, undulating, caddies.

Chimanimani — 2,654 metres (2,903 yards) 9–36. One and a half kilometres (one mile) from Chimanimani Hotel, clubhouse, caddies.

Chipinge — 5,650 metres (6,179 yards) 9–72. Adjacent to village, sloping, water hazard, sand greens, clubhouse, caddies.

Above: War Memorial, Chipinge.

Trout Fishing Paradise

The only fly-fishing — wet or dry — in Zimbabwe is during the October to April trout season in the tarns, man-made lakes, and cool gushing streams of the Eastern Highlands. These are an ideal environment for three species of trout introduced from other parts of the world.

Rainbow trout is the most widespread of the trout family and a favourite sporting fish. The largest rainbow caught in the Nyanga area weighed almost four kilos (eight and a half lbs).

Brown trout are considered by many to be the most canny. The record Nyanga catch was slightly more than three kilos (six and a half lbs). American brook trout are not widespread, but since they are easier to catch they are popular with beginners.

Constantly monitored and restocked, these waters ensure good fishing throughout the year, particularly in **Nyanga Mountains National Park's Nyangwe**, **Udu**, and **Nyanga dams**. In nearby **Lake Gulliver** and **Saunyami Dam**, anglers cast for some of the largest fish in the national park.

There are also private lakes and streams in the Nyanga area where visiting anglers may fish for a fee. Private lakes at Zimbabwe Sun's **Troutbeck Inn** and **Montclair Casino Hotel** are stocked for the benefit and pleasure of their guests. Good trout fishing can also be enjoyed at **Lake Alexander**, thirty-seven kilometres (23 miles) north of **Mutare**.

The most ideal stretches are the reaches of the sparkling **streams** and **rivers** of **Chimanimani National Park**, where one **fishing camp** provides **shelter** for those enthusiastic enough to walk into these remote areas.

Trout fishing can be enjoyed all year-round at the Nyangwe and Nyanga dams, but only between October and May in the rivers, streams, and other dams. In Chimanimani National Park the season runs between October and April (the winter season is from May to August).

Zimbabwe's trout fishing is among the cheapest in the world. Permits are available at the local wardens' offices, where visitors can also check on current regulations and conditions.

Coarse fishing for bream, black bass, tigerfish, and other species may be enjoyed at **Fern Valley Lake**, eight kilometres (five miles) from **Mutare**.

Fishery research and development are carried out in Nyanga Mountains National Park by the Department of National Parks and Wild Life Management. The **trout hatchery** and **research station** are located near Nyangwe Dam. The hatchery is open for a limited number of hours each day to the public.

Brood stock, which mature at two years, are chosen for their high yield, rapid growth rates, body conformation, coloration, and disease resistance. Breeding takes place during the winter months of June, July, and August. Males are kept upstream because the female hormones induce fighting that causes excessive injuries.

Three months before spawning, the fish are placed on a diet of specially-formulated pellets containing Carophyll Red, used to give colour to a popular brand of orange soda which — besides quenching human thirsts — improves the production and fertility of trout eggs.

Since each female is only ripe for about three days of the year they are checked twice a week. When ready, the females are taken into the hatchery building together with the males. Stripping is carried out under artificial light. Ultraviolet sunlight, which under natural conditions is shielded by water and the nest, damages or destroys eggs.

Fertilization is almost immediate. Expansion, which starts when the eggs come into contact with water, lasts about twenty minutes. To initiate the expansion and harden the shells, a little water is added.

Later, the fertilized eggs are washed two or three times to remove excess milt and debris, measured, and placed in the incubation trays.

Initial development of the embryo takes place between forty-eight and seventy-two hours after stripping. Depending on water temperatures, the eyed stage — when two little black dots, the embryo's eyes, can be seen through the egg shell — is reached eight to nine days later.

Above: Nyanga Dam, near Nyanga National Park headquarters, swarms with trout.

Next the eggs are siphoned out and swirled around in a plastic bucket, a shock treatment guaranteed to kill any eggs that have not developed and so avoid infection of the healthy eggs. The eggs then take between three and five weeks to hatch.

After the fry have absorbed the yolk sac and reached the "swim up" stage, they are taken to the raceways where, initially, they are fed on daphnia, pellet powder, minced meat, and lungs mixed with gelatin. Daphnia, water fleas, are bred in special ponds.

Trout have variable growth rates. To ensure uniformity of size, fry and fingerlings are graded frequently in a rectangular box with spaced, parallel bars along its base. Small fish slip between the bars separating them from the larger fish.

Fingerlings are reared in circular ponds until they are more than twenty centimetres (eight inches) long. To protect them from the hammerkop and the giant kingfisher, two major predators in Nyanga, the ponds are covered with wire mesh. Another savage predator active during winter months is the clawless otter.

Unprotected, these unwary fish are easy prey for the raider. Shadows on the breeding ponds turn the waters into a raging maelstrom as the trout, with Pavlovian reflex, swarm in avaricious schools ready for the first scattering of food.

Trout depend on high oxygen levels. Aeration increases the dissolved oxygen content in water — and aerated ponds can hold double their normal capacity. During the long, hot summer months, when Nyanga trout often suffer from bacterial infection, this aeration helps reduce stress. Heat makes them miserable and sluggish. The best fishing is when the rains are plentiful, the temperature low, and the trout are lively and eager to take the fly.

North-East and North: A Green and Pleasant Land

The massive plateau that stretches from Chinhoyi in the north to Shurugwi in the south, and from Redcliff in the west to Marondera in the east, encompasses much of the highveld. At the centre of the plateau is the capital, Harare.

Spreading roughly west, north-east across the middle of Zimbabwe its broad, open grasslands are cooler than the low country to the north and south.

The plateau's deep soil, good rainfall, warm summers, temperate winters, and freedom from tropical pests such as malarial mosquitoes, makes it among the most productive farmland in southern Africa. The surrounding countryside is both green and pleasant, with many interesting features easily accessible by first-class roads.

One of the most popular places is Ewanrigg Botanical Gardens, home of the largest aloe collection in this part of Africa. To the north, maize and dairy farms flourish in the fertile Mazowe Valley where water from the dam that was built in 1920 irrigates the neighbouring farms, including the vast Mazowe Citrus Estate. In addition, the dam itself is renowned for the size of its carp and is a popular fishing resort.

The road that heads eastward from Mazowe winds through fields of maize and cotton to the small town of Bindura. From there, its course leads through rugged, compelling scenery to the picturesque old mining town of Shamva, named for the tsamvi trees (a variety of wild fig) that flourish there.

Getting there

There are many excellent roads and frequent rail and bus services.

When to go

It is pleasant all year-round.

Where to stay

There are many first-class hotels in Harare and excellent hotels and motels in centres like Chinhoyi. See Listings for "Hotels". Many urban centres also have caravan parks and campsites. See Listings.

Sightseeing

Two roads run **north-east** from **Harare**. One ends after thirty-two kilometres (20 miles) at **Arcturus**, named after one of the syndicates that was formed to prospect for gold in the early days.

The town was established around some 550 gold claims acquired in 1911 by the Planet Arcturus Gold Mine Company which developed three mines — **Planet, Arcturus,** and **State**.

Arcturus is at the centre of a farming and mining district popularly known as **Enterprise**, although the district headquarters is at **Goromonzi**, seven kilometres (four miles) **south**.

A **dirt road** from the town leads to the **Harare–Mozambique** road which, eighty-seven kilometres (54 miles) from Harare, arrives at the administrative centre of **Murewa**, located beneath a huge **granite kopje** that resembles the shape of an elephant.

There are some exceptional examples of **rock art** in the extraordinarily large **Murewa Cave**, set on a **hillside** seven kilometres (four miles) from the town. The cave, which is a **national monument**, has many paintings depicting animals, people, plants, and trees.

Murewa also has a small **cemetery** containing the **graves** of settlers, officials, and police who died there around the turn of the century. One small **monument** honours the memory of a former official who was murdered, then thrown into a nearby river, never to be found.

Fifty-six kilometres (35 miles) beyond this centre stands **Mtoko**. Founded in 1911, and named after the local chief, it is the last town before the **Mozambique border** and for

Above: Ewanrigg Botanical Gardens.

many years was the customs and immigration post. The **office** has long since been moved to the border at **Nyamapanda**.

Mtoko, known mainly as a fountain-head of rock art, boasts **several caves** in the wild countryside around the town that are significant for the number and quality of their ancient **cave paintings**. The most important form a group — **Charewa**, **Ruchera**, **Manemba** — found a few kilometres to the **east**. Another important cave, **Gambarimwe**, twenty-three kilometres (14 miles) to the **north**, was proclaimed a **national monument** in 1949.

The paintings depict remarkably stylised birds, snakes, lizards, elephant, antelope, and buffalo, as well as hunters and women.

The countryside in this administrative district, which extends beyond the **Ruenya River** into the northern portion of **Nyanga**, is known as **Makaha**. It was one of the richest lodestones of gold for the ancients, who quarried the hills of schist and greenstone for centuries.

Ancient **fortifications** built by early mining communities crown many of the hills. An outstanding archaeological example near the Ruenya River, **Makaha Fort**, has a **circular wall** seven metres (24 feet) in diameter.

The indigenous tribes were not the only ones adept at constructing strongholds. On the **Nyamsizi River**, some eighty kilometres (50 miles) beyond Mtoko, not far from the **Nyamapanda border post**, stand the **ruins** of a small seventeenth-century fort built by the Portuguese to defend their gold traders.

To Karanda

Twenty-one kilometres (13 miles) from Harare, along the Mozambique road there is a **left fork** to **Shamva** and **Mount Darwin**. Nineteen kilometres (12 miles) beyond the fork, close to the popular **Mermaid's Pool picnic spot**, is one of the natural treasures of the country, the three square kilometres (just over one square mile) of **Ewanrigg Botanical Gardens**.

Established in 1920 by Basil Christian, who bequeathed it to the nation after his death in 1950, the gardens contain what is perhaps the world's most famous collection of aloes and cycads. During June, when the aloes flower, the gardens draw thousands of visitors from all around the world.

Above: Weekend watersports at Harare's Lake Chivero resort, formerly Lake McIlwaine.

There are more than fifty species of aloe, several cycads, and many other colourful plants, including a substantial collection of cacti, bougainvillaea, fuchsias, and a **herb garden**.

Fifty-two kilometres (32 miles) **north** of Ewanrigg is **Shamva**, a gold-mining centre originally known as Abercorn after the Duke of Abercorn, President of the British South Africa Company. The name was changed to avoid confusion with Abercorn in Zambia (then Northern Rhodesia).

The Shamva **police camp, magistrate's court**, and **hospital** stand on a **hill** overlooking **Shamva Mine** two kilometres (just over a mile) away. The townspeople have seen many mines come and go. The Abercorn mine, one kilometre (over half a mile) **north-east** of the police camp, opened in 1906 and closed in 1913.

If gold gave Shamva birth, nickel sustains its life. When the yellow seams ran out, the Anglo American Corporation developed a large **mine** to exploit the area's abundant **nickel deposits**. The nickel concentrates are shipped twenty-seven kilometres (17 miles) by rail for treatment at the **Trojan Nickel Mine** processing plant in **Bindura**.

Originally named Kimberley reefs, after a local gold mine, Bindura remains at the centre of one of the oldest mining regions in the country. For years its citizens slept to the lullaby of the crushing plants as they pounded the gold-bearing ore around the clock.

From Shamva, it is sixty-seven kilometres (42 miles) to **Mount Darwin**, the town that sits on the slopes of a hill known to the local communities as *Pfura*, meaning large rhino. The town was named by the hunter Frederick Selous after Charles Darwin.

In the communal lands well to the **north** of Mount Darwin the Evangelical Alliance has established a number of missions, including a large **hospital** at **Karanda**.

The area became the site of what was perhaps the earliest missionary endeavour in southern Africa when Father da Silveria, a Jesuit priest who landed at Sofala in 1560, travelled inland as far as Karanda. His message was not well-received. One year later, in March 1561, the missionary was strangled and his body thrown into the **Musengezi River** as an offering to the crocodiles.

Above: Eland, the largest of Africa's antelope.

A single road runs twenty-seven kilometres (17 miles) from Harare to end at the barrier of **Domboshawa**, a massive granite rock covered with yellow and brown lichens and pierced by a massive **cave**.

Witch doctors used the cave and the valley below for their secret rainmaking rituals, which involved lighting a fire in the mouth of the cave and a considerable knowledge of local weather lore.

For when the wind was in the right direction for rain, it forced the smoke through a small opening in the top of the rock. Those watching below considered this a signal from the spirits that rain was on the way.

Both the cave and surrounding woodlands were sacred to the local people, but for casual visitors the greater interest will be the cave's **rock art**, some of which has unfortunately been destroyed by the rainmakers as well as more recent vandals.

To Mazowe

Mazowe, forty kilometres (25 miles) north of Harare, is the village headquarters of **Mazowe Valley**, Zimbabwe's largest citrus fruit growing area as well as an important

maize, cotton, and tobacco producing region.

Portuguese explorers, who recognised the gold wealth inherent in the countryside, travelled up the **Mazowe River** for more than three centuries. Old crushing **stones**, used to smash the gold-bearing rock in hollowed-out bowls of surface rock, can still be found, especially near the streams. These suggest that the precious metal was worked by slaves chained together in rows, after the fashion depicted on Egyptian monuments.

Traces of a cement-type smelting **furnace**, similar to those discovered at Great Zimbabwe, were also found, indicating that crushing, washing, and smelting were carried out on the spot.

The rustic **Mazowe Hotel**, now with two **swimming pools**, is one of the oldest hotels in the country. It opened in 1895 and the ambience of its settler-pioneer days is steeped in every beam and brick.

At Mazowe one road forks **north-east** through **Glendale** to Bindura, while the main road to **Centenary** continues ten kilometres (six miles) **north** to **Jumbo**, which grew from a **siding** established on the **Mount Hampden branch line**.

Above: Leafy sonnet of purple and gold as a jacaranda flowers.

While the railroad may claim responsibility for the town's origins, the **Jumbo Mine** — named after London Zoo's largest elephant — gave the place its impetus. Registered in October 1890 by Thomas Maddocks, the mine stands on the site of some extensive ancient gold workings.

Following that first claim, more than 100 gold mines were established and most of the gold was produced within a radius of seven kilometres (four miles) around the station.

Fragments of old **Delft pottery** and **nankin china** have been found in the vicinity of the Jumbo Mine — an indication of Portuguese presence. Further evidence is found in the shape of **old foundations** and extensive **terracing**, marking the site of a settlement of some considerable size. These were uncovered in the 1960s on a commanding hill, close to the **Marodzi River**.

A few kilometres beyond Jumbo a road leads **north-east** to **Concession** and **Amandas**, a gold and chrome mining centre. The nearby **Iron Duke Mine**, lying in the **gorge** of the **Yellow Jacket River** that flows through the **Iron Mask Mountain**, is Zimbabwe's only major source of iron pyrites. Originally a gold mine, the pyrites were discovered by accident when a crosscut to pick up the gold reef failed to do so.

Just beyond Concession and Amandas, a **road** forks **west** for five kilometres (three miles) to reconnect with the Centenary road, and twenty-six kilometres (16 miles) further along it flashes by the one-store **hamlet** of **Msonedi**. Another eight kilometres (five miles) brings you to **Mvurwi**, which was originally known as Dawsons and later became Umvukwes. It is an important farming and mining centre on Zimbabwe's Great Dyke.

Some six kilometres (three and a half miles) before Mvurwi, a **junction** strikes **west** twenty kilometres (12 miles), mostly across gravel, to **Mtoroshanga**, the bustling centre of a prosperous tobacco farming and chrome mining region. From there a **good road** leads forty-five kilometres (28 miles) **south** to **Mpinga** on the main **north-west Harare–Zambia road**.

North-West to the Zambezi

After passing through forty kilometres (25 miles) of cultivated farmland, the road leading north-west from Harare — towards Lake Kariba and the Zambian border — reaches a long, flat-topped ridge.

This is an outcrop of the Great Dyke of Zimbabwe, one of the most extraordinary geological features in southern Africa. Born 700 million years ago in a subterranean upheaval, this geological marvel left a gigantic trough up to seven kilometres (four miles) wide and 500 kilometres (311 miles) long extending almost the entire length of the country (See "The Land: Diamonds and Coal, Wheat and Tobacco", Part One).

Beyond the dyke is a pleasant savannah of tobacco, maize, and cattle farms. Its urban centre is the village of Chinhoyi, site of the famous and spectacular Chinhoyi Caves.

Sightseeing

The tall **hill** which stands eighteen kilometres (11 miles) **north-west** of Harare, was named **Mount Hampden** after John Hampden by his friend the hunter and explorer Frederick Selous.

During the Second World War a flying school was established in its shadow as part of the Empire Air Training Scheme. When it closed at the end of the war the school was converted into a hostel for civil servants, then subsequently became a reform school while the old hangars were used to store grain. Since 1973, it has been known as Charles Prince Airport.

Today the chameleon-like **complex** is Harare's second airport, the busy base of most of Zimbabwe's light aircraft companies, once again a flying school, and home to the **Mashonaland Flying Club**.

Forty-eight kilometres (30 miles) to the **north-west**, at **Gresham**, the road cuts over the mineral-rich **Great Dyke** and through the productive farmlands and gold fields of the **highveld**.

From Gresham it is twenty-five kilometres (15 miles) to **Banket**, the centre of an important agricultural area that produces tobacco and maize in large quantities.

It is in this region that a winter wheat irrigation project recently gave birth to the country's second-largest lake. The waters that have backed up behind **Mazvikidei Dam**, just over an hour's drive from the capital, have created a playground rivalling Lake Kariba.

Another twenty-three kilometres (14 miles) beyond Banket the road arrives at **Chinhoyi**, famed for an outstanding natural feature eight kilometres (five miles) **north** of the town — a thirty-metre-wide (100-foot), forty-six-metre-deep (150-foot) **limestone shaft**, joined by several **passages** and **caves**, at the foot of which lies a **large pool** of clear water ninety metres (300 feet) deep. The labyrinth served as refuge for the local people from raiding warrior parties.

It was "discovered" by Frederick Courtney Selous who, in May 1888, gave a dissertation on the subject to the Royal Geographical Society in London. The caves and pool form one of those rare places where reality actually exceeds travel brochure hyperbole.

Climbing down the steep **granite steps**, it is easy enough to imagine you are approaching the entrance to Hades and the river Styx. All light vanishes. The silence is both eerie and profound, the dimensions gargantuan and vertiginous.

Then, at a twist in the **tunnel**, the revelation: there at the bottom it stands, limpid and translucent, a fathomless pool of deepest blue. If you are lucky enough to catch it when the mid-morning sun is directly above it, the water sparkles with the hidden fires of a priceless turquoise.

There is another formidable **hole in the ground** sixteen kilometres (10 miles) **west** of Chinhoyi along the **Copper Queen Road**, at the **site** of the largest and most impressive ancient mine workings in the country.

The area is marked by the **large slabs** of monolithic rock removed from the depths by those miners of old when they gouged out the hole. It measures half a kilometre (one-third of a mile) long, 150 metres (495 feet) wide, and twenty-four metres (80 feet) deep.

Opposite: Chinhoyi Cave — 150 feet deep, where a pool of clear blue water fills another 300 feet of this natural limestone shaft.

Above: Sounding hippo surges through a flock of ducks.

Closer to Chinhoyi, lying to the **west** and **east** of the town, **Alaska** and **Eldorado** — names that ring out the gold-rush romance — both have interesting histories.

Eldorado, in fact, is a misnomer: this was no city of treasure, just proof that all that glisters is not gold.

Nonetheless, in 1904, after the discovery of a possible gold formation that some thought might be of the same size and value as that on the Witwatersrand in South Africa, one astute share pusher used the lure of its name, from that fabled city of gold in Latin America, as the bait to make a fortune.

Although the find was untried, he proceeded to peg claims along several kilometres of the "gold reef" and word of this new discovery soon spread. The operator then manipulated the share market and a new rush began. Hundreds of gullible treasure hunters from South Africa and Europe flocked to buy his claims, only to find their stake worthless.

In recent years, copper mining at nearby Alaska and **Mangula** has contributed to the prosperity of Chinhoyi. Copper, in fact, has been worked in this area for centuries.

Lower Zambezi: Old Man River Keeps Rolling Along

Strange footsteps, imprinted in the sands of time and now laid bare in the fossils of the Zambezi Valley, reveal that dinosaurs — meat-eating, reptilian giants which walked on two legs — roamed this region more than 150 million years ago. The footprints measure forty centimetres (16 inches) from heel to toe.

Why the dinosaurs vanished from the face of the earth remains a mystery. While it is clear that some unexpected, natural catastrophe caused their sudden extinction, science has yet to discover what it was.

This apart, the Zambezi Valley's fossil records do tell of the many other dramatic changes that have taken place over hundreds of millions of years. Prised from the wind-blown sands, ashes, and rocks of the valley's steep gorges and gentle plains, these frozen moments in history narrate epic stories of glacial activity, earth movements, and climatic disturbance.

Above: Hippos cluster in the shallows of the Zambezi.

They tell of a time when the valley had abundant water and was covered with temperate forest; and of another time when it was nothing but a desert streaked by massive lava flows.

No doubt many more prehistoric secrets are drowned by the deep waters of the man-made lake that covers 5,000 square kilometres (1,930 square miles) of the middle Zambezi Valley between Victoria Falls and Kariba Gorge.

The Kariba Dam has caused profound change, particularly downstream in the middle Zambezi Valley where the fairly constant year-round water flow has had a profound and sometimes disturbing effect on river life.

Until the 1980s, the floodgates were opened frequently and the artificial, sediment-free floods caused extensive erosion. Large amounts of fertile, alluvial soil were washed away and fish species that breed under cover of flooded vegetation, where the young are relatively safe from predation, faced extinction.

In twenty years, one thirty-kilometre (19-mile) stretch between Mana Pools and the confluence of the seasonal Sapi River and the Zambezi saw twenty square kilometres (eight square miles) of fertile flood plain vanish. The telltale signs are in the near-vertical river cliff. During the last decade, however, the floodgates have remained closed and the erosion and river widening have stopped.

For centuries the Zambezi has attracted explorers. Today's adventurers, including game-viewers and bird-watchers, who come to explore it by canoe, by vehicle, and on foot also discover its excitement — and its sense of timelessness.

The most popular waters for these safaris are the 256 kilometres (159 miles) stretching downstream from the Kariba Dam, under the Otto Beit Bridge at Chirundu, to Kanyemba on the Mozambique border. A busy trading post in the seventeenth century, Kanyemba was a port of call for the Portuguese merchants who followed the river's course into the interior. (See "The Gold and the Silver, Part One).

Getting there

Chirundu, a border post on the banks of the

Zambezi, is 347 kilometres (216 miles) from Harare on an excellent main road.

When to go

The Zambezi Valley can be extremely cold in winter and excessively hot in summer. But between the two extremes it enjoys a gentle climate.

Where to stay

In Karoi, Karoi Hotel (2-star). See Listings for "Hotels". There is a caravan park and camp-site. See Listings.

In Makuti, Cloud's End Hotel. See Listings for "Hotels".

In Chirundu, Chirundu Valley Motel and Resort. See Listings for "Hotels".

Sightseeing

Chirundu is 251 kilometres (156 miles) from Chinhoyi on one of the finest roads in southern Africa. At a **junction** twenty kilometres (12 miles) **north-west** of Chinhoyi, another road leads forty-six kilometres (29 miles) **north** to **Mhangura**, home to the largest **copper mine** in Zimbabwe, which came into operation during 1957. The company town has its own **hospital** and fine **sports grounds** for cricket, tennis, swimming, squash, and bowls.

Karoi, which lies on the Chirundu road sixty kilometres (37 miles) beyond the junction, announces itself with a **signpost** depicting a witch riding a broom. Passers-by may wonder why this is the town emblem and why, unlike all the other towns in Zimbabwe, there is no word of welcome or farewell. In fact, the name derives from the Bantu word *karoyi*, little witch. Long ago it was the practice in these parts to throw witches into the river.

Now one of the greatest tobacco growing areas in Zimbabwe, Karoi was regarded as unsuitable for human settlement well into the twentieth century. Not until Robbie Robertson established **Buffalo Downs Farm** in 1938 — after protracted arguments with civil servants who considered the tsetse fly-infested scrub too unhealthy — was the spell broken.

Robertson's first tobacco crop in 1939, planted on forty hectares (100 acres), produced more than 1,100 kilos (2,425 lbs) a hectare — double the normal yield — and its quality was so high that it sold at almost thirty per cent more than the top price, provoking a Parliamentary debate.

At once farmers began to clamour for land around Karoi, then known as Urungwe. The area's real development (and change of name), however, took place after the Second World War. The approaches to the town, with its well-planned **landscaped gardens** and smart streets, reflect Karoi's prosperity and efficiency.

Eighty-seven kilometres (54 miles) after leaving this bewitching town that wishes neither welcome nor goodbye, you arrive at **Makuti** with its one **petrol station**, one **store**, and one **motel**, standing at the **junction** with the Kariba road that runs **west** for seventy-four kilometres (46 miles) to **Kariba**.

Continue along the **Chirundu road** another twenty-four kilometres (15 miles) — to the junction with the **gravel road** that runs seventy-five kilometres (47 miles) **north**, **north-west** to **Mana Pools National Park headquarters** — then another thirty-nine kilometres (24 miles) to **Chirundu**, where the swift-flowing **Zambezi River** funnels through a 370-metre-wide (1,221-foot) **gap**.

Until 1939, the only way you could cross the river was by pontoon. Before that, travellers made the perilous crossing across the raging waters by dugout canoe, which was first paddled a considerable distance upstream against the main current, then turned downstream and aimed with furious strokes at the distant landing stage.

Designed by Sir Ralph Freeman of Sydney and Birchenough Bridge fame, the 415-metre (1,370-foot) **bridge** that now spans the river was built just before the Second World War. It was funded by the Beit Trust and named after Alfred Beit's brother, Sir Otto Beit, whose widow, Lady Lilian, opened it on 24 May, 1939.

It remains the fastest land link between **Harare** and the Zambian capital of **Lusaka**, situated 125 kilometres (78 miles) beyond the **border**. There are **customs and immigration posts** at the bridge.

Mana Pools: Theatre of the Wild

Though it lies in unbearably hot tsetse fly-infested forest, riddled with a daunting array of tropical diseases including sleeping sickness, bilharzia, and malaria, Mana Pools National Park, seventy kilometres (44 miles) downstream from Chirundu, is considered by many to be the jewel in Zimbabwe's crown.

There the river, flowing slowly north towards Zambia for thousands of years, has left behind the remains of old river channels forming small seasonal ponds and pools spread over an area of several hundred square kilometres. These extend several kilometres back from the river where, on fertile terraces, huge mahogany and acacia trees cast luxuriant shade.

Today Mana Pools, one of Zimbabwe's four World Heritage Sites, is the stage for one of Africa's greatest natural spectacles — a classic theatre of the wild, attracting hordes of animals during the long, hot African summer, drawn by the abundance of water and the lush grazing along its banks.

The national park, lying between 400 and 900 metres (1,300–3,000 feet) above sea-level, is a timeless legacy of wilderness that may yet be the last vestiges of a unique ecosystem.

A hydroelectric dam planned for the Mupata Gorge would have created an 850-square-kilometre (330-square-mile) lake, destroying most of the flood plain, and halving the carrying capacity of Mana Pools — the ecological heart of this great natural treasury.

Other critical pressures remain. Poaching, especially of the Zambezi's unique fish populations, ivory, and rhino horn, is still endemic despite the dedication of the country's game wardens, rangers, and scouts: many have given their life in the war against poachers. Elephants, like humans, also destroy their environment and wreak great change in the forests and woodlands.

A plan to eradicate tsetse fly in the Mana Pools and Sapi wildlife areas, to satiate the incessant demand for land for human settlement, would also affect great areas on which the wildlife depends. And, finally, oil prospecting companies have been given large tracts for exploration.

All these factors pose an immense threat to the viability and survival of this marvellous and unique ecosystem. Reconciling the different interests may prove insurmountable, but few would count the cost of attempting to do so. Mana Pools deserves to survive unspoilt as it has throughout the centuries.

Many animals flourish under its benign protection: thousands of zebra, kudu, eland, impala, and other antelope species among which the lion and the leopard, the hyena and wild dog find easy pickings.

The sanctuary, one of only two pockets of nyala in the country, is also home to 16,000 buffalo and more than 12,000 elephant — Zimbabwe's largest concentration after Hwange. Many female elephants in the Mana Pools region do not have tusks and are much more aggressive than those with tusks.

Sadly, what was once Zimbabwe's finest population of black rhino has been badly hit by poachers crossing the river from Zambia. For years the desperate scenario has been one of shoot to kill — the wardens, the poachers; the poachers, the wildlife.

Along the river bank, where one of the greatest varieties of bird life in the world flourishes, hippos warm themselves in the morning sun. Later in the day, they keep cool by remaining all but submerged in the river, sharing their hidden sandbanks with silent and almost unseen crocodiles.

The great reptiles, survivors from the age of the dinosaurs, are seen most often during the winter months between May and August when, because of the cold weather, they bask more frequently to raise their body temperatures to their preferred 30°C (86°F).

Croc families live in harems, between eight and twelve females to one male. There are no sex chromosomes in crocodiles and to a great extent the temperature at which the eggs incubate governs the sex of the newborn. The ideal temperature for incubation is 31°C (88°F). The colder the nest, the more females the eggs produce. The warmer the nest, the more males.

Formidable predators that move with amazing suddenness, a full-grown creature can easily kill a full-grown Cape buffalo. Tenacious of life, crocodiles do not die swift-

Above: One of many seasonal ponds in Mana Pools National Park.

ly either. The heart of one continued to beat thirty minutes after it was cut from its body.

Distant mountains, the escarpment wall of the valley, and reed-edged backwaters and sandbanks all flank the slow-moving Zambezi. The great number and variety of its woodland and water birds — more than 380 species — is enough to draw the breath of any ornithologist. Its banks flutter with Goliath herons, Egyptian and spurwing geese, cormorants, storks, brilliantly coloured bee-eaters, and kingfishers.

Vultures, plovers, Nyasa lovebird, yellow-spotted nicator, white-collared pratincole, Livingstone's flycatcher, banded snake-eagle, and the clichéd symbol of Africa, the black and white fish eagle, haunt the riverine forest and mopane woods (See "Bird Life: An Ornithological Treasure House", Part Four).

In the river, tigerfish, bream, tilapia, vundu, nkupi, chessa, cornish Jack, and lung-fish sport and prey upon one another.

The richness of the forest trees and plants is the vital link in Mana Pools chain of continuity. The apple ring acacia keeps the elephant herds alive during the fierce October–November dry season.

High up on the trees, almost fourteen metres (45 feet) above the ground, you can see the browse line where the elephants, standing on their rear legs, have raised their trunks to pluck the protein-rich pods. The seeds are recycled through the creature's dung to renew their pledge of plenty the following year.

Most ubiquitous of all, however, is the odd-looking sausage tree with its pendulous fruit, weighing up to ten kilos (22 lbs). It can give quite a meaty blow when it falls on an unsuspecting head — as it often does.

Apart from causing headaches, the tree has a great many uses that promote health. Applied to the flesh, its crushed and pulped fruit has been found to relieve skin cancer and all over Africa it is an essential ingredient in herbal medicines concocted to treat a variety of ailments.

Animals such as baboon, rhino, and porcupine relish the fallen fruit and the beautiful, reddish-purple, trumpet-shaped flowers, pollinated by bats (almost one-third of Zimbabwe's 190 mammal species are bats), are a delicacy for many antelope and

194

Above: Zambezi canoe safari through Mana Pools National Park.
Overleaf: Waterbuck take flight across the shallows of the Zambezi River.

other animals. The wood is used to make the traditional dugout canoes of the local people (See "Flora: A Land of Flaming Colour", Part Four).

Mana Pools National Park covers 2,196 square kilometres (848 square miles). The adjoining Safari Areas cover a total of 4,570 square kilometres (1,764 square miles).

Getting there

Many visitors drive, and another popular way in and out of Mana Pools or Chikwenya is by forty-five minute charter flight from Kariba. There are airstrips at the park headquarters and Chikwenya.

From the Chirundu Road, it is some seventy-five kilometres (47 miles) along a good dirt road. There is a limit to the number of vehicles allowed into the park, so check with national parks' headquarters in Harare for availability and for road conditions as they often wash away. There are only a few dirt roads.

The winding dirt road from Mana Pools National Park Headquarters to Chikwenya runs twenty-five kilometres (15 miles) through dry river drifts and impenetrable mopane forest on clogging sand. For some of this distance the road traverses part of the safari area, adjacent to the park, where hunting is allowed.

When to go

Mana Pools is only open between April and October. The number of visitors is strictly controlled.

Where to stay

There is limited accommodation at the park headquarters and several campsites. There is a safari camp at Chikwenya, just outside the park boundaries at the confluence of the seasonal Sapi River and the Zambezi. See Listings. There are many first-class hotels at Kariba. See Listings for "Hotels". Kariba also has many caravan parks and campsites. See Listings.

Sightseeing

Even in the broiling heat of early October, days at **Chikwenya** are idyllic. The **safari camp** is a masterpiece of simplicity. The basic mud-wall, lime plastered **thatch huts**

Above: Zimbabwe's rare and endangered black rhinos.

are well spaced out on a **terraced glade** above the dry watercourse of the **Sapi River**, with shower and toilet open to the sky.

Camp fires blaze throughout the season — from the cold frosty nights of the May-June-July winter to the 35°C (95°F) evenings of late October and early November.

In the first weeks of April and May, when the park reopens after the six-month closure, the animals are shy and easily disturbed. By the end of the season, the animals are so used to people and vehicles that they stand unmoving. Returning giant elephant, given nicknames by the resident staff, roam frequently through the camp investigating breakfast tables and guests, cookhouse and storerooms, providing memorable photo sessions for the tourists.

During a game drive in the forest a leopard moves — in an all too brief flash of feline grace and sinew — from tree bole through an open gully into thick grass. The driver leaves the open vehicle and stalks through the grass, hoping to flush it out, as the tourists hold their breath in almost unbearable tension.

Nobody notices the frenzied bites of the tsetse flies until the next day, when swollen ankles and arms are given the relief of a dawn river cruise aboard **three fibreglass canoes** joined together and bridged with a high deck to create a unique **Zambezi stern-wheeler**.

The boat drifts on down the broad sweep of the **Zambezi**, five kilometres (three miles) wide, carried on the swift-flowing currents raging beneath the deceptively-still surface.

Chikwenya island, all two square kilometres (under a square mile) of it the haunt of elephant and buffalo, is soon left behind as the boat veers into an island-strewn **backwater** on the **northern side** of the river where a profusion of stilts, plovers, egrets, the lily-trotting jacana, herons, and waders stalk water gardens of hyacinth and weed.

Masses of buffalo, elephant, impala, and other antelope haunt the thornbrush and open glades of the **banks** against the smoky-grey **Zambian mountains**. During the season of the grass fires, the air is misty with smoke that limits visibility.

As the boat swings round an **island peninsula,** a startled grazing hippo takes off at a canter and plunges ten feet into the water with a resounding, thunderous smack

Above: Buffalo on the shores of the Zambezi River.

— a live, two-ton submersible in a startling high dive demonstration.

Other hippos raise their heads and yawn, revealing their frightening incisors. The yawn is not an intake of breath, but an aggressive warning.

In this enchanted valley the season of drought is no more. Held back behind the wall of the Kariba Dam, the Zambezi flows strong year-round, undercutting **miniature cliffs** of sand that occasionally crumble and avalanche into the water. Elsewhere, the honeycomb nests of the gregarious bee-eaters aerate the fragile cliffs, prelude to another cycle of erosion.

Their food chains secure and abundant, all life continues to prosper in this paradise where scores of aquatic plants of overwhelming beauty — water primroses and yellow water peas among them — drift along many secret backwaters.

As you turn for home, the delicate pastel lavender of the morning glory water plant glows luminously in the weak and watery sun, yet another in an endless sequence of images that will never fade from the memory.

Above: Kariba woodcarver shapes image of Nyaminyami, the river god.

Lake Kariba: The Jade Sea

Though awesome to all those who behold it close up, the Kariba Dam seems all too puny for the task of containing the world's second-largest man-made inland sea.

Indeed, when you stand on the slender crest of the dam, the mind struggles to comprehend what it has achieved — an irrevocable change not just in the shape and character of the Zambezi Valley, but of the Zimbabwe nation.

It was at Kariba, no higher than 366 metres (1,200 feet) above sea-level, that the Zambezi suddenly funnelled into the narrow neck of a 100-metre-wide (330-foot) gorge, carving its way through a large granite block leaving the top to form a natural bridge. The arch looked like a large traditional fish trap and the river people called it *kariwa*, the Shona word for the stone snare they use to catch birds and mice.

The first known, written mention of the gorge is in a despatch of 11 December, 1667, from the Portuguese explorer Manuel Baretto. Almost 200 years later, on 20 October, 1860, David Livingstone and his brother shot the rapids. One century later, on 17 May, 1960, Britain's Queen Elizabeth, the Queen Mother, switched on Kariba's generators.

In a note to Lord Russell, Livingstone described his hair-raising three-hour ride. "The wind rose and entered the gorge with great force, waves half filled my canoe and swamped Charley's, but being near shore, nothing was lost."

In 1877, after trekking along the Zambezi's north bank from Victoria Falls, Frederick Selous visited the gorge on another of his hunting expeditions. In 1892, William Keppel Stier surveyed the gorge as part of a study for a proposed railway along the Zambezi Valley to link the river's navigable stretches.

Nothing came of the idea, but twenty years later, H. S. Kergwin, a government officer, suggested that it was an ideal place to dam the river for irrigation. The idea was eventually consigned to limbo, only to be revived in 1941 when J. L. S. Jeffares made another survey, this time to determine the feasibility of a hydroelectric scheme.

The prospects appeared excellent, but it took another thirteen years to hammer out the details. Finally, in 1954, the civil engineering firm of Richard Costain was awarded the contract to build a town for 10,000 engineers and construction workers. Impresit, an Italian consortium, then set about building the dam.

When the work began elders of the Tonga tribe, who lived on the shores around the gorge, petitioned the construction company to abandon the project. They said it would anger *Nyaminyami*, their river god, who would take revenge.

According to their tribal lore, *Nyaminyami* is the direct descendant of the Tonga soothsayers and witch doctors who communicate with him telepathically and perform many miraculous cures. The Tonga believe that *Nyaminyami* is a benevolent spirit, the guardian of the river and all that it bestows life upon.

In 1958, when the river level rose more than thirty metres (100 feet), and over thirteen million litres (3.5 million gallons) a second raced through the gorge — washing away bridges and damaging the coffer dam — the elders claimed it was the vengeance of *Nyaminyami*.

On 20 February that year, when the flood was at its height, seventeen men — fourteen Africans and three Italians — were swept away by a wall of cement. Their bodies are still entombed within the tapering 128-metre-high (420-foot) dam wall that measures twenty-six metres (85 feet) at its base and thirteen metres (43 feet) at its crest.

Dry season conditions were equally appalling. When temperatures reached more than 50°C (122°F), workers had to keep their tools in buckets of water so that they could be handled.

Altogether, more than seventy people (the first an Italian, Pietro Giovanna, on 7 October, 1956, and the last an African named Felikisi, on 15 December, 1961) died during the five years it took to complete the dam.

Six flood gates are contained within the wall that stretches more than half a kilometre across the gorge and contains more

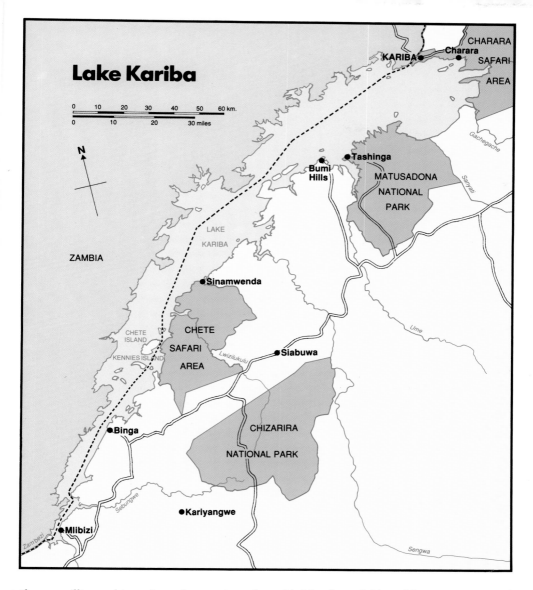

Lake Kariba

0 10 20 30 40 50 60 km.
0 10 20 30 miles

N

CHARARA

KARIBA Charara CHARARA
SAFARI
AREA

Tashinga

Bumi
Hills

MATUSADONA

NATIONAL

PARK

LAKE
KARIBA

ZAMBIA

Sinamwenda

CHETE
ISLAND

CHETE

SAFARI

KENNIES ISLAND

AREA

Siabuwa

Lwizilukulu

CHIZARIRA

NATIONAL PARK

Binga

Kariyangwe

Mlibizi

Zambezi

Sebungwe

Sengwa

Gachegache

Sanyati

Ume

than a million cubic metres of concrete and 11,000 tonnes of steel.

Lake Kariba itself was born on December 3, 1958, when the diversion tunnel and temporary openings in the dam wall were closed. It was not until another five years, in September 1963, that the lake assumed its present dimensions.

Covering more than 5,000 square kilometres (1,930 square miles), the lake is 281 kilometres (174 miles) long and at its widest point more than forty kilometres (25 miles) across. Its jade-coloured waters are studded

with islands and fringed by mountains and forests.

As its waters rose during the five years it took Lake Kariba to form, "Operation Noah" — one of the most dramatic animal rescue stories in history — evolved. The slowly rising waters trapped many animals on rapidly disappearing islands. Led by game warden Robert Fothergill, game rangers kept vigil, organizing a mercy mission that stirred the world's imagination.

By the time that "Operation Noah" ended, the team had ferried 5,000 creatures to safety.

The operation involved the capture of antelope and smaller creatures like the endearing bushbaby — as well as literally steering larger animals like elephant and rhino to game sanctuaries along the southern shores.

Lake Kariba wrought astonishing economic, as well as physical change. Before its formation the Zambezi Valley was an infertile furnace, almost physically uninhabitable. Now it has become a playground for watersports enthusiasts, its shores and islands teeming with countless animals and birds.

Lake Kariba's waters support more than forty different varieties of fish, including a sardine species endemic to Lake Tanganyika and Lake Victoria that has formed the basis of a major fishing industry. And of course, the generators it drives are vital to Zimbabwe's national growth.

The dusty, rowdy construction camp that developed on the seven hills around the southern side of the Kariba Gorge (and subsequently the shores of the lake) has become one of Africa's smartest holiday resorts.

More than just a sunny, idyllic getaway, Kariba offers the supreme beauty of its surrounding landscapes, magnificent watersports — including some of the most exciting fishing in the world, water-skiing, sailing, and scuba diving — and a wildlife spectacle that has few, if any, equals. When you weary of the outdoor life, experience the area's sophisticated hotels, casinos, and restaurants.

The greatest transformation that Lake Kariba has wrought upon the Zambezi Valley is in the new and distinct ecosystems it has created. The harsh, broken country of the rugged surrounding hills, combined with infertile soils and poor rainfall, attract browsers.

The lush shoreline vegetation, a mixture of aquatic and land grasses, supports a profusion of life. Extensive pastures of nutritious grass between the high- and low-water levels have led to dramatic increases in elephants, buffalo, rhino, and smaller animals.

The drowned forests of the permanent shallows with their mats of Kariba weed, *Salvinia molesta*, encourage a proliferation of insects that attract many birds — and allow hippo and crocodile to increase without inhibition.

Out in the main lake, the depths teem with huge shoals of bream and predatory tigerfish. Kapenta, the tiny, protein-rich sardines that were introduced in the late 1960s, yield around 12,000 tonnes a year. The species has also become a vital link in the food chain of the tigerfish.

Feeding deep down on Kariba's endemic plankton during the day, the kapenta schools are lured to the surface at night by lights — one above the surface, and one beneath — hanging from the fleets of curiously-shaped fishing rigs. The rigs are basically a steel deck welded onto two enormous pontoons. The net is lowered overboard by winches to a considerable depth.

When these tiny fish are alarmed, they sound and dive back down to the depths. The lights draw them in large schools and, when enough fish are concentrated above the net, the alarm is triggered by suddenly dousing the lights. The fish swim down into the net in millions as it is quickly winched to the surface.

Conditions for the three-man crews are harsh, but the rewards are comparatively high. At night, the darkness out on the lake is alive with thousands of bobbing, twinkling lights.

Before Kariba was formed, 1,000 square kilometres (386 square miles) of land were cleared of trees to aid future trawling operations. It was thought that they would be useless and could also damage this new artificially-created ecosystem. In fact, what no ecologist could have known was just how important the drowned trees would become.

Research by the national parks' Fisheries Research Institute at Kariba, which monitors fish populations, has shown that the flooded trees, which constitute an area twice as large as the bottom surface and play a major role in Lake Kariba's productivity, support dozens of invertebrate species and algae.

Opposite: Cruising yacht heels to the wind on sparkling Lake Kariba.

Previous pages: Luxury pleasure craft moored at Caribbea Bay Marina, Kariba town.

Below: Poinsettia flowers.

Above: Little bee-eater.

These essential links in the food chain sustain Kariba's impressively high fish populations and also many water bird species. Lake birds include egrets, kingfishers, bee-eaters, black-collared barbets, fish eagles, and herons such as the Goliath.

Eventually, of course, the trees will disap-

pear and Kariba will undergo another major change of character, but not for a long time. Although they have been weakened by woodborers at water level, and broken down by the lake's sometimes fierce and unpredictable storms, the trees rot remarkably slowly. Thirty years after they were immersed by waters thirty metres (100 feet) deep, the bark on some is still supple. Many trees have become fossilised after absorbing various minerals from the water.

As the trees continued to decompose beneath the surface, the fairly constant lake levels of the 1980s encouraged new growth and the spread of large and important trees — Natal mahogany, tamarind, and acacias in particular — along the shoreline.

Though a freshwater lake, Kariba has the same volatile nature as the sea. Its unpredictable waters can be extremely dangerous. Often glassy calm, in minutes sudden storms spring up and gale force winds drive waves as high as four metres (14 feet). Waterspouts rising to ninety metres (300 feet) create another perilous hazard.

Kariba undergoes constant change. Waves continue to pound away earth cliffs on some shores and islands, but in other areas they throw up sandy beaches.

When the lake was first formed, the swamped vegetation swiftly raised the water's nutrient levels, causing such a sudden and unpredicted increase in the growth of *salvinia* that it threatened to engulf the entire lake.

At one time the weed covered fifteen per cent of the surface, but fears of a major ecological disaster proved groundless. As the vegetation rotted away, the nutrient levels fell and the grotesque floating carpets of weed shrank. They now cover less than two per cent of the water.

In fact, what remains serves as a catalyst for the spread of the nutritious torpedo grass that provides valuable grazing for fish when submerged and for ungulates when exposed.

Taking root on the little mats of floating *salvinia*, the grass spreads across the lake. The *salvinia* is an ideal seedbed that helps the grass to establish itself on the shoreline between the low- and high-water mark. Now as the lake rises and falls, the exposed

Above: Kapenta fishing rig on Lake Kariba.

pastures sustain enormous numbers of herbivores.

The new ecosystems have proved to be benign and protective, creating an enormous wildlife sanctuary the entire length of Kariba's southern shores, interspersed by protected safari areas where licensed hunting is allowed.

Beyond Kariba, on the islands and in the wilderness that surrounds the town, permanent safari camps and lake-shore resorts provide seclusion with first-class accommodation. They also offer game-viewing, fishing, and photographic excursions. Experienced operators offer a range of craft for charter, from fishing boats to fast cruisers to sail boats, all under qualified supervision.

With or without a boat, you can experience some of the finest freshwater fishing on Lake Kariba. The ultimate prize is the beautifully marked, fighting tigerfish found throughout the lake, though the best specimens have been taken in the area around Sanyati Gorge, the venue for an annual international tiger fishing tournament.

Tigerfish, one of the world's fiercest game fish, is not the only quarry for the angler; bream, chessa, nkupi, and the giant vundu also provide excellent sport.

Excellent accommodation is provided in the Matusadona National Park in the form of luxury lodges and well-equipped camping sites.

Getting there

Kariba, 366 kilometres (277 miles) from Harare, 1,244 kilometres (773 miles) from Victoria Falls (by road), and 806 kilometres (500 miles) from Bulawayo, is served by road and air. Air Zimbabwe operates a daily "bus" service from Harare, Hwange, and Victoria Falls. The Kariba ferry, *Sealion*, provides a twenty-two-hour service for both passengers and their vehicles up or down the length of the lake. Meals or overnight accommodation are provided aboard. Charter planes and boats operate between Kariba and lodges on its islands and shores. See Listings.

When to go

Kariba and the lake are open year-round, but the summer heat from late November until February can be unbearable. Winter months are crisp and sharp, so the best time is late

Above: Game drive on Fothergill Island.

April to May and September to early October.

Where to stay

The Cutty Sark Hotel (2-star), Caribbea Bay (with casino) (3-star), Lake View Inn (2-star), Kariba Breezes Holiday Resort, Zambezi Valley Hotel, Most High Hotel. There are others. See Listings for "Hotels".

There are many caravan parks and camp-sites and a national parks' caravan park and campsite at Nyanyana, near Kariba Crocodile Farm. See Listings.

On Lake Kariba, Spurwing Island safari camp, Fothergill Island safari camp. See Listings.

Sightseeing

The road from **Makuti** descends the first leg of the seventy-four kilometres (46 miles) to **Kariba** through the hills that form the **Charara Safari Area**.

The **sign** announcing that the visitor is now in a **nature reserve**, warning that it is dangerous to leave the car, is immediately justified. Two kilometres (just over a mile) out of Makuti, tuskers browse along the verge of the road.

Three kilometres (two miles) later a pride of lion enjoy the warmth of the **asphalt**.

Grudgingly they stir themselves and lope lazily off into the underbrush. The flash of a leopard's eyes in a tree beyond this point leaves no doubt that you have entered the wilderness.

Descending though the wild and arid countryside, the humidity rises up to meet you until, finally, you swoop into town past the airport.

The most up-market residential area in Kariba is on the Heights, where the smart, former executive residences of the construction company straddle the peaks and slopes of the hills.

The **summit** — at the end of a spectacular **hairpin road** — offers tremendous panoramas over the **lake**, **dam wall**, and **downstream gorge**. Baboons crowd the forests and frequently cross the road. Throughout the seasons the hills are aflame with jacaranda.

On the summit, close to the neat little **shopping centre** with its **supermarket** and **evangelistic hotel**, stands the **Church of St. Barbara**, built to honour those who died building the dam.

Above: Elephants and young at Matusadona National Park.

The unique design — in the shape of a coffer — means there are no exterior walls, only **archways** that serve as **entrances**. Inside, the names of those who died are inscribed on **commemorative plaques**.

Seen from the **The Peak** on the other side of the summit, the **dam** itself also stands as tribute to these brave men. At first sight it is hard to comprehend. By comparison with the lake behind it, the elegantly curved wall of the dam seems far too slender to have been the catalyst for such a large inland sea.

Three decades of polishing have almost erased the inscription on the **brass plaque** unveiled by Queen Elizabeth, the Queen Mother, but the sun beating off it reflects the gleaming pride of the achievement that she honoured. Standing on the **roadway** that crosses the dam into **Zambia**, you feel the structure tremble from the power of the giant turbines buried deep inside the **wall** of the **gorge**.

On the **lake surface**, more than twenty-four metres (80 feet) below the top of the dam, weed collects in the **barriers** that sieve the 107-metre-deep (350-foot) waters.

Andora, over on the **south side** of the gorge, is Kariba's busiest **harbour**. Large houseboats, majestic yachts, and kapenta fishing rigs berth there. The Kariba car ferry, *Sealion*, discharges its passengers and cars at the end of its twenty-two hour voyage down the length of the lake.

In 1990, the cost of chartering a floating pleasure palace with a maximum of twelve passengers was around Z$800 a week. Charter and commercial craft are governed by strict regulations. After one vessel sank with loss of life, more than sixty vessels were deregistered. Lake police, in sleek power launches, maintain regular patrols.

From Andora, **marinas** and **hotel resorts** stretch along the **coves** and **inlets** of the lake shore, including the sublimely graceful architecture of the exotic Spanish-style **Caribbea Bay Hotel**, managed by Zimbabwe Sun.

Located outside the township, **Kariba Crocodile Farm** breeds crocodiles for commercial and restocking purposes. The farm and a **curio shop** selling an assortment of crocodile skin products are open to the public.

Matusadona National Park: Wildlife Beyond Compare

Matusadona National Park, where elephant, buffalo, impala, kudu, and waterbuck roam its 1,370 square kilometres (529 square miles), is the real showpiece of this unparalleled wilderness region, perhaps because only one-third of the park is easily accessible to vehicles and then only for six months to a limited number of visitors.

Formed out of the gaunt plateaux above the lake on the Zambezi Escarpment, and the undulating hillocks of the lake shore, it is virtually inaccessible by road. The park's southern boundary is studded with many hidden bays, coves, inlets, and backwaters.

The Ume River forms the western boundary and the flooded Sanyati Gorge, carved by the Sanyati River, the eastern boundary. Waterfalls plunge almost soundlessly 610 metres (2,000 feet) down the gorge's granite cliffs, where only the sound of the fish eagle and the baboon break the silence.

Matusadona is home to at least 400 black rhino, more than a thousand elephant, several thousand buffalo, sable and roan antelope, greater kudu, bushbuck, eland, waterbuck, hippopotamus, hyena, leopard, impala, lion, and many crocodile. Its birds include the fish eagle, African darter, heron, cormorant, stork, plover, lily trotter, and many woodland species.

The shores in the park border Lake Kariba's eastern basin. The basin forms the largest area of open water on the lake and it is the most developed part. For fishermen many rivers offer fine sport, and for the holiday-maker there is the magnetic lure of the basin's many islands and the Sanyati Gorge.

Getting there

By air or boat charter from Kariba. The flight takes fifteen minutes.

Above: Tourists game-viewing from close range on the surface of Lake Kariba.

Opposite top: Buffalo graze on Lake Kariba's shore.

Opposite: Majestic greater kudu at Bumi Hills.

Overleaf: Sports fishermen in search of tigerfish drift in the shallows of Lake Kariba's drowned forest.

Above: Caribbea Bay Resort on the shores of Lake Kariba.

When to go

The park is open all year-round.

Where to stay

Bumi Hills Safari Lodge (3-star); Tiger Bay, a fishing resort.

Sightseeing

Whether you travel by boat or air, either is an ideal way to acquaint yourself with the **lake**. From a height of 150 metres (500 feet) you look down on **one island** after **another**, small and large, some simply sand and scrub where the former water lines are clearly marked.

Extensive **forests** of **drowned trees** — stand in the **shallows** that stretch away from their **shores**.

The plane flies over the **resort islands** of **Spurwing** and **Fothergill**, and the **Tiger Bay fishing camp** on the Ume River. At Spurwing's **chalets** you wake to memorable vistas of the **Matusadona Mountains** and **Sanyati Gorge** across the water.

The experience is much the same at Fothergill — which also operates Chikwenya

camp — except that guests sleep in African-style **thatched chalets**. In 1990, Fothergill was no longer an island. Because of falling lake levels it was once again an extension of the mainland to which it used to belong.

Tiger Bay fishing camp speaks for itself. The ultimate prize is the ferocious and lively tigerfish — the best specimens are found in Sanyati Gorge.

By contrast, from the minute the rocky **landing strip** lying between two **granite hills** hoves into view, you are left with no doubt that **Bumi Hills Safari Lodge**, just outside the park on the hills above the **south-western banks** of the **Ume River**, is all about wildlife.

Usually there's an impressive collection of elephant, buffalo, or other animals that have to be chased away by lodge staff before the plane can land. Once the landing is performed, those in search of wildlife should need no more convincing that they have come to the right place.

Those with any doubts remaining need only take a five-minute game drive with one of the lodge's resident rangers. Elephant come close enough to the open vehicle for the brave or foolhardy to lay their hand upon them.

Greater kudu, sporting what are perhaps the most magnificent horns in the animal kingdom, stand motionless in the thicket. Only male kudu carry horns and their majestic lyrate proportions proclaim both beauty and masculinity. Wart hog, tails erect, trot briskly away and buffalo cover the grassy river banks and the forest thickets in thousands.

At sundown, Daniel, a Zimbabwean ecologist, parks the vehicle and offers beers or soft drinks as the sky is burnished red beyond a herd of 200 buffalo at the **water's edge**.

Next day you drift on the gentle Kariba swell in a **powerboat** no more than three metres from two young bull elephants who for the last three hours have been frolicking in mock combat a kilometre **offshore**. Ivory clacking and clicking as they wrestle, the two frequently submerge before bobbing up. Nowhere else in the world can you watch this behaviour at such close quarters.

Older animals of the herd migrate regularly between the mainland and the islands, some preferring a solitary life on their own desert strip to the vagaries of mainstream "city" life.

When elephants swim they move slowly in a running movement, the herd in single file, against each other's rumps or holding the tail of the animal in front. Underwater, they have an uncanny sense of direction.

It has been recorded that two elephants once travelled forty kilometres (25 miles) across the lake from Zimbabwe to Zambia, virtually submerged all the way with their trunks serving as snorkels, on a swim that lasted twenty-three hours.

As you make your way back to your **room** later that evening, after nightcaps in the lodge's **garden bar**, the shadowy tree standing by the **path** turns out to be a full grown tusker. The golden rule says "don't move". Overruling instinct sends you sprinting down the nearest staircase. At Bumi Hills, man remains ever the intruder.

The lodge is also the base for perhaps the most unforgettable experience of any in Zimbabwe — tranquil nights under the stars at **Water Wilderness**.

First thing in the morning, the fibreglass

boat leaves the **harbour**, pitching and tossing as it corkscrews through a wild sea beneath racing clouds. Bow thrusting into the breakers, under half power, the vessel makes its way out into the lake before the helmsman adroitly judges the pitch of the waves and turns beam on to race for the shelter of the **Matusadona shoreline**.

Soon the sea slackens and the boat cruises between **drowned trees** and **marker buoys** to the "**mother ship**", moored in a deep lagoon. Around it, tethered to the stumps of drowned trees, each floating on its own steel pontoons, are four comfortable, self-contained rooms.

From these, you literally paddle your own canoe to meals, and on game voyages. As you drift only two metres (six–seven feet) offshore, five bull elephants stand in the shallows, plucking out clumps of torpedo grass and clearing away the mud from the roots with a rhythmic swish-swish of their trunks.

In the hours of tranquillity there are always adrenalin-charged experiences — be it the snout of a crocodile nosing by your canoe at night or the sudden emergence of a hippo coming up for air as you drift through a moonspun silver thread on the still water of the lagoon.

Next morning, at dawn, you follow the guide, Indian file, in your fibreglass canoe and beach it on the shore of a hidden **backwater** for another session of tranquillity and adrenalin in equal measure.

Gun in hand, he leads the party inland over a rise, through scrub and stunted **woodland**, pausing to point out the **spoor** of a recent leopard, the **tunnel trap** of the driver ant, and skirt two lone but ferocious buffalo.

Though they are more than 100 metres (330 yards) distant, two guests choose to head for a **hide** perched in a tree to await the party's return. The bark of the baboon pack startles them. The leopard is still around. And the adrenalin pumps through their veins like a Zambezi flood.

Late that afternoon, the sun burns its haunting vermilion insignia into Lake Kariba — a flaming arrow that sears the forest of drowned trees and turns the water a molten crimson.

Above: An undisturbed Eden — the shores of Lake Kariba beneath Bumi Hills.
Previous pages: 128-metre-high Kariba Dam contains more than a million cubic metres of concrete.

Westward Ho!

There is much to do, see, and enjoy all along Lake Kariba and its shores. Many **fishing camps** and little **harbours**, hidden away from the eyes of the outside world, offer untrammelled outdoor joys.

Chalala, a tiny kapenta **fishing village** nestled among the hills of the **Sibilobilo Lagoon south-west** of Bumi, is populated by the local fishermen and their families.

From their pretty little **harbour** set against a background of thatched houses, verdant lawns, and sere brown hillsides and savannah, the boats sail out each night into the often stormy waters of the **Sengwa Basin**.

Offshore, **twelve islands** — the crests of a submerged range whose wildlife was cut off from the mainland — form the twenty-two square kilometres (eight square miles) of **Sibilobilo Safari Area**, where hunting is occasionally allowed. The islands boast impressive populations of buffalo, impala, sable antelope, zebra, and greater kudu.

The Sengwa Basin, which lies **westward** of these islands, is notorious for its unpredictable waters. Often mirror calm, the surface can turn in seconds into churning, mountainous seas that can easily swamp a small boat. The delta of the **Sengwa River**, which feeds into the stormy basin, is marked by a **safari camp**, kapenta fishing operation, and **crocodile farm**.

South-west of the river, the **Sengwa Institute of Wildlife Research**, established in 1970 by the University of Zimbabwe, overlooks the **point** where the lake narrows. The institute has developed sophisticated radio-tracking systems to monitor the movements of large animals like elephant and rhino, and research studies of wart hog, elephant, impala, tsetse fly, bats, small mammals, lion, buffalo, and kudu have been undertaken.

The Institute marks the **boundaries** of the 1,080-square-kilometre (416-square-mile) **Chete Safari Area**, set aside in 1963. There licensed hunters stalk a wide spectrum of animals characteristic of the Zambezi Valley, including elephant, buffalo, leopard, black rhinoceros, eland, sable antelope, greater kudu, bushbuck, duiker, impala, wart hog,

Above: Pleasure craft cruises the blue waters of Lake Kariba.

and baboon. Bird species include fish eagle and marabou stork.

The **Lwizikululu River** bisects the safari area and at its mouth there is an intriguing and tiny **island** in the centre of a wide, circular **lagoon**. If you want to camp, the abandoned **safari camp** on the island makes an ideal spot, but you need permission from the Chete game ranger to land there.

With its rich and varied trees of Natal mahogany, wild fig, marula, mopane, and baobab, the lake shoreline takes on an especial beauty. It is inadvisable to step ashore, however, for the plentiful wild animals and the risk of being accidentally shot by a hunting party could bring a premature end to your holiday.

Where the lake narrows by **Chete Gorge** lies **Chete Island**, the largest island on the lake, renowned for its many elephant. Rarely will anybody sail by without sighting at least one herd.

Above the gorge stands the Chete game ranger **headquarters** and **safari camp**. Beyond the gorge, another wide **basin** is studded with many fascinating islands where large crocodiles can be seen lying motion-less in the water. During the breeding season, they come ashore to bury their eggs in the many sandy **beaches** of this region.

The **mouth** of the **Sengwe**, thought by many to be the most beautiful of the rivers that feed into the lake, lies **south** of this basin and marks the border between the Chete hunting area and a **forestry reserve** where hunting safaris also operate.

In the **hills** of the **eastern escarpment**, above the lake and beyond the safari area, the well-wooded, broken country of remote **Chizarira National Park** makes game viewing difficult. The park, which has a range of wildlife including elephant, black rhinoceros, lion, leopard, cheetah, roan, and tsessebe, is dominated in the **north-east** by 1,371-metre-high (4,500-foot) **Mount Tundazi**.

As an "island" of rivers, perennial springs, and natural springs, the Chizarira, in fact, has extended the westerly range of several bird species including the rarely-seen Taita falcon (present in some gorges), crowned eagle, fish eagle, brown hooded kingfisher, red-billed woodhoopoe, golden-tailed woodpecker, and Meyer's parrot.

But few visit the remote park. Written

permission is needed to enter it and the park can only be reached by four-wheel drive vehicle. It lies fifty kilometres (30 miles) **east** of **Binga**, a small **village** and **harbour** at the **western** end of the lake.

Hunting rights in the neighbouring **Chirisa Safari Area**, dominated by the valley that has been cut over the aeons by the large but seasonal stream that drains **northwards** into Lake Kariba, are leased by a safari hunting company.

The wide range of animals on hand, including almost 10,000 elephant, wart hog, buffalo, impala, black rhinoceros, leopard, lion, cheetah, wild dog, bushpig, zebra, and various antelope species, makes Chirisa a hunter's paradise.

The **lake basin** that leads to Binga is marked by an unusual **forest** of trees that came crashing down in one of the frequent landslides that occur along the lake shores. The trees, however, took root again at once.

Binga, sprawled across a range of **low hills**, has a splendid **rest camp** and a shady **caravan park** and **campsite**. There is also a **harbour, restaurant, pub, supermarket, petrol station, post office, government offices**, and **lake safety station. Holiday houses** along the lakeshore can be rented, and there is also a flourishing **crocodile farm** and a successful kapenta fishing operation.

Ironically, although it is set on the shores of the largest hydroelectric scheme in southern Africa, Binga still uses kerosine lamps and candles for light.

Binga marks the last leg of the boat safari along the lake as the forested, rolling hills disappear from view and the sheer rock walls of the Zambezi Gorge, where monkeys, dassies, and klipspringer scamper about, close in. Strega and wild hibiscus flower freely and an occasional hardy pawpaw tree struggles to keep a roothold in the steep **cliffs**.

Riven by many lovely little **bays** and secret **inlets**, the Zambezi Gorge offers holiday sailors some fine **moorings**. From these, they can go exploring ashore during the day and spend the evening listening to the lake lapping against their boat to the lullaby of chirping cicada, croaking frogs, and the sound of fish breaking water.

Soon the gorge ends abruptly, and the grassy shoreline that spreads out into the flat distance is marked by the thatch of an occasional **fishing camp**.

South-west of the extensive mouth of the **Sebungwe River**, the remarkable **Sebungwe Narrows** begin, and no more than 200 metres (600 feet) separate the Zimbabwean and Zambian shores. Leaving the narrows, you sail into the **Mlibizi Basin** very near to the end of your voyage of discovery. The charming **harbour** at **Mlibizi**, on the **south-western shore** of the basin, has given life to a **rest camp** with **chalets, campsite, shop** and **bottle store, restaurant**, and **two swimming pools**. You can hire boats and rafts for fishing.

The harbour marks the end of Lake Kariba and is also the **western terminus** for the Kariba Ferries, *Sealion*, which makes regular return trips up and down the lake. Kariba Yachts also make occasional cruises to Mlibizi.

Above: Grey duiker.

The River People

The lake has had profound effects on the communities that have made their home in the Zambezi Valley for centuries, particularly the Tonga people.

Forced to resettle many kilometres inland, the Tonga were expected to adapt their lifestyle from a fishing culture to that of agriculturist, on a stretch of land as mean as any in the world.

On the sixty-kilometre journey inland from lakeshore Bumi Hills, skirting the borders of Matusadona National Park, the stony leached soil of the Tonga reflects back the hammer-heavy heat in shimmering waves.

The baked earth and tsetse fly thicket is cruel and unrelenting, and the traditional mud and thatch rondavel homesteads sit amid fields of choking dust. It's a harsh existence, yet the people are cheerful and welcoming, anxious to please with the gift of a smile and a precious mug of water that they have had to carry perhaps eight or ten kilometres (five–six miles).

Although boreholes, dams, clinics, schools, administrative offices, and about 1,600 kilometres (1,000 miles) of roads were built to serve the new area in the Zimbabwe hinterland, the move was traumatic. Before the lake was formed, their traditions and lifestyles had changed little throughout the centuries.

The Tonga people eke out a mean existence from the arid, infertile soils bordering the Matusadona National Park. But the Tonga are hungry for progress. Within a few years they established more than sixty schools.

Nonetheless, much of their lifestyle remains untouched. The *nganga* (witch doctor) plays a major role. But no chauvinism affects the pipe-smoking women of the matrilineal Tonga, whose children adopt the maternal totem and whose sons inherit from the maternal uncle.

Tonga women love adornment. They pierce their ears and insert thorns, which are subsequently replaced by sticks of steadily increasing size to enlarge the hole.

During their initiation ceremonies, it is traditional to remove the six upper front teeth. Although men now spurn this ceremony, Tonga women still follow the practice. As soon as the second teeth have settled, girls are taken by their mother to the tribal "dentist" who uses two axes to remove the teeth — one levered between them, the other to hammer them out. Hot porridge is served to ease the pain.

Tonga women also pierce holes in both lips which they enlarge by placing wooden plugs in them. Another custom is for children around the age of ten to pierce holes in their noses — girls use a mimosa thorn, boys a porcupine quill.

The solid wooden doors of Tonga homesteads are inscribed with delicate carving. When someone dies they are buried close to the front door with all their personal possessions, and the family then awaits the return, in a year or two, of the spirit. To expedite the return, goats and chickens are sacrificed, beer is brewed, and the mourners dance on the grave — not with joy but to compact the earth — accompanied by singing.

Above: Young Tonga mother carries home a harvest of bananas.

PART THREE: THE CITIES

Above: Sundown's golden salute to the Harare Sheraton Hotel and International Conference Centre.
Opposite: Harare city centre from the air.

Harare: The Garden Capital

Founded in 1890, the Zimbabwean capital of Harare has developed into a modern and attractive city, with wide streets, avenues of flowering trees, leafy parks, verdant sports fields, and modern shops and hotels.

Its elegant high-rise buildings add yet another splendour to a city that could arguably claim to be, if not the most beautiful, one of the world's most pleasant capitals.

Lying 1,500 metres (4,875 feet) above sea-level, the city's climate is pleasant and temperate. The rainy season occurs between November and March, but there is sunshine throughout most of the year. The coolest months are June and July; October is the hottest.

Entertainment is provided by the many theatres, cinemas, and nightclubs, and the city features a comprehensive selection of restaurants. In addition to the varied sights of Harare, several tour operators offer excursions to the surrounding districts.

Harare's 1990 population of 850,000 was about seventy-five per cent African and twenty-two per cent European, with the remaining three per cent Coloured (mixed race) and Asian.

The city's centennial was celebrated on 12 September, 1990 — 100 years to the day after the BSAC's 500-strong mercenary expedition, the Pioneer Column, arrived at the end of their 600-kilometre (372-mile), three-month trek from Fort Tuli, located on the Botswana-Zimbabwe border.

Raising the British flag the next day in what is now African Unity Square, the Pioneer Column Commander, Colonel Edward Pennefather, named the new settlement Fort Salisbury in honour of the incumbent British Prime Minister, the third Marquis of Salisbury.

The site originally chosen for the new fort was near Mount Hampden, but when Pennefather surveyed the locality, however, he found that the land around a small granite outcrop rising from the plain, today known as the Kopje, was more suited to the expedition's needs.

The nearby Mukuvisi River would provide abundant water for the new town that was soon to rise up on the open, fertile plain that stretched from the foot of the Kopje to the edge of the horizon. Such level land, with its granite bedrock, was ideal for the future city Pennefather envisaged.

The township at first grew as a series of huts and simple buildings near the foot of the Kopje, but in 1891 it was decided that because the land there was too marshy, the main centre should be moved to the Causeway, the area where the Government buildings now stand. These two parts of town merged some years later to form the central portion of the rapidly expanding township.

Pennefather's faith was not misplaced. From the top of the Kopje, with its landscaped garden and plaques commemorating the city's history, the visitor can enjoy a panoramic view of Harare today, a reality that more than honours the century-old dream of the Pioneer Column.

Laid out across 540 square kilometres (208 square miles), with many islands of green — sports grounds, parks, and recreation areas — the capital's streets, lined with avenues of jacaranda and flame trees, are as broad and elegant as those of Bulawayo.

Contributing their own colour and diversity to the floral scene are the National Botanic Gardens, just four kilometres (two and a half miles) from the city centre, and Harare Gardens, located within the city centre itself.

The admirable year-round climate makes sport an important part of city life. Horse-racing and trotting take place at Harare's superb tracks, while in their seasons, soccer, rugby, cricket, tennis, flying, gliding, and many other recreations can be enjoyed. There are also more than a dozen challenging golf courses.

At the international-standard Donnybrook Track on the city's outskirts, motor-racing, from Formula 1 Grand Prix to motorcycles (including motocross scrambling), are held regularly throughout the year.

Sailing, water-skiing, and other watersports take place on Lake Chivero (formerly McIlwaine), only thirty-five kilometres

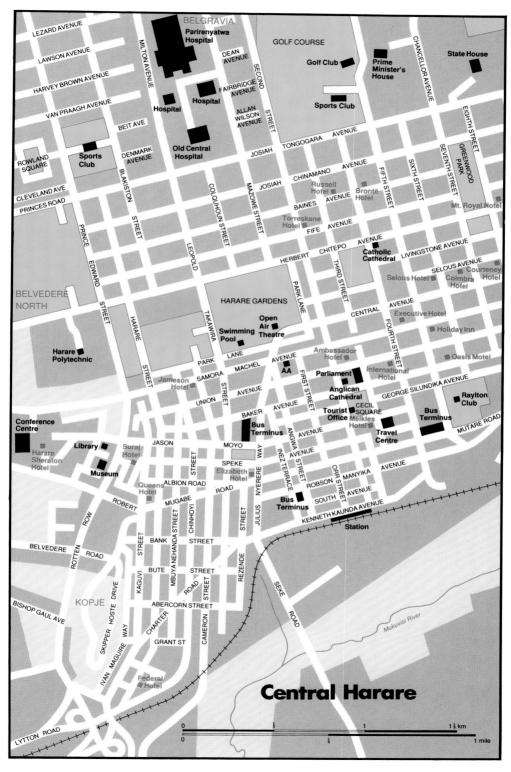

Central Harare

Above: Samora Michel Avenue at the heart of downtown Harare.
Opposite: Mountain of fruit in Harare's popular Mbare market.

(22 miles) from the city. This stretch of water and its shoreline form the Lake McIlwaine Recreational Park, which also contains an extensive wildlife reserve.

One of Harare's most impressive sights stands twelve kilometres (seven miles) south of the city centre at Epworth. There, massive boulders eroded over aeons by wind and rain are balanced in fantastic formations.

Pleasant suburbs with smart shopping centres, nostalgically named with such Anglo-Saxon nomenclature as Kensington, Belgravia, Milton Park, and Belvedere, stretch in every direction.

Many old street names — Speke and Baker avenues — also remain. The English imprint is indelibly stamped, nowhere more evident than in the pedestrian-only shopping mall at the city's heart and the window displays of the many chain stores.

Despite severe foreign exchange restrictions, the windows showcase contemporary fashions (virtually all designed and made in Zimbabwe) and a wide range of modern consumer goods.

Parliament Buildings, where the demo-cratically-elected, black majority government meets, is a link in the historical chain of Zimbabwe's colonization dating from the last decade of the last century. It was designed as a hotel — then known as Cecil Building — just a few metres from the spot where Pennefather and his pioneers raised the British flag.

The land that they claimed for the BSAC and themselves, in fact, was originally occupied by the Harava people, a Shona group under Chief Mbare, after whom one of the city's main suburbs is named.

When the pioneers arrived the land was in the possession of another Shona group, under Chief Gutsa, which had conquered the Harava, killing Chief Mbare.

Almost simultaneous with the 1896 Ndebele uprising in Bulawayo, the Shona took to arms in the first of Zimbabwe's wars of liberation, the first *Chimurenga*.

While Bulawayo's European settlers were retreating into a laager to take refuge from

Overleaf: Zimbabwe's elegant capital of Harare.

227

the Ndebele, Salisbury's new immigrants sought refuge from the Shona in the town gaol, which they fortified. There they waited, prepared for siege. After six weeks, faced by superior arms and the arrival of troop reinforcements under Colonel Anderson, the settlers' will prevailed and the Shona were forced to concede (See "The Gold and the Silver", Part One).

At the time of the first *Chimurenga*, the new hotel was just an empty shell. It had been commissioned by two carpetbaggers from the Kimberley gold fields, Robert Snodgrass and Daniel Mitchell. Although the building was far from complete, Colonel Anderson requisitioned it as barracks for his men when the rains began in late 1896.

Two years later, when Snodgrass and Mitchell ended their partnership, the building — dining room, billiard hall, and eighteen bedrooms — was still unfinished and the BSAC, which had loaned the partners £7,000 to build it, confiscated the hotel with the intention of turning it into the new town's General Post Office.

Within weeks, however, a legislative council to rule over this "new territory" was established and the hotel's dining room was earmarked as the assembly chamber, the bar and lounge as legislative offices, and the upstairs rooms — though some were still without floors — as government offices.

The Public Works Department was assigned to complete the work and the first meeting of the new legislative council took place on 15 May, 1899, surrounded by builders, carpenters, and plumbers.

The meeting coincided with the arrival of the railway and three years later, with the completion of the line to Bulawayo in 1902, Salisbury was proclaimed the new capital. It was granted city status in 1935.

Little more than two decades after that first meeting, Rhodesia was proclaimed a self-governing colony and the chamber declared too small. The first opening of Parliament was held instead in the capital's Princess Hall. Yet after many acrimonious debates about building a new Parliament, the members finally decided to expand Cecil Building.

In the years since, there have been many more improvements to the Parliament Buildings, culminating with expansions in 1969 that raised the structure to six storeys. There, eleven years later on 14 May, 1980, President Caanan Banana performed the first State opening of independent Zimbabwe's Parliament.

A decade later, Zimbabwe's 100 members of parliament voted to merge the two-chamber Westminster-modelled independent Parliament into one house, abolishing the unelected forty-seat Senate for an enlarged single chamber of 150 MPs, 120 of whom contest their seats in the general elections. The other thirty seats are occupied by the governors of Zimbabwe's eight provinces, ten traditional chiefs, and twelve members nominated by the President.

Almost a century after Snodgrass and Mitchell gave shape to their grand vision of an elegant hotel, the interior of Parliament Buildings is still surprisingly intact — with the original doors, windows, floors, and ceilings in place.

Despite its sturdy structure, however, the buildings' historic role is drawing to a close. Plans for a new parliamentary complex on top of the Kopje are well-advanced.

Conservationists, however, are hopeful that the old Parliament Buildings will be preserved as a national monument. As the one visible link between Zimbabwe's British colonization and its first decade of independence, the old hotel is one of the most significant buildings — architecturally and historically — in the country.

Many other historic monuments, mostly of a colonial nature, retain their place in Harare's architectural legacy: the staff where Pennefather raised the British flag marks the entrance to African Unity Square; cenotaphs to the heroes of two world wars dominate Harare Gardens (and also a 1913 drinking fountain commemorating Britain's King George V); and the city's excellent Queen Victoria Museum is now the headquarters of the National Museum.

Opposite: Finely woven traditional shawls and wicker baskets draw many residents and tourists to Harare's lively markets.

As the second decade of independence opens, Harare is developing swiftly. Its population now approaching one million people, new factories and suburban estates are extending the city's peripheries.

Careful planning by city officials, however, should ensure that the spaciousness and cleanliness of Harare's broad and sunny streets will endure all change — to add more than a measure of delight, not only to its ever-increasing number of citizens but to the ever-increasing number of visitors it welcomes each year.

Getting there

Harare, 439 kilometres (273 miles) from Bulawayo, 580 kilometres (360 miles) from Beitbridge, and 878 kilometres (546 miles) from Victoria Falls, is well-served by many international flights. Domestic and regional air, rail, and road services link it with major centres in Zimbabwe and southern Africa.

When to go

The city is pleasant all year-round.

Where to stay

Sheraton Harare (5-star), Monomotapa (5-star), Meikles (5-star), Holiday Inn (4-star), Cresta Jameson (4-star), Cresta Oasis (3-star), Machipsa Park Lane Hotel (3-star), Feathers Hotel (2-star), Red Fox Hotel (2-star). There are many other hotels with varying degrees of quality and service and many guest-houses. See Listings for "Hotels". There are many excellent caravan parks, and camp-sites. See Listings.

Sightseeing

Bounded in the **south-west** by the **railway yards** and **industrial area**, central **Harare's** southernmost limits are marked by **Kenneth Kaunda Avenue** on which the **railway station** stands.

The railway reached Harare in May 1899 (it was linked to Bulawayo and South Africa three years later), but the 1990 station dates from more modern times.

If you **turn east** out of the station and take the **second road north** onto **Second Street**, a pleasant stroll brings you close to the heart of the city, to **Meikles Hotel**, for many decades flagship of the outstanding entrepreneurial dynasty that founded its fortune on shanty stores and crude lodging houses built and operated in the earliest Pioneer days.

Meikles' early colonial two-storey ver-andahed original was demolished in the 1960s to make way for the **concrete edifice** that now stands on **the corner** of Third Street and **Jason Moyo** (formerly Stanley) **Avenue**. The hotel faces **African Unity** (formerly Cecil) **Square**, the location of Harare's humble beginnings a century ago.

The Pioneer Column rounded **the Kopje** on the morning of 12 September, 1890, coming to a halt where the **Anglican Cathedral** now stands. The next morning the men, in full dress, raised the British flag to a gun salute and named the area **Fort Salisbury**.

The fort was built at once in what is now African Unity Square, later laid out patriotically in the shape of the Union Jack. It remains the city's central motif.

With magnificent trees, cascading fountains, and dazzling flower beds, this natural haven in downtown Harare is bounded to the west by the **offices** of the *Zimbabwe Herald* (note the display of **old linotype machines** at the side of the building), and on the north side by the **Anglican Cathedral** and the mellow **Parliament Buildings**.

The *Herald* is almost as old as the city. It first appeared on 27 June, 1891, edited by W. E. Fairbridge, a South African stockbroker who became the first Mayor of Salisbury in June 1897.

Fairbridge was sent from Cape Town by the Argus newspaper group to launch the paper titled *The Mashonaland Herald and Zambesian Times*. The first editions were nothing more than two or four cyclostyled sheets printed on both sides and stapled together by Fairbridge himself who then made the delivery rounds.

Long-term project

The cathedral, on the corner of **Baker Ave-**

Opposite: Floral clock outside Harare's Town House in Julius Nyerere Way.

nue and Second Street, was built on the same spot that an Anglican minister, Canon Balfour, constructed Fort Salisbury's first church out of pole and daga in 1890.

One year later a procathedral was built out of brick and corrugated iron by an Archdeacon Upcher. The building was heartily disliked, and by the end of the nineteenth century its early parishioners were actively planning a new stone cathedral.

Trying to complete the house of worship was enough to tax the patience of a saint. The **foundation stone** was laid on St. George's Day, 1913 — the service of thanksgiving for the cathedral's successful completion was celebrated on 20 December, 1964!

The only surviving relic of Canon Balfour's church — the Altar Cross, made from cigar boxes by a Trooper Purdon — is preserved in the cathedral's **St. George's Chapel**. There you can also see a carved altar rail depicting the "Last Supper", believed to have come from a seventeenth-century Dutch church.

The foundation stone can be seen in the cathedral's **Lady Chapel**. The cathedral **Bell Tower**, containing **ten bells** cast by the Whitechapel Foundry, London, was completed in 1961.

The cathedral is open daily — times of services in English and Shona are on the notice board — and on special occasions the building is floodlit.

Standing **east** of the cathedral, on **the corner** of Baker Avenue and **Third Street**, are Parliament Buildings. The exterior is pleasant and modest, but its corridors echo with history.

So much of what shapes modern Zimbabwe has taken place within these walls, from the ill-fated federation of the 1950s to Ian Smith's Unilateral Declaration of Independence — UDI — that led to the final confrontation between the European settlers and African nationalists.

Many historical items line its walls. Hanging in the **member's lounge** are **oil portraits** of all of Rhodesia's administrators, governors and prime ministers. **Busts** of Rhodes, Selous, Jameson, South African soldier and statesman Jan Smuts, and Britain's Lord Malvern are located in the **pub-**

lic corridor** leading to the **strangers' gallery**.

The members' **dining room** contains a thirty-metre-long (100-foot) **tapestry** recreating a sequence of historical scenes, embroidered by the women's institute of what was then Rhodesia. The former **debating chamber** of the Federal Parliament is now the **reading room**. Visits to Parliament Buildings can be arranged.

Opposite Parliament, on the corner of **Third Street** and **Baker Avenue** is the **old Lonrho Building**, built in 1910.

The building retained its original interior until a 1984 renovation, but much of what still stands is the original. Today the building is used for commercial offices.

Shopping mall

Go west along Baker Avenue, off Second Street north of Meikles, and you will cross **First Street Mall**, Harare's attractive pedestrian-only **shopping centre** featuring many attractive open-air cafes and coffee shops.

Go **east** along Union Avenue across Second Street and you arrive at the new **headquarters** of the London Rhodesia Company — Lonrho.

Great efforts have been made to preserve many of the older buildings that have played a role or brought colour to the city's history. One such edifice, lost during a bitter struggle between Zimbabwe's Reserve Bank and the city fathers, was **Jameson House** on **Samora Machel Avenue**.

The bank bought Jameson House, which was built in 1896, with the intention of demolishing it. The city served the bank's management with an order to preserve Harare's first double-storey building, but the order was overruled and the building demolished.

One of the most interesting early buildings, **Cecil House**, at the corner of **Central Avenue** and Second Street, was built in 1901. It was rescued from decay by the Mining Industry Pension Fund in 1976, and not only carefully restored, but joined by a **new office block** built immediately behind it in the same Victorian style. Both buildings are floodlit at night.

The mining industry has done much to enhance public awareness of the historic value of Harare's old buildings. Another

Above: Bowling match at Harare Club.

building that belongs to the Department of Mines is the **Macgregor Geological Museum** on **Fourth Street.** It contains **gemstone displays**, a comprehensive **collection** of **rock samples**, and maps showing the localities where they are found. The museum is open during normal hours every weekday and admission is free.

Lying on **Julius Nyerere Way,** between **Speke** and Jason Moyo avenues, stands **Town House,** built between 1931 and 1933, home of the **Mayor's Parlour** and the Town Clerk's department.

It is notable not only for its architectural style, but for the unusual **floral clock** incorporating the national symbol, the Zimbabwe Bird. It was built in 1950 in the gardens in front of the **main steps** to commemorate the city's first sixty years.

Dominating the city centre skyline, the curved, slender profile of the eighteen-storey **Monomotapa Hotel** overlooks to the **south** the slender steel and glass lines of Harare's most modern landmark, **Karigamombe Centre**, at the corner of Samora Machel Avenue. To the **north,** the hotel overlooks one and a half square kilometres (half a square mile) of the city's main park, **Harare Gardens**.

Christmas fairytales

Harare Gardens is enjoyed year-round for its treasured recreation area of leafy avenues, **open-air theatre, bandstand, children's playground, bowling greens, cenotaphs** to the dead of two world wars, and a **miniature model** of **Victoria Falls.**

Every year, in December, the gardens are the setting for a fascinating collection of nursery rhyme characters, part of Harare's Christmas lights display.

The park is flanked by the metropolitan **Les Brown swimming pool** to the **west, Park Lane** to the **south, Herbert Chitepo** (formerly Rhodes) **Avenue** to the **north,** and the **National Art Gallery** to the **east.**

The gallery, built in 1957 and regarded as one of the largest and most modern in Africa, is designed to foster interest in art and culture generally, and to act as a medium for Zimbabwe's own artistic communities. In addition to exhibitions the gallery stages lectures, films, slide presentations, workshop demonstrations, and live theatre.

Above: Modern Zimbabwe stone sculptures at Chapungu Kraal Craft Village, Harare.

Many permanent and temporary exhibitions are presented and a **workshop** attached to the gallery helps Zimbabwe sculptors develop their skills. There is also a **sales gallery** where contemporary **stone sculptures** from established and unknown artists can be bought (See "Sculpture: Collected the World Over", Part Four). The gallery is open on Tuesday to Friday from 09.00 to 12.30 and 14.00 to 17.00.

Other art galleries in Harare include the **John Boyne Gallery**, located in the **Standard Bank** at the corner of Speke Avenue and **Inez Terrace**, which honours John Boyne, the founding chairman of the Standard Bank in Zimbabwe. The gallery is open to artists who wish to mount their own exhibitions — by prearrangement with the bank. Admission is free.

Sandwiched between a **delicatessen** and a **men's outfitters** on **Robert Mugabe** (formerly Manica) **Road** is the **Gallery Delta**, which stages lively exhibitions and occasional plays.

Turn **north** into Park Lane from the gallery and take the first turn **east** (not possible by car as it is one-way) into Herbert Chitepo

Avenue. On the north side, between **Seventh** and **Eighth streets** and Herbert Chitepo and **Josiah Chinamano** (formerly Montague) avenues, is another inner-city recreation area, **Greenwood Park**, a pleasant oasis for the many flat dwellers in this area of Harare.

One section has been developed by the Round Table charitable organisation as a **children's playground** with a **miniature railway**, **boating pool**, and many other attractions that are open during weekends. Money generated by the park is donated to local charities.

The **western end** of Jason Moyo Avenue leads across **Rotten Row** (another mark of Anglo-Saxon nostalgia, it is named after the London landmark) into **Pennefather Avenue**, which commemorates the city's founding father. Leading south off Pennefather Avenue is **Willoughby Crescent**. There you will find the **National Library** and **National Museum**, headquarters of the National Museums and Monuments.

Among a wealth of exhibits on display are examples of **rock art**, an authentic **Shona village** of the nineteenth century containing tools, weapons, and household

Above: Sculpture at Harare's Heroes' Acre honours those who died in the struggle to liberate Rhodesia.

goods; a **freshwater aquarium**; and fascinating **models** of animals in their natural habitat.

The Museum Club, which caters to young people aged between seven and sixteen, meets fortnightly and activities include talks, film shows, and practical demonstrations. The museum is open daily throughout the year.

Facing the museum is the **Civic Centre** and the **municipal offices**, located in the **Rowan Martin Building**. The building stands on what was once the city racecourse, run by the Mashonaland Turf Club, before its move to the Borrowdale suburb.

On the south side of the museum is the **Courtauld College of Music,** and along Rotten Row (crossing Robert Mugabe Road) is the modern, circular **Magistrates' Court**.

Sports centre

Pennefather Road is a cul-de-sac that leads into Harare's magnificent 4,000-seat **International Conference Centre**. Completed in 1986, it adjoins the **Sheraton Hotel**. The space-age centre, the continent's largest, clad in burnished gold panelling, has three other **meeting rooms** of various sizes, **VIP section**,

press centre, and administration block. The basement of the building houses its extensive maintenance workshops.

The conference hall has been designed so that it may be separated into individual rooms, enabling different events to be held simultaneously. The latest sound system and the use of marble within the hall enhances the excellent acoustics, while remote-control television cameras monitor all doors and approaches to the VIP section. The centre has its own fully-equipped medical clinic.

Continue west along Robert Mugabe Road and **turn south** onto **Rekayi Tangwena** (formerly Sir James McDonald) **Avenue**. The first **turn west** off Tangwena brings you to **Glamis Stadium**, the spacious **showground** of the **Zimbabwe Agricultural Society**, founded in 1899, and the setting for the colourful **Harare Agricultural Show** held each August.

The second **turn west** off Rekayi Tangwena Avenue leads to the **National Sports Centre's indoor stadium**, which offers facilities for wrestling, boxing, volleyball, karate, and many other indoor sports. The playing surfaces and the lighting are up to international standards and **bars** and **refreshment areas** are provided. Pop festivals and stage shows seating up to 5,000 are also held at the centre.

But pride of place among the city's stadia must go to the Chinese-built **National Sports Stadium** on the main **Harare-Bulawayo road**. One of the major show-pieces of sporting Africa it was built by Chinese and Zimbabwean workers. The stadium, completed in 1986, has a crowd capacity of 60,000.

Leave the National Sports Centre, crossing Rekayi Tangwena Avenue heading **east** along **Belvedere Road** which leads to the intersection with Rotten Row. Continue **east** across the intersection into **Skipper Hoste Drive**, which circles Harare's first bastion — the **Kopje**.

From its **summit** there are fine views over Harare and the surrounding countryside. A **toposcope** indicates the direction and distance of various points of interest.

The Kopje became a **memorial** to the founders of the city at the end of the last century, and it was there that the Eternal Flame of Independence was lit on 18 April, 1980, to commemorate the birth of Zimbabwe. There are plans to build a new parliament on its summit.

South-west of the Kopje lies Harare's **Workington industrial area** where Zimbabwe's colonial past is kept alive in such prosaic street names as **Birmingham**, **Glasgow**, **Barrow**, and **Plymouth roads**.

South-east of the Kopje, following **Cripps Road** (an extension of Rotten Row), estates such as **Mbare**, **Graniteside**, and **Arcadia** allow visitors to experience Harare's vibrant African ambience in local **craft markets** that display a fascinating range of traditional, indigenous carvings, fabric, basketwork, metalwork, and agricultural produce.

Trotting

For sports lovers, there can be few cities that provide such a range of recreational opportunities as Harare. Along with indoor facilities at the Sports Centre and outdoor facilities at the National Stadium, there are many spectator sports, such as horse-racing. Slightly more offbeat, at least by African standards, is trotting.

Where Cripps Road crosses **Seke** (former-ly Hatfield) **Road** to become **Dieppe Road**, head **south** along Seke Road for five or six kilometres (three–four miles) to the **National Trotting Club's Waterfalls Stadium**. Race meetings were held virtually every Sunday of the year.

The only trotting track in Africa, it was laid out — and maintained — to international standards with an 800-metre (2,625-foot) **circuit**. The sport was well-established (and well-run) with some 150 registered horses. Bar, bookmakers, and totalisator facilities operated at all meetings. But, lacking sufficient support, it closed down in 1990 and was turned into a greyhound racing track.

For the outdoor enthusiast, Harare boasts a variety of tennis clubs, bowling greens, cricket grounds, rugby and soccer fields, as well as a total of fourteen golf courses — seven rated up to championship standard — within a thirty-kilometre (nineteen-mile) radius of the city centre. Visiting golfers can rent clubs, and some clubs also have caddie-carts for rent. All courses have caddies available for hire.

From the railway station or city centre, follow **Second Street north** to the intersection with **Josiah Tongogara** (formerly North) **Avenue** and **turn east**. Take the next **turn north** into **Fifth Street**.

The first **sports ground** to the **left** is that of the **Harare Sports Club**, an international cricket venue where an England touring side played Zimbabwe in 1990.

The next **turn left** is the entrance to the **Royal Harare Golf Club**, one of a handful around the world to have been given the royal accolade. Its beautiful fairways and immaculate greens are the annual setting for the Zimbabwe Open, one of the major events in the African Safari circuit, that takes place sometime between April and May.

Though seemingly mundane from the fence, the landscaping of this course seen from the patio that overlooks both the first tee and eighteenth hole is a tribute to the designer and nature's form.

Opposite the club are the spacious grounds of what was the **Prime Minister's official residence** until the post was abolished. The entrance is on **Chancellor Avenue**, the next **turn north** off Josiah Tongogara Avenue.

The **turn** after this is the **entrance** to **State**

House, the official residence of the President. It was built in 1910 and has been considerably extended in the years since.

Botanical gardens

Bordering the fence surrounding the Prime Minister's residence, to the **east** of Fifth Street is the long-established **plant research experimental station**. Next to it stands almost seven square kilometres (three square miles) of land that was reserved as a recreation area in 1902. In 1962 it became the **National Botanical Gardens** under the direction of Dr. Hyram Wilder.

Half of the gardens are devoted to indigenous plants from Zimbabwe's woodlands and include most of the 750 species found in the country. Other areas contain a selection of plants typical to the African continent, including rare and endangered species, as well as exotics from South America, India, Australia, and the Far East. The **National Herbarium**, situated in the Botanical Gardens, is surrounded by shrubs of exotic origin.

These gardens are close to the splendid **National Archives**. Built in 1961, it is the repository for Zimbabwe's pre-colonial, colonial, and post-colonial history containing more than 40,000 books, many rare **manuscripts** and **documents**, and a comprehensive **photographic collection**.

The National Archives, founded in 1935, is open daily to the public and admission is free. The **Reading Rooms** and **Gallery** are open from 07.45 to 16.30, Monday to Friday, and from 08.00 to 12.00 on Saturday.

Ten kilometres along **Borrowdale Road** (which is an extension of **Chancellor Avenue**) stands the verdant **Borrowdale racecourse**, centre of the Turf Club of Mashonaland's multimillion dollar enterprise that includes tote and off-course betting shops.

Borrowdale Park, home to thoroughbred racing in Zimbabwe, is considered one of the best tracks in Africa. The course is two and a half kilometres (one and a half miles) in circumference, with a 1,400-metre (4,593 foot) straight. Mobile starting stalls, accommodating up to twenty horses, are used for all distances.

The Mashonaland Turf Club stages more than forty race meetings a year, each card featuring up to nine races involving approximately 100 horses. The club operates its own totalisator both on the course and at seven other centres within the city.

Borrowdale is named after one of the city's first settlers, Henry Borrow, a bored ostrich farmer who migrated from South Africa.

University

Harare University also lies in the city's **northern suburbs** on 180 hectares (450 acres) of pleasant park land at **Mount Pleasant**. Britain's Queen Mother laid the foundation stone in July 1953 and it was incorporated by Royal Charter on 11 February, 1955.

With 10,000 students in its nine faculties — agriculture, art, commerce and law, education, engineering, medicine, science, social studies, and veterinary science — the university has strong links with the city. The public are frequently invited to lectures given during the evenings in the **Llewellin Lecture Hall**.

The northern suburbs also have their own small slice of African wilderness in **Ballantyne** and **Blair parks** — two small reserves situated in **Highlands** that are owned and managed by the City Council. Open to the public throughout the year, there is no charge for admission. Ballantyne has a number of small antelope and both parks have a wide variety of indigenous waterfowl on their **lakes,** which are stocked with bream. Fishing is allowed.

A taste of the wild can also be experienced at **Hillside**, seven kilometres (four miles) **east** of the city centre. There the **Mukuvisi Woodland Society** presents "a touch of the wild in the heart of the city" with guided foot safaris through unspoilt indigenous woodland off **Glenara Avenue South**. Facilities include **game-viewing platform** and **picnic area**. Many species of wildlife can be seen, along with a wide variety of birds, plants, and flowers.

No suburban tour would be complete without a stop at **Willowvale**. There you will find the largest single tobacco auction centre in the world. The Harare suburb's US$6 million auction hall was opened in 1986. The amazing speed at which bids from national and overseas buyers are reeled off by the auctioneers astonishes all first-time visitors to these colourful auctions.

Below: Lone poppy blooms in a sea of gold and yellow.

Above: Colourful blooms in downtown Harare Gardens.

The crop, first planted in 1895, is the country's largest single foreign currency earner — realising around US$150 million a year. Until the Unilateral Declaration of Independence — UDI — in 1965, Zimbabwe was the world's second-largest producer of tobacco.

Since independence, production has constantly increased and the country now produces well above 110,000 tonnes a year.

Another suburban tourist attraction is **Chapungu Kraal** located at **Doon Estate** in the suburb of **Msasa**. Featuring an authentic nineteenth-century Shona village and a gallery for modern **Shona sculpture**, the kraal's other attractions include spectacular tribal and traditional dance shows every weekend, accompanied by a live marimba band.

The traditional village — named after the bateleur eagle, a symbol of good luck — comprises **six huts** including a **granary**, a **witch doctor's hut**, and a **cattle kraal**. The witch doctor's hut, which has a resident *nganga*, is situated near the top of a small kopje on the thirty-hectare (86-acre) site to the **east** of the city centre.

Twelve kilometres (seven and a half miles) **south** of the city centre, along **Chiremba** (formerly Widdecombe) **Road**, stand the spectacular **Epworth Balancing Rocks**, which provide novice rock climbers with a splendid summer's evening challenge.

Two attractions not to be missed before leaving handsome Harare are the ceremonial **Independence Arch** that greets the visitor on the road south to the city's **international airport** and the moving splendour of **Heroes' Acre**, a ceremonial burial ground on a forested ridge some kilometres **west** of the city centre, opposite the National Sports Stadium on the Bulawayo road. There the martyrs who laid down their lives for freedom, and those who have died since independence in the service of their nation, are buried in peace.

The granite walls are built in the style of those at Great Zimbabwe. The monument is marked by a slender, soaring column visible for many kilometres around. Magnificent bas relief representations of the independence struggle flank either side. Permission to visit this national shrine must be obtained from the Ministry of Information in Harare.

Bulawayo: Parks and Power Stations, Fountains and Factories

Spacious, sunny, and friendly, Zimbabwe's second-largest city, Bulawayo, with a population of around half a million, lies halfway between Beitbridge and Victoria Falls at the main axis of the country's major road, rail, and air routes. Since its birth a century ago, Bulawayo has continued to develop as one of southern Africa's most attractive cities.

Although it is the country's principal railway junction and marshalling yard, and contains a major proportion of its industrial capacity, Bulawayo's wide, tree-lined streets and avenues, together with a pleasant mixture of early and modern architecture, lend the city a unique character.

The site of Bulawayo was chosen by Mzilikazi's successor, Lobengula, in 1870. He called it *Gubulawayo*, meaning "the place of slaughter", to commemorate his battle victories. By 1890, Bulawayo was a large capital consisting of many grass huts and a population of between 15,000 and 20,000.

Lobengula's well-fortified personal kraal, three kilometres (two miles) away at Mvutja on the banks of the Mguza River, drew crowds of carpetbaggers, hunters, and prospectors seeking permission to trade, hunt, or search for gold.

The first stage of Rhodes's strategic design for a far-reaching British empire in Africa was to send a delegation to Bulawayo to negotiate a concession with Lobengula and his people, the Ndebele, that would allow his British South Africa Company — BSAC — to operate in Matabeleland (See "The Gold and the Silver", Part One).

When Rhodes despatched a mercenary army three years later the destruction had begun. With the Ndebele in disarray, hundreds of settlers poured in and Bulawayo was born. The first houses were built about one and a half kilometres (one mile) from the ashes of Lobengula's capital.

In 1894, however, for reasons known only to himself, Dr. Leander Starr Jameson decided to move the European settlement to a spot five kilometres (three miles) away.

When Rhodes heard of this, he ordered Jameson to build a rondavel on the site of the royal kraal, token of his acknowledgement of Ndebele bravery.

Bulawayo's first native-born European citizen, Lilian Tempofsky, was born two months after Jameson's decision to move the town.

The new Bulawayo streets were extremely wide, broad enough to allow a full team of oxen, twenty-four pairs, to make a 180 degree turn. Fast-growing trees, particularly jacaranda, were planted along each side to create avenues of leafy shade, as brick and stone buildings for houses, shops, and bars began to rise everywhere. Sports fields were cultivated for soccer, cricket, rugby, and a racecourse for horse-racing.

On 1 June, 1894, only seven months after the flag was raised, Jameson stood on the steps of the settlement's first hotel, Maxim's (it no longer exists, but a bronze plaque marks the spot), opposite what is now City Hall and declared: "It is my job to declare this town open, gentlemen, I don't think we want any talk about it. I make the declaration now. There is plenty of whisky and soda inside, so come in."

Hotels with high-sounding names, such as the Palace and the Imperial, opened their doors, and churches, stores, and clubs sprang up. The town could also boast a lending library, a taxidermist that offered stuffed birds and animal skins, and a new stock exchange. Business was brisk.

Newspapers soon followed. *The Chronicle*, which first appeared twice weekly in October 1894, covered most of the professions and services and by May 1895 it had become a daily.

The bustle and movement in the dusty streets gave an air of life and vigour to the new town. Traders abandoned their stores at Tuli, Fort Victoria (now Masvingo), and even Salisbury (now Harare), to cash in on the new-found prosperity of Bulawayo.

Within months, 400 gold diggers had

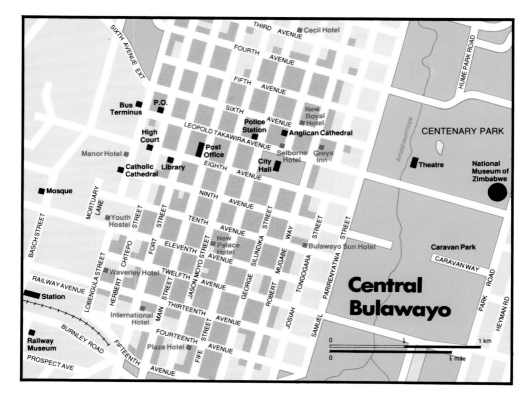

Central Bulawayo

been given licences to prospect, 11,000 claims were registered, and the population had risen to more than 1,500.

In October 1897, following the 1896 defeat of the Ndebele, Bulawayo was elevated to a municipality. The town's new status coincided with the arrival of the railway from Mafeking. Bulawayo became a city in 1943 to mark the fiftieth year of its founding.

The city's colourful history is so recent that you feel you can almost reach out and touch it. And indeed you can lay your hand on the bark of the tree under which Lobengula held his *indaba* (meeting) in the gardens of State House where Rhodes's rondavel still stands.

Wherever you go in this handsome provincial capital, history constantly comes to life and confronts you — both inside and outside, with its splendid museums, relics, and monuments that are zealously maintained and guarded.

In Centenary Park, which also contains Bulawayo's modern theatre, is the Colosseum-style building of the National Museum, considered by many to be one of the finest institutions of its kind in southern Africa.

The Railways Museum, near the National Railways' headquarters complex, houses steam engines, rolling stock, and machinery dating back beyond the turn of the century when the Europeans swept across this land.

Brave and tragic — and some may well think noble — Lobengula has even been immortalized in the city's 1943 coat of arms with three hyrax ("rock rabbits") courant and a crest composed of an African elephant "with trunk elevated proper". The hyrax are the totem of the Ndebele royal family and symbolise the Ndebele nation; the elephant, the emblem of Lobengula whose title among the Ndebele was *Ndhlovu*, meaning "the elephant".

Also on the shield, on a red background signifying bloodshed, is the city's Sindebele motto, "Si yi pambili", which translates into "We go forward".

Much of Bulawayo's historical past still exists in the present. The tree where the first British flag flew blooms by the small building that was Dawson's Store — now part of

242

a private hotel — run by trader and miner James Dawson, who also served as an envoy for Lobengula.

The BSAC lion that once adorned the Rebellion Memorial at the junction of Main Street and Leopold Takawira (formerly Selborne) Avenue, is now in Bulawayo's State House gardens, which are the impressive venue for the city's annual Independence Day celebrations.

Some early businesses also survive. Haddon and Sly, founded in 1894, is today one of the best-known shops in the city. Another business that dates from the nineteenth century is that of Smart and Copley pharmaceutical chemists.

Issels engineering business was founded in 1894. During the first *Chimurenga* the firm repaired guns and gun carriages as well as making searchlights for the top of the market building. Osborne's bakery was established as a small tearoom along Jason Moyo Street in 1897.

After touring the city's historical sites, museums, and parks, you may well want to explore all the sporting life that Bulawayo has to offer. There is fortnightly horse-racing at the Ascot Race Course and, although little used these days, Bulawayo also boasts an international motor racing circuit.

Speedway, stock-car racing, bicycle racing, athletics, boxing, and yachting regattas are regular events on the city's sports calendar. For golf enthusiasts the city boasts three verdant, eighteen-hole courses. On Bulawayo Golf Course a memorial recalls the *Silver Queen*, a plane that crashed just after taking off in March 1920, on the last leg of the pioneer London to Cape flight. The flight was finished by a replacement plane.

As well as golf, there are several cricket and rugby grounds, tennis and squash courts, bowling greens, swimming pools, and other sporting and recreational facilities, including two first-class football stadiums.

As the nation's second-largest city, capital of Matabeleland Province, and Zimbabwe's industrial dynamo, Bulawayo has a lively nightlife. There are many fine restaurants, four cinemas, two drive-ins, two fine theatres, nightclubs, many discos, and a wide choice of accommodation, from luxury hotels to more modestly priced establishments.

Indeed, in 1990, 100 years after the city's first beginnings, Bulawayo is all that a city of the twenty-first century should be.

Getting there

Bulawayo, 439 kilometres (273 miles) from Harare, 321 kilometres (200 miles) from Beitbridge, and 439 kilometres (273 miles) from Victoria Falls, is well served by air, road, and rail services. Domestic and regional flights, bus, and train services link it with major centres in Zimbabwe and southern Africa.

When to go

Bulawayo is pleasant all year-round.

Where to stay

Bulawayo Sun (3-star), Cresta Churchill (3-star), Bulawayo Holiday Inn (3-star), New Royal Hotel (2-star), and Selborne Hotel. There are other hotels with varying degrees of service and quality. See Listings for "Hotels". Bulawayo has a centrally located caravan park and campsites. See Listings.

Above: Elder of Bulawayo's Zion Christ Church annoints a worshipper.

Above: Zimbabwe's National Railways' headquarters building dominates the downtown heart of Bulawayo.

Sightseeing

As a city that owes much of its prominence and prosperity to the railway line that arrived there in 1897, it is perhaps a good idea to start sightseeing at Bulawayo's **railway station**.

Set at the **south-west corner** of the **city centre**, it lies fittingly enough off **Lobengula Avenue** in the shadows of the imposing **headquarters** of Zimbabwe National Rail-ways and the **cooling towers** of the city's **power station**.

The 1990s station postdates the original by several decades, but it reeks with the nostalgic sights and smells of the great days when steam locomotion ruled the countryside. Steam is perhaps the greatest legacy that the National Railways of Zimbabwe inherited at independence.

Its fleet of ninety-five steam locomotives were to have been phased out by the end of

Station Road), steam engines are always at work shunting, as well as arriving and departing.

Bulawayo's original station, built on the former headquarters occupied by one of Lobengula's crack regiments (the King's eldest son also lived there), boasted the longest railway platform in the world. The workers who dug the foundations discovered a number of caves.

The **foundation stone** of the original railway **headquarters building** was laid on 2 April, 1913, by Mrs. Rochfort Maguire, whose husband negotiated the concession to occupy Matabeleland from Lobengula in 1888 with Frank Thomson and C. D. Rudd.

The fascinating **Railway Museum** lies at the back of the station, between **Customs** and **Prospect avenues**. One of its most impressive exhibits is Rhodes's beautifully-preserved private **Pullman coach**.

This complete Victorian suite on wheels, befitting the grand, egocentric fancies of the man who allotted himself the task of empire builder, gives substance to the now fading shadows of that empire and his unfulfilled dreams. After his death in 1902, the coach carried Rhodes's body from the Cape to Bulawayo.

Evidence enough of Rhodes's ambition is contained in another **exhibit**: a **written proposal** of 28 April, 1898, from Rhodes, seeking British Government support to extend the railway another 800 miles (1,288 kilometres) to Lake Tanganyika.

Steam engines

Other exhibits include the 1900 **staff register, menus**, and **table settings** from the British Royal train of 1953; a **letter** of 28 May, 1897, from Rhodes appointing J. L. Bissett general manager of the Bechuanaland Railway at a salary of £1,200 a year; and old locomotives and rolling stock.

One **steam engine**, *Jack Tar*, served the Mashonaland Railway Company Limited. Another steam engine on display, known as **number 257**, was made at the Falcon Engine and Car Works, Loughborough, England, in 1897. It is a two-foot gauge loco that worked for many years on the Beira to Umtali (now Mutare) line before ending its life on a private forestry line in Zimbabwe.

the 1970s, but economic restraints, such as the high cost of spare parts for diesel locomotives and Zimbabwe's plentiful supplies of coal, together with the skills available in the Bulawayo **steam workshops**, have ensured their continued viability.

Apart from taking much of the strain off the diesel and electric locomotive fleets, steam also stimulates tourism. Special steam safaris draw thousands of steam train buffs to Bulawayo every year. As the country's principal **railway junction** (the city's large **Mpopoma marshalling yards** are located on

Above: Woodcarvers with their curios on a Bulawayo sidewalk.

Outside, in mint condition, are the **coaches** and **locomotives** of later eras — including one of the powerful **1929 Beyer Peacock** steam giants designed by H. W. Garratt. Near these nostalgic machines are **notices** that evoke those days of old, such as one headed "Prevention of Consumption" that earnestly exhorts passengers "to abstain from the dangerous and objectionable habit of expectorating".

Rhodes's empirical ambition also sought to impose what he considered the "civilizing" benefit of Christianity across Britain's sphere of influence in Africa, and until 1962, a mobile mission constantly travelled the length and breadth of the railway network.

The **coach** that was attached to one of the regular trains to carry the missionaries about their work — with its inscription, "They brought light to the line" — is preserved inside the museum.

One final exhibit, a **piece of twisted metal**, is all that remains of either railway or train after a dynamite load blew up on 15 June, 1940, leaving the landscape over several square kilometres in a state of devastation approaching that of a nuclear catastrophe.

Lobengula Avenue is in two separate sections. Along the **northward extension** lie the **Convent School**, **Catholic Cathedral**, **Manor Hotel**, **Scout Hall**, and **Bus Terminus**.

From the railway station, you can cross Lobengula Avenue into **Thirteenth Avenue**. The first intersection after this is **Herbert Chitepo** (formerly Jameson) **Street**. Head **north** along this street and to the **left** you will see the impressive **High Court** building. The city's **War Memorial** is on the **right**.

The **Post Office** is nearby — on the **corner** of **Main Street** and **Eighth Avenue**. At the **corner** of **Jason Moyo** (formerly Abercorn) **Street** and **Ninth Avenue**, **OK Bazaar** occupies the spot where Rhodes's Bulawayo office stood.

City Hall

Continue **east** along Ninth Avenue to the intersection with **George Silundika** (formerly Rhodes) **Street**, and the office of *The Chronicle*. **Turn north** into George Silundika Road and you arrive at the very heart of the city, the elegant **City Hall** complex set in manicured lawns and pretty **flower gardens**, beautiful at night under floodlights.

Above: Woodcarvings and wicker baskets draw tourists to a downtown Bulawayo street market.

The complex stands on the **site** of the 1896 laager where the first European population was besieged by the Ndebele. The **well** they sank for water can be seen in the gardens. The City Hall complex, where the **Tourist Information Bureau** can be found, is bounded to the **south** by Eighth Avenue, to the **west** by **Fife Street**, to the **east** by **Robert Mugabe Way** (formerly Grey Street), and to the **north** by **Leopold Takawira** (formerly Selborne) **Avenue**.

West along Leopold Takawira Avenue, at the corner of Fife Street, is the **Police Station**.

Facing the City Hall on the opposite side of the avenue, at the **corner** of Robert Mugabe Way, is the splendidly comfortable **Selborne Hotel**, which in 1990 celebrated fifty years of traditional Anglo-Saxon inn-keeping in Africa.

Nostalgia seeps from its timber beams, nowhere more so than in the **King's Head**, one of its five bars, with its chauvinistic but popular "men only" ambience. No longer legally enforceable, the tradition is strictly maintained with shouts of "stranger in the house" whenever a welcome or unwelcome woman enters. Further along Robert Mugabe Way is Bulawayo's attractive **Anglican Cathedral**.

To the east of City Hall stands the **Bulawayo Art Gallery** with its impressive collection of **tapestries** and **paintings** reflecting both western and African techniques.

The splendid **National Library** lies to the **south-east** of the city centre, at the point where **Twelfth Avenue** becomes **Third Street**.

Princes Park and the magnificent Olympic-size **Municipal Swimming Bath** lie between Leopold Takawira and Ninth avenues. Leopold Takawira leads **east** toward Bulawayo's two major inner-city **recreation parks**: **Central** and **Centenary**.

Cut by the waters of the **Amatsheumhlope River**, both parks are renowned for the beauty of their gardens and tree-lined, flower-filled **paths** alongside **streams** and **waterfalls**.

Central Park was developed to commemorate Bulawayo's city status on 4 November, 1943. Apart from being graced by a variety of handsome trees and magnificent flowers, it contains one of the finest **caravan parks** in southern Africa.

Above: Mechanics service one of Zimbabwe's steam locomotives.
Opposite: One of the old steam giants preserved in Bulawayo's rail museum.

The park is also home to one of the most skilfully designed **illuminated fountains** in southern and central Africa, a constantly changing pattern of water and colour that creates a delightful rainbow in the early morning light.

The fascinating variations of form, height, and colour of the fountain, built in the 1960s to celebrate the seventy-fifth anniversary of the founding of the city, are located by the side of Leopold Takawira Avenue for passing drivers and pedestrians to enjoy.

The beautiful grounds of Centenary Park, forty-five hectares (111 acres) of once arid land, were opened as a sylvan city retreat in 1953 to mark the centennial of the birth of Cecil John Rhodes.

A large man-made **lake** draws a rich vari-

Above: Sculptor fashions a tribal elder from clay at Bulawayo's Mzilikazi Craft Centre.

ety of waterfowl and there is also an **aviary**. For children there is a **miniature railway** and a small fenced **game park** with some smaller wildlife species.

Natural History Museum

For a real introduction to African wildlife, a visit to Bulawayo's outstanding **Natural History Museum**, which lies within Centenary Park, is a must. The museum is at the **intersection** of Leopold Takawira Avenue and **Park Road**.

Its mammal collection, which numbers approximately 75,000 specimens, is the largest of its kind in the southern hemisphere and the eighth-largest in the world. Adjoining the museum is an **open-air display** of **mining antiquaria**.

The awesome **centrepiece** of the museum is the second-largest mounted pachyderm in the world, known as the **Doddieburn elephant**. It stands more than three metres (11 feet) high at the shoulder and its two tusks weigh forty and forty-one kilos (88 and 90 lbs) respectively.

The **exhibition hall** which houses this is a stunning work of three-dimensional art.

A family of guinea fowl struts through the undergrowth where a pride of mounted lions are poised on the bloody entrails of a wildebeest kill. Plaster-cast trees throw shade over the animals to the recorded sounds of babbling streams and forest bird calls. Soft light bathes and brings to life the panoramic background painted in luminous pastel colours by artist Terry Donnelly.

Imagination reflects itself in every hall of this magnificent museum: from the displays of **African mammals** and **birds** (including the 2,000-year-old **fossil egg** of an extinct Madagascan bird); to the **gallery** of an underground **gold mine**; through to the **pony express coach** built by Abbot, Downing Company of Concord, New Hampshire, USA, which was used by Royal Mail contractor C. H. Zeederberg.

Missionary John Moffat, who quit the Inyati mission in 1865 and returned to Matabeleland in 1887 as British Representative to Lobengula's court, established the first mail service, between Mafeking in South Africa and Bulawayo, a year later on 21 August, 1888.

The **first letters** were postmarked

Above: Black rhinos at Chipangali Wildlife Orphanage near Bulawayo.

"Gubulawayo Bechuanaland", but for one day only. There are only thirteen extant copies of this postmark. Fearing it would offend Lobengula, the word Bechuanaland was removed from the stamp immediately.

Among the other antiquities in the museum are exhibits from Robert Moffat's Inyati Mission, which still exists, and the **gun carriage** that bore Rhodes to his funeral in the Matobo Hills on 10 April, 1902.

The museum also houses all the **flags** that have fluttered over Rhodesia and Zimbabwe since Rhodes's enterprise was launched: the first from 1890 to 1923, the flag that flew from 1923–52, the federation flag of 1953–63, the UDI flags of 1964–68 and 1968–79, the six-month flag of 1979 to 18 April, 1980, and finally the Zimbabwean flag that has flown throughout the country ever since.

Beyond the city centre

From the artistic visions of the Natural History Museum, explore the more contemporary works at the **Mzilikazi Art and Craft Centre**. It lies in a **suburb** of the same name four kilometres (two and a half miles) **north-west** of the city centre. There, new generations of artists, potters, sculptors, and other craftsmen are earning national and international recognition for the outstanding beauty of their work.

Along **Third Street**, three kilometres (two miles) beyond the **eastern edge** of the city centre, the lush, green going of the **Ascot racecourse** attracts punters and turf enthusiasts in large numbers for its twice a month meetings. Horse-racing, with a turnover of more than US$2.4 million a year, is a major industry employing several thousand people.

The permanent **showground** of Zimbabwe's annual International Trade Show, with its landmark **spire**, lies at the **southern periphery** of the city centre, along **Hillside Road**, which is an extension of Robert Mugabe Way.

The show's history dates back to 1953 when Bulawayo staged the **Rhodes Centenary Exhibition**, an event that drew people from all over the world and was opened by Britain's Queen Mother.

Seven years later, in 1960, Bulawayo staged the Central African Trade Fair, when once again the Queen Mother opened the event.

Above: Bulawayo's Central Park.
Opposite: Winner's laurels for Rolls Royce in Bulawayo's annual Vintage Car Rally.

Since then the fair has been developed by the Bulawayo Agricultural Society into an international showcase for Zimbabwe and its products.

Also considered a showcase are Bulawayo's many wildlife parks and bird sanctuaries. Four kilometres (two and a half miles) **south** of the city centre, **Hillside Dam Nature Reserve** and **bird sanctuary,** located in the delightfully named **Fortune's Gate** suburb, makes an enjoyable picnic spot. There is an **aviary**, **tea room**, and **picnic site**.

Also **south** of the city centre, eight kilometres (five miles) along **Matobo Road**, is the **Tshabalala Wildlife Sanctuary**, run by Zimbabwe's Department of National Parks and Wildlife Management. The park is home to giraffe, zebra, and many antelope including tsessebe, impala, wildebeest, kudu, and many local birds.

Other green and inviting recreational areas near the city centre include the **Ncema**, **Mzingwane**, and **Khame dams**.

Continue **south** of the city centre to the outer suburbs and **Hope Fountain**, one of the oldest missions in southern Africa. Established in the 1870s by Robert Moffat and his colleagues under Lobengula's aegis, the mission still exists today.

Like his father, Mzilikazi, Lobengula tolerated the missionaries, but did not allow his people to become Christians, fearing that the gospel might weaken the structure of his military kingdom.

The site for the Hope Fountain Mission, in a beautiful, well-watered valley, was chosen with the help of the hunter Henry Hartley and the artist-explorer Thomas Baines.

The mission buildings were damaged during the first *Chimurenga,* when the Ndebele set fire to the thatched roof. The buildings were soon repaired, however, and Hope Fountain Mission continued to grow and prosper spiritually throughout the next century. Today the excellent **school**, **medical facilities**, and beautiful **church** at the mission provide another living link between the Ndebele royal family and modern twentieth-century Bulawayo.

Mutare: City of Mountains and Flowers

Encircled by graceful hills and granite mountains, Mutare lies in a natural bowl that forms the gateway between the lowlands of Mozambique and the highlands of Zimbabwe. Beautifully laid out, its broad, pleasant streets are ablaze with colour all year-round.

Designed to exploit its incomparable setting, this lively and prosperous city contains a striking theatre and concert hall, superb civic centre, and first-class sporting amenities.

Mutare is arguably Zimbabwe's most colourful city. During the Christmas season the flame trees are at the peak of their brilliance. In winter, aloes and cycads are in flower, while September and October are the months for jacaranda and bougainvillaea.

Mutare is an international city, separated from the Mozambique border by a chain-mesh fence, wasteland, and floodlights. It is also the terminal of the oil pipeline from Beira that discharges its products at Feruka, a few kilometres west of the city.

Farming and mining are the mainstays of the city's economy, although the manufacturing section has developed rapidly and now includes a vehicle assembly plant, glass, timber, paper, textile, and food processing industries.

Despite the rapidly expanding industrial sprawl, nothing diminishes Mutare's glory. As a major city it suffers no overcrowding. In terms of population — far outranked by Bulawayo, Chitungwiza (Harare's satellite) and Gweru — Mutare at most has a scarce 75,000 residents (indeed it is said that Mutare is most suited to the newly-wed or nearly-dead).

Yet although fifth in number of people, it claims third place in terms of importance. Mutare has always prided itself on its role in national history.

The original settlement was built in 1888, seventeen kilometres (10 miles) from the present city near the kraal of the powerful Manica chief, Mutasa, whose favours and support were courted by both the British and the Portuguese.

Abandoned in 1891, a second township was established near the Mutare River at the proposed headquarters for the railway from Beira through Fort Salisbury to Bulawayo, where it would link up with the line from South Africa. The rail would then move north to complete the Cape to Cairo link that Rhodes planned as part of the British conquest of Africa.

Contractor George Pauling began construction at Fontesvilla in September 1892. The narrow-gauge line, following the course of the Menini River Valley from Macaque, reached the place where Mutare now stands on 4 February, 1898.

And there it faced an insurmountable barrier — the daunting climb over Christmas Pass (named by the army engineer assigned to build a road over it after he made camp there on Christmas Day, 1891). The incline was too steep and a tunnel was unfeasible.

Pauling suggested to Rhodes that Mutare (known until independence as Umtali) would have to be moved a second time. Promising compensation totalling around $100,000 to all those who agreed to move, Rhodes organised the transfer under a government notice of 1 October, 1896 (See "The Eastern Highlands: Mountain and Moor, Forest and Waterfall", Part Two).

Many wood and iron buildings from the old town were carried over Christmas Pass and laid out on the Sable Valley, Waterfall Mountain View, and Berkeley farms established by three of the original settlers.

The governing Sanitary Board held its first meeting in the "new" Umtali on 29 September, 1887, and the railway established its headquarters and the locomotive workshops that served the entire system for many years.

Development was swift. The BSAC built a Z$6,000 dam for town water and in 1899 the town fathers built a tramway, the only one ever to operate in Zimbabwe, between the railway station and the town centre by way of Herbert Chitepo (formerly Main) Street. It was maintained by railway engineers who also carried out work in the neighbouring mines and farms.

Six months after the inauguration of the

Above: Three Steps was the first house to be built when Umtali, now Mutare, was founded in the 1890s.

Salisbury–Umtali line, the original narrow-gauge track was replaced on 1 August, 1900, with a standard-gauge line and the Beira Railway company amalgamated with the Mashonaland Railway Company. The railway brought increasing numbers of settlers. By 1904, despite the endemic malaria, the population totalled more than 1,000 (of which only a quarter were women).

In 1910, the wood and iron railway headquarters were dismantled, loaded onto special trucks, and taken to Bulawayo. The Mutare workshops, however, continued to maintain the Garrett steam locomotives for many years afterwards and, much later, assumed responsibility for major overhauls of the modern diesel-electric fleet.

Mutare became a municipality in June 1914, and a city on 1 October, 1971, during the war for independence.

Getting there

Mutare, 263 kilometres (163 miles) from Harare, 577 kilometres (359 miles) from Bulawayo, 992 kilometres (616 miles) from Victoria Falls, and 585 kilometres (364 miles) from Beitbridge, is well-served by road and rail services. There is a regular night train between Mutare and Harare and a luxury passenger coach service by road five days a week. It does not run on Tuesdays and Thursdays. Mutare is the main border post between Mozambique and Zimbabwe.

When to go

Mutare is pleasant and beautiful all year-round, but particularly colourful between November and December when its flame trees and flamboyants burst into bloom. Between May and July aloes and cycads are in flower and its many jacaranda trees and bougainvillaea blossom between September and October. Mutare is never short of nature's colour.

Where to stay

The Manica Hotel (3-star), Christmas Pass Hotel. There are other hotels with varying degrees of service and some splendid hotels in the nearby Vumba Mountains. See Listings for "Hotels". Mutare has a beautiful caravan park and excellent campsites. See Listings.

Above: The Vumba Mountains are the back drop to Mutare's Herbert Chitepo (formerly Main) Street.

Sightseeing

The main road from Harare into Mutare, a modern **dual carriageway**, begins its climb over **Christmas Pass** from the plains just beyond the **northbound Penhalonga Road**. There is a **hotel** where the road begins to climb. In earlier times the pass was a formidable barrier, so severe it took the early settlers a whole day and sometimes longer to make the trek over it.

At the crest of the pass there is a **viewpoint** which is also the start of a **gravel road** that leads precariously up to the 1,520-metre (5,000-foot) **summit** of **Mutare** (formerly Umtali) **Heights**. It is a snaking, hairpin road with steep drops on either side.

At the summit, soldiers and police guard a **radio mast**. The sunset from this point is superlative.

It was at the Christmas Pass viewpoint on 8 July, 1953, that Britain's Queen Elizabeth, the Queen Mother, unveiled a **monument** raised to Kingsley Fairbridge, an ardent South African-born advocate of white settlement in the British Empire.

Fairbridge organized the migration of thousands of British orphans and unwanted children to Canada, Australia, and what was then Rhodesia. The monument was removed after independence and is now on view in Mutare's **Utopia Museum**, in the house where Fairbridge was born.

A small distance beyond the viewpoint, where the road descends into the city, is the superb **caravan park** and **campsite**. Beyond that, to the **south** of the road, is the beautiful **Murahwa Hill Nature Reserve** run by the Zimbabwe National Trust.

Within its leafy interior, there is evidence of prehistoric settlement in this area, a **protected village** (monument to the second *Chimurenga*), and a sanctuary for rare birds, trees, and butterflies. You can also reach the reserve down a **steep path** from Christmas Pass.

As you enter Mutare itself, a modern **motel** stands to the **west** of the road before the **west turn** into **Magamba** (formerly Jan Smuts) **Drive**. This leads to the Mutare Agricultural and Horticultural Society's excellent **showground**.

Mutare still depends on farming and mining for much of its prosperity and the yearly

Top: Vintage steam traction engine stands outside Mutare National Museum.
Above: Utopia House National Museum, Mutare, depicts the lifestyles of the early European settlers in the region.

Agricultural and Horticultural Society Show, first staged in 1900, draws thousands of visitors from all around the country.

After the showground turn, there is another **intersection** to the **north-east** along **Jason Moyo** (formerly Rhodes) **Drive**. It circles the attractive fairways of **Mutare Golf Club** and comes out on **Herbert Chitepo** (formerly Main) **Street**.

Turn north off Herbert Chitepo Street along **Arcadia Road** which leads to **Cecil Kop Nature Reserve**. Cecil Kop's seventeen square kilometres (seven square miles) of pristine African landscape supports a wide variety of antelope, elephant, rhino, zebra, and wildebeest — a stunning spectacle to find in any city, even in Africa.

Within Cecil Kop, **Thompson's Vlei** lies along the **eastern boundary** of the city — which also forms the **Mozambique border** — and has giraffe, buffalo, wart hog, nyala, blue duiker, and other antelope. Only three kilometres (two miles) from the city centre, Cecil Kop Nature Reserve is open daily from 09.00 until sundown.

At the **intersection** with Jason Moyo Drive the Harare Road becomes **Robert Mugabe Avenue** (formerly Churchill Road). The next **intersection** brings you to **Aerodrome Road**. Robert Mugabe Avenue then continues to the **junction** with **Simon Mazorodze** (formerly Meikles) **Road**.

Mutare's superb **civic centre**, to the **west** of **Simon Mazorodze Road**, adds charm and dignity to the city. Surrounded by manicured lawns and flowerbeds, the city's showpiece is the legacy of Sir Stephen and Lady Courtauld whose old home, "La Rochelle", some way outside the city on the Penhalonga Road, is open to the public (See "The Eastern Highlands: Mountain and Moor, Forest and Waterfall", Part Two).

The civic centre includes an Olympic **swimming pool**, the **Courtauld Theatre** (one of the finest amateur theatres in Africa), **Turner Memorial Library**, **Queen's Concert Hall**, and **Post Office**.

In contrast to the modern civic centre, **Utopia Museum**, which stands on **Fourteenth Avenue**, is in the third house to be built in Mutare. The house was the birthplace of Kingsley Fairbridge, the Rhodes scholar and poet who died prematurely at the age of thirty-nine.

His father, Rhys Fairbridge, was the man who surveyed and laid out the new Mutare. The house, which has been restored to its original condition, presents a clear picture of the way the early pioneers lived at the turn of the century. The Fairbridge family donated it to the National Museum of Zimbabwe.

It is only a street away from the first house built in the new town, **Three Steps**, which is still a fashionable city residence, as are many of Mutare's original buildings.

A history of the city and the Eastern Highlands is graphically displayed at the **Mutare Museum**, **south** of **Aerodrome Road**, which matches Bulawayo's for the quality of its exhibits.

One of the museum's displays, located in the **Transport Gallery**, has an outstanding number of exhibits including a London **telephone kiosk** (large enough to be a bedsit), **horse-drawn carriages**, **early locomotives**, and **vintage cars** and **motorcycles**.

The **Boultbee Gallery**, named after the first curator, Captain E. F. Boultbee, OBE (Order of the British Empire), contains a range of **armour** and **small arms** covering the past 500 years.

At the **natural history** displays (for many the most compelling), you can open a hatch and study a live **bee colony** at work in its hive, or walk through a door into an **outdoor aviary** that contains almost 600 birds representing more than fifty species from four major families. Other displays in this superb museum focus on cultures and landscapes.

One **road** leads **east** from Mutare down to the Mozambique **border post** and, beyond that, the village of **Machipanda**. Along the way you can catch some outstanding views of **Cross Kopje**, its **summit** crowned with a floodlit, ten-metre-tall (33-foot) **cross** that honours the memory of the African soldiers from Zimbabwe (then Rhodesia) who fell alongside their East African brothers during the First World War.

Opposite: Mutare banana plantation.

Gweru: Zimbabwe's Industrial Heart

Gweru, the country's third-largest city with more than 80,000 people, traces its humble roots back to 1894 when Dr. Leander Starr Jameson established a coaching station along the Harare–Bulawayo road. Within the year there were six hotels and it had become a settlement for gold prospectors combing the seams of the Great Dyke.

Gweru's first bank opened in 1896, followed two years later by the Stock Exchange that still stands in the town centre. One of the country's pioneer newspapers, the *Northern Optimist*, now the *Gweru Times*, was launched in 1897.

The arrival of the railway in 1902 — from both the north and the south — was the catalyst that triggered Gweru's initial development. Then called Gwelo (the name was changed in 1982), the town was elevated to municipal status in 1914 and became a city in 1971.

Until the end of the 1930s it remained mainly a farming centre, serving the many cattle, dairy, and arable farms that flourish in the region. A second catalyst then transformed Gweru from an agricultural to a major industrial centre — the 1939 decision of the Bata Shoe Company to establish a factory there.

Now the largest shoe-manufacturing plant in Southern Africa, it produces more than ten million pairs of shoes a year for both the local and export market. In the years since, following in the company's footsteps, so to speak, many more large industries have established manufacturing units at Gweru.

Gweru is also an important army and air force training centre. The establishment of an Air Training School at Gweru during the 1939–45 war, as part of the Empire Air Training Scheme, gave the town a big boost, and laid the foundation for further growth in the postwar years.

Getting there

Gweru, 164 kilometres (102 miles) from Bulawayo, 183 kilometres (114 miles) from Masvingo, 471 kilometres (293 miles) from Beitbridge, and 275 kilometres (171 miles) from Harare, is centrally situated. It is well-served by daily rail and bus services.

When to go

Gweru is pleasant all year-round.

Where to stay

Midlands Hotel (3-star), Fairmile Motel (3-star). There are other hotels with varying degrees of service. See Listings for "Hotels". There is an excellent caravan park and campsite.

Sightseeing

Gweru's wide streets with their graceful buildings, attractive green lawns, colourful flowerbeds, and stands of tall and shady trees, come as a revelation to those preconceived images conjured up by its reputation as the industrial centre of the country.

The pleasant **city centre**, guarded on one side by the **Midlands Hotel** and by the old **Stock Exchange building** on the other, still retains its farming ambience. Dating back to 1898, the Stock Exchange in **Main Street** is the city's oldest building. Dominating the city centre is **Boggie's Clock Tower** with the hands standing at 10.50. The clock

Above: Boggie's Clock Tower, Gweru.

and tower were raised in memory of Scottish-born Major W. J. Boggie by his widow, Mrs. Jeannie Boggie, in 1937, nine years after his death.

Town legend says that his remains were interred in the tower and that when, one day in 1981, they were removed at 10.50, the clock stopped — never to move again.

Mrs. Boggie was well-known for her vocal remonstration to the authorities and letters to the press against the noise created by the training aircraft that flew low over her farm. The noise, she claimed, prevented her hens from laying and the cows from being content.

The elegance of Gweru's early colonial architecture is perhaps best seen in the old 1905 **magistrate's court** on **Lobengula Avenue**, now a government administrative office.

From a more recent era, the graceful curved profile of the city's splendid **municipal offices** on **Robert Mugabe Way** (formerly Livingstone Avenue), is set in a delightful **rose garden** containing a **stone** from London's **Waterloo Bridge,** presented to the city fathers by the London County Council.

Close by, in a secluded avenue, stands another antiquity, more of interest for what it represents than for its design. Gweru's **Dutch Reformed Church**, a branch of the South African faith that espoused and spread the gospel of apartheid, still serves worshippers, tangible proof of the country's commitment to freedom of worship.

As an important army and air force training centre, it is appropriate that the outstanding **Midlands Museum** on **Lobengula Avenue** (within walking distance of the city centre) should serve as Zimbabwe's **National Military Museum**.

The **weapons hall** and **open-air displays**, featuring different generations of aircraft and ground armour — tanks, personnel carriers, field guns — are striking visual exhibitions.

Among the biplanes and early jet fighters is the strange-looking **"pou du ciel"** — Flying Flea — built by Aston Redrup of Bulawayo in 1933 and powered by a 540 cc two-stroke motorcycle engine.

With a top speed of 100 kilometres (60 miles) an hour, this odd plane needed less than 100 metres (330 feet) for take off and landed at a speed of thirty kilometres (19 miles) an hour. It had a flying time of three hours and a ceiling of 1,520 metres (5,000 feet).

The most interesting historical exhibition, however, is contained in the **Military History gallery**. Attractive graphics detail the wars of freedom fought in Zimbabwe ending with a display that salutes the martyrs and heroes of the most recent struggle for independence.

A tribute to other heroes in another war are the **Memorial Swimming Baths**, located off Robert Mugabe Way behind the magnificent **auditorium** of **Gweru Theatre** (noted for its carved wooden mural depicting theatre through the ages). These were built as a 1920 memorial to those who fell in the Great War and were the first public swimming baths constructed in Rhodesia.

Gweru offers much in the way of recreation. There is another **swimming pool** on **Birchenough Road**, **cinemas**, a comfortable and comprehensive **library**, **music academy**, a **golf course**, sailing, riding, and almost eighty members' clubs.

To commune with nature, **Antelope Game Park,** nine kilometres (five and a half miles) from town, offers forty-five kilometres (28 miles) of game-viewing roads and abundant wildlife, in particular sable and giraffe.

Above: Gweru National Military Museum.

PART FOUR: SPECIAL FEATURES

Above: Colourful collection of Zimbabwe butterflies. Opposite: Baby giraffe.

Wildlife: Where the Game Still Roams Wild and Free

Since independence, Zimbabwe has gained a justified reputation as one of the finest game-viewing countries in Africa. More than twelve per cent of its land is set aside solely for wildlife conservation and, with a few exceptions, virtually all species of mammal, bird, reptile, and insect indigenous to the region are well represented.

Most of the 291 known land mammals recorded south of the **Zambezi** and **Cunene rivers** occur naturally in Zimbabwe, including the large and spectacular animals for which Africa is famous. In many cases, Zimbabwe can boast some of the finest remaining populations on the continent.

Where poaching has virtually destroyed the **elephant** in several neighbouring countries, Zimbabwe has an overpopulation of these magnificent pachyderms. Their numbers have developed from an estimated 5,000 or so animals at the turn of the century, to over 50,000 today, mainly — but not entirely — confined to the country's major national parks and other protected areas.

The **Hwange National Park** and associated areas, which together form a wildlife complex that extends several hundred kilometres south of **Victoria Falls**, contains Zimbabwe's largest elephant population, exceeding more than 20,000.

During the rains the animals tend to disperse throughout the park, crossing the border into Botswana. During the dry season the large herds return, concentrating near easily-accessible pans such as **Nyamandhlovu**, close to the park's **Main Camp** headquarters.

Several other major conservation areas also comprise large elephant populations. There are an estimated 13,000 elephants in the **Zambezi Valley** wildlife complex, which includes the well-known and exceptionally beautiful **Mana Pools National Park**; 12,000 in the remote **Chizarira National Park** and neighbouring **Chirisa Safari Area**; and 5,000 in the **Gonarezhou National Park** in southeastern Zimbabwe.

Less significant but nevertheless important herds can often be seen on the shores of **Matusadona National Park** at **Lake Kariba**.

Zimbabwe also shelters the world's largest surviving population of the endangered **black rhinoceros**, with approximately 1,500 animals concentrated mainly in the Zambezi Valley and the Chizarira-Chirisa complex, and a scattering of smaller herds in several other park areas. Unfortunately, the Zambezi Valley group came under heavy pressure from poachers early in 1985, and rhino poaching has since spread.

The Department of National Parks established "Operation Stronghold" to contain the poaching, while the private sector assisted by providing funds and equipment through the "Rhino Survival Campaign".

"Operation Stronghold" has three main components: anti-poaching operations in the field, relying heavily on anti-guerilla tactics; the establishment of semi-captive breeding programmes in areas less vulnerable to poaching; and captive breeding both within Zimbabwe and abroad, especially in the United States.

White rhinoceros

Zimbabwe also has a small but — in this case — growing population of **white rhinoceros**, *Ceratotherium simum*. This species was exterminated in Zimbabwe early in the century and almost became extinct throughout Southern Africa.

A few tenacious rhinos managed to survive in South Africa's Umfolozi-Hluhluwe complex, and were regenerated until there were enough animals to translocate to other areas in the region.

Zimbabwe's white rhinos all originate from this South African population and can be seen in such well-protected areas as the **McIlwaine Recreational Park** near Harare, the scenic **Matobo Hills** near Bulawayo, near **Main Camp** in Hwange, and in **Lake Kyle Recreational Park**.

National Parks Recreational Parks, Botanical Gardens & Reserves

ZAMBIA

LAKE CABORA BASSA

MOZAMBIQUE

CHIRUNDU · Mana Pools

KARIBA

Charara Safari Area

CENTENARY

KAROI

MT. DARWIN

Matusadona

Chinhoyi Caves · CHINHOYI

BINDURA

SHAMVA

Ewanrigg Botanical Gardens

BINGA

Chizarira

Darwendale · HARARE

Lake Chivero

Zambezi

Victoria Falls

MLIBIZI

CHEGUTU

KADOMA

MARONDERA

NYANGA

Nyanga

Kazuma Pan

HWANGE

RUSAPE · Mtarazi Falls

Ngezi

MUTARE

Hwange

KWE KWE

Sebakwe

CHIVHU

MVUMA · Vumba Botanical Gardens

GWERU

Chimanimani

BULAWAYO

Mushandike Sanctuary

MASVINGO

Lake Mutirikwi

Rusitu Forest Botanical Reserve

PLUMTREE

Umzingwane

ZVISHAVANE

Great Zimbabwe Ruins

CHIPINGE

Chiranda Forest

Matobo

Bangala

Manjirenji

BOTSWANA

GWANDA

WEST NICHOLSON

TRIANGLE · CHIREDZI

RUTENGA

Gonarezhou

0 100 200 300 km
0 100 200 miles

BEITBRIDGE

SANGO

SOUTH AFRICA

MOZAMBIQUE

It is not always easy to distinguish between black and white rhinos at a glance; the white rhino is more heavily built, has a longer head, a square mouth, and a pronounced "nuchal hump" at the shoulder.

It also feeds exclusively on grasses, whereas the black rhino is predominantly a browsing animal, preferring the leaves, shoots, and twigs of shrubs and bushes.

Unlike the rhino, **buffalo** are extremely common in most large national parks and other conservation areas, and herds up to 2,000-strong are regularly seen in Hwange, the Zambezi Valley, and the Matusadona National Park.

At Matusadona, the buffalo population underwent an explosive expansion during the 1980s, when several years of drought caused Lake Kariba to fall to its lowest level since the dam was built back in the 1950s.

Dense swards of torpedo grass developed along the exposed shorelines, creating a vastly increased food supply for buffalo and other grazing animals. The buffalo population responded by increasing at a rate of about ten per cent a year for several years.

Matusadona and Lake Kariba also have one of Zimbabwe's largest populations of **hippopotamus**. Usually seen in schools or pods (a term borrowed from the whale world) of females accompanied by a dominant male, hippo are grazing animals.

They emerge from the water at night and, in times of drought, may travel several kilometres during the evening to feed. Their passive appearance when resting in the water belies a potential for ferocious aggression, as several Zimbabwean canoeists can testify. They are especially dangerous out of the water and cause many injuries and deaths each year.

The Zambezi River has an excellent hippo population, and they can also be seen in most other major rivers, both within and outside the park estate.

Big cats

For many visitors on safari in Zimbabwe, a top priority will be to see the "big cats", and **lion** in particular. As with most other species, the country has a balanced population of these superb creatures, again located mainly within the formal park and wildlife sanctuaries.

Good lion sightings tend to result from a combination of patience, luck, and a willingness to get out of bed early in the morning. Unlike the East African plains, where animals can often be seen from great distances, most Zimbabwean parks are covered with dense bush or woodlands and contain few open areas.

Kills usually take place at night, often in these more open expanses, and prides generally remain close to their victims for an hour or two after sunrise before retreating into the bush.

Prime areas for lion sightings during a short visit include Hwange, Mana Pools, and the torpedo-grasslands along the shores of Matusadona.

The Matobo Hills, south of Bulawayo, have one of Africa's densest populations of **leopard**, and most other parks also have good numbers. Again, however, the area is largely covered with dense bush and sightings are usually a matter of luck.

Two other exceptionally beautiful species, the **cheetah** and the **wild dog**, are unfortunately less well-represented. There are only about 500 cheetah in Zimbabwe, largely because of the few open but well-grassed habitats this species prefers.

Most Zimbabwean cheetah are presently located on private ranch lands. Habitats tend to be more suitable, and there is — fortunately — a large artificial food supply in the form of cattle, and few competing predators.

The Zimbabwean wild dog, like the cheetah, today numbers in the hundreds. Relentlessly persecuted in the past, it was often shot on sight both inside and outside the park boundaries. In Hwange and the Zambezi Valley, packs numbering between fifteen and thirty animals are sometimes seen near Mana Pools.

Research continues on ways of protecting and regenerating the two species, which are in grave danger of local extinction.

The cheetah and wild dog aside, many other large mammals occur in good numbers throughout the park and wildlife estates. **Giraffe** are plentiful in most areas except the Zambezi Valley, where — for as yet unknown reasons — they seem never to have been present.

Wildebeest is another species that does not occur in the Zambezi Valley, although they are plentiful elsewhere and are often seen in the company of zebra.

Of the antelopes, the most plentiful and prolific — and maybe the loveliest — are the **impala**, which occur throughout the wildlife reserves and often outside them as well.

Impala are easily recognised by their silky golden coats, black and white markings on the rump, and the lyre-shaped horns carried by the males.

Most large groups are composed of females, with one dominant ram in attendance. The rams fight for control during the rut in March and April, then attempt to retain groups of females on their terrain while unsuccessful males form small, loosely structured "bachelor groups".

Of the larger antelopes, **kudu**, **waterbuck**, **eland**, and **reedbuck** are common in much of Zimbabwe, while **gemsbok** — a species that prefers more arid habitats such as the Kalahari in neighbouring Botswana — only occur in the extreme west.

There are small populations of **tsessebe**, **Lichtenstein's hartebeest**, and **red hartebeest** in several areas; while smaller antelopes such as **duiker** and **steenbok** are common.

The strange little **klipspringer**, with its cylindrical hooves and spiny coat, inhabits the rocky hills and outcrops, while the tiny little **blue duiker** is confined to the montane areas of Zimbabwe's Eastern Highlands.

Top: Sable herd at waterhole in Hwange National Park.
Above: Impala — perhaps the loveliest of all antelope.

Twelve orders

Taxonomically Zimbabwe's mammals represent twelve orders. The elephant is the sole representative of the *Proboscidea*, while the black and white rhinos and the **zebra** are included in the *Perissodactyla*, or odd-toed hoofed mammals.

The *Artiodactyla*, or even-toed hoofed mammals, include the buffalo, hippopotamus, all the antelopes, the giraffe, **bush pig** and **wart hog**, while the *Primates* are represented by the **chacma baboon** and the **vervet** and **samango monkeys**. The big cats, wild dog, and many other less spectacular species are, of course, all *Carnivora* or meat-eaters.

The *Insectivora* include species such as the **shrews** and the **hedgehog**, while the shy, nocturnal, and odd-looking **aardvark**, though insectivorous, is the sole representative of the *Tubulidentata* order. The **pangolin** — also insectivorous — belongs to the *Pholidota* order. More than fifty species of **bat** are contained in the order *Chiroptera*, while the *Rodentia* are represented by the **porcupine** and a multitude of **rat**, **mice**, and **gerbil** species.

Hares and **rabbits** belong to the *Lagomorpha*, and the elephant's closest — if distant — relatives are the two species of **dassie** or **rock rabbit** (hyrax) that are members of the *Hyracoidea*.

Zimbabwe also has 153 reptile species divided between six suborders; the **tortoises** and **turtles** (*Cryptodira*), the **terrapins** (*Pleurodira*), the **amphibians** (*Amphisbaenia*), the **lizards** (*Lacertilia*), the **snakes** (*Serpentes*), and the **crocodile** (*Crocodylia*).

Visitors often ask about snakes, especially if they are undertaking a walking safari. Snakes are certainly plentiful in Zimbabwe and some of the more spectacular of the country's seventy-six species include the **Egyptian cobra**, the **black** and **green mambas**, and the **python**.

They are seldom seen, however, preferring to avoid humans whenever possible. The main exception to this rule is the **puff adder**, which may hiss in warning without moving away, and then bite if its warning is ignored.

The beautifully-marked python is Zimbabwe's largest snake, sometimes reaching a length of six metres (20 feet). They are

Opposite: Giraffe reach heights of more than five metres and their blood pressure is controlled by a complex system of valves.

Below: Chameleon on bare branch.

Above: Monitor lizard.

mainly nocturnal, feeding off birds and mammals ranging in size from rats and mice to small antelopes. The snake is neither aggressive nor venomous, but can inflict a painful bite if disturbed. Pythons were once in great demand for their skins and today they are the only Zimbabwean snake that has legal protection.

Also in demand for their skins are Zimbabwe's crocodiles. An essential part of the ecology in which they occur, these ancient reptiles were almost exterminated in some areas earlier in the century, greatly disturbing the equilibrium of fish populations and numerous other species.

In these depleted areas, crocodile numbers have been revitalised by a combination of protective legislation and the crocodile farming industry that is compelled by law to return a percentage of its hatchlings to the wild if necessary.

There are abundant crocodile populations in Lake Kariba, in the Zambezi, and in most other major rivers, both inside and outside park boundaries.

Though they may spend much of the day basking on sandbanks, these giant lizards are often shy, slipping quietly into the water when humans approach and staying submerged for long periods. It is inadvisable to swim in these waters, even if crocodiles cannot be seen.

Smaller crocodiles prey mainly on fish, particularly barbel; larger specimens may take mammals such as antelopes and even buffalo, launching an extremely rapid attack on their prey as they drink or swim and then pulling it underwater until the quarry drowns. Crocodiles are also valuable scavengers, swiftly disposing of carcasses and other wastes.

Conservation

In Zimbabwe the proper conservation of wildlife has become a matter of national priority. The term wildlife is now used to include all flora and fauna, even though there is still a good deal of emphasis on the larger mammals — the foundation on which Zimbabwe's parks and much of the country's economic approach to wildlife — is based.

Concern over the survival of large mammals was first expressed early in this century.

Opposite: Lioness grooms cubs.

Below: Young python. The largest snake in Zimbabwe reaches lengths of more than six metres when mature.

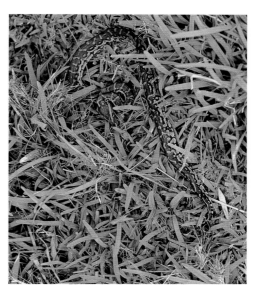

Above: Ground squirrel.

Opposite: Young cheetah — the fastest land animal in the world.

Many species, including rhino and elephant, had suffered severely from several decades of uncontrolled hunting. The spread of commercial agriculture and human settlement also destroyed animal habitats.

The government responded by setting aside large "game reserves" solely for wildlife, the forerunners of today's national parks system. Locals were removed from these areas and forbidden to hunt for any reason. As a result, the rural communities became hostile to both wildlife and wildlife areas.

Despite this hostility, expansion and development continued through the 1960s. During the 1970s, however, it became obvious that action must be taken to dissipate the growing tensions between the rural inhabitants and preserved areas.

The turning point was the farsighted 1975 Parks and Wild Life Act. Hitherto — as is still the case in many countries — wildlife had been State property, the equivalent of the royal game of Europe.

The act allowed landholders to take responsibility for wildlife management and use on their land. Many predicted that this would lead to wholesale extermination. Instead there was a steady increase in wildlife populations on private lands as ranchers and farmers began to gain financial returns through carefully controlled sport hunting.

This philosophy has more recently been extended to the country's "communal lands". Districts and even individual villages have been given full responsibility for wildlife management, and in many cases have already gained substantial benefits in both cash and animal population growth.

Thus Zimbabweans have, once again, a positive incentive to conserve wildlife and its habitats.

Above: Spotted hyena are formidable predators as well as scavengers.

Opposite top: White rhino mother and calf at Hwange National Park.

Opposite: Baboons.

Following page: Ostrich, the world's largest bird.

273

Bird Life: An Ornithological Treasure House

As with most of southern Africa, Zimbabwe has a large and varied avifauna. To date, approximately 640 species — including both residents and migrants — have been recorded in the country. Some bird families are exceptionally well-represented, such as the warblers with fifty-three species and the diurnal birds of prey with forty-seven.

Human activity, notably the clearing of land for settlement and cultivation, has had a profound effect on Zimbabwe's bird life. Though no species has yet become extinct within the country, many — such as the **bateleur eagle** — have declined in numbers or disappeared from certain areas.

At present, more than forty species have "Special Protection" under Zimbabwean law, a status that theoretically precludes the capture, maiming, or killing of these species except under strictly controlled circumstances.

Whether protected or unprotected, most of Zimbabwe's bird life can be found in several major habitat areas, each characterised by the particular bird community that resides there. Patches of relict forest, especially in the east and south-east, often shelter endemic species. Woodland birds inhabit the mopane of the low-lying river valleys such as the Zambezi, as well as much of the low-veld, the teak woodlands of Matabeleland, and the miombo woodlands and wooded savannahs characteristic of the plateau region. Savannah grasslands, montane grasslands, and freshwater habitats also harbour their own specific populations.

About seventy-five of the recorded species are palaearctic migrants that breed in Europe and Asia and visit Africa during the European winter. These migrants include twenty-two varieties of **passerine**, nineteen of **sandpiper**, and fourteen different **birds of prey**.

Another sixty species are pan-African migrants, visiting Zimbabwe from other parts of the continent. This group includes nine types of **cuckoo**, five of **swift**, and seven species of **swallow**. Most of these pan-African migrants breed in Zimbabwe before heading north during their non-breeding season.

In forest habitats, bird communities are likely to include **doves, louries, barbets, bulbuls, robins, flycatchers, shrikes, sunbirds**, and **waxbills**. Two species in particular — **Swynnerton's robin** and **Robert's prinia** — are confined to forests in Zimbabwe's eastern districts and found nowhere else in the world.

Woodlands are often characterised by a wide variety of arboreal passerines, such as **drongos, cuckoo shrikes, warblers, flycatchers**, shrikes, and sunbirds; many non-passerines such as doves, **parrots**, cuckoos, louries, **woodhoopoes, kingfishers, bee-eaters, hornbills**, and **woodpeckers**; and also ground birds that include **francolins, korhaans, buttonquails**, and some **coursers**.

Grasslands are characterised by francolins, korhaans, **larks, cisticolas, longclaws, pipits, bishops**, and **widow-birds**. Freshwater habitats harbour **ducks, coots**, and **cormorants**; **ibises** and **darters** prefer open stretches of water; and bare shorelines attract **plovers, sandpipers, herons**, and various other **waterfowl**.

Impressions

The casual visitor is likely to have three immediate impressions, particularly if they hail from the more temperate part of the world such as Europe or North America.

The first will be the great variety of brightly coloured birds — much more than the 150 or so species of the fowl-impoverished north.

A second observation will be the frequency with which large species, including many raptors, herons, the **kori bustard** — and of course the **ostrich** — are casually sighted.

And thirdly, visitors from afar will notice the ever-present background music, typified by several species of dove and **pigeon**, that is an inescapable feature of any visit to the bush.

The avifauna acoustics can also be enjoyed in the suburbs of any major city where a wide variety of birds have become accustomed to human activity, and indeed thrive in city gardens and parks.

Top left: Weaver bird.

Top right: Crested crane.

Centre left: Lilac-breasted roller.

Above: Ground hornbill.

Left: Secretary bird.

Early risers are unlikely to be out of hearing distance from the **Heuglin's robin**, which has one of the most beautiful calls of any Zimbabwean species. The bird is recognized by its olive-brown above, white eye-stripe, and dull orange under-parts.

Contained within the same family are two other common garden birds, the **kurrichane** and **groundscraper thrushes**. Both species may be seen hopping across lawns and bare flowerbeds in search of food, and both are easily distinguishable.

The kurrichane has a grey crown, mantle, back, rump, tail, and wing coverts; orange bill and flanks; and a white abdomen. The groundscraper is grey and has white under-parts spotted with black.

Sunbirds, louries, and finches all frequent gardens, as do several doves and pigeons, including the extremely common **Cape turtle dove** with its ubiquitous call, often anthropomorphised as "where's FA-ther, where's FA-ther".

The call of the brightly-coloured **crested barbet**, often seen hopping around the branches of trees or foraging on lawns, is quite accurately described as an alarm clock with the bell removed.

By dark the cry of the fiery-necked **nightjar** is also a common feature of both suburban and bush surroundings; a mellow, whistling phrase characterised as "good Lord deliver-us". The **spotted eagle owl**, a largish species reaching around forty-five centimetres (18 inches) in length, may also be heard. Males of this breed have an easily-recognised, two-syllable call, "VOOO-huu", with the second note lower in pitch than the first.

Travellers by road, especially at night, are also likely to experience "close shaves" both with nightjars, which often lie on road surfaces (especially dirt or gravel), and owls, including the **marsh** and **grass owls**, which have a predilection for perching on fence posts and scavenging for small animals.

By day, **yellow-billed kites** also hunt the roads and tracks, while the smaller **black-shouldered kite**, Zimbabwe's most common and widespread bird of prey, can be seen on fence and telegraph poles, perhaps flanked by a variety of other species including bee-eaters, **rollers**, swifts, and swallows.

Away from the suburbs and into the major wildlife areas, it is often the larger raptors and herons that attract immediate attention. Of the seventeen species of eagle found in Zimbabwe, the most intensively studied is the **black eagle**, *Aquila verreauxii*.

There is a particularly high density of these large birds in the **Matobo Hills**, south of **Bulawayo**. Magnificent flyers, they often perform spectacular aerial displays from prominent outcrops in their large territories.

Though disappearing from other areas, the striking bateleur eagle, *Terathopius acaudatus*, is still common and easily seen in many protected regions.

This is the only eagle of which male and female can be easily distinguished in flight: both are white under the wing, but the black trailing edge is broader in males than females. Bateleurs spend much of the day flying, often circling in thermals, thus making identification a simple matter.

A striking species, found near marshy woodland areas throughout much of the country, is the **long-crested eagle**, *Lophaetus occipitalis*. Reaching fifty-five centimetres (22 inches) in length, the bird is black with white leg feathers and a long, floppy crest.

Above: Fledgling darters at Lake Kariba.

Above: Distinctive fish eagle — known for its haunting cry — with freshly caught prey.
Opposite: Kori bustard, thought to be the largest flying bird in the world.

It catches its prey, mainly rodents, by dropping straight down from its perch upon them.

Martial Eagle

The largest eagle in Zimbabwe is the **martial eagle**, *Polemaetus bellicosus*. Reaching eighty centimetres (32 inches) in length, this species is brown with white-spotted under-parts and bright yellow eyes. They are powerful birds that hunt from the air, often at great heights, and their prey includes small antelopes and birds.

Zimbabwe's most famous raptor, featured widely in the media and conspicuous at many tourist resorts, is the **fish eagle**. With a white head, black upper-parts, and chestnut under-parts, the bird closely resembles the bald eagle of North America.

It prefers to build its untidy nest in the branches of bare trees and, though it can be seen along most rivers in the wilder parts of the country, it is a particular attribute of **Lake Kariba**.

There the partly-submerged "drowned trees", together with a greatly expanded food supply, have combined to create an excep-tional population of this magnificent bird.

As their name implies, fish eagles feed mainly on fish caught in their talons during shallow dives from perches beside the water. In some areas, notably the **Sanyati Gorge** on Lake Kariba, local guides have trained fish eagles to stoop for bream thrown from a boat, providing superb opportunities for viewing and photography.

It is undoubtedly the fish eagle's call, often uttered on the wing in duet between members of a pair, that is its most memorable feature: a piercing "KHOW-kyow-kyow", falling in pitch and volume towards the end.

The largest living bird in the world, the **ostrich**, can be found on Zimbabwean grasslands and in lightly wooded savannah. Though once well distributed throughout the country, they are now restricted to **Matabeleland**, parts of the south-east, and the central plateau.

A thriving ostrich ranching and farming industry has recently developed in Zimbabwe, mainly to satisfy the demands of the fashion world for its skin. The bird's low-cholesterol

279

meat has also found a ready market, mainly in the health conscious United States.

Another Zimbabwean species, the kori bustard, can weigh up to twenty kilos (44 lbs), and is thought to be the biggest flying bird in the world. Kori bustards are usually seen in pairs at Matabeleland or **Hwange National Park**, and are unmistakable because of their enormous size.

Although not as large as the kori, many of Zimbabwe's herons and **storks** are towering, spectacular birds. To tell the difference, incidentally, storks fly with their necks outstretched; herons fold their necks in flight, bringing their heads closer to their bodies.

Of the eight species of stork that occur in Zimbabwe, two — the **white stork** and **Abdim**'s **stork** — are migrants. The white stork, the legendary bringer of babies, breeds in Europe and Asia but migrates to Africa during the European winter and may be seen in flocks numbering several thousand.

Abdim's storks are also a common sight during the Zimbabwean summer; easily recognised by their black and white colouring, they are often seen in large flocks on highveld grasslands and cultivated fields.

Other storks include the **marabou** (probably the ugliest) and the **saddlebilled** (the most spectacular). The marabou, a predominantly predatory bird, is black above, white below, and has a large, pinkish pouch hanging from its throat. The saddlebill,

though also black and white, is a strikingly handsome bird with a distinctive yellow "saddle" on its red and black bill. It is usually seen in the low-lying river valleys and is a common resident of Lake Kariba.

The largest of the herons — the **Goliath** — is another extremely handsome bird, found along the larger river systems and on Kariba. Though predominantly grey, it is not to be confused with the smaller — and much more common — **grey heron**, *Ardea cinerea*, often seen hunting along the margins of watercourses.

Another interesting, but less common, member of this family is the **black heron** or **egret**, *Egretta ardesiaca*, a totally black species about sixty-five centimetres (26 inches) long that forms its wings into an "umbrella" when fishing in the shallows of lakes and rivers.

Bee-eaters

Many other families are well-represented in Zimbabwe. The beautiful **carmine bee-eater** arrives during August or September, forming large colonies in burrows along the riverbanks.

Several species of **vulture** may be sighted on the remains of kills made by predators; the most common being the **white-backed vulture**. And **weavers** of several species manufacture the distinctive tree-suspended nests, often seen in colonies hanging over water.

The serious ornithologist should obtain an authoritative book on the subject, such as Robert's or Newman's guide to the birds of the region; and the Ornithological Association of Zimbabwe is always keen to acquire new members and pass on its substantial body of knowledge.

Most ornithological research in Zimbabwe is presently directed towards conservation. Several species, such as the bateleur eagle, the kori bustard, the **wattled crane**, and the **Lilian**'s and **black-cheeked lovebirds**, are vulnerable to extinction. Some of the endemic species of the eastern districts are actually threatened. Their disappearance is almost always the result of habitat destruction, sometimes combined with illegal capture for the wild bird trade or by illegal killing.

The **Natural History Museum** in

Above: Augur buzzard. These birds of prey prefer a lofty perch from which to search for food.

Above: Bateleur Eagle with distinctive neck ruff. The bird's name derives from the 17th-century French word for acrobat because of its spectacular stalling and somersaulting flight.

Bulawayo has the largest ornithological collection in the southern hemisphere, with 92,000 skins, 15,000 clutches of eggs, 20,000 nest record cards, and 800 skeletons.

The Ornithological Association has over 12,000 field cards, publishes a regular magazine, *The Honeyguide*, and is currently undertaking a project to produce a massive, nationwide bird atlas.

While waiting for the book to be publish-ed, Zimbabwean species can be studied live at the **Larvon Bird Gardens**, a few kilometres outside **Harare**. It contains a magnificent collection of indigenous and well-kept exhibits including an outstanding walk-through **aviary** in which man and bird can view one another in harmony.

Flora: A Land of Flaming Colour

The **Save Star**, the **flame lily**, the magnificently grotesque **baobab** — these are just a few of the flowers and trees included in Zimbabwe's diverse repertoire of flora and vegetation.

Though much of the country has been greatly modified by human activities, notably commercial and subsistence agriculture, Zimbabwe still has extensive areas of natural vegetation.

Biologists recognise six major physiognomic types — forest, thicket, savannah woodland, tree savannah, shrub savannah, and grassland — and twenty-five vegetation varieties.

Most of central Zimbabwe is characterised by savannah woodlands known locally as miombo woodland or *Brachystegia* woodland, because of the dominance of this genus.

In these areas, which have an average annual rainfall of between 750 and 1,000 millimetres (30-39 inches), the **msasa** (*Brachystegia spiciformis*) and **mnondo** (*Julbernardia globiflora*) predominate in open stands growing up to ten metres tall (33 feet).

Both of these trees are superficially similar in appearance, but can easily be identified. In the *msasa* the pair of "terminal leaflets" — at the tip of the main leaf — is larger than the other leaflets; in the *mnondo* they are visibly smaller.

These trees, and many others associated with this woodland type, can be seen on virtually any drive through the Zimbabwean highveld, or in areas close to major cities such as the **McIlwaine Recreational Park** near **Harare**.

They are at their most spectacular in August, when their new flush of foliage erupts in the russets and golds associated with autumn rather than spring in more temperate climates.

Both also grow large numbers of seed pods, which explode in a phenomenon known as "dehiscence", scattering seeds beneath the trees and for several metres around. As rainfall decreases, the **msasa** gives way to the **mfuti** (*Brachystegia boehmiil*),

and on the Zambezi escarpment to a hybrid (*Brachystegia allenii*).

One of Zimbabwe's most striking geological features, the **Great Dyke**, also on the central plateau, deserves mention for its unique flora. The Dyke runs 530 kilometres (329 miles) north to south, bisecting the highveld plateau.

It is a source of several valuable minerals, including chrome and platinum, and its exposed rocks — mainly gabbro, pyroxenite, and serpentine — produce distinct soils that support a vegetation markedly different from the rest of the region.

The serpentine areas, which make up about seventy-seven per cent of the Dyke, are devoid of trees and are covered instead with short, stunted grasses.

About twenty plant species, including an **aloe** (*Aloe ortholopha*), are endemic to these parts of the Dyke. Other areas support woodlands more similar to those covering the rest of the plateau.

Above: Magnificent Zimbabwean orchid.

Above: Harare Botanical Gardens — *Dombeya rotundifora*.

Also associated with the Dyke are two small **botanical reserves** — the **Tingwa** and **Mwari** — found at its northern end. There, rooted on swampy ground beside streams flowing off the Dyke, are Zimbabwe's only examples of the spectacular **raphia palm**, growing to a height of about ten metres (33 feet) with single leaves reaching twenty metres (66 feet) in length.

Though little-known, these reserves are well worth visiting. Apart from the interest of the palm groves themselves, they lie in the midst of spectacular Dyke scenery.

Amazing baobab

Zimbabwe's drier regions, such as the Zambezi Valley and the south-eastern lowveld, are often dominated by woodlands of **mopane** (*Colophospermum mopane*).

Deep and extensive root systems, water storage organs, and small leaves tend to be features of woody plants that thrive in these drier regions, and the amazing baobab has all these characteristics.

The baobab is Zimbabwe's sole representative of a family with the appropriately resounding name of *Bombaceae*, and —

at least when mature — needs no description.

It is sometimes known as the "upside-down tree" because of its branches' resemblance to an exposed root system. Young trees are more difficult to identify, as their trunks taper sharply and the leaves are simple, not compound as in older specimens.

Baobabs are among the world's longest-living plants and a tree with a diameter of ten metres or more may be 2,000 years or older.

Though they look sturdy, the baobab has little real substance. Their stout trunks conceal a relatively soft, pithy interior composed of thin-walled cells for water storage. Baobabs have been shown to expand in girth after good rains and to contract during droughts.

The baobab's large white flowers last no longer than twenty-four hours and are thought to be pollinated by bats. Among many local legends associated with the baobab is a belief that picking the flowers will bring bad luck.

However, the baobab itself has brought good luck to many early bush pioneers. Its bark can be formed into a very durable string

Above: Yellow daisies bloom in Nyanga Garden.

and its pith can, if chewed, provide at least some moisture for the thirsty, as can water-retaining crevices and hollows in its trunk.

The seeds are filled with a pith that is rich in tartaric acid and can be sucked or soaked in water to provide a refreshing drink. Seeds can also be ground to flavour soups, or roasted and used as a coffee substitute.

Unfortunately, Zimbabwe's elephants are also aware of the benefits that baobabs can provide, and many fine specimens have been destroyed.

The mopane, also a favorite fodder of elephants, has amazing powers of survival and regeneration in the semi-arid regions in which it occurs. It is not uncommon to see several "new" trees growing up from a fallen trunk. In some areas the combination of elephants, fire, and soil types combine to maintain these trees as shrubs, while in other areas, such as the **Zambezi Valley**, they may mature into the magnificent "cathedral mopane", spreading their branches in arbor-eal splendour.

Riverine areas in the lower-lying parts of the country also support some interesting trees, including the **winterthorn** (*Acacia albida*) and the **sausage tree** (*Kigelia africana*).

There are extensive winterthorn wood-lands beside the Zambezi in **Mana Pools National Park**. This unusual tree has a "reverse foliage cycle", bearing leaves during winter when many other species are bare, and hence providing shade. As a legumi-nous plant, winterthorn's other benefits include its ability to fix nitrogen in the soil, thus helping other species gain a foothold on the sandy ground it prefers; and the production of large crops of pods, which are much sought after by elephants and other animals.

The sausage tree carries spectacular mauve flowers in August and September and its unmistakable seed pod — rather like a straight cucumber in shape — is said to have several medicinal properties and may be efficacious in curing skin cancer.

Forests

In Zimbabwe's eastern districts, abundant rainfall has created a mosaic of grassland and forest communities. The forests typically occur on steep, windward slopes and in shel-tered valleys. The high humidity beneath the

Above: One of Mutare's many colourful tree blossoms.

tree canopies promotes the growth of epiphytic ferns, fungi, lichens, and mosses.

This part of the country has several other interesting botanical reserves. For instance the **Chirinda Forest Reserve**, thirty-five kilometres (21 miles) south of **Chipinge**, protects one of Zimbabwe's few remaining examples of primaeval subtropical forest and is particularly well known for its specimens of **red mahogany** (*Khaya nyasica*).

In the "**Valley of the Giants**" within the reserve, one mahogany, thought to be more than 1,000 years old, stands almost sixty metres tall (197 feet) and has a girth of sixteen metres (53 feet) at its base. Other reserve species include **ironwood**, **figs**, **mosses**, ferns, and a rare **orchid**, *Calanthe natalensis*.

Zimbabwe hosts a variety of spectacular flowers and flowering trees, some of which are exotic and others indigenous. For example, many city streets are lined with **jacarandas** (a native of Brazil) that flower in September turning the streets and avenues into a riot of mauve.

Another tree that has equally spectacular flowers is the **lucky-bean** (*Erythrina abyssinica*), which produces a magnificent show of red flowers in September and October, and exceptionally hard red and black seeds — the lucky beans themselves — that are often made into necklaces or bracelets.

Eight species of **protea** can be found in Zimbabwe, all with attractive flowers that bloom between April and July. Five of these species occur only in the **Nyanga** and **Chimanimani** mountains. The other three — *P. Gaguedi*, *P. Welwitschii*, and *P. Angolensis* — can be seen in open woodlands across most of the highveld. Several flowering aloes are a particular feature of rocky outcrops in many parts of the country.

The Save star (*Adenium multiflorum*) is a beautiful member of the oleander family that is widespread at lower altitudes in sandy or rocky habitats, while its relative the **Runde star** (*Pachypodium saundersii*) is common in the south-east.

But pride of place among the flowers must go to the beautiful flame lily, Zimbabwe's national flower. The flame lily lies dormant through most of the year, then springs to life with a brief flash of red during the rains.

Sporting Zimbabwe

Zimbabwe, one of the most sporting countries in Africa, offers a wide range of facilities and athletics, nearly all promoted by amateur organisations.

As a novice in the world sporting arena, Zimbabwe made a giant leap into the international limelight when the women's hockey team struck gold, the country's first ever, at the 1980 Moscow Olympic Games. During the 1982 Commonwealth Games in Brisbane, Australia, the women's bowling team gained another gold medal.

Soccer, the most popular sport in the country, was plagued by many defeats until the national team won the prestigious East and Central African Challenge Cup in October 1985.

Since independence, the national sport has spread throughout the country and at cup finals and internationals crowds of more than 30,000 are common.

At a world level, Zimbabwe's most consistent successes have been achieved on the cricket field and the country is pressing hard to become the eighth major cricket playing nation. The country has won the International Cricket Conference trophy three times in ten years to take its place alongside the leading cricketing nations in the World Cup competition.

Zimbabwe's fastest-growing sport, rugby, has attracted more African players in schools than any other sport since 1980. Three or four international teams visit the country each year.

There has also been renewed interest in tennis, since Zimbabwe is again participating in the Davis Cup after years of isolation during the Unilateral Declaration of Independence (UDI) period. Africa's new regional competitions have given the game impetus through a new crop of youngsters fighting for national honours.

Golf, as well, has experienced a major revival and the Royal Harare Golf Club's course, laid down in 1930 and regarded as one of the best in the world, is the scene for the annual Zimbabwe Open, part of the famous Safari Golf Circuit that attracts the world's top players for tournaments in Kenya, Nigeria, Zambia, and Zimbabwe.

For those who prefer to watch rather than participate, Harare's new Olympic-sized National Sports Stadium, with a seating capacity of 60,000, was completed in 1986 to provide a venue for the country's rising young talent.

Athletic records are being broken continuously at the provincial level, but national marks have stood for some time. The country's most notable recent successes are in distance running, and with the growth of technical coaching in field events the sport is destined to continue along its bright path.

Amateur boxing, once a major contributor to the country's sporting honours, has faded into insignificance, although the professional code has continued since independence.

Horse-racing has a strong following in Zimbabwe, with regular meetings at Harare and Bulawayo. Other equestrian sports that attract a strong but small following are gymkhana, jumping, dressage, polo, and cross-country.

Strangely enough, Zimbabwe has had Olympic and Commonwealth Games successes at sailing and rowing, but in landlocked Zimbabwe these pastimes will always remain minor sports.

Other sports in which Zimbabwe has excelled include baseball and softball, shooting, motorcycle racing, car racing, squash, and badminton. Minor sports that thrive in the country include body building, netball, flying, gliding, skydiving, cycling, archery, darts, snooker, billiards, chess, and motocross.

Athletics

Many Zimbabwean athletes have begun to attract international attention and sports are thriving in schools. Athletics are run by an elected board, the Amateur Athletic Association of Zimbabwe (AAAZ).

Zimbabwe competes at a regional level in the East and Central African championships yearly, but the country's participation in Commonwealth and Olympic Games has been sporadic.

As Rhodesia, a team took part in the 1960 Rome Olympics. The Smith regime sent a team to the 1972 Munich Olympics, but it was not allowed to participate. While

Above: Tennis is Zimbabwe's fastest growing participant sport after soccer.

Zimbabwe missed out in 1976, a team was present at the 1980 and 1984 Olympics, and at the 1982 Commonwealth Games.

Soccer

Soccer has an annual turnover of more than US$1 million, and attendances at the major grounds in Harare and Bulawayo for important international league and cup matches vary between 30,000 and 45,000.

Association football was first played in the country in 1890 and the first soccer league — the Salisbury Association League — was formed in 1898.

The game was taken up enthusiastically by Africans in even the most remote rural areas, where players often had to make their own footballs from a bundle of thin soft bark covered with animal skin, and by the 1940s the Rhodesian Bantu Football Association was established.

The National Football League, to which all clubs are affiliated, was formed in 1953. The ruling soccer body is the Zimbabwe Football Association (ZIFA).

All provinces have their own leagues. The players in the amateur leagues that com-pete in Division Five seek promotion right up to the First Division, the Super League, which offers tough competition and substantial prize money. The Super League season, with fourteen teams taking part, begins in February and ends in November.

Among the most popular teams are the Dynamos (which draw crowds of between 10,000 and 30,000), the Highlanders, the Zimbabwe Saints, CAPS United, and Zimbabwe's army team, the Black Rhinos.

There are also four major annual cup competitions in Zimbabwe: the Chibuku Trophy, the BAT Rosebowl, the Rothmans Shield, and the Natbrew Cup.

Soccer achieved its greatest success to date in 1969, when Zimbabwe made their first World Cup. Placed in group fifteen (the Asian-Oceanic group) for the qualifying rounds, Zimbabwe (then Rhodesia) held Australia to two draws in their bid to qualify for the final sixteen in Mexico but lost the third encounter 3–1.

The major soccer highlight since independence has been Zimbabwe's home victory in the 1986 East and Central Africa Senior Challenge Trophy tournament, against

Above: Testing fairways and immaculate greens of the Troutbeck Inn's nine-hole golf course.

Zambia, Malawi, Tanzania, Kenya, and Uganda.

In 1982, the Zimbabwe national junior team, Young Warriors, reached the semi-finals of the Africa Zone World Cup, losing 2–3 to Nigeria. A year later they reached the finals of the COSAFA youth tournament before going down to Zambia 3–5.

Rugby

Since its introduction to Zimbabwe at the turn of the century, rugby has been one of the country's main winter sports. The first match was played on the sandy bed of the Shashi River in July 1890 (See "The Lowveld: Sugar and Citrus, Heat and Hazard", Part Two), and the first national team to tour travelled to South Africa in 1900 to take part in the Currie Cup.

The sport is run by the Zimbabwe Rugby Union (ZRU), which oversees the national league made up of the top club teams.

In secondary school, rugby is the major winter sport for boys. Before independence, rugby was confined to European schools, but since 1980 many African schoolboys have taken up the sport. In 1986 more than seventy-five per cent of the players from the top twenty-six rugby playing schools were African.

The Inter-City League is the premier national competition. There is also a country district league as well as a provincial league. Close to 1,000 senior players take part in league matches throughout the country each week.

The major domestic trophies are the Lawson Shield for the Harare League, the Edwards Cup for the Harare First League, and the McGregor and Lawson Shields for the Bulawayo First League.

An average of three major tours a year are made to Zimbabwe by top overseas clubs and nations. Past competitors include the Soviet Union; Paris University; Portugal; Swansea, Wales; and the Northern Irish province of Ulster.

In 1987, Zimbabwe was one of sixteen countries that took part in the inaugural rugby World Cup, co-hosted by New Zealand and Australia.

Cricket

Cricket ranks as Zimbabwe's most successful

Above: Horseriding in the forests around Troutbeck.

sport. The game was first played in Zimbabwe in August 1890, near Masvingo. Today the sport is run by the Zimbabwe Cricket Union (ZCU), which raises about US$250,000 a year to provide coaching and send teams abroad. The major league is the Rothmans National League, consisting of eight clubs.

Cricket's popularity at the local school level has increased significantly since independence, with the help of the ZCU which has established an extensive coaching structure.

Each year the top seven league teams and the Zimbabwe School teams battle up and down the field for the Logan Cup during a two-day competition. There are also provincial matches and the District Associations compete annually for the Lithurbridge Cup, the major winter league trophy.

In the 1983 World Cup competition, Zimbabwe was declared the best fielding team, beating Pakistan in a warm-up match and defeating Australia in one of their group matches.

The following year, Zimbabwe lost only two of its six first-class matches during their tour of England. In 1985, Zimbabwe won the ICC Trophy a second time, thus qualifying for the 1987 World Cup. It was a feat that they repeated in Holland in 1990 to qualify for the 1991 World Cup.

Tennis

First played in Zimbabwe in 1890 and well-established before the turn of the century, tennis suffered more than most sports from the isolation of the UDI period.

The sport's resurgence was marked in 1985 by Zimbabwe's 3–2 Davis Cup victory over Poland, followed in 1986 by the staging of the Africa Zone Davis Cup matches where Zimbabwe defeated Libya and Morocco. By 1990, tennis had become Zimbabwe's most popular participant sport after soccer.

Golf

Golf is another of Zimbabwe's favourite sports, dating back to 1895 when the first golf club in the country was formed. The Royal Salisbury (now the Royal Harare) Golf Club was founded in 1930 — and the Henry Chapman Golf Club (also in Harare), Harry Allen Golf Club in Bulawayo, the

Top: Novice rock climber learns new skills on a training face near Harare.

Above: Off to a flying start on the lush going of Harare's Borrowdale horse-racing circuit.

Above: Angler wins joust with a fighting Zambezi tigerfish.

Bulawayo Golf Club, and clubs in Mutare, Gweru, and Masvingo were all established soon afterwards.

Among the world's top professional golfers from Zimbabwe in the 1980s were Nick Price, Dennis Watson, Simon Hobday, Mark McNulty, and Teddy Webber.

The first Zimbabwe Open, held in 1985, posted prize money of US$100,000, the richest sporting purse in the country. This annual event is now part of the African Safari Circuit which brings top golfers from around the world to Africa.

The course at Royal Harare was rated one of the best by champions like Gary Player and Tony Jacklin, and most of the leading courses are of impeccable quality. Several also qualify as the world's most beautiful courses by virtue of their scenic setting, particularly those in the Nyanga area.

Horse-racing

Horse-racing, one of the most popular spectator sports in Zimbabwe, has an annual tote and course turnover worth millions of dollars and both the Mashonaland and Bulawayo Turf clubs run a professional,

world-standard industry. Top jockeys and trainers can earn up to US$100,000 or more in a good year.

The first race meeting in Zimbabwe took place in 1889, when a detachment of Royal Horse Guards arrived in Gubulawayo (Bulawayo) with a letter from Queen Victoria for King Lobengula, announcing the granting of a Royal Charter to the British South Africa Company. The race meeting arranged to celebrate the event included a Zimbabwe Plate and a Gubulawayo Handicap.

In July 1891, the Gymkhana Club was formed in Harare. A year later it was renamed the Mashonaland Turf Club but it was not until 1897 that the first Turf Club race was held. The Bulawayo Turf Club was formed in 1894. Stakes were small until after the Second World War when locally bred horses began to make a showing.

Horse-racing in Zimbabwe is mainly confined to two venues — Ascot at Bulawayo and Borrowdale Park at Harare (the latter has been compared with the finest courses in the world for facilities and efficiency).

May, June, and July are the principal

racing months, although there are feature races throughout the season. The numbers of entries for each race fluctuate between seven and twenty horses, with more than 100 horses involved each week. Crowds vary from 5,000 at an average Saturday meeting to 15,000 for the major events.

Mountaineering

Zimbabwe offers some scintillating challenges for serious climbers — from the mountains of the Eastern Highlands to the vertical granite kopjes around Masvingo and in the Matobo Hills. There are rock climbs of varying difficulty scattered throughout the country, many of them yet unexplored.

The Mountain Club of Zimbabwe, which has about 200 members, organises regular forays, and members have represented Zimbabwe in international meetings. The club has climbed Mulanje in Malawi and the ice-capped main peaks of Batian and Nelion on Mount Kenya. Some members have also climbed in the Alps, the Himalaya, and the Andes.

The club continues to attempt new climbs in the country, many of which compare favourably with overseas mountaineering in terms of difficulty. There are 400 climbs of varying challenge at Hatfield's boulder outcrops and 120 at the club's training and practice area at Cleveland Quarry near Harare.

Twelve ascents at Cleveland Quarry are grade six climbs (the most difficult according to the international scale). Probably Zimbabwe's most famous and most spectacular rock climb is Chiweshe's Bare, a smooth, huge dome rising some 300 metres (990 feet) high.

Fishing

Zimbabwe is well-endowed with water, a superb climate, and a good road network, all essential factors that have combined to make fishing a popular sport in this country of ninety angling clubs.

Fishing ranges from the warm waters of Lake Kariba to the cold, clear streams of the Eastern Highlands. In between are more than 8,000 small and large dams, and many rivers including the Zambezi, Limpopo, and Save.

Medium-sized lakes such as Lake Mazvikidei, Lake Mutirikwi, Lake Manyame, Lake Chivero, Sebakwe Dam, and Inyankuni Dam are popular boating and fishing waters, well within reach of major urban centres.

Anglers thus have a choice of fly-fishing for trout in the Eastern Highlands or coarse fishing for exotic and indigenous species at lower altitudes.

Lake Kariba has about twenty angling species, including several bream (tilapia and allies). The Kariba waters also contain tigerfish, eels, various catfish, the giant vundu, labeos, chessa, nkupe, bottlenose, and Cornish Jack.

A greater variety of fish occurs upstream from Victoria Falls, where the African pike and several largemouth bream species are popular. The fighting yellowfish can also be caught in many small to large rivers.

The best fishing competitions are the annual international tigerfish tournament at Lake Kariba and the annual Mutirikwi and Inyankuni bass fish tournaments.

There is also an annual spearfishing tournament on Lake Kariba where tigerfish, bream, labeo, and chessa are the species most frequently harpooned.

Sailing

For landlocked Zimbabwe, sailing holds a special place in the sporting public's affections. *David Butler*, crewed by Chris Bevan, finished first across the line during one of seven races in the 1960 Olympic Flying Dutchman class and placed fourth overall. This achievement guaranteed untold sailing publicity and the sport grew in popularity.

Formed in 1929, the Matobo Sailing Club at Matobo Dam, about 25km (16 miles) from Bulawayo, was the first of its kind in Zimbabwe. By the 1930s there were five clubs: Mazowe, Gweru, Kwe Kwe, Matobo, and Umgusa (Bulawayo).

In recent years, junior sailing has attracted enthusiastic support and Zimbabwe is continually represented at the annual World Championships in the Optimist Class and at the Commonwealth Games.

Hunting: Stalking the Big Game

Hunting is not only a popular sport, but it also helps to manage surplus game populations. In some areas controlled hunting is essential to proper wildlife management.

There are several safari areas in the Zambezi Valley below Kariba Dam, where elephant, buffalo, lion, leopard, and all species of antelope are found. Many of these may be hunted by prior arrangement with the Department of National Park and Wild Life Management. These areas are normally open from the beginning of May to the end of September and cater to approximately 200 hunters a year.

The other safari area open to hunting is at Tuli, in the south-west of Zimbabwe, which accommodates up to four hunters for periods of ten days.

Though wildlife hunting is banned across much of the African continent, the thrill of big-game hunting is still available — at a price — for those who seek adventure in the style of old-time hunters like Frederick Courtney Selous who roamed the country's wilderness more than a century ago in search of ivory and lion mane.

Free-spending "great white hunters" can pay up to US$21,000 each for a twenty-one-day Zimbabwean safari — and the privilege of shooting lion, elephant, leopard and buffalo — although the average cost of a hunting safari in 1990 ranged between US$5,000–10,000. Trophy fees paid to the government averaged around US$4,000 for each safari.

Only the rare rhino, whose population has sunk dangerously low due to the activities of well-armed poachers supplying high paying horn markets in the Middle and Far East, is protected from legal hunting.

Zimbabwe's Ministry of Natural Resources and Tourism strictly controls and monitors hunting safaris which are divided into three categories: "Big Game", "Plains Game", and "Ranch Hunt" (hunting on privately owned land). The strict regulations even specify which type of weapon and bullet must be used for an individual species. The minimum calibre for elephant is .458, most other animals require a minimum calibre bullet of .375. All weapons and ammunition must be declared and will be inspected by customs which provides the temporary import licence.

The hunting season runs from late April to late September. By October, most areas are too hot and the rainy season, with prolonged as well as torrential downpours, starts in November.

The choice area for big game — elephant and the big cats — is the Zambezi Valley and its catchment area, including Matetsi and the lowveld, which has the largest concentration of leopards. These spotted felines are also found in good numbers in south-western Zimbabwe. Other animals are dispersed throughout the country in reasonable numbers, with the largest concentrations in the Midlands and the least in the Eastern Highlands.

Professional hunters and guides are licensed by the country's Department of National Parks and Wild Life and all are members of the Zimbabwe Association of Tour Operators (See Listings).

To qualify, each professional must spend years in the bush under a qualified hunter and pass written examinations on wildlife law, use of firearms, zoology, flora, tracking animals, identifying spoor, trophy measurements, and natural history. They operate under the strictest controls and must ensure that only those beasts for which licences are held are hunted, and that the rules are scrupulously observed.

Their millionaire clients come mostly from America, West Germany, France, Canada, Austria, Spain, South Africa, Britain, Australia, Denmark, and Italy.

The professional hunter's knowledge of wildlife and bush lore is profound. They can read the spoors and signs in the drifting sands like a surveyor reads a map. One grizzled Zimbabwean tracker looked at a few scuff marks in a dry river bed and described an unsuccessful attack by lions on a buffalo.

"This is where two lionesses lay in wait", he said indicating some flattened grass. "Probably a male lion went upwind and urinated which made the buffalo move in this direction."

He pointed to an area of scuffed sand and

some specks of blood: "Here the lions attacked — they were dragged along here but thrown off and the big buffalo escaped."

Zimbabwe, which has more than 65,000 elephants and a carrying capacity for only 35,000, argues that controlled hunting is of more use to the environment than no hunting and brings in badly needed foreign exchange, part of which is ploughed back into anti-poaching squads and conservation projects.

Not unnaturally the professional hunters also take this view. Many say that because of the ban on hunting in the late 1970s the once flourishing wildlife sanctuaries of Kenya and Tanzania became a poachers' paradise. Hundreds of elephants and rhinos were slaughtered, there was no money for anti-poaching patrols, and roads and tracks became totally overgrown.

Zimbabwe wildlife authorities and hunters argue that they are the best protection against poaching as the poachers remain far away when they and their clients are operating.

Unlike the poachers, who kill as many animals as possible, including immature ones for their horn and ivory, the great white hunter is interested in a trophy or perhaps a skin and will carefully select the animals he wants.

On a recent hunting safari in a special area of the Zambezi Valley, an experienced American hunter wanted "big ivory" — an elephant with tusks weighing perhaps forty-five kilos (100 lbs) each.

Cow elephants have thinner ivory and are ignored. Young breeding bulls are also passed by though they may have tusks of perhaps twenty-three to twenty-seven kilos (50–60 lbs). The hunter wanted one of the solitary and wily old bulls who are on their last set of teeth (known as "six-molar" bulls) and no longer breed.

During the course of two days, constantly checking the wind, the trackers took the hunter through or around perhaps 100 elephants in five or six herds but not one was considered "suitable". A few days later though, the hunter got his bull.

Elephants grow six, or very occasionally seven, sets of foot-long teeth in their lifetime. They use them to grind up bark and branches supplementing their diet of grass

and leaves — a full grown elephant consumes perhaps 317 kilos (700 lbs) of vegetation a day.

At the age of fifty or sixty they lose their last set and then, depending on the area, death is often near. Without the molars, the elephant must depend on grass and leaves but in the dry season these may be sadly lacking and the animal grows weaker and weaker until it dies.

The most dangerous and exciting animals to hunt today are buffalo and leopard. During his safari the American and his guides spotted a couple of big old "buff" browsing about one kilometre (half a mile) away on the far bank of a river. The wind was against them and as the Landrovers pulled up the beasts merely raised their heads and then continued eating.

Through the glasses, one was seen to have a magnificent boss — set of horns. The professional hunter, his client, tracker, and game scout set off with their rifles across the river, and through the high grass on the other bank.

Suddenly they came upon the buffalo half hidden in the grass. One was just twenty metres (60 feet) away. Frank, the American client and an antique gun dealer by trade, lifted his big .458 magnum rifle and fired. The shot caught the beast high in the shoulder — a little too high — while the recoil slammed Frank's own shoulder back about thirty centimetres (12 inches). The heavy bullet knocked a spurt of dust from the beast's hide, but it did not fall. It just raised its huge head, located the hunters, snorted and charged. More than half a tonne of pure muscle made the ground vibrate.

Frank fired again, as two other shots boomed out almost simultaneously from the game scout and professional hunter. The "buff" crashed to the ground in a cloud of dust just three metres (10 feet) from where the group stood. The animal had taken four bullets — two of them soft-nosed dumdums from the world's most powerful rifle — to knock it off its feet.

Leopard present a different problem. Unlike lion, the cat tends to hunt and prowl at night and spends most of the day sleeping. They have a keen sense of smell and eyesight. Leopards move silently and will attack if wounded, cornered, or if someone inadvertently walks under a tree where they are resting.

Poachers catch their leopards with cruel snares and traps, but the big-game hunter must lie in wait for his prey, which demands skill, iron nerve, and endless patience.

First, the trackers search for a tree used by leopards — it will have claw marks on the bark, a long horizontal branch affording a view over a wide area, and backed by thick bush or cover. Preferably, the setting should also be near water.

Then a gazelle or wart hog is shot for bait and hauled up onto the branch where it hangs from a rope. Leopard generally take their kills into trees to eat and, in theory, a leopard will soon discover the dead animal, hook it up onto the branch with a paw, and start eating.

Hyenas and most lions do not climb trees and vultures, unable to hang upside down like bats, are also denied access to the bait.

The following day the hunters return to the tree to see if the lure has been touched. If it has, trackers build a hide of grass and branches. They carefully smear mud over the broken ends of the twigs so they do not show white wood and try to blend the construction into a bush.

A clear view of the branch from the hide is essential and, as the shot may be taken in almost total darkness, the leopard tree must also be silhouetted against the sky. The hide must be downwind of the heavy cover through which the leopard likes to approach the tree.

Hunter and tracker enter the hide in the afternoon. They must sit in total silence, not daring to move a limb, to sneeze, or to flick away biting tsetse flies or ants. One hunter described how a large snake actually slithered across his feet while he was frozen to the spot with fear.

There can be few more eerie experiences than squatting in a hide, surrounded by the mysterious, muttering night sounds of the African bush. Suddenly a leopard coughs nearby. The low grunt can carry a long way on the still air and it is impossible to tell how close the animal is.

The leopard moves silently to the tree. The hunter, with pounding heart, hands slippery with sweat, almost fails to believe his eyes when the big cat appears like magic on the branch twenty metres (60 feet) away. A well-placed shot from a small calibre, high-velocity rifle will kill it. If in his excitement, the hunter misses the lethal spot or his bullet is deflected by a twig, the leopard may leap to the ground wounded.

This is the most dangerous moment of all for any hunter. The cat will make for the long grass and he must follow its trail of blood specks. The wounded beast can spring at him from only a few yards away.

One man who survived a leopard attack in such circumstances said all he recalled was a blur of movement as the beast flashed towards him in total silence. Its tail appeared to windmill round and round as it kept its balance. The hunter had only a split second to aim and fire his magnum revolver or shotgun loaded with heavy double buckshot.

Zimbabwean officials say the country earned around US$20 million from hunting safaris in 1990. A good proportion of this is ploughed back into wildlife protection and anti-poaching squads to save many more animals from death — including the rhinos. It also provides spin-off industries, such as taxidermy, leather work, and carving that demand highly skilled craftsmen.

Above: Elephant trophies are the major prize of a Zimbabwe hunting safari.

Rock Art: The Priceless Legacy

Thousands of years ago the San, those prehistoric pioneers of Zimbabwe, used rock faces and caves across the country as a canvas for their unique and extraordinary art. These paintings are found throughout Zimbabwe, wherever there are outcrops, and although more than 4,000 sites have been identified and catalogued, experts believe that many more priceless Stone Age art treasures have yet to be discovered, particularly within the awesome Matobo Hills area.

The rock paintings, which are from a similar era to those discovered hidden deep in caves in France and Spain, are usually found in Zimbabwe on the exposed granite faces of kopjes, open to the wind, sun, and rain.

The processes of the earth's cooling three billion years ago affected the granite in many different ways: some split in regular vertical and horizontal cracks that were enlarged over the centuries by water and weather. As a result, many became a series of great boulders balanced one on top of the other.

In other instances, upright sheets of granite simply fell away leaving a fresh, clean vertical face — an ideal "canvas" for those early artists. Another erosion process turned some of the granite slabs into large, shallow caves, whose smooth concave and convex walls and ceilings provided the San painters with their greatest opportunity. Such caves are the richest repository of these earliest art forms.

Almost inevitably, the views from these caves located high above the ground were panoramic, some views stretching for at least 100 kilometres (60 miles), providing a great deal of artistic inspiration.

The San artists belonged to the group of hunter-gatherers who lived in southern Africa beginning 20,000 years ago until the early Iron Age about 2,000 years ago. None of the paintings have been dated effectively, but experts agree that they belong to the Late Stone Age.

The most recent works incorporate the different media used throughout the past: polychrome figures, landscapes, complicated cryptographs, and finally plastered kaolin works. When the kaolin clay fell off, etched in white among the black lichens were impressive and dramatic works of art.

The colours used in the rock art were derived from iron oxides: haematite provided the red, limonite the yellow, and the monochrome whites and greys came from various clays and organic matter.

How these were mixed and prepared is not fully understood, but the "paint" was not only remarkably smooth but incredibly durable. It had to be to survive thousands of years of weathering.

While exact dating of the paintings is still to be confirmed, archaeologists have used stratified deposits to form educated guesses. Judging from the stratum in which it lay, for instance, one painted stone uncovered in Nswatugi Cave is thought to be 18,000 years old. Most rock art, however, is believed to be much more recent.

The sequential development of this art form through the millenniums has been (and still is) the subject of much conjecture and postulation. There is, however, a clear line of evolution. The earliest monochrome forms depict animals in silhouette and "matchstick" people.

In a second form, the animals are almost caricatured — depicted in outline profile only, while people are shown in much greater form and detail. A third style, which introduced the use of white pigment, has a great variety of animals and a greater use of colour.

Polychrome paintings, with a deft use of both colour and detail, are common. The fourth, more sophisticated style, uses strong outlines and contrasts, subtle shading, and infilling. Many consider this to have been the apogee of rock art.

One constant theme in virtually all these works is the relationship between man and animal. Other common subjects include animal and human forms depicted with their

Opposite top: Zimbabwe's highly stylised rock art produced between the last 20,000 and 2,000 years.
Opposite: Thousands of years old, late Stone Age San masterpiece at Silozwane Cave.

297

tools, weapons, domestic goods, and crude jewellery.

Among the most frequent animal portrayals are antelope (particularly kudu and sable), elephant, rhino, zebra, and wart hog. In rare instances there are illustrations of reptiles, birds, fish, and insects, along with surrealistic animal forms and objects.

Zimbabwe has one of the highest concentrations of rock paintings in Africa (found throughout the country wherever there is bare granite), and eight major sites in the Matobo Hills represent all that is best in this highly stylised and unique art form. Bound up with the life of prehistoric man — his hunting, dances, and spiritual beliefs — these paintings include the rituals that heralded puberty, circumcision, marriage, births, and deaths.

Kudu, for instance, were a symbol of potency. Bees and honey also appear to have had a deep ritual or spiritual significance. It is thought that illustrations of elephants and abstract animals were linked to rainmaking celebrations and rituals.

More important than an understanding of what the pictures symbolise or narrate, however, is the need for an extensive and continuing survey to discover other rock art sites throughout Zimbabwe. Experts feel that the surface of this vast Stone Age treasury has barely been scratched and estimate that at least double the number of known sites have yet to be found and identified.

In addition to the numerous known and unknown paintings, Zimbabwe also has some outstanding rock engravings — petroglyphs — where the images are carved into the rock and not painted.

A three-metre (10-foot) engraving of a giraffe on a flat sandstone outcrop near Beitbridge is perhaps the most outstanding example of this art form that is contemporaneous to the rock art era.

The origins of these extremely basic carvings is unclear and little attention has yet been given to any interpretation of this art form.

Although it is impossible to list or describe all the rock painting and engraving sites in Zimbabwe, the most outstanding are well-documented (See National Museums and Historical Sites, "In Brief").

Sculpture: Collected The World Over

The earliest known Zimbabwean sculptures were discovered at Great Zimbabwe, including the seven soapstone birds that were plundered, eventually returned, and are now kept in the national museum.

Several monoliths, many with geometric designs carved into them, were also found at Great Zimbabwe. Other works said to come from Great Zimbabwe are the anthropomorphic figures presently in the British Museum and in the Tishman Collection in New York, but so far this claim has not been authenticated.

Several centuries later, Zimbabwe has assembled perhaps the world's greatest generation of contemporary sculptors — seven out of the top ten stone sculptors — and *Newsweek* magazine declared in 1987 that Shona sculpture was one of the most important new art forms to emerge from Africa this century.

Michael Shepherd, art critic for the London *Sunday Telegraph*, wrote: "It is extraordinary to think that of the ten leading sculptor-carvers in the world, perhaps five come from one single African tribe [Shona]."

In 1988, when Shepherd reviewed a London exhibition of Sylvester Mubayi's work, he named Mubayi, Joseph Ndandarika, and Nicholas Mukomberanwa as the leading three Zimbabwean sculptors.

Frank McEwen, one of the men who helped found the Shona school of stone sculpture, added: "Certainly when I knew him [Sylvester Mubayi] he was by far the greatest sculptor there." He also described Joseph Ndandarika as "a great genius . . . a universal genius who worked in every possible medium".

Nicholas Mukomberanwa, the third on Shepherd's artistic hit list, is also universally accepted as one of Zimbabwe's very first sculptors, along with such people as John Takawira, Thomas Mukorabgwa, and Henry Munyaradzi.

Each has stood the test of time: all have been sculpting since the 1960s and are still very prominent today. Other artists such as Moses Masaya, Damian Manuhwa, Bernard Takawira, Bernard Matemera, Albert Mamvura, and Norbert Shamuyarira have recently begun attracting international attention as well.

"What the Shona school of sculpture now desperately needs", writes Michael Shepherd, "is informed recognition of its highest quality of work to spur it on into the twenty-first century. Otherwise it may simply dwindle into airport art."

It would be a great pity if this happened. The recently formed Shona school is the first distinct school of sculpture to emerge in southern Africa.

There is little evidence to suggest that any other sculpture on the scale of that found at Great Zimbabwe developed between the fifteenth century and the emergence of the Shona school in the second half of this century.

Indeed, sculpture did not become a serious art form in Zimbabwe until the 1940s and 1950s, when various mission schools established art classes. Yet the medium developed at remarkable speed, particularly in the transmission of carving skills.

Religious iconography was the basic theme of this work. Two leading centres in the development of this medium were the Serima Mission in Masvingo and the Cyrene Mission in the Matobo Hills. Both schools' students participated in national and international exhibitions and developed their talents at home, while gracing the remarkable interiors of their chapels. Several former Serima and Cyrene pupils, such as Nicholas Mukomberanwa and Sam Songo, later became widely acclaimed sculptors locally and internationally.

The National Gallery, which was opened in 1957, began to foster stone sculpture largely because of the reaction to Joram Mariga's work in the 1960s.

Mariga travelled to the gallery from Nyanga to ask for critical judgement of his stone-carved bowls. His innate skills and finished work so impressed the Director, Frank McEwen, that he founded the National Gallery Workshop School — a loose association of artists eager to experiment with carving. At first the group concentrated on fashioning the soft and malleable local soapstone but

soon the fledgling sculptors began to work Zimbabwe's magnificent, indigenous hard rock such as serpentine and granite.

It was an ideal material that gave unique form and direction to their abstract and expressionist themes. So versatile did the artists become, and so distinctive was their work, that in the ten years between 1962 and 1972 they attracted international attention from critics, art dealers, and collectors at exhibitions in London, New York, and Paris.

The quality of their work and its inherent spiritualism was so outstanding that several hard-headed "patrons" in Zimbabwe established sculpting groups on their farms. Notable among these was Tom Blomefield of Tengenenge farm, who in 1965 put many of his labour force to carving. Pat Pearce opened her Nyanga farm to sculptors in 1961 and McEwen established a rural recluse for artists at Vukutu in Nyanga.

His National Gallery became the main marketing agent for these sculptures, and not entirely from altruism. The gallery made a handsome profit, even during the sanctions imposed during Smith's UDI. The sculptors were given just a third of the selling price.

Many of the practitioners involved in the "Shona" school, however, were in fact farm

Above: Striking example of Shona sculpture.

labourers from neighbouring countries who had become sculptors, and their output was proliferate. More than 7,000 major pieces were sold between 1962 and 1972. As the war of liberation intensified, however, many abandoned the craft, leaving the country and the medium to a handful of committed artists.

Earlier work produced during these early years included a range of small simple busts in soapstones; humorous heads from Joseph Ndandarika, natural portraits by Tubayi Dube, and strong monumental characters from the hands of Boira Mteki. Together these artists shaped the acknowledged parameters of this artistic medium.

With the end of the 1970s and Zimbabwe's independence, sculptors of international renown began producing what is now known as Zimbabwean stone sculpture.

The foremost single factor in this development, apart from the skills of the carvers, has been the properties inherent in Zimbabwean stone. It has led to a unique style, one where static, solid forms are so compact that they seem to displace space and yet dispense a sense of the infinite universe.

Often idiosyncratic, these superb sculptors fashion their pieces into sometimes familiar, but mainly abstract, animal and human forms, or spiritual images drawn from Zimbabwe's rich traditional folklore and religious beliefs.

John Takawira's work is obsessed with the monumental. Geometry and its precision inspires that of Nicholas Mukomberanwa. In contrast, Henry Munyaradzi's work is one of diminishing scale. Joseph Muzondo emphasises collectivism and Bernard Matemera enhances fecund forms in classical African proportion.

Stone sculpture continues to occupy a prominent position in Zimbabwe. International interest and patronage remain high and local and international promotion are growing increasingly professional and effective.

The second generation of stone sculptors has received considerable backing from art dealers. Many now hold annual one-man exhibitions in some of the most prestigious art centres in the world.

Where to see the best

Stone Dynamics in **Samora Machel Avenue**, Harare, provides a platform for talented new artists to establish themselves nationally and internationally.

However, the best works by Zimbabwe's most famous artists are also on display to give the gallery what it terms a "unique blend of young and old, of master and pupil". Sculptures by Henry Munyaradzi, Nicholas Mukomberanwa, Richard Mteki, and other acclaimed artists can be seen alongside the "second-generation" works of Brighton Sango, Ernest Chiwaridzo, and Lefati Gonde.

The owners of **Vukutu Galleries** on **Harvey Brown Avenue**, Harare, have given much encouragement and support to young artists, many of whom have since become masters in their fields. They say that "the gallery is an outlet for the best of their work and a place of encouragement and instruction for the young".

The doors of the **National Gallery of Zimbabwe** are graced on the left by John Takawira's "Chapungu" — a rugged piece of stone that appears to contain the shape and presence of an eagle. On the right is Bernard Matemera's "Sleepwalker" — winner of the Director's Award of Distinction in the 1988 Zimbabwe Heritage Exhibition.

Above: Harvest celebration in serpentine stone.

Above: Seven Shona sculptors rank among the world's top ten with works such as this.

The National Gallery is committed not only to the promotion of Zimbabwean stone sculpture but also to the sculptors themselves, and is concerned with meeting their educational and economic needs. Besides buying sculpture for its permanent and overseas collections, the gallery sells work through exhibition and the Gallery Market.

The National Gallery has helped establish the public esteem in which national sculptors are held today, both inside and outside the country. The winners of prizes and awards at the Zimbabwe Heritage Exhibition receive generous press and television coverage, and the gallery sends sculptors and their exhibitions outside Zimbabwe.

Gallery Director Cyril Rogers says that the 1988 Zimbabwe Heritage Exhibition saw changes in the direction of stone sculpture in response to social and cultural changes, an indication of diversity in the tradition which bodes well for the future.

Tastes of Zimbabwe

Most Zimbabwean hotels offer conventional European or English menus, and a visitor would be hard-pressed to find one that did not serve the traditional beef and Yorkshire pudding. The roast and two-veg conservatism runs deep throughout the nation's culinary highways and byways.

Yet the visitor who wants to wander beyond the confines of steak (admittedly of excellent quality) and chicken can find plenty to titillate their taste buds, if they use a little imagination.

Bream from Lake Kariba comes in many guises — even as kippers or "smoked haddock" — and is excellent in any form it takes. Bream features on most hotel and restaurant menus, but several other fish — often just as tasty — may not.

The humble kapenta, or freshwater sardine, is often denigrated but, when fresh and fried it is the equal of whitebait. Even the tigerfish, supposedly stuffed with tiny bones, can be converted into tasty dishes, and is also canned for local supermarkets.

Crocodiles are not fish — in fact they prey on them — but the meat of this prehistoric reptile has become an interesting addition to the Zimbabwean food scene in recent years. The meat comes from crocodile farms and ranches and can be turned into an amazing variety of dishes, from meatballs to stews and soups.

While the unitiated may blanch at the thought, crocodile meat is much nicer than it sounds, with a flavour variously described as resembling chicken, veal, and fish. You can buy it smoked and sliced in city delicatessens, and increasingly it can be found on the menus of the country's more adventurous restaurants.

Several other species traditionally regarded as "wildlife" are farmed on ranches in Zimbabwe, and — again — their meat sometimes appears in supermarkets or on the menus of some hotels and restaurants. Impala meat, particularly a choice loin, is the most common. Provided it is well prepared — it usually needs marinading for a while — it compares well with the best venison. Eland, zebra, and buffalo meat (often more tender than prime beefsteak) are sometimes available and, depending on your tastes, well worth a try.

For snacks, many local people are more or less addicted to biltong, the ubiquitous southern African dried meat that may even include elephant (legally culled and eaten in Zimbabwe). Up-market versions of biltong include a variety poached in peanut butter.

The traditional ethnic dishes are basic and simple but serve both carnivore and vegetarian. Oxtail stew is the country's meat staple, while rape in peanut butter is the most popular vegetarian dish.

The "national dish" is, of course, sadza — maize ("mealie") meal — served with relish. Every visitor should try it at least once, preferably as a guest in a rural home, eating it with the fingers and garnished with a variety of tasty relishes and vegetables not often found in more conventional tourist surroundings.

And don't shy away from such local delicacies as mopane worms, flying ants, or smoked barbel if they are offered to you. They are nicer — much nicer — than you might think.

Vegetarians can also delight in the fact that Zimbabwean farmers and horticulturalists grow more than sixty kinds of fruit and vegetables. Citrus fruits, accounting for the largest percentage of horticultural produce, include oranges, tangerines, lemons and grapefruit. Apples, apricots, nectarines, peaches, pears, plums, and quinces will probably be familiar to most visitors.

Those visitors from cooler climes may not have experienced the pleasures of Zimbabwe's range of subtropical fruit, easily available in season, that includes kiwi fruit, superb avocados, guavas, bananas, litchis, granadillas, mangoes, juicy pawpaws, and pineapples. Also try to get hold of a baobab fruit, if you can: when ripe, its pith — cream of tartar — has an exceptionally delicate and pleasant taste.

The bush has its fruits as well. Wild loquats grow over many square kilometres of the

Above: Some traditional Zimbabwean dishes. Clockwise: Crocodile stew; mealie meal (*Sadza*); oxtail stew; roast loin of impala; biltong in peanut butter; rape in peanut butter; and (centre) smoked crocodile tail.

highveld and their fruit, known locally as *mahobahoba*, is sold by the side of the road during September and October. Unripe, it is bitter and unpalatable, but when ripe both juicy and flavourful.

The same can be said of the monkey orange, again a highveld fruit. It looks like a grapefruit, and grows on smallish trees of the *Strychnos* genus. Don't try one unless it is really ripe — the hard outer shell should be a deep yellow.

The locally brewed beers are first class if you like light, lager-type beers, while "shake-shake" — a beer brewed specifically for indigenous taste-buds — has a unique but pleasant flavour and texture.

Some decades ago Zimbabwean wines were a bad joke. The story is often told of the visiting expert who, after tasting a local wine produced from a vineyard on a nearby hill, remarked: "Doesn't travel very well, does it?"

Things are much better today. Zimbabwean wineries have acquired the knack of turning locally produced grapes into a variety of wines with a surprisingly wide range of taste and bouquet. Prices vary from a few Zimbabwean dollars for a sturdy house red or white (often sold in the bistro-style restaurants that abound in Harare and Bulawayo) to substantial sums for an excellent pinotage or pseudo-Champagne.

PART FIVE: BUSINESS ZIMBABWE

The Economy

Zimbabwe's economy is based on abundant supplies of mineral and agricultural raw materials, a highly developed infrastructure, experienced management, and a relatively skilled labour force. Agriculture is the country's leading source of income. Agricultural output was up forty per cent the year following the 1987 drought. Strong prices and good demand for the country's main mineral exports — nickel, asbestos, ferrochrome, and gold — also aided the 1988 economic upturn which Zimbabwe experienced.

Development in these and other sectors of the economy has been guided by the government's second economic agenda, the First Five-Year National Development Plan (1986–1990).

A recent development in Zimbabwe's economic policies is a new economic reform programme announced in June 1990 by Finance Minister Dr. Bernard Chidzero involving foreign loans of about two billion US dollars.

An Open General Import Licence (OGIL) system would replace the old system of allocating foreign exchange for import licences, allowing importers to bring in goods virtually as they like, without the need to go through the time-consuming official channels. The World Bank, African Development Bank, and International Finance Corporation are supporting the reform in the form of 400 million US dollars from the World Bank and 130 million US dollars from both other organizations. The Zimbabwe government has also promised to bring its budget deficit down to a reasonable six and a half per cent of the GDP. Adding to the new reforms, the establishment of the Foreign Investment Centre has produced a more efficient system.

Though these new reforms should boost the economy overall, mortgage rates continue to rise due to inflation, causing a depression in the property market.

To a large extent, Zimbabwe's GDP depends on the growth of its agricultural sector and the international economy.

The country's chief imports are iron and steel plates and sheets, power machinery and switch gear, telecommunications equipment, construction and industrial machinery, and vehicle kits, as well as spare parts for agriculture and textiles. Zimbabwe's chief trading partners include South Africa, the UK, West Germany, the USA, Japan, and Italy.

Zimbabwe belongs to a number of international organizations which raise finance for development — the International Monetary Fund, the World Bank, the Southern Africa Development Coordination Conference (SADCC), the Preferential Trade Area for Eastern and Southern Africa (PTA) — and is signatory to the Lome II Convention grouping the EEC countries with African, Carribean, and Pacific countries.

The government was set to move socio-economic development away from the ownership structure in favour of local enterprise, both public and private. It hopes that more emphasis on investment in the productive sectors will, in the long run, ensure continued, positive development of the economy.

Foreign investment, either solely or as a joint venture with either the public or private sector, is welcome under certain specified conditions and areas.

The government, on its own part, is actively involved in laying the requisite basic infrastructure, like electricity, roads, water supply, and other services in the rural areas.

Opportunities

Agriculture

Although agriculture accounts for less than twenty per cent of GDP, it is by far the most important economic activity in Zimbabwe, with eighty per cent of the population dependent on it, and twenty-six per cent of the labour force directly employed by it. This sector provides forty per cent of the raw materials for industry and accounts for between forty and fifty per cent of total exports.

Of the total land area, about forty per cent is considered arable (although only six per cent is cultivated). In the drier parts of the middleveld and the lowveld, the land is only fit for ranching. Droughts occur regularly, and in many areas farmers depend heavily on extensive water conservation.

The most common food crop is maize, but drought-resistant sorghum and millet have also been grown successfully in drier areas. Tobacco is the largest foreign exchange earner in the whole economy, followed in the agricultural sector by cotton, sugarcane, coffee, and tea. There is a diminishing difference between largely white-owned commercial farming and black communal or subsistence farming.

Tobacco

There are basically two different kinds of tobacco grown in Zimbabwe: Virginia and Burley, although Oriental (Turkish) tobacco is also cultivated.

Virginia tobacco is best grown on sandveld soils. When ripe, the leaves are reaped and cured in heated barns (flue-cured). Burley is a larger plant that can grow in red soil areas. It is reaped whole and the plants are sun-cured by hanging them across poles in ventilated sheds. Both crops are then graded, baled, and sold at auction floors in Harare between April and September. About ninety-five per cent of the total crop is exported.

During the Liberation War, tobacco exports were reduced by international sanctions. After independence, a steady recovery took place. Virginia tobacco — grown on large-scale farms as it requires extensive drying and curing facilities — significantly increased production.

Some 1,200 farmers employ thousands of seasonal workers during the tobacco season, which in 1986 produced 117,000 tonnes.

Cultivation of Burley tobacco on smallholdings is encouraged in communal lands and settlement schemes.

There are tobacco research stations in Kutsaga (near Harare), Banket, and Masvingo (especially for Oriental tobacco). There are also training schools near Harare.

Maize

Zimbabwe's staple food — maize — is an important subsistence and commercial crop. It is estimated that some 15,000 square kilometres (5,792 square miles) are under cultivation.

It grows best in red soil areas with at least 600 millimetres (15 inches) of rainfall a year and a warm climate. In the north-west, where rainfall is more dependable than in other parts of the country, maize is extensively cultivated, sometimes as an irrigation crop.

It takes about four months to ripen and early planting is essential for good results. The communal farmers produce fifty per cent of the total maize crop, though yields vary. The poorer farmers who cannot afford good seed and fertilizer can expect a considerably lower yield than the farmer of better means, even in the same area.

Zimbabwe is normally self-sufficient in maize and produces a surplus for export. Farmers sell to the Grain Marketing Board (GMB), which has more than fifty collecting points and many silos spread throughout the country. The GMB resells to local millers and can export any surplus.

In years with normal rainfall, Zimbabwe exports maize to a number of African countries such as Malawi, Mozambique, and Zambia. About one million tonnes a year are consumed within the country, while in a good year production can be twice as much. During the droughts of the early 1980s, however, yields were reduced drastically and Zimbabwe was forced to import maize for local consumption.

Cotton

Cotton became Zimbabwe's second most important cash crop (after tobacco) during UDI, with a tenfold increase in production between 1965 and 1975.

It is grown particularly in Chegutu, Kadoma, Gokwe, the Save Valley, and the lowveld, mostly on big commercial farms but increasingly on smallholdings by peasant farmers.

The Cotton Marketing Board, which purchases the harvest, operates ginneries (in Banket, Shamva, Glendale, and Kadoma) where the lint is separated from the seed.

The lint is sent on to spinning and weaving factories, and the seeds are pressed into cooking oil and margarine (up to 20,000 tonnes of oil a year). Stock feeds are also an important by-product.

Almost 300,000 tonnes of cotton were produced in 1985, forty-five per cent by communal farmers. Some seventy-five per cent is exported, valued at more than Z$100 million, the balance being consumed by a thriving textile industry with factories in Harare, Bulawayo, Gweru, Mutare, Kadoma, and Chegutu.

Irrigation crops

There are several large irrigation schemes in Zimbabwe, most notably the Save River system in the lowveld, utilizing rivers like the Mwenezi. Most of Zimbabwe's dams were built, entirely or partly, for irrigation.

Sugarcane is perhaps the most important perennial irrigation crop, where the soil and the hot humid climate of the south-eastern lowveld has proved to be ideal.

Large estates have been created at Triangle, Hippo Valley, and Chiredzi where refineries turn the cane into sugar, molasses, and ethanol. Zimbabwe exports between 100,000 and 200,000 tonnes of raw sugar a year.

Wheat was introduced rather late as a major irrigation crop in Zimbabwe, grown in winter. The grain is sold to the Grain Marketing Board. Total production is about 150,000 tonnes a year.

Citrus fruits, such as orange, lemon, and grapefruit, are grown on a large scale in the lowveld and in the Mazowe Valley (north of Harare). Grapes are cultivated on irrigated vineyards (at Mazowe, Marondera, Bulawayo, and Odzi), from which indigenous wine is made.

Animal husbandry

Cattle can be kept throughout Zimbabwe, except in the north-west along the Zambezi and in the south-east, where tsetse fly makes animal husbandry impossible. More than half of the five to six million head of cattle are owned by communal farmers, who keep them both as a sign of wealth and as a source of livelihood. Overgrazing is a serious problem.

From very early times there have been three main indigenous breeds: the *mashona* of the humped-back Sanga type, the *tuli* which has adapted to the dry pastures of Matabeleland, and *nkone* cattle. In recent years all three have been improved by scientific rearing.

Commercial farmers sell their beef cattle on the hoof to the Cold Storage Commission, which runs slaughterhouses plus a large cold store in Gweru. Generally, supply meets demand, and there is normally a small surplus for export (especially to EEC countries), which is handled by the commission.

About 100,000 dairy cows produce milk for the Dairy Marketing Board. Demand exceeds supply and efforts are being made to increase milk production by setting up more collection depots and organizing a wider transport system.

There are more than a million goats in Zimbabwe (mainly in communal lands), nearly half a million sheep, and 200,000 pigs, making the country self-supporting in pork.

Forestry

The timber industry in Zimbabwe employs more than 14,000 workers and is based on natural forests of teak, other indigenous hardwoods, and large-scale plantations of pine, eucalyptus, and wattle, which are grown mainly in the eastern mountains.

Large scale afforestation with softwoods has been undertaken in the Eastern Districts. To date, more than 630 square kilometres (255 square miles) of softwoods have been planted, of which more than 200 square kilometres (80 square miles) are State-controlled. The area is still being expanded.

Some 130 square kilometres (53 square miles) of black wattle are grown for tan bark production by private growers in the Eastern Districts. Eucalyptus plantations in the country total some 300 square kilometres (120 square miles). Some plantations are in compact blocks, but many form farm woodlots. They make a substantial contribution to the country's economy, providing locally needed fuel and poles. In some cases they support small lumber mills. Of the total, about twenty-six square kilometres (10 square miles) are state-owned.

Some 70,000 tonnes of teak, mahogany, and *mukwa* (kiaat) logs have been taken annually over the past five years from the natural woodlands of the Kalahari sands in the west and north-west. These go to make railway sleepers, parquet flooring, and furniture. Over 8,240 square kilometres (3,336 square miles) of these forests are under the control of the Zimbabwe Forestry Commission, the state forest authority.

The Forestry Commission undertakes research and training up to diploma standards for the benefit of forestry in the country. It is involved, with the Department of Agricultural Technical and Extension Services, in large-scale plans to extend rural and farm woodlots under a World Bank Afforestation Project to replace severely depleted supplies of indigenous wood in the communal lands.

Industry

Processing of agricultural products and the manufacturing industry together account for about thirty-five per cent of the GNP. About eighteen per cent of the labour force is employed in the manufacturing sector (two per cent of the population).

There is a great concentration of industry in Harare (fifty per cent) and Bulawayo (twenty-five per cent). Kwe Kwe and Redcliff are centres of iron and steel works. Gweru has textile and shoe industries, and textiles are also centred at Kadoma and Chegutu. Mutare is a centre for the timber industry and a large vehicle assembly plant.

Zimbabwe's manufacturing industry is the largest in sub-Saharan Africa, next to South Africa's. It made great strides during the Federation years, and then suffered a setback when sanctions were imposed in 1966, but quickly recovered and expanded. The number of made products increased tenfold between 1965 and 1982.

The State is taking a more active part in the manufacturing sector, especially through the 100 per cent publicly owned Zimbabwe Development Corporation. The State today has an eighty per cent stake in the Zisco steel plant, and substantial interests in the pharmaceutical industry, the production of edible oils and fats, textiles, furniture, film processing, and the mining industry.

Mining

The Zimbabweans have a long tradition of mining dating back to the Middle Ages. Gold was mined on the Zimbabwean plateau by the twelfth century, but it is likely that alluvial gold was washed from river sediment centuries earlier.

To a great extent, gold was bartered for goods and exported to Asia and Europe via Indian Ocean ports such as Sofala, controlled by the Arabs and, later, by the Portuguese.

The gold trade declined, however, as the mines became exhausted or were more and more difficult to work with the limited technology then available. Historically, gold mining played an important part in the Great Zimbabwe and the Monomatapa (Mutapa) states.

Iron mining and smelting were introduced by the original Bantu immigrants. Iron was available in many parts of the country but there were specialists in metallurgy, notably the Njanja in the south-west along the Save River. Other centres were Chirumhanzu, Redcliff, Mount Buhwa, Matobo Hills, and various places in the Zambezi Valley.

The sponge iron from the furnace was repeatedly

heated and hammered into a pure and malleable material for making weapons and tools. The most important tools were the hoe or *badza*, along with knives and spearheads.

Today mining occupies a crucial position in the economy of the country, with minerals and metals accounting for forty per cent of exports and seven per cent of GDP. Gold is still the most important metal (forty per cent of total value). Other minerals are asbestos, nickel, coal, and copper. As a result of modern methods, mining has become diversified, with more than forty minerals and metals being produced.

There are a few large multinational companies engaged in mining, as well as a large number of individually-owned small workings. In some areas farmers dig for alluvial deposits.

Zimbabwe is fortunate in having large deposits of coal at the Hwange Colliery which are large enough to provide for both domestic needs and export.

Multinational companies dominate the mining sector, though the government is increasing its involvement and stake. It has established the Minerals Marketing Corporation as the sole agent for sales and exports of minerals produced in the country, and has also set up the Mining Development Corporation for public investment in mining. Existing mining operations are being expanded either by private investors, by the government, or by both in joint ventures.

Transport

Zimbabwe boasts an international airline, a rail network that is the envy of its neighbours, and a good road network. There is little water transport. Overall, the national transport system is based on a sound infrastucture backed up by careful maintenance and, where possible, modern equipment.

Tourism

With almost 400,000 arrivals in 1986 and an annual value in the region of US$100 million, tourism is one of Zimbabwe's most important growth industries. Apart from Victoria Falls, which have attracted overseas visitors for many decades, tourism is concentrated on the outstanding national parks, the Eastern Highlands, Lake Kariba, and a number of historical sites, particularly Great Zimbabwe.

The Zimbabwe Tourist Development Corporation (ZTDC) is responsible for coordinating and promoting the entire industry, including hotels, tour and safari operators, travel agents, and all tourist areas and attractions.

Current government policy is to develop Zimbabwe for relatively expensive quality tourism from overseas. Efforts to introduce mass tourism and low-cost package tours, which could damage sensitive environments, have so far been resisted. The ZTDC is, however, promoting low-cost domestic tourism.

Power

Zimbabwe's power consumption is currently growing at a rate of at least six per cent a year.

The generation and distribution of electricity is undertaken by the Zimbabwe Electricity Supply Authority (ZESA), a parastatal.

ZESA is a result of an amalgamation of the former Electricity Supply Commission and four municipal electricity undertakings (Harare, Bulawayo, Mutare, and Gweru). ZESA will eventually take over the generation functions of CAPCO at Kariba South when the reconstitution of CAPCO is completed.

The sources of electricity in Zimbabwe are hydro power and thermal power. There is one hydroelectric generating station, Kariba South, and a coal-fired generating station at Hwange. Other thermal stations at Munyati, Harare, and Bulawayo, in place for twenty years, are nearing the end of their economic life. Studies will be carried out to look into the possibility of extending their life spans.

Further projects on the Zambezi River are under investigation. The river has potential hydroelectric capacity of approximately 2,500 megawatts.

Zimbabwe has in the past exported power to neighbouring Zambia to meet that country's power needs.

Water resources

The planning and development of the country's limited water resources is a major concern for the government.

The growth of population, industry, mining, and agriculture has contributed to the increase in the demand for water throughout the country.

Technicians monitor the development of water utilization, search for new groundwater sources, and improve river yields by building dams. There are thousands of small and medium sized dams and boreholes throughout the country, each adding to Zimbabwe's water resources and improving the watering facilities for human and animal consumption and also providing for small irrigation schemes. Major dams have been constructed to satisfy the demands of urban water supply, industry, and mining, and many more dams were to be completed by the end of this decade.

The National Master Plan for Rural Water Supply and Sanitation has been composed, offering a long-term strategy aimed at providing portable water within reasonable walking distance to the whole population of the communal and re-settlement areas of Zimbabwe by means of construction of 576 piped water schemes and about 36,000 new boreholes or wells fitted with handpumps.

To combat contamination, the construction of a total of 1,402,000 latrines has also been proposed in this plan.

Much thought has been given to the possibilities

of developing irrigation to introduce both a greater degree of certainty into crop production and to improve yields. The success of many smaller schemes has led to the planning and introduction of more ambitious ones, and water resources development assisted the increase of irrigated area from 20 square kilometres (7.7 square miles) up to 170 square kilometres (65 square miles) during the last twenty-five years.

Mazvikidei Dam, yielding 100 million cubic metres, has been completed and proposals have been submitted for eight more major dams to be constructed for irrigation purposes at the end of this decade.

Protection of the developed water resources against contamination by human activities is the responsibility of the Water Pollution Control Section, which regularly inspects existing waste water treatment works and maintains a close liaison with related authorities.

An additional aspect is the use of the large dam reservoirs as fisheries for the supply of fish protein.

Labour

The Ministry of Labour, Manpower Planning, and Social Welfare is dedicated to the development of Zimbabwe's human resources. It records and reviews these human resources to initiate relevant development programmes.

The Ministry of Labour, Manpower Planning, and Social Welfare has a Technical and Vocational Training division which takes a direct responsibility in skills training and runs the nation's technical colleges and polytechnics. There are seven technical training colleges: Harare Polytechnic, Bulawayo Technical College, Kwe Kwe Technical College, Mutare Technical College, Gweru Technical College, Kushinga-Phikelela School of Business, and Secretarial Studies and Masvingo Technical College.

A National Vocational Training Centre has been established at Belvedere, in Harare. Saint Peters Kubatana, which started as a private school in 1963, is now a vocational training school financed by the government.

The Ministry of Agriculture runs six agricultural training colleges in Chibero, Gwebi, Esigodini, Rio Tinto, Mlezu, and Kushinga-Phikelela.

The national needs for high-level manpower are being supplied by the University of Zimbabwe, which has faculties of agriculture, arts, commerce and law, engineering, education, medicine, science, social studies, and veterinary science.

Investment

Government policy

• To develop to the full the potential of the agricultural, mining, commercial, and industrial sectors so as to expand their productive capacities, thus promoting growth, generating employment opportunities, and uplifting the standards of living of the people.
• To increase state participation in the development process through direct investment and acquisition of shareholdings in the corporate business sector.
• To develop the private sector which has a sense of social responsibility alongside the developing public sector.
• To support investment from within Zimbabwe and to encourage investment from foreign sources both public and private. (The Government expects foreign investors to provide for domestic equity participation within a reasonable period of time).
• To enter into joint ventures with foreign investors particularly in key sectors affecting strategic facilities or basic infrastructural development.

Foreign Investment

Applications for the approval of foreign investment are considered by the Foreign Investment Committee, and the Ministry of Finance, Economic Planning, and Development. The Government welcomes foreign investment and offers a number of incentives and guarantees. Proposals are considered on their merits against criteria established by the Foreign Investment Committee.

Emigrants' Settling-in Allowance

The maximum settling-in allowance granted is Z$1,000 a family unit. However, applications to exceed this amount can be considered on their merits by the Exchange Control Authorities.

Release of Dividends, Branch, and Partnership Profits

Dividends, branch, and partnership profits on venture capital qualify at fifty per cent net after tax.

Incentives

Special initial allowance

Zimbabwe has a special initial allowance of 100 per cent of capital expenditure on farm equipment, industrial buildings, railway lines and articles, implements or utensils, staff housing, and tobacco barns.

Depletion allowance

There is a provision for a depletion allowance of five per cent of value of minerals produced by mining operations.

Mining capital allowance

A mine owner may claim either 100 per cent of current capital expenditure or spread the allowance over the life of the mine.

Incentives for rural industry

In addition to the special initial allowance, there is provision for a fifteen per cent investment allowance on capital expenditure on commercial and industrial buildings and equipment at growth points in rural areas. The Government also provides refunds of sales tax or import tax on goods of a capital nature bought or imported by industry, particularly mining, for investment in designated growth points.

Investment Protection

Protection for investments, both local and foreign, is contained in the constitution. Section sixteen of the constitution provides for the protection from deprivation of property. It requires that property may only be expropriated in terms of a law and that such a law must require, *inter alia*, that:
• Reasonable notice of intention to acquire the property is given to the owner.
• The acquisition is reasonably necessary on one or other of certain specific grounds such as defence, public safety, or order.
• Adequate compensation is paid promptly. In the event that the parties fail to agree on what is adequate compensation, the owner of the property can apply to the courts for judicial arbitration.

Getting Started

Company legislation

The Companies Act provides for the constitution of public and private companies, and the registration of foreign companies, as well as both the voluntary and compulsory winding up of companies and judicial management.

A company incorporated abroad may establish a place of business and carry on its activities in Zimbabwe without having to form a separate, locally registered company. Before establishing a place of business, there must be lodged with the Minister of Justice, Legal, and Parliamentary Affairs:
• A certified copy of its memorandum and articles of association.
• A list of directors resident in Zimbabwe and particulars of the person responsible for the management of the business.

• If the foreign company is a subsidiary of another company or companies, the particulars of such holding company or companies as the case may be.

Company registration fees

Company registration fees are twenty cents for every Z$100 of the nominal capital, with a minimum of Z$63 for a private or nonprofit company and Z$200 for any other company. Fees for registration on increases of capital will be 20 cents for every Z$100 of the additional capital. The cost of a company registration certificate is Z$3. The registration fee for a foreign company is Z$53, irrespective of the nominal capital. For those requiring to register their prospectus, an additional Z$33 is payable.

Business licences and permits

The Shop Licences Act stipulates that a licence should be held by any person who in any shop, store, or other fixed place of business carries on the trade or business of selling or letting for hire any goods.

The licence is issued by the local licensing authority, i.e. local authorities for the area, if it is satisfied that the premises concerned (or machines) are suitable for the conduct of the trade or business in question. The fee for the issue or renewal of a licence is Z$225 for an urban area.

Work permits

Foreign recruitment is a temporary policy adopted by the government to resolve the skilled manpower problem.

Before an employer embarks on a foreign recruitment exercise, permission in principle must be received from the Manpower Planning Committee on Foreign Recruitment of the Ministry of Labour, Manpower Planning, and Social Welfare. Once a suitable foreign recruit has been identified, the employer must submit an application for work permit to the Immigration Department. The applicant should remain outside the country while the application is being processed. The recruit should be able to transfer skills to an identified Zimbabwean understudy, or undertake a training programme for the company or organization concerned.

Work permits are normally valid for up to two years with a possibility for an extra year's extension upon application. Work permits become invalid if an expatriate worker changes employers without obtaining prior approval from the Immigration Department and the Manpower Planning Committee on Foreign Recruitment.

Import Controls and Procedures

Import controls are operated in terms of regulations made under the Control of Goods Act. An amendment allows a few items to be imported without an import licence:
• Workshop appliances.
• Garden and farm implements, including tractors and farming machinery.
• Motor vehicles and motorcycles, only one for each family.

This list does not include any appliances, machinery, or vehicles which are for industrial, commercial, or mining use, or goods which are to be sold.

Customs duties

The customs duty-free allowance for passengers baggage is Z$200. An additional Z$4,800 is dutiable. Thus, returning residents are entitled to import up to Z$5,000 worth of goods without being required to produce an import licence.

Beginning January 1988, a new Customs and Excise Tariff and Valuation system was introduced. Importers are now required to furnish, with each entry, documentary evidence of:
• Seller's invoice for the goods.
• Inland freight and insurance charges.
• Sea freight statement.
• Wharfage charges.
• Port terminal handling charges.
• Port agents and clearing fees.
• Rail Advice Note from NRZ showing all external charges.
• Road Consignment Note showing all external charges.
• Insurance premium.
• Airway bill.
• Bill of landing.

Lack of documentary evidence may delay clearance, resulting in unnecessary demurrage charges; or a heavy monetary deposit may be called for before the goods are released. The importer should submit to Customs all the documents required to support the declaration made.

A combined "Customs Valuation and Containerisation Guide" is available from Government Publication Offices.

Foreign exchange applications

All applications for foreign exchange to establish or expand an existing wholesale-retail operation or a commercial service are considered by the Commercial Projects Committee. This Committee is not, however, concerned with industrial or mining projects.

In examining applications, the committee considers two separate criteria — one for emergent businessmen and the other for established companies. The current criteria for both emergent and established companies now stand as follows:

Established Companies

• Whether the goods to be imported are of the commercial service which is to be sustained, would serve an essential need, ameliorate some deficiency in domestic supply of an essential item, and/or lead to a sustained net gain in foreign exchange.
• Whether the applicant can show that he would be able to import, on a continuing basis, at a substantially lower foreign exchange cost than any existing importers of the item concerned, with comparable standards of quality and after-sales-service.
• Whether following a change of franchise, resulting in the right to import an essential product being transferred from one firm to another, the existing holder of the allocation is not able to import satisfactory substitute product.
• Whether a continuing need has arisen for the importation of additional spare parts or other materials to service plant, machinery, vehicles, or equipment for approved industrial or mining project.

Emergent Businessmen

• The applicants must either be a registered company or a registered co-operative.
• The applicants must already be trading or providing a service which is in line with the goods they wish to import for a period of at least 12 months.
• The applicants must be operating from premises suitable for the type of business they are conducting.
• The applicants must produce proof that they have made adequate arrangements to finance their imports.
• In cases where after-sales-service is required, the applicants must show that they have made adequate arrangements to provide this service.

No allocations of foreign exchange are granted for locally produced items and low priority items such as luxuries. When considering applications the committee always takes into account the availability of foreign exchange at the time. In order to promote the government's decentralisation policy and to avoid overtrading in certain areas, the committee further gives higher priority to applications from firms based in centres other than Harare.

Furthermore, the committee requires detailed information on all relevant aspects of the business. Owing to the widely varying circumstances of each application, there is no special application form and applicants are free to include additional information which they feel will assist the committee in making a decision. The application should cover the following points:
• Tariff item and description of the goods to be imported.

- The name in which the business is registered, physical and postal address, and whether or not it is resident for exchange control purposes.
- The date of registration and registration number of the company, including the date of commencement of business in Zimbabwe. A copy of the certificate of incorporation has to be attached.
- The names of all directors and/or partners. Each director and/or partner should further declare and state the names of other companies in receipt of commercial and/or industrial foreign currency allocations of which he/she is a director and/or partner.
- The designation, name, address, and telephone number of the company officer responsible for the application who must himself/herself sign it.
- The gross annual turnover of the company for the past two years, together with audited balance sheets and profit and loss accounts. If the company has been trading for a period of less than two years, then a provisional balance sheet together with profit and loss accounts has to be provided for the period which the company has been trading.
- Details of any links with any other company outside Zimbabwe.
- The nature of the main business presently conducted by the company and what proportion of its present activities is concerned with the type of goods for which the application is being made. Also state to what extent will the nature of the business be changed if the application is approved.
- The size of the staff and labour employed and if this will increase if the application is successful.
- Details of any allocations for any other tariff item.
- Details of any previously imported goods in the tariff item concerned, including any transfers into this tariff from other tariffs.
- Details of any past imports on a "no currency involved" basis or through the Preferential Trade Area in the past.
- State the market arrangements for the goods to be imported and give an indication by name and allocation of the end users and, where appropriate, the specialized after-sales-service that can be provided.
- The name of the supplier of the goods and assurance of landed price, and the selling price both initially and for each six-month quota period, based on job/for values.
- Details of any allocations withdrawn.

Applications, in duplicate, should be forwarded to the Secretary for Trade and Commerce, PO Box 7708, Causeway, Harare.

Export Controls

Export procedures vary between different export territories and also from one customer to the next. Forms generally required by an exporter are:
- Standardised bills of entry export form (No. 34) — obtainable from stationers.
- Exchange control forms. CDZ for household goods and personal effects, CDI for any other goods — obtainable from exchange control sections of local banks.
- Export licences — obtainable from Ministry of Trade and Commerce. Some items such as agricultural and wildlife products require a permit from the respective government department prior to applying for an export licence.
- Consignment notes — obtainable from the carrier.
- Duty drawback application form (No. 44) — obtainable from stationers.
- Packing sheet.
- Commercial invoices — obtainable from stationers.
- Declaration of origin form (DA 59) for export of goods to the Republic of South Africa — obtainable from stationers.
- Certificate of origin form (No. 18) for goods exported to Malawi — obtainable from stationers.
- Custom union forms C and D for goods exported to Botswana originating from Zimbabwe, South Africa, Lesotho, Swaziland, and Namibia. Forms A and B for the goods originating from any other country.
- Port shipping instructions — may be prepared by the exporter or obtained from a printer to the exporter's specification.

Export Promotion Programme

The Government of Zimbabwe reached an agreement with British commercial banks for a sterling £70 million facility. These funds will be used to extend the existing Export Revolving Fund which already caters for raw material and balancing equipment requirements for industrial exporters and includes the Mining and Agricultural sectors. These allocations are only earmarked for export-generating activities.

Manufacturing

Industrial exporters will continue to benefit from the original Export Revolving Fund in compliance with the "Circular to all Manufacturers" and applications must continue to be submitted through Industrial Import Control. However, all "Top UP" applications must now be accompanied by copies of CDI forms, and not schedules listing CDI numbers as before. This will enable Export Promotion Monitoring Unit at the Reserve Bank of Zimbabwe to verify the details submitted against Exchange Control records and to check on the imported content applied for.

Industrial exporters are to be granted a supplementary allocation for the domestic market, based on twenty-five per cent of increased export earnings. Exporters can now apply for the supplementary allocation to buy imported inputs for the domestic market, based on the increase between their 1985 and 1986 export.

Mining

With the introduction of the extended Export Promotion Programme, the procedures for applying for funds have been changed, with allocations now being made directly to the mining company. As the thrust of this programme is to increase exports, only exporting mines will qualify for allocations.

Applications for mining continuation equipment and spares (for Z$50,000 and below) must be submitted through Commercial Import Control. Applications for Mining projects (in exceess of Z$50,000) must be submitted through the Chamber of Mines. The applications will then be considered by the appropriate authority or committee.

Agriculture

In this sector, imports which can be applied for are:
• Anthelmintics and other veterinary products.
• Essential stockfeed ingredients.
• Requirements for the horticultural sector.
• Machinery and spare parts.
• Crop chemicals.
• Fertilizer.
• Dip chemicals.

Applicants should enclose copies of *pro forma* invoices or telex confirming the order and a letter of justification for their requirements.

The Ministry of Lands, Agriculture and Rural Resettlement will inform importers through the press of imports available for financing.

Applications, in duplicate, should be marked EPP-Export Promotions Programme and addressed to the Secretary for Lands, Agriculture and Rural Resettlement, PO Box 7701, Causeway, Harare.

Finance

Local borrowing by nonresident owned companies are based on a formula obtainable from the RBZ. The formula considers, among other things, the percentage of foreign capital introduced, profits retained in Zimbabwe and that repatriated.

The Zimbabwe Stock Exchange

Trading on the Zimbabwe Stock Exchange takes place on its floor in Harare. The Stock Exchange is open every business day of the week.

Prices of locally listed companies are continuously available to investors and the exchange issues daily turnover figures for shares and money changing hands. In addition, indices of mining and industry counters are compiled and published on a daily basis.

Figures of the numbers of shares of each listed security traded are compiled on a weekly basis and released to the press for publication in the financial sections. The exchange also lists Zimbabwe Government and local municipal loan stocks.

Taxation

Income tax

The tax assessment year runs from 1 April to 31 March in the next succeeding year. Employees' salaries or wages are normally subject to Pay As You Earn (PAYE) deductions.

As from 1 April, 1988, Zimbabwe abolished different tax rates for married and single persons. The main change is the adoption of a separate taxation system which involves a single rate structure over seven bands of income from a zero rate band up to sixty per cent rate band.

Individuals earning Z$2,500 or more a year from employment are subject to PAYE. Taxable income includes income from employment, rentals, taxable interest in excess of Z$500, and business profits.

Tax rates

The rates of tax are fixed annually after the Minister of Finance, Economic Planning and Development presents his budget to Parliament.

Tax credits

The abatement system, which gave a reduction of tax by means of an amount of taxable income deductable at the lowest rates of tax, has been replaced by a credit system which is more equitable, as everyone who qualifies gets the same amount of tax deducted. These are as follows:
• A tax credit of Z$120 is granted for each minor child of a taxpayer up to a maximum of six children.
• A Z$120 tax credit will be granted for each minor child, other than the minor child of a taxpayer, who is wholly maintained throughout the period of assessment.
• A tax credit of Z$360 will be granted to family taxpayers whose spouses have no taxable income.
• A tax credit of twenty per cent of insurance premiums and medical aid contributions can be claimed with a maximum of Z$400 insurance credits, and twenty per cent of the excess of Z$250 medical expenses will be claimable.
• A Z$500 tax credit will be granted to taxpayers who are physically or mentally disabled to a substantial degree or whose children are disabled.
• A Z$500 tax credit will be granted to taxpayers who are blind or whose spouses are blind.
• A Z$50 standard dependents credit will be granted to every taxpayer.

An exemption will apply for the first Z$500 of interest received by individuals in addition to the existing exemptions on interest from the Post Office Savings Bank and Building Society's two-year Paid Up Permanent Shares.

Company tax

• Companies are subject to a flat rate on taxable income of forty-five per cent and a surcharge of twenty per cent (i.e. fifty-four per cent).

• Dividends distributed by companies incorporated in Zimbabwe to persons not ordinarily resident in Zimbabwe and to residents of Zimbabwe are subject to a twenty per cent nonresident shareholders tax or twenty per cent resident shareholders tax withheld at source. Branch profits tax, at fifteen per cent of fifty-six per cent of taxable income, is payable by branches of companies in addition to the tax mentioned above.

Sales tax and import tax

The rate of sales tax on local purchases and import tax on imported goods, other than those exempted, such as basic foodstuffs, is ten per cent on all general items and twenty per cent on certain listed durable goods. Orthopaedic appliances and other appliances to compensate for a defect or disability, invalid carriages, literature for the blind, braille typewriters, and braille watches are exempt from sales tax.

Holiday currency tax and airport tax

A tax of twenty per cent of the allocation of foreign exchange for holiday purposes is chargeable to residents. The holiday allowance currently stands at Z$450 a year. An airport tax of Z$10 for each passport is payable by residents embarking on international flights. Nonresidents pay US$10 or the equivalent in denominated currency.

Royalty, capital gains, dividends

A tax on royalties of twenty per cent is applicable. The capital gains tax currently stands at thirty per cent. Foreign dividends accruing to residents are subject to a twenty per cent tax. Relief is available for foreign tax deducted at source.

Fringe benefits tax

Fringe benefits are taxed on the basis of the cost to the employer, except in the case of housing and use of furniture where the taxable benefit is the value to the employee. Details of the benefits tax in respect of loans and use of motor vehicles are as follows:

Loan from an employer

• The benefit is based on the following deemed interest rates per annum for the year of assessment — where indebtedness does not exceed Z$12,000 (twelve and a half per cent) — where indebtedness exceeds Z$12,000 (thirteen and a quarter per cent).

• If the actual cost of a loan to the employer exceeds the above rates, the taxable value of the free benefit is based on the actual cost. In all cases the taxable value is reduced by any interest paid by the employee to the employer for the loan.

• Loans for education, technical training, or medical treatment are excluded.

Private use of motor vehicles

• With effect from the year ended 31 March, 1985, the standard benefits in respect of motor vehicles are as follows:

Not exceeding 1500cc	Z$1,500
1501cc to 2000cc	Z$2,000
Exceeding 2000cc	Z$3,000

• The taxable value shall be at these rates unless the employee can show the taxable value to be less or the Commissioner of Taxes considers that the taxable value based on its cost to the employer is higher. The taxable value is reduced by the amount of any payment made by the employee for the use of the vehicle.

Double Taxation Agreement

Zimbabwe has double taxation agreements with the United Kingdom. Except where they are income effectively connected with the permanent establishment on fixed base in Zimbabwe of a resident of the UK, the following types of income are subject to a Zimbabwean tax, including branch profits tax and withholding tax at the following restricted rates which are calculated on the gross amount of the income:

Type of income	Maximum Rate
Interest	10 per cent
Technical Fees	10 per cent
Royalties	10 per cent

Dividends distributed by a Zimbabwean company to a company resident in the UK which controls twenty-five per cent or more of the voting power in the Zimbabwean company are subject to NRST at the reduced rate of five per cent. For all other dividends the rate of twenty per cent applies.

Relief from double taxation

Where income from sources in a country other than Zimbabwe is taxed in both countries, relief is granted against Zimbabwean tax regardless of whether there exists an agreement with the country of origin for the avoidance of double taxation.

PART SIX: FACTS AT YOUR FINGERTIPS

Visa and Immigration requirements

Visa applications may be obtained at Zimbabwe diplomatic missions located in Brussels, Ottawa, Bonn, Paris, Berlin, Tokyo, Geneva, New Delhi, Bucharest, Stockholm, Moscow, Canberra, Washington DC, New York, Belgrade, London, and throughout Africa. In countries where Zimbabwe has no representation, applications can be lodged at the British High Commission or Embassy.

Nationals of the following countries must obtain the proper visa prior to arrival: Afghanistan, Albania, Algeria, Andorra, Angola, Bhutan, Bulgaria, Burma, Cape Verde Islands, China, Iran, Iraq, Israel, Kampuchea, North Korea, South Korea, Laos, Lebanon, Libya, Mali, Mozambique, Mongolia, Philippines, Poland, Portugal, Romania, Senegal, Somalia, South Africa, Spain, Sudan, Syria, Taiwan, Tibet, USSR, Vietnam, South Yemen, North Yemen, and Zaire. This should be done well in advance as applications can take time to process.

Citizens of other countries and most Commonwealth citizens are granted visas at the ports of entry on presentation of a valid passport, a return or onward ticket, and proof of sufficient funds to support their travel plans.

Any visitor intending to take up work or residence in Zimbabwe must have the authority of the Chief Immigration Officer.

Health requirements

All visitors (including infants) are required to possess a valid yellow fever vaccination certificate. Malaria is endemic throughout the country — particularly the lowveld. Visitors should begin taking a recommended prophylactic two weeks before their arrival and continue for six weeks after their departure. Bilharzia (*schistosomiasis*) is common throughout Zimbabwe, but is easily avoided by drinking treated water — tap water in major centres is safe to drink — and by not swimming in lakes and rivers, particularly where there are reeds.

International flights

Zimbabwe is served internationally by Air Zimbabwe and sixteen other international airlines. The flying time to Harare from London is ten hours; from New York (via London) seventeen hours; from Bombay nine hours; from Tokyo twenty-three hours; and from Sydney sixteen hours (flight times may vary slightly).

Zimbabwe's major point of entry by air is Harare International Airport. A regional air service to Johannesburg operates from Bulawayo Airport. Harare International Airport is quite modest, but does provide full passenger facilities — twenty-four hour currency exchange, post office, duty-free shop, restaurant, and bar service. A porter service is available for the traveller's convenience.

For transport into Harare, Air Zimbabwe provides regular bus services; taxis and rental cars are available; and for those on a group tour, there are minibuses provided by the tour operator.

Air fares

The usual range of fares is available: business and economy class; excursion fares, bookable any time for stays of between fourteen and forty-five days; an APEX fare, bookable one calender month in advance, allowing for stays of between nineteen and ninety days. The price of cheaper APEX fares varies according to the season. Stopovers *en route* are possible when arranged with the airline for all but APEX fares. Reductions are available for children.

Departure tax

The airport departure tax is US$10 a person, payable only in US dollars.

Arrival by rail

There are five points of entry into Zimbabwe by rail — at Plumtree on the Zimbabwe-Botswana border, Victoria Falls on the Zimbabwe-Zambia border, Mutare and Sango on the Zimbabwe-Mozambique border, and Beitbridge on the Zimbabwe-South Africa border. Arrivals undergo full customs and immigration checks.

Arrival by road

There are ten points of entry by road into Zimbabwe from the country's five neighbours. From Botswana the border post is at Plumtree and Mpandamatenga; Kasungula serves as the border post from Namibia; Zambia has three border controls to Zimbabwe: Victoria Falls, Chirundu, and Kariba. Mount Selinda, Nyamapanda, and Mutare are the points of entry from Mozambique; and Beitbridge from South Africa. All have full customs and immigration checks, some only for limited periods.

Customs

All visitors must fill in a currency declaration form on arrival and retain it until departure.

Personal items such as clothing, toiletries and cosmetics, one watch, hairdryer, calculator, camera, etc. may be temporarily imported duty-free. Gifts worth not more than Z$150 per person, five litres of alcohol (but not more than two litres of spirits); and an unlimited supply of tobacco may be carried in by visitors.

Domestic air services

Air Zimbabwe operates a comprehensive network of regular daily flights between Harare, Bulawayo, Masvingo, Gweru, Buffalo Range, Kariba, Hwange National Park, and Victoria Falls. Charter companies also offer flights at reasonable costs to all main airports and to many landing fields not served by the national airline.

Road services

There are some 78,400 kilometres (48,725 miles) of road throughout Zimbabwe, of which 5,000 kilometres (3,000 miles) are first-class, two-lane surfaced roads. The rest of the country relies on single lane, all-weather gravel, and dirt roads. All tourist centres are linked by asphalt roads.

A luxury coach service operates between Johannesburg and Harare via Bulawayo, and from Bulawayo to Victoria Falls. There are daily bus services between Harare and Bulawayo and five days a week between Harare and Mutare. Other routes are Harare–Kariba; Harare–Nyanga; Harare–Great Zimbabwe, and Masvingo–Bulawayo.

Taxi services

Taxi services are immediately available at Harare International Airport. They can also be found outside of most hotels in Harare and at the country's major centres. Licensed taxis are metered and a ten per cent tip is usually added directly to the meter.

Car rental

There are many car rental companies in Zimbabwe. The major agencies have representatives throughout the country. Avis and Hertz both operate out of Harare International Airport. Everything from small two-door sedans to spacious four-wheel drive vehicles are offered at a flat weekly or daily rate, plus mileage and insurance. Some agencies offer vehicles on a self-drive basis or with a driver.

Driving

Drivers require a valid International Driving Licence. Those with their own vehicles will require a *Carnet de Passage*, *Triptique*, and International Certificate of Insurance. Driving is on the left.

Rail services

The National Railways of Zimbabwe operate a total network of 3,400 kilometres (2,110 miles) through the following lines: Harare–Gweru, Harare–Lions Den (branch line to Kildonana),

Harare–Shamva (branch line to Trojan), Harare–Mutare (continues to Mozambique), Gweru–Masvingo, Gweru–Rutenga (branch line to Zvishavane), Gweru–Bulawayo, Bulawayo–Victoria Falls, Bulawayo–Plumtree (continues to Botswana), Bulawayo–West Nicholson, Rutenga–Beitbridge (continues to South Africa) and, Rutenga–Mozambique (branch line to Chiredzi). All main passenger trains have full dining-car facilities and sleeper accommodation.

Climate

Temperate conditions prevail all year-round, moderated by the altitude and inland position, which keeps the humidity comfortably low. The average day temperature is 25°centigrade (77°F). During the evening the temperature drops substantially.

There are four distinct seasons: winter from May to August, when night temperatures can drop below freezing point, with little or no rainfall; a warm and normally dry spring between August and November; a rainy season (summer) between November and April; and a transitional autumn during April and May.

Currency

The Zimbabwe dollar is divided into 100 cents. Notes are issued in denominations of Z$2, 5, 10, and 20. There are six different coins: 1, 5, 10, 20, 50 cents, and Z$1.

Currency regulations

There is no limit to the amount of foreign currency imported to Zimbabwe, but it must be declared on arrival. Up to Z$40 may be legally imported or exported. Always retain exchange receipts, as these are your only record of legal exchange and are necessary to reconvert unused local currency to foreign currency at departure. Avoid changing large sums of money as the process of reconverting can be time-consuming.

Banks

Banking hours are from 08.30 to 14.00, Monday to Friday (except Wednesday). Wednesday bank hours are from 08.30 to 12.00. Banks are also open on Saturday mornings from 08.30 to 11.00. All the major banks offer currency exchange.

Credit cards

Visa, MasterCard, Access, Diners Club, and American Express are accepted throughout Zimbabwe. Representatives are located in Harare should you need to contact them for any services, cash advances, or to report a lost or stolen card.

Government

Zimbabwe, a member of the United Nations, Organization of African Unity, and the Commonwealth, is an independent republic operating under an executive President who also serves as Head of State and Commander-in-Chief of the Defence Forces. He is elected by the Members of Parliament and holds office for a period of five years, with no restriction on the number of terms he may serve.

Parliament is unicameral and has 150 members, of whom 120 are directly elected. The remaining thirty consist of eight provincial governors, ten traditional chiefs, and twelve members who are nominated by the President.

The Cabinet decides on policy and prepares legislation for consideration by the Parliament. This consultative body consists of twenty-two appointed Ministers and eight Deputy Ministers. Each Ministry is headed by a Permanent Secretary who is a civil servant.

The judiciary has three divisions: Magistrates courts, High Court, and Supreme Court. The Supreme Court acts as the only court of appeal. A system of assessment replaces trial by jury in Zimbabwe. In addition to Common Law and Statute Law, Customary Law still operates. This law generally applies to disputes over *lobola* (dowry), dissolution of marriage, custody of children, damages in cases of adultery and seduction, and inheritance.

Local government consists of seven Provincial Councils, thirty-five District Councils, fifty-seven Rural Councils, four Town Councils, seven Municipal Councils, and two Local Boards.

Village Development Committees (representing communities of about 1,000 people) and Ward Development Committees (representing communities of about 6,000 people) form the basis of the system. It has been transformed into a development-orientated system with powers to run income-generating projects.

Language

English is the official language of Zimbabwe and is understood within most populous areas. In other areas indigenous languages are likely to be spoken. The most common of these are Shona and Ndebele — while minority languages such as Tonga, Tshindao, and, Hlengwe are also spoken.

Religion

Although more than half the population subscribes to Christianity, many Zimbabweans still adhere to traditional beliefs. Spirit mediums are consulted to give advice in times of ill-fortune, as they are believed to have direct contact with the ancestors. All prayers to *Mwari* (God) are channelled through the ancestors.

There are also some new movements, originating from other parts of Africa, that are gaining ground. The most important is the Zionist or Apostolic Church, a kind of revival movement dependent on charismatic leaders.

The Asian minority is either Muslim or Hindu.

There are Jewish congregations in Harare and Bulawayo.

Time

Zimbabwe is two hours ahead of Greenwich Mean Time (GMT). Time remains constant throughout the year.

Daylight

Daylight varies by approximately one hour between winter (May–August) and summer (November–March), when there are twelve hours of daylight.

Business Hours

Normal business hours are Monday to Friday from 08.00 to 16.00 or 17.00. Most shops remain closed on Saturday and Sunday, while a few are open for business until noon on Saturday morning.

Security

Harare is one of the safest African capitals. You need not hesitate to walk through the city during the day, though at night you should consider taking a cab to get around. Do not leave valuables in hotel rooms and do not carry large sums of cash. Make use of the hotel safe-deposit box.

Communications

The Posts and Telecommunications Corporation (PTC) runs a comprehensive network of postal, telephone, telex, and radio services locally and worldwide at rates comparable to those found abroad. International direct dialling is available through the earth satellite station at Mazowe.

Media

The Zimbabwe Government has committed itself to the free flow of information, the media are therefore free from censorship.

There are two daily and Sunday papers, as well as a number of national and local periodicals. These are published weekly, fortnightly, or monthly. The Zimbabwe Mass Media Trust, a government body formed in 1981 to decrease the dependancy on foreign-controlled newspapers, owns the two Sunday and daily papers and one weekly.

The national news agency is ZIANA. Foreign bureaux operating in Harare include the BBC, AFP, UPI, AP, and Reuters. Zimbabwe-based foreign correspondents are required to register yearly.

The Zimbabwe Broadcasting Corporation provides the country's radio and television services. ZBC operates four radio channels broadcasting for about seventeen hours a day. Radio 1 (English) and Radio 2 (vernacular) can be considered the general home service. Radio 3 is a pop music channel and Radio 4 educational. Two television channels broadcast six hours a day. TV One provides a general service, while TV Two is devoted to more serious programming and education.

Energy

The electric supply is 220V AC, using three square-pin plugs. A flashlight is recommended as there are brief but frequent power cuts outside the main centres. Carry plenty of batteries, as locally made batteries only last a few hours.

Medical services

Medical facilities in Zimbabwe are better than in most African countries. With well distributed hospitals and clinics, medical attention is always nearby. Standards range from private hospitals and clinics with sophisticated equipment and specialist personnel, to fairly basic government hospitals and clinics. Prices vary accordingly. All medical practitioners speak English, so you should have no difficulty explaining your problem. The names and addresses of physicians and dentists are listed at the beginning of the Harare telephone directory and at the front of each listing by town.

Medical insurance

Cover can be bought in Zimbabwe from local agencies, as well as locally based multinational insurance firms, but it is usually cheaper and more practical to buy it in your own country before departure. Given the high cost of specialist medical services, insurance is advisable.

Chemists/Pharmacies

Medical supplies are quite expensive and fairly basic. Those on regular medication should carry adequate supplies with them. Those wearing glasses should carry an extra pair — just in case — or failing that, a prescription.

Most chemists and pharmacies maintain regular business hours. Some are open on Saturday mornings.

Liquor

Zimbabwe has four brands of lager-style beer, all fairly cheap. Imported spirits are expensive. Local spirits are cheaper, but quite rough. Zimbabwe has some good domestic wines and the quality is improving.

Tipping

Tipping is optional. Service still comes with a smile without a tip, but an acknowledgement of good service is warmly accepted. Porters should be given 50 cents a bag. Most hotels provide a staff box at the cashier's counter where you can pay all at once at the end of your stay.

Clubs

Clubs are a prominent feature of Zimbabwean social life. Some are organised around sport, some are philanthropic — and there are even traditional English "gentlemen's clubs". Most have excellent facilities and welcome visitors, especially members of international clubs and societies, with reciprocal arrangements. Others charge a temporary membership fee.

Sport club activities include: angling, archery, athletics, badminton, baseball and softball, basketball, billiards and snooker, body building, bowls, boxing, bridge, chess, cycling, cricket, darts, gliding, golf, hockey, horse-racing, judo, motor-cycling, motor racing, netball, polo, rowing, rugby, sailing, shooting, show jumping and dressage, sky-diving, soccer, squash, swimming and diving, table tennis, tennis, volleyball, and waterpolo.

ENGLISH–SHONA

Hello (sin.)	Mhoro
Hello (pl.)	Mhoroi
How are you?	Makadii
I am well (good, fine, etc.)	Ndiripo makadiiwo
Thanks	Ndatenda
Thank you	Ndinotenda
Goodbye (when staying)	Fambai zvaakanaka
Goodbye (when leaving)	Chisarai
Hotel	Hotera
Room	Imba
Bed	Mubhedha
Something to eat	Zvokunwa
Coffee	Kofi
Hot	pisa
Water	Mvura
Hot water	Mvura inopisa
Cold	tonhora
Tea	Tii
Meat	Nyama
Fish	Hove
Bread	Chingwa
Butter	Bhata
Sugar	Shunga
Salt	Munyu/sauti
Today	Nhasi
Tomorrow	Mangwana
Now	Zvino
Quickly	Nokukurumidza
Slowly	Zvishoma zvishoma
Hospital	Hospitari

MORE WORDS

Mr	Va
Mrs	Mai
Grandmother	Ambuya
Mother	Mai
Grandfather	Sekura
Sir	Changamire
Father	Baba
Friend	Shamwari
I	Ini
You	Iwe
You (pl)	Imi
What?	Chi-i?
Who?	Ndiani?
Where?	Kupi?
When?	Rini?
How?	Sei?
Why?	Sei?
Yes	Hongu
No	Aiwa/Kwete
To eat	dya
To drink	nwa
To sleep	rara
To come	uya
To go	enda
To stop	mira
To buy	tenga
To sell	tengesa
Street/road	Mugwagwa
Shop	Chitoro
Money	Mari
One	Motsi/poshi
Two	Piri
Three	Tatu
Four	China
Five	Shanu
Six	Tanhatu
Seven	Nomwe
Eight	Sere
Nine	Pfumbamwe
Ten	Gumi
Hundred	Zana
Thousand	Churu
Monday	Mu-vhuro
Tuesday	Chi-piri
Wednesday	Chi-tatu
Thursday	Chi-na
Friday	Chi-shanu
Saturday	Chi-tanhatu
Sunday	Zuva

PHRASES

Where is the hotel?	Hotera iri kupi?
Good morning	Mangwanani
Good afternoon	Masikati
Good evening	Manheru
Come in!	Pindai!
Please sit down	Chigarai pasi
Welcome!	Titambire!
Where do you come from?	Munobva kupi?
I come from . . .	Ndinobva ku . . .
What is your name?	Munonzi ani?
My name is . . .	Ndinonzi . . .
Do you speak Shona?	Mu-no-taura chiShona here?
I do not speak Shona	Handitauri chiShona
It is very good	Zvakanaka zvikuru
It is bad	Zvakaipa
I am sorry	Ndine urombo
Excuse me (apology)	Ruregerero
Where is the toilet?	Chimbuzi chiri kupi?
What is the time?	I-nguva-i?
How much money is it?	I-mari-i?
It is expensive	Zvi-no-dhura
Wait a bit	Mirai zvishoma
Go away!	Ibvaipo!

In Brief

Zimbabwe National Parks

Zimbabwe National Parks are those areas of interest by virtue of ecological value and exceptional scenic beauty; from the cool mountains of the Eastern Highlands to the sun-washed grasslands of Hwange National Park. They are protected by law to preserve their aesthetic value and to prevent commercial exploitation. Foreigners and Zimbabweans visit the 44,688 square kilometres (18,000 square miles) — over twelve per cent of the country's total land — set aside as parks for educational and recreational enjoyment.

Parks and Reserves Legislation

The Parks and Wild Life Act provides for establishment of national parks, safari areas, recreational parks, sanctuaries, and botanical reserves and gardens. The various areas combine to form the Parks and Wild Life Estate.

National Parks are established to protect landscapes, conserve ecosystems and their elements (with particular emphasis on large mammals and their habitats), and to protect important sites for research, education, and their aesthetic value.

Controlled sport hunting is permitted in safari areas. Wild populations may be harvested or otherwise used providing that this is not in conflict with species-ecosystem conservation, the wilderness qualities, or the future resource values of the area. Recreational parks are established to preserve and protect the natural features they contain for the enjoyment, long-term benefit, cultural inspiration, and recreation of the local people and visitors.

Parks and Reserves Administration

The Department of National Parks and Wild Life Management, within the Ministry of Natural Resources and Tourism, is responsible for management, administration, and development of the protected areas system. The department is a scientifically based and ecologically orientated land-use agency with a special responsibility to ensure the proper conservation and use of the nation's parks and wildlife resources.

All bookings and enquiries may be made at the department's headquarters in Harare (tel: 706077).

World Heritage Sites

There are little more than 100 World Heritage Sites strictly protected by international law. These are either unique cultural sites — the Pyramids, Acropolis, Taj Mahal — or unique natural sites such as Australia's Great Barrier Reef and Tanzania's Selous National Park.

In Zimbabwe, Great Zimbabwe and the Khame Ruins are cultural World Heritage Sites, while Mana Pools National Park and Victoria Falls Rainforest National Park are natural World Heritage Sites.

Botanical Reserves

Within the Parks and Wild Life Estate, botanical reserves have been established to protect rare or endangered indigenous plants, or representative plant communities growing naturally in the wild. These reserves exist in their own right or within other areas of the estate.

Visitors who have a greater-than-average interest in botany may obtain details of these reserves from the Department of National Parks and Wild Life headquarters in Harare.

Safari Areas

Hunting is not only a poplular sport but also helps to manage surplus game populations. In some areas controlled hunting is essential to proper wildlife management.

There are several safari areas in the Zambezi Valley below Kariba Dam where elephant, buffalo, lion, leopard, and all species of antelope are to be found. Many of these may be hunted by arrangement with the Department of National Park and Wild Life Management. These areas are normally open from the beginning of May to the end of September, and cater to approximately 200 hunters a year. Non-hunters may view and photograph game in the adjacent game reserves, fish in the Zambezi River, or merely enjoy the magnificent scenery.

The other safari area open to the public is at Tuli, in the south-west of Zimbabwe. This area can accommodate up to four hunters at any one time for periods of ten days during the open season from May 1 to September 30.

National Parks Accommodation

There are over 250 chalets, cottages, and lodges in the Parks and Wild Life Estate, providing accommodation for over 1,000 visitors nightly. All are equipped with basic furniture, including refrigerators and bedding, and have paraffin pressure-lamps, gas, or electric lighting. Firewood must be purchased from park authorities. There are also caravan and camping facilities in almost every area. These are usually situated in picturesque surroundings, with ablution blocks (bath, showers, basins, all with hot and cold water, and toilets) and braai sites.

Some accommodation is located within game areas that only open seasonally. The opening and closing times indicated are liable to vary depending upon road conditions.

Types of accommodation vary, and detailed, up-to-date information can be obtained from the Central Booking Office (tel: 706077).

Chalets: One- or two-bedroom units with cooking utensils, external cooking facilities, and communal ablution blocks. Guests must supply own cutlery and crockery.

Cottage: One- or two-bedroom units with refrigerator, bathroom, and toilet. Guests must supply their own crockery and cutlery.

Lodges: One or two bedrooms, lounge/dining room, kitchen with stove, internal bathrooms and toilet, bedding, cooking utensils, cutlery, and crockery.

Caravan Parks and Camping Sites: All have communal ablution blocks, braai sites, and occasionally electric lighting.

Exclusive Camps: Units of permanent accommodation for twelve persons (fully equipped, but visitors must provide and cook their own food). Set within the Chizarira, Matusadona, and Hwange national parks, these camps include the exclusive use of a five-kilometre area where visitors may game-view on foot.

All accommodation is serviced. Please note that entry fees are charged in addition to the accommodation charge.

Advance Bookings

Visitors organizing their visit independent of a travel agent are advised to book well in advance for any accommodation. Advance bookings may be made up to six months ahead (e.g. on 1 January you may book for the succeeding months up to and including the following June). Bookings are allocated on either a "draw" or "first come" basis. January, April, May, August, September, and December bookings are all done by draw. February, March, June, July, October, and November bookings are on a first come basis. Due to the exceptional demand for the Mana Pools Lodges, their bookings are always allocated by draw. Only one application per group is considered. You may request a specific unit of accommodation (or site) but these may not be reserved or guaranteed. Central Booking Office will notify you in writing whether your application has been booked or not.

A fifty per cent deposit of the total accommodation fees is due at the time of booking, the balance due payable thirty days prior to taking up the accommodation. For caravan and camping sites, the full fees are due at the time of booking.

Advance bookings should be addressed to the Central Booking Office, Travel Centre, Jason Moyo Avenue, Harare, Zimbabwe, PO Box 8151, Causeway, Harare; phone 706077 or Bulawayo Booking Office, PO Box 2283, Bulawayo; phone 63646. Advance bookings may not be made at local park offices.

Visitors are reminded that they must report to the park office on arrival (by 5:30 pm) and at departure, even if the booking has been made and confirmed with the Central Booking Office. You will not be accommodated if you arrive at the park with more people than you originally booked.

Firearms

Visitors entering any area under the control of the Department of National Parks and Wild Life Management must declare any firearms in their possession. If they wish to take these with them into the area, an officer will seal the weapons and levy a fee of Z$3 per seal. This does not prevent the weapon from being fired, but an attempt to do so will break the seal.

Boating

Local and visiting holiday-makers are reminded that power and sailing boats used on estate waters must be registered at the Department of National Parks and Wild Life Management head office.

Wilderness Trails

Wilderness trail walks are led by experienced park staff and are available during the dry season within selected national parks — Mana Pools, Matusadona, Hwange (Sinamatella), Hwange (Robins), Chizarira, and Gonarezhou (available to Zimbabweans only). Groups of up to six persons, over the age of sixteen years, may take part in these backpacking adventures.

The goal of these walking trails is to bring the visitor in direct contact with the wilderness both educationally and recreationally. Game-viewing is not specifically emphasised, instead the entire environment is investigated — from tiny crawling insects to the towering trees above them. The guides that accompany you are all highly knowledgable and experienced. They can answer your inevitable and numerous questions as well as prepare you for a possible encounter with dangerous game.

These treks are not for the amateur. You are required to carry all your own equipment, including your backpack, food, and water. You should be in fit condition to take part in these hikes over rough terrain that usually last four days.

For the less-adventurous, but equally curious, escorted day-walks are available in many parks for durations of between one and three hours. These are led by armed Game Scouts and are arranged on request at the parks themselves.

Remain in your car

Visitors to game areas are not permitted to leave their cars while on game-viewing drives. This requirement is to protect the visitors, who often do not appreciate how dangerous a wild animal can be. Visitors who break the rule may be required to leave the park, in addition to paying a fine.

In certain areas exceptions to this rule are made, and these are detailed under the individual locations.

Restrictions on Dogs

Dogs are not allowed in any accommodation area including caravan parks and camping sites without prior permission from the warden. Such permission will be granted only in exceptional cases, such as a guide dog for a blind person. Under no circumstances will a dog be allowed in any game area. Where dogs are permitted, they must be under the effective control of their owners at all times.

Addresses

- Department of National Parks and Wild
  Life Management
  PO Box 8365
  Causeway
  Harare

- Forestry Commission
  PO Box 8111
  Causeway
  Harare

- Zimbabwe Tourist Board
  PO Box 8052
  Causeway
  Harare

National Parks	Square Kilometres
Chimanimani	171 sq km
Chizarira	1,910 sq km
Gonarezhou	5,053 sq km
Hwange	14,651 sq km
Kazuma Pan	313 sq km
Mana Pools*	2,196 sq km
Matobo	424 sq km
Matusadona	1,407 sq km
Nyanga	330 sq km
Victoria Falls*	23 sq km
Zambezi	560 sq km
TOTAL	27,038 sq km

* World Heritage Sites

Botanical Reserves	Square Metres
Bunga Forest	4,950,000 sq m
Chirinda Forest Reserve	9,490,000 sq m
Chisekera Hot Springs	950,000 sq m
Haroni Forest	200,000 sq m
Mawari Raphia Palm	340,000 sq m
Mazowe	460,000 sq m
Pioneer	380,000 sq m
Rusitu Forest	1,500,000 sq m
Sebakwe Acacia Karoo	600,000 sq m
Sebakwe Great Dyke	1,650,000 sq m
Sebakwe Mountain Acacia	530,000 sq m
South Camp	260,000 sq m
Tingwa Raphia Palm	2,900,000 sq m
Tolo River	440,000 sq m
Vumba	420,000 sq m
TOTAL	25,070,000 sq m

Botanical Gardens	Square Metres
Ewanrigg	2,860,000 sq m
National Botanic	670,000 sq m
Vumba	2,000,000 sq m
TOTAL	5,530,000 sq m

Sanctuaries	Square Kilometres
Chimanimani Eland	18 sq km
Manjinji Pan	3 sq km
Mbaze Pan	0.4 sq km
Mushandike	129 sq km
Nyamanyetsi (Nyamaneche)	25 sq km
Tshabalala	11 sq km
TOTAL	186.4 sq km

Safari Areas	Square Kilometres
Charara	1,692 sq km
Chete	1,081 sq km
Chewore	3,390 sq km
Chipinge	261 sq km
Chirisa	1,713 sq km
Dande	523 sq km
Deka	510 sq km
Doma	945 sq km
Hartley 'A'	445 sq km
Hurungwe	2,894 sq km
Malapati	154 sq km
Matetsi	2,955 sq km
Sapi	1,180 sq km
Sibilobilo	44 sq km
Tuli	416 sq km
Umfurudzi	760 sq km
TOTAL	18,963 sq km

Recreational Parks	Square Kilometres
Bangala	27.0 sq km
Chibwatata	0.1 sq km
Chinhoyi Caves	1.2 sq km
Kavira	0.5 sq km
Lake Cunningham	41.7 sq km
Lake Kariba	2,872.0 sq km
Lake Kyle	169.0 sq km
Lake Matobo	29.0 sq km
Lake Robertson	112.0 sq km
Manjirenji	34.0 sq km
Ngezi	58.0 sq km
Robert McIlwaine	61.8 sq km
Sebakwe	26.0 sq km
Umfuli	127.0 sq km
Umzingwane	12.3 sq km
TOTAL	3,571.6 sq km

Other Areas	Square Kilometres
Cecil Kop Natural Reserve	17.40 sq km
Great Zimbabwe National Monument*	7.4 sq km
Gweru Antelope Park	12.14 sq km
Imire Game Park	10.00 sq km
Iwabe Game Park	200.00 sq km
Mtarazi Falls	24.95 sq km
Sengwa Wildlife Research Area	373.00 sq km
TOTAL	644.95 sq km

* World Heritage Site

World Heritage Sites

Great Zimbabwe National Monument

Size: 7.46 sq kms
Province: Masvingo
District: Masvingo
Geographical location: Near Kyle Recreational Park, south-west of Lake Mutirikwi (Kyle), 29km from Nyanda
Altitude: 1,140m
Physical features: The area is in a rugged kopje-strewn valley.
Vegetation: Bushveld
Fauna: Greater kudu, bushbuck, duiker, steinbuck, klipspringer, leopard, and baboon
Bird life: Hornbills, green pigeon, freckled nightjar, and purple-crested heron
Cultural heritage: Great Zimbabwe was first occupied in the 8th century AD but most of the 'dzimba dzemabwe', or houses of stone, were built by the Karanga, ancestors of the present Shona people, between the 11th and 15th centuries. During this era it was the royal capital of a state that dominated the central plateau and the gold trade to the coast. A solid stone conical tower forms the centrepiece of a huge elliptical building, wall, and hut complex. The outer wall is 249m in circumference and in parts over 10m high and 5m thick. Excavations have yielded articles from China, India, and Asia, but the most spectacular find was the soapstone Zimbabwe birds adopted as the symbol of Zimbabwe.
Visitor facilities: It is a major tourist attraction and there is a site museum, 40 sq m of aloe gardens, and a hotel nearby.

Khame Ruins

Province: Matabeleland North
District: Bulawayo
Geographic location: 22kms west of Bulawayo
Physical features: Declared a World Heritage Site in 1986, Khame was a successor to Great Zimbabwe. The methods employed in the building of the dry stone walls that date from the 15th to the 17th centuries resemble those at Great Zimbabwe, but the use of varied decor indicates an improvement in design techniques. The majesty of the buildings and the wide range of artefacts of regalia nature suggests that this was once the headquarters of a state that historians know as Torwa.

Mana Pools National Park and Associated Safari Areas

Size: Mana Pools National Park 2,196 sq kms (Chewore Safari Area 3,390 sq kms, Urungwe Safari Area 2,870 sq kms, Sapi Safari Area 1,180 sq kms, Dande Safari Area 523 sq kms, and Doma Safari Area 764 sq kms).
Province: Mashonaland West
District: Hurungwe
Geographical location: North-east of Lake Kariba in the Zambezi Valley on the south bank of the river (which forms the border with Zambia)
Altitude: Under 500m to 1,062m
Physical features: The areas (excluding Dande) have extensive frontages along the lower Zambezi River, from Kariba Dam to near the Mozambique border, and include large areas of the rugged Zambezi escarpment, which rises to 1,000m from the valley floor. Mana Pools are former channels of the Zambezi. Much of Chewore is heavily dissected, with Mupata Gorge (30kms long) along the northern boundary. Between the gorges of Kariba and Mupata the river is broad and sandy. Mean annual rainfall is 700mm, falling mainly in summer. Mean annual temperature is 25°C.
Vegetation: Well-grassed communities dominate the mountainous escarpment and higher Chewore areas. The valley floor is dominated by mopane woodlands or dry, highly deciduous thickets known as jesse. Seasonal tributaries crossing the valley floor support extensive riverine communities. On the younger, sandier alluvial deposits along the Zambezi are well-developed communities of acacia and diverse woodlands on the higher deposits (old islands or levees).
Fauna: The rich and varied fauna mammal populations tend to concentrate on the flood plains during the dry season when water elsewhere (except in the escarpment) is scarce and when the numerous acacia shed their protein-rich pods. Mammals include black rhinoceros (Chewore has one of the most numerous populations in Africa), elephant, hippopotamus, lion, wart hog, bush pig, zebra, cheetah, wild dog, and a wide range of antelope species including mixed herds of greater kudu, bushbuck, nyala, eland, waterbuck, sable antelope, grysbok, and steinbok. Nile Crocodile are also present. Common fish include tigerfish, tilapia, vundu, nkupi, chessa, Cornish Jack, and lungfish.
Bird life: There are over 380 species including Nyasa lovebird, yellow-spotted nicator, white-collared pratincole, banded snake-eagle, and Livingstone's flycatcher.
Population: There is virtually no permanent human habitation due to an array of tropical diseases including sleeping sickness, bilharzia, and malaria.
Visitor facilities: The areas provide opportunities to experience some of the greatest seasonal mammal concentrations in a natural environment and it is ensured that recreational hunting will not impair the essential wilderness qualities and resource values for future generations. The number of cars allowed into Mana Pools National Park at any one time is limited. Mana Pools is only partially developed as a tourist centre, but is so popular that the available facilities are prone to saturation. There is a tourist camp at Chikwenya on the confluence of the Sapi and Zambezi rivers, but there are no tarred roads and visitors are strictly confined. There are

airstrips at Chikwenya and Mana Pools. Visitors are allowed to walk in the riverine woodlands in the park. Open 1 May – 31 October. Visitors are advised to be well-equipped with mosquito nets and repellent when visiting camping sites along the river.

Victoria Falls Rainforest National Park

Size: 23 sq kms
Province: Matabeleland North
District: Hwange
Geographical location: In the extreme west on the southern bank of the Zambezi River, which forms the border with Zambia
Altitude: 913m
Physical features: The park contains Victoria Falls: the largest sheet of falling water in the world — over 545 million litres a minute during the flood season, hence the African name of 'Mosi oa Tunya' — the smoke that thunders. The park includes the Zambezi River above and below the falls within Zimbabwe and the upper Batoka Gorges. Annual rainfall is 600–700mm and mean annual temperature is 20°C. The spray thrown up from the falls is partly responsible for sustaining the rainforest.
Vegetation: Dominant types are riverine communities associated with the upper Zambezi River, the Victoria Falls rainforest, and open grassland of several different species. Scrubland adjacent to the gorges gives way to Kalahari woodland.
Fauna: Many large mammal species, including hippopotamus, lion, wart hog, and numerous antelope species. Victoria Falls forms a geographical barrier between the distinct fish faunas of the upper and middle Zambezi River. Fish species include several species of bream, chessa, tigerfish, and barbel.
Bird life: Cormorant, darter, heron, duck, egrets, bitterns, pygmy geese, and white-fronted bee-eaters along the river. In the rainforest there are Heuglin's robin, Knysna lourie, and trumpeter hornbills. The gorges provide breeding places for the rare Taita falcon.
Visitor facilities: These are well-developed, with hotels available in Victoria Falls town. Visitors to the falls and rainforest area are limited to about 1,000 persons a day. There are good paths to the falls and through the rainforest.

National Parks

Chimanimani National Park

Size: 171 sq kms
Province: Manicaland
District: Chimanimani
Geographical location: Eastern Highlands of Zimbabwe, 75kms south of Mutare, on the border with Mozambique
Altitude: Up to 2,400m
Physical features: The park includes the main massif of the Chimanimani Mountains within Zimbabwe, an area of rugged grandeur with peaks rising to over 2,400m and deeply dissected gorges with magnificent waterfalls. The region is subject to sudden storms and mists. It is an important water catchment area.
Vegetation: Mainly montane plant communities including open grassland and relict forest patches in sheltered areas with some woodlands. The flora includes elements of the south-western Cape flora that spreads north along the eastern mountain chain of Southern Africa. There are also some low-altitude rainforests, uncommon in Zimbabwe.
Fauna: Sable antelope, eland, oryx, blue duiker, klipspringer, and an occasional leopard
Bird life: Violet-crested turaco, malachite sunbird, laughing dove, trumpeter hornbill, secretary bird, francolins, and eagles
Visitor facilities: Camping is allowed in the park. There is a base camp and information office 20kms from Chimanimani Village. There are no access roads beyond the base camp. Easier access and more public facilities are available in the extreme north. An Outward Bound School adjacent to the park uses the area extensively. Food must be carried in by the visitor. Trout fishing in the Bundi River from 1 October – 21 April.

Chizarira National Park

Size: 1,910 sq kms
Province: Matabeleland North
District: Binga
Geographical location: East of Lake Kariba
Altitude: 648–1,433m
Physical features: Most of the park is on an undulating, dissected plateau decending in the north from wooded ridges, mountains, and rocky valleys to the 500m escarpment overlooking Lake Kariba. Rivers from ridges on the plateau have cut deep gorges in their passage through the escarpment. The area is a well-watered "island" of rivers, perennial springs, and natural springs in the fairly arid Zambezi Valley, and forms an important catchment area. The park includes some low-lying country along the Busi River in the south-east. Mount Tundazi (1,370m) is a prominent feature in the north-east.
Vegetation: Due to the generally higher rainfall of

the plateau areas, the vegetation has affinities with that usually found further east in Zimbabwe. Much of the plateau is dominated by drier miombo woodland with mopane and open grasslands. Scrublands occur towards the west and at low altitudes in the south-east. The gorges support riverine communities.

Fauna: Elephant, buffalo, black rhinoceros, lion, leopard, cheetah, zebra, wart hog, and a range of antelope including roan and tsessebe

Bird life: Taita falcon, crowned eagle, fish eagle, brown-hooded kingfisher, red-billed wood-hoopoe, golden-tailed woodpecker, and Meyer's parrot

Visitor facilities: Few visitors use the park, which is remote and difficult to reach. There is an airstrip at park headquarters in Manzituba to the east, but no visitor facilities in the park. Visitors must obtain permission to enter from the Provincial Warden. Game-viewing is permitted on foot. Roads suitable for four-wheel drive vehicles only.

Gonarezhou National Park

Size: 5,053 sq kms
Province: Masvingo
District: Chiredzi
Geographical location: On the south-east border of Zimbabwe adjacent to Mozambique
Altitude: 162–578m
Physical features: The flat to undulating country is interrupted by the valleys of the Mwanezsi, Runde, and Save rivers, and by isolated hills including the Chikunja Range. Chilojo cliffs form a spectacular backdrop on the south bank of the Runde for about half its distance through the park. The park includes Gorheve Pans, 30kms north of Mabalauta (filled with water during the rainy season). Rainfall is low and falls mainly between November and April.

Vegetation: There is a wide variety of vegetation types including mixed woodland, mopane, acacia, aloes, evergreen forest and thicket patches, deciduous woody species, and a patch of relict riverine forest.

Fauna: Elephant, black rhinoceros, hippopotamus, nyala, suni, Lichtenstein's hartebeest, steinbok, grysbok, grey duiker, Livingstone's suni, oribi, klipspringer, red squirrel, and common bush squirrel. River fauna includes freshwater turtle, lung fish, a threatened top minnow, tigerfish, and tilapia. Marine tarpon and swordfish have been taken in the Runde River many kilometres from the sea. There is a significant crocodile population.

Visitor facilities: The park is open to visitors in the dry season from May to October. Well-established rest camp at Chinguli in the centre and campsites throughout the park. Only four-wheel drive vehicles are permitted on park roads. Game-viewing on foot is allowed. Prior written permission must be obtained before entering the Mabalauta Area. The nearest store is 40kms from camp in Chikombedzi.

Hwange National Park

Size: 14,651 sq kms
Province: Matabeleland North
District: Hwange
Geographical location: On the border with Botswana, about 200kms north-west of Bulawayo
Altitude: 938–1,152m
Physical features: Kalahari sands cover some 9,470 sq kms of the park area. The gently undulating country has "fossil" river lines draining south-west towards the great Makgadikgadi Pans in Botswana. Parallel "fossil" dunes occur in the centre and west. The park contains temporary seasonal pools or pans with high salt content. The more broken country in the north is where streams and rivers rise and drain north towards the Zambezi River. The climate is dry and tropical with annual precipitation about 655mm decreasing towards the south and west. The dry winter is followed by a hot, dry season, then rains between November and March. Mean maximum temperature reaches 35°C in October. The mean minimum temperature drops to 3.5°C in June and July and frost is frequent.

Vegetation: Vast teak forests in the north give way in the south to the Kalahari sandveld that supports some typical woodland areas. Fires and frost sometimes lead to thicket conditions. The areas surrounding "fossil" rivers are characterised by areas of open grassland often fringed with acacia. Mopane and commiphora woodlands occur in the north with open grassland in the marshlands.

Fauna: There are 35 large mammal species recorded (jackal-sized or larger) and 401 bird species. The fauna represents a merging of elements from the southern savannah and south-west arid faunal elements of Africa with species typical of the Kalahari penetrating into the park from the south-west. Black rhinoceros and white rhinoceros have been reintroduced and appear to be prospering. There are strong populations of elephant (20,000), buffalo (30,000), giraffe, zebra, hippopotamus, wart hog, and a wide range of antelope including wildebeest, greater kudu, impala, and sable. Other mammals include lion, leopard, cheetah, wild dog, and hyena.

Bird life: Varies with seasonal flocks of waxbills, canaries, doves, francolin, guinea fowl, sandgrouse, and starlings during the dry season. Migrant cuckoos, swallows, swifts, warblers, nightjars, Egyptian geese, red-billed teal, and knob-billed ducks on the pans during the wet season. Raptors include bateleur eagles, lappet-faced vultures, white-backed vultures, Cape vultures, white-headed vultures, and hooded vultures.

Visitor facilities: The area is an internationally popular tourist destination. Development for visitors includes roads, shops, caravan parks, and campsites concentrated in the north of the park, which is also served by five hotels near the park. Access is by paved and gravel roads, rail, and an airport located outside the park. There is a network of game-viewing roads, but the number of vehicles in the park is limited. Other facilities include observation platforms and hides.

Kazuma Pan National Park

Size: 313 sq kms
Province: Matabeleland North
District: Hwange
Geographical location: On the border with Botswana
Altitude: 900–1,200m
Physical features: There are flat grassland plains of basalt clays and gravels with large seasonally inundated natural pans in the southwest.
Vegetation: The open grassland in the east is fringed by mopane and Kalahari woodland.
Fauna: There is a wide spectrum of large mammal species, but populations are generally sparse and seasonal. Locally threatened species have a high incidence and include gemsbok, tsessebe, roan antelope, oribi, and cheetah. This is the only area in Zimbabwe where the western population of the southern African oribi occur. Game tends to concentrate in the more watered and tree-covered western sector of the park. The pans are important to waterfowl.
Visitor facilities: Game-viewing on foot is allowed, but there are no other tourist facilities. The area is remote and four-wheel drive vehicles are essential. Visitors must obtain prior permission from the Provincial Warden.

Mana Pools National Park

(see "World Heritage Sites")

Matobo Hills National Park and Lake Matobo (Matopos) Recreational Park

Size: 465 sq kms
Province: Matabeleland South
District: Matobo
Geographical location: 54kms south of Bulawayo in south-western Zimbabwe
Altitude: 1,300–1,466m
Physical features: The complex occupies the core of the Matobo Hills, an agglomeration of granite kopjes with numerous caves. Geological faults have created domes (*dwalas*) that sometimes have huge isolated boulders on their smooth surfaces. The hills are an important water catchment area for the southern Matabeleland, feeding tributaries of rivers such as the Tuli, Mtsheleli, Maleme, and Whovi. The hills are interspersed by valleys with deeper soils, marshlands, and streams.
Vegetation: The flora reflects a wide diversity of habitats and includes cacti on exposed granite; well-wooded clefts on the kopjes with *Euphorbia candelabrum*, mnondo trees, and golden-flowered *umsehlas* around the bases; open woodland in well-drained valleys; grassy marshlands; and swamps. There are several species of trees, shrubs,

flowering plants, ground orchids, and over 100 species of grass. Lichens are common on the massive boulders.
Fauna: The 88 recorded mammal species include high densities of leopard, klipspringer, hyrax, and red hare. Twelve large mammal species have been reintroduced. There are 71 reptile species, of which 39 are snake species, including a thriving population of the highly venomous black mamba. There are 27 amphibian species and 16 fish species, which include several exotics introduced to the streams and dams such as tilapia, black bass, barbel, and Hunyani salmon.
Bird life: Over 300 bird species occur, which is over half the number known to exist in Zimbabwe. They include 40 raptor species such as black eagle (highest known density), Wahlberg's eagle, tawny eagle, banded harrier, secretary bird, black-shouldered kite, snake eagle, little sparrow-hawk, gabar goshawk, peregrine falcon, and lanner falcon.
Cultural Heritage: The biological diversity of this important catchment area has attracted inhabitants from the Stone Age to the present, notably the San bushmen and the Ndebele. The area has great archaeological, historical, and spiritual significance. Caves in or near the park include Nswantugi (with bushmen giraffe paintings), Bambata (the first cave to be excavated in Africa), and Silozwane (which was once used by the Ndebele for rainmaking ceremonies).
Visitor facilities: Matobo Hills National Park was a gift to the people of Bulawayo by the late Cecil John Rhodes. Facilities in the park include nine lodges at lower Maleme Dam, four caravan and campsites, a network of gravel game-viewing roads, and horse trails. Fish licences must be obtained from the park office prior to fishing. Boating is allowed, but details should be obtained from the warden.

Matusadona National Park

Size: 1,407 sq kms
Province: Mashonaland West
District: Kariba
Geographical location: On the southern shore of Lake Kariba
Altitude: Up to 1,201m
Physical features: Matusadona comprises an abrupt and rugged escarpment separated from the lakeshore by an apron of flat land. Most of the park is inaccessible by road and extends over the upland area high above the lake. The numerous bays of the lakeshore are formed by drowned valleys. The Ume River forms the western boundary and the flooded Sanyati gorge the eastern boundary.
Vegetation: Well-grassed communities dominate the mountainous two-thirds of the park. Elephant have modified this environment by destroying many large trees. Below the escarpment fairly dense, woody vegetation dominates, comprising mainly small mopane trees and bushes. Lake Kariba is a man-made lake with evolving shore communities

where swamp grass is conspicuous.

Fauna: Black rhinoceros (estimated 400), elephant (1,000), buffalo (several thousand), sable and roan antelope, greater kudu, bushbuck, eland, waterbuck, hippopotamus, lion, leopard, impala, hyena, and crocodile (estimated 400 adult crocodile). Lake fish include tilapia, vundu, tigerfish, and Tanganyika sardine (*kapenta*).

Bird life: Fish eagle, African darter, comorants, heron, stork, plover, African jacana, and numerous woodland birds

Visitor facilities: Only one-third of the park is open to the public. Organized tourism facilities include three lodges, bush camps at Muwu and Ume River and an airstrip at Tashinga. Boat, canoe, and walking safaris are operated from Fothergill Island and Spurwing, which provide excellent game-viewing opportunities following Operation Noah in the late 1950s when thousands of animals were rescued from the rising waters of Lake Kariba. Entry by boat is allowed all year, but entry by road is restricted to 1 May – 31 October. No supplies can be provided. Some camping equipment may be hired, but this should be booked well in advance of any visit.

Nyanga Mountains National Park

Size: 314 sq kms (Nyanga Mountains National Park 339 sq kms and Mtarazi Falls 25 sq kms).
Province: Manicaland
District: Nyanga
Geographical location: Situated in the Eastern Highlands on the Mozambique border, about 200 kms east-south-east of Harare
Altitude: 880–2,592m
Physical features: Nyanga National Park comprises a giant volcanic plateau and includes part of Mount Inyangani (highest peak in Zimbabwe). This mountainous area is the source of several important rivers (Pungwe, Odzi, Gairezi, Inyangombe, and Mtarazi) and includes a number of waterfalls. In Mtarazi Falls National Park the river cascades 762m down the cliff face into the Honde Valley. Many of the rivers have been dammed to form small lakes.
Vegetation: The area contains stunted woodlands, patches of submontane lowland forest, introduced pines and wattles, and high altitude heathlands.
Fauna: Nyanga is an important mountain sanctuary for wildlife in a region where plantations of exotic conifers and wattle tend to dominate the landscape, and contains an interesting montane fauna which is unique in Zimbabwe. In Mtarazi Falls National Park the rainforest created by spray from the waterfall provides a home for the blue duiker. There are relatively few large herbivores on the veld, although lions are present. Stream fish include trout.
Bird life: Cisticolas, waxbills, mannikins, widowbirds, buzzards, and eagles
Cultural Heritage: There are certain important archaeological sites indicating past high-density occupation of the area by an agricultural culture of

remarkable technical sophistication.
Visitor facilities: The parks are essentially scenic but also provide for a range of outdoor recreational activities including quality angling for introduced rainbow, brown, and brook trout in specially built dams. Other facilities include a hotel and lodges in the park, six hotels near the park, caravan and campsites, and well-maintained gravel roads.

Victoria Falls Rainforest National Park

(see "World Heritage Sites")

Zambezi National Park

Size: 560 sq kms
Province: Matabeleland North
District: Hwange
Geographical location: In the extreme west on the southern bank of the Zambezi River, which forms the border with Zambia
Altitude: 1,000m
Physical features: The Kalahari sand sheet has been eroded to expose underlying basalt in the north along the Zambezi River frontage (about 50kms). It forms undulating country in the remainder of the area, with two extensive marshy systems draining towards the Zambezi below the Victoria Falls.
Vegetation: Kalahari woodland typifies the sand sheet between the open grassed marshlands and has been modified in parts by past logging and fire. A mixed scrub community has developed on the basalt areas, giving way to riverine vegetation dominated by acacia and tamarind watercourses, especially along the Zambezi. Papyrus swamps occur among the riverine communities.
Fauna: Large mammals include elephant, hippopotamus, black rhinoceros and white rhinoceros (reintroduced), lion, leopard, spotted hyena, giraffe, zebra, wart hog, and some 12 antelope species including sable and waterbuck. River fish include tigerfish, tilapia, and vundu.
Bird life: Fish eagle, Goliath heron, malachite kingfisher, egrets, and darters
Visitor facilities: The park is closed to visitors in the wet season from November to April. Facilities in the park include lodges on the banks of the Zambezi, fishing camps, and a road network.

Botanical Reserves

Bunga Forest

(see "Vumba Botanical Reserve")

Chirinda Forest Botanical Reserve

Size: 9.5 sq kms
Province: Manicaland
District: Chipinge
Geographic location: Eastern Zimbabwe 35kms south of Chipinge on the Mozambique border

Physical features: Tropical forest
Vegetation: The area is noted for many unique types of flora, including the nation's tallest indigenous tree — a red màhogany, *Khaya nyasica* — over 60m high. This is one of the last remaining areas of primeval forest within the country.
Visitor facilities: None

Haroni Forest

Size: 200 sq kms
Province: Manicaland
District: Chimanimani
Geographical location: 30kms south-east of Chimanimani
Altitude: Undocumented
Physical features: Rare lowveld forest
Vegetation: Similar to that found further east in Mozambique
Bird life: Includes species found nowhere else in Zimbabwe
Visitor facilities: None

Rusitu Forest

Size: 1.5 sq kms
Province: Manicaland
District: Chimanimani
Geographical location: 50kms south of Chimanimani
Altitude: Undocumented
Physical features: A low altitude area of dense forest
Vegetation: Many varieties of plants make this a botanist's haven.
Visitor facilities: There are no visitor facilities and the final access to the forest is on a poor gravel road.

Sebakwe Acacia Karoo, Sebakwe Great Dyke, Sebakwe Mountain Acacia

(see "Sebakwe" under "Recreational Parks")

Vumba Botanical Reserve and Garden and Bunga Forest Botanical Reserve

Size: 7.4 sq kms (Vumba Botanical Garden 2 sq kms, Vumba Botanical Reserve 420 sq m, and Bunga Forest Botanical Reserve 4.5 sq kms).
Province: Manicaland
District: Mutare
Geographical location: About 30kms from Mutare on the road to Chimanimani
Altitude: Up to 2,000m
Physical features: Wooded granite hills, located in the Vumba Mountains (known as the "mountains of mist"), overlook the plains of Mozambique. The annual rainfall is 1,676mm.
Vegetation: Thick montane evergreen forest and open scrub vegetation with aloes occur on steep rocky slopes. The Botanical Garden contains cycads, orchids, and many trees and shrubs found nowhere else in Zimbabwe.
Fauna: Blue duiker, bushbuck, bush pig, and samango monkey

Bird life: Orange ground thrush, wood owl, red-winged starling, bronze sunbird, augur buzzard, forest weaver, Nyasa crimsonwing, Swynnerton's robin, and 2 species endemic to Zimbabwe — chirinda apalis and Robert's prinia.
Visitor facilities: The reserves have camping facilities, scenic drives, and a network of footpaths. There is a hotel nearby.

Botanical Gardens

Ewanrigg Botanical Garden

Size: 2.83 sq kms
Province: Mashonaland East
District: Harare
Geographic location: 40kms from Harare on the road to Shamva
Vegetation: This garden has an international reputation for its extensive displays of aloes and cycads, growing along the sides and crest of a small ridge dominating the other collections of plants in their setting of green lawns and indigenous woodland. The best time of year to view these multitudes of aloes unique to Ewanrigg Botanical Garden is during July. The peak of the flowering season for the Barberton daisies, fuchsias, and begonias is September – October. There is also a wide selection of cacti and staplieae.
Visitor facilities: There are no overnight facilities within the park though picnic sites exist.

National Botanical Garden

Size: 550 sq kms
Province: Mashonaland East
District: Harare
Geographical location: Situated in Alexandra Park, Harare
Altitude: 1,455m
Vegetation: Some sections of the park are dedicated to plants from different climatic areas. The park also contains the National Herbarium.
Visitor facilities: None

Vumba

(see "Vumba" under "Botanical Reserves")

Sanctuaries

Chimanimani Eland Sanctuary

Size: 18 sq kms
Province: Manicaland
District: Chimanimani
Geographical location: Near the town of Chimanimani in eastern Zimbabwe
Altitude: Undocumented
Physical features: The mountainous terrain includes Bridal Veil Falls. Annual rainfall is high.

Vegetation: The area is in the undifferentiated afromontane vegetation zone with a diverse canopy flora.

Fauna: There is a relict eland population, the species being the only large antelope to adapt to the artificial environment of pine plantations. The sanctuary also has waterbuck and zebra.

Visitor facilities: There are no tourist facilities in the sanctuary, but there is a hotel and caravan-campsite at Chimanimani.

Manjinji Pan

Size: 3 sq km
Province: Matabeleland South
District: Beitbridge
Geographic location: 160kms east of Beitbridge on the Mwenzi River
Altitude: Undocumented
Bird life: This is an area on the Mwenzi set aside as a bird sanctuary where all bird life is protected.
Visitor facilities: None. A four-wheel drive vehicle is recommended as the area is accessible by secondary road only.

Mushandike Sanctuary

Size: 129 sq kms
Province: Masvingo
District: Masvingo
Geographical location: 26kms west of Masvingo, centred on the Mushandike Dam
Altitude: Undocumented
Physical features: Mushandike Dam is ringed by mountains. The annual rainfall is under 1,000mm.
Vegetation: The area lies within the drier Zambezian miombo woodland and contains a complexity of habitats.
Fauna: White rhinoceros, sable, grysbok, waterbuck, duiker, greater kudu, klipspringer, wildebeest, zebra, and leopard. Fish in the dam include black bass, tilapia, and barbel.
Bird life: Red-billed teal, comb duck, herons, and cormorants
Visitor facilities: Internal gravel roads (subject to seasonal flooding), caravan and camping facilities, and licensed sport fishing

Safari Areas

Charara Safari Area

Size: 1,692 sq kms
Province: Mashonaland West
Districts: Hurungwe and Kariba
Geographical location: Eastern shores of Lake Kariba near the border with Zambia
Altitude: 490–1,209m
Physical features: The broken Zambezi Valley escarpment country gives way to limited areas of flat land along the shores of Lake Kariba.
Vegetation: Similiar to that of the Mana Pools National Park and other Zambezi Valley conservation areas, mopane woodlands and dry decidious thickets with localised riverine communities.

Fauna: The fauna is similar to that of Mana Pools National Park and the Zambezi Valley conservation areas, but with limited riverine communities. Mammals include elephant, black rhinoceros, lion, leopard, greater kudu, bushbuck, and eland.

Visitor facilities: Lake Kariba is an important visitor destination and benefits substantially by the proximity of the Charara Safari Area, which offers good game-viewing and is popular with anglers. Limited recreational hunting permitted. Game-viewing is permitted by foot. Nyanyana Camp is on the mouth of Nyanyana River, almost 3kms from Kariba. Caravan and camping sites are within 100m of the lake shore.

Chete Safari Area

Size: 1,081 sq kms
Province: Matabeleland North
District: Binga
Geographical location: Along the southern shores of Lake Kariba
Altitude: 300–900m
Physical features: Broken country in the east gives way to more undulating country overlain with Kalahari sand in the west. The area is dissected by numerous watercourses flowing into three seasonal river systems (Ruziruhuru, Senkwi-Murambare, and Mwenda). Soils are generally poor, stony, and shallow. The artificial Lake Kariba has inundated the northern fringe of the area and the lakeshore is characterised by many bays formed in drowned valleys.
Vegetation: Generally scrub or mopane communities with open miombo woodlands occuring on the deeper sands. Riverine vegetation along the watercourses with steeper slopes is characterised by species of commiphora and occasional baobabs. Grass cover is varied. Water ferns are common along the lakeshore.
Fauna: Elephant, buffalo, leopard, black rhinoceros, eland, sable antelope, greater kudu, bushbuck, duiker, impala, wart hog, and baboon. Nile crocodile are present.
Bird life: Fish eagle and marabou stork
Visitor facilities: None. Strictly controlled recreational hunting is permitted.

Chewore Safari Area

Size: 3,390 sq kms
Province: Mashonaland West
District: Hurungwe
Geographic location: 48kms downstream from Mana Pools
Altitude: Undocumented
Fauna: Most species of game are found in this reserve, including the rare black rhinoceros.
Visitor facilities: None. The park is open from May

to October. Visitors must report to the warden at Marongora. A four-wheel drive vehicle is recommended as the roads are not regularly maintained. Recreational hunting is permitted by licence. There is also an airstrip.

Chipinga Safari Area

Size: 26 sq kms
Province: Manicaland
District: Chipinge
Geographical location: 63kms from Birchenough Bridge
Altitude: Undocumented
Fauna: Most species of game are found in this safari area.
Visitor facilities: None. Hunting is permitted by licence and arranged through authorized safari companies.

Chirisa Safari Area

Size: 1,713 sq kms
Province: Midlands
District: Gokwe
Geographical location: In north-west Zimbabwe adjacent to Chizarira
Altitude: 600–1,200m
Physical features: The area is dominated by the valley of the Sengwa River, a large but somewhat seasonal stream draining northwards into Lake Kariba. The rivers are usually in deeply incised valleys or canyons. The topography varies from rough, steep broken scarps and hills to gently undulating sandveld.
Vegetation: The vegetation is characterised by a diversity of well-defined communities including open grassland on the flood plain of the Sengwa and scrub, tree thickets, and woodland on clays. The woodlands are on sandy soils with mopane thickets on heavier soils. Riverine communities occur along some of the tributaries of the Sengwa, but have generally been severely modified by elephant.
Fauna: Elephant (12,000), buffalo, impala, black rhinoceros, lion, leopard, cheetah, wild dog, wart hog, bush pig, zebra, and various antelope species
Visitor facilities: The area caters for a range of outdoor activities, including recreational hunting outside the research area. There is an airstrip at Gokwe.

Dande Safari Area

Size: 52 sq kms
Province: Mashonaland Central
District: Guruve
Geographical location: In north-western Zimbabwe, east of and adjacent to Chewore
Altitude: Undocumented
Fauna: Many species of game are found within the safari area's boundaries, including the black rhino.
Visitor facilities: None

Deka Drum Fishing Resort

Size: 51 sq kms
Province: Matabeleland North
District: Hwange
Geographical location: 50kms north of Hwange where the Deka and Zambezi rivers converge
Altitude: Undocumented
Fauna: Well-known fishing area
Visitor facilites: Caravan and camping facilities available. There is an airstrip.

Hurungwe Safari Area

Size: 2,894 sq kms
Province: Mashonaland West
District: Hurungwe
Geographical location: Situated in the north-west of the country, between Kariba, Mana Pools, and Hurungwe Communal Land
Altitude: Undocumented
Fauna: It has a sizeable population of most of the game species found in the Zambezi Valley.
Visitor facilities: None

Malapati Safari Area

Size: 15.5 sq kms
Province: Masvingo
District: Chiredzi
Geographic location: In south-eastern Zimbabwe, it adjoins the southern end of the Gonarezhou National Park and lies on the Mwezeni River.
Altitude: Undocumented
Fauna: A selection of game indigenous to the area
Visitor facilities: None

Matetsi Safari Area

Size: 2,955 sq kms
Province: Matabeleland North
District: Hwange
Geographical location: North-west Zimbabwe on the border with Botswana and Zambia
Altitude: 1,000m
Physical features: The area occupies the almost imperceptible watershed separating the Zambezi and the inland drainages of the great Makgadikgadi salt pans in Botswana. It is the source of several rivers including the Matetsi, Gwai, and Deka. About 75 per cent is well-watered with perennial streams and rivers, while the remaining area is overlain with Kalahari sands. On one side is a 30-kilometre stretch of the Zambezi River.
Vegetation: Dry deciduous forests on the deep sands. The basalt soils provide a complex of vegetative communities including mopane woodlands and scrub communities. Open grassland can be found on the marshlands.
Fauna: Lion, leopard, zebra, buffalo, greater kudu, bushbuck, reedbuck, waterbuck, klipspringer, impala, and wart hog. The area is renowned for sable antelope.
Visitor facilities: Facilities include lodges and

game-viewing walks. Access is by road or rail and there is an airstrip. Controlled recreational hunting is permitted.

Tuli Safari Area

Size: 41.5 sq kms
Province: Matabeleland South
District: Beitbridge
Geographical location: 90kms west of Beitbridge
Altitude: Undocumented
Fauna: Populations of game indigenous to the area
Visitor facilities: None. Limited hunting.

Recreational Parks

Bangala Recreational Park

Size: 12 sq kms (Bangala Dam has a capacity of over 140 million cubic metres).
Province: Masvingo
District: Masvingo
Geographic location: 103kms from Chiredzi in south-eastern Zimbabwe (last 24kms on a gravel road)
Altitude: Undocumented
Physical features: The park was created around the Bangala Dam and provides irrigation water for the Hippo Valley and Triangle Estates.
Visitor facilities: None. The area's attractions are boating, fishing, and unspoiled surroundings.

Chinhoyi Caves Recreational Park

Size: 1.2 sq kms
Province: Mashonaland West
District: Makonde
Geographic location: 8kms west of Chinhoyi on the Kariba road
Physical features: A 30m-wide by 45m-deep shaft in limestone rock, at the foot of which lies a large pool of clear water over 90m deep. Stalactites overhang the pool.
Visitor facilities: There is a petrol station and a motel at the park, and full shopping facilities are provided at the town of Chinhoyi (8kms away). There is also a caravan and camping site.

Lake Kariba Recreational Park

Size: 290 sq kms
Provinces: Mashonaland West and Matabeleland North
Districts: Kariba and Binga
Geographical location: On the north-west border with Zambia in Mashonaland and Matabeleland North Province. It excludes the waters contained in Matusadona National Park.
Altitude: 482m
Physical features: Kariba is a man-made lake resulting from the damming of the Zambezi River at Kariba in 1958. The water covers 5,180 sq kms of what was once the Gwembe trough. The lake has

currents and sudden storms. The Mlibizi, Zambezi, Sanyati, Ume, and Sebungwe rivers still flow through it.
Vegetation: 1,000 sq kms of forest were cleared prior to flooding. Explosive growth of the exotic floating salvinia on the lakeshore acted as a stabiliser. The weed once covered fifteen per cent of the lake surface but has now declined to under two per cent. Emergent vegetation is not particularly well-developed, apart from extensive beds of torpedo grass that provide valuable grazing for fish when submerged, and for ungulates when exposed.
Fauna: The lake is not particularly productive, but 42 fish species are known to exist including tilapia, vundu, Hunyani salmon, nkupi, chessa, bottlenose, and Cornish Jack. Tigerfish are a popular sporting species. The Tanganyika sardine (*kapenta*) has been introduced and is prospering in the vacant lacustrine habitat. The lake is rich in crocodile.
Bird life: Egrets, kingfishers, little bee-eaters, black-collared barbets, fish eagles, and herons such as the Goliath heron
Visitor facilities: The lake is a popular tourist destination served by the town of Kariba. Facilities include lodges, campsites, walking and canoe trails, watersports, boat hire, and various safaris.

Lake Kyle Recreational Park

Size: 170 sq kms
Province: Masvingo
District: Masvingo
Geographical location: 32kms south-east of Masvingo in eastern Zimbabwe
Altitude: 1,200m
Physical features: Lake Mutirikwi is an artificial lake constructed to provide water for the vast irrigation schemes of the lowveld. It is located at the confluence of the Mshagashe and Mutirikwi rivers. The park is bounded on three sides by tributaries of the Mutirikwi.
Vegetation: The grassy plains are interrupted by densely wooded ravines.
Fauna: Many mammals have been reintroduced including white rhinoceros, giraffe, buffalo, wildebeest, greater kudu, nyala, bushbuck, eland, reedbuck, impala, sable antelope, zebra, oribi, duiker, steinbuck, hippopotamus, wart hog, and Lichtenstein's hartebeest. Crocodiles are present. Fish include black bass, tilapia, yellowfish, and bottlenose.
Bird life: Includes ostrich
Visitor facilities: There are many visitors because of high-quality gameviewing. Facilities include caravan and campsites, four hotels on the lakeshores, pony trails, and watersports. The lake is renowned for bass fishing. Licences must be obtained from national parks staff prior to fishing.

Lake Matobo (Matopos) Recreational Park

(see "Matobo National Park" under "National Parks")

Lake Robertson Recreational Park

Size: 112 sq kms
Province: Mashonaland East
District: Harare
Geographic location: 85kms from Harare, off the Bulawayo road, 30kms downstream from the Lake McIlwaine Recreational Park
Altitude: Undocumented
Visitor facilities: No development has yet taken place. The park's principal attraction lies in fishing, boating, and the restful natural surroundings.

Manjirenji Recreational Park

Size: 35 sq kms
Province: Masvingo
District: Chiredzi
Geographic location: In south-eastern Zimbabwe, 65kms from Chiredzi (62kms on gravel road)
Altitude: Undocumented
Physical features: Encompassing Lake Manjirenji (formerly Lake McDougall) which has a 285 million cubic metres capacity
Visitor facilities: None. The park's attractions include boating, fishing, and unspoiled scenic surroundings.

Ngezi Recreational Park

Size: 58 sq kms
Province: Mashonaland West
District: Kadoma
Geographic location: 64kms from Featherstone on the Kwe Kwe road
Altitude: Undocumented
Physical features: This park includes the Ngezi Dam area.
Visitor facilities: Caravan and camping sites are available, though no supplies are available. Game-viewing by foot and fishing are offered.

McIlwaine Recreational Park

Size: 62 sq kms
Province: Mashonaland East
District: Harare
Geographical location: On the shores of Lake Chivero about 30kms south-west of Harare
Altitude: 1,300m
Physical features: The park is located on a 14.5-sq-km-long lake created by a dam across the Hunyani River. A ridge of ironstone hills forms the northern boundary. The lake supplies water to Harare. Fairly uniform topography with scattered granite kopjes and dolerite dyke intrusions. Soils are generally sandy. Water temperatures range from 14° to 27°C and the lake stratifies in summer.
Vegetation: Woodlands dominated by *msasa* and *mnondo* communities are associated with the granite kopjes and numerous termitaria. The remaining area is mainly grassland varying from generally dry to marshy. It is proposed to introduce a number of indigenous trees to the area, including acacia species. *Msasa* veld is retained in its natural state in certain parts of the park and does not occur in other conservation areas in Zimbabwe. Dense algal blooms occur in the lake.
Fauna: Reedbuck, steinbuck, duiker, sable antelope, leopard, olive baboon and other monkeys, buffalo, oribi, and wart hog. Introduced mammals include giraffe, zebra, greater kudu, eland, blue wildebeest, impala, waterbuck, and tsessebe, some of which have become well-established. Crocodile are present. At least 23 fish species have been recorded in the lake including tilapia, yellowfish, barbels, tigerfish, and Hunyani salmon.
Bird life: The 250 bird species include ostrich, fork-tailed drongo, northern grey tit, spotted creeper, blue-eared glossy starling, white-throated robin, chat, Mashona flycatcher, darters, cormorants, herons, egrets, and ducks.
Cultural heritage: Many Bushman paintings have been found in the area.
Visitor facilities: Lake Chivero is Harare's premier recreation park and tourism is encouraged with game-viewing, watersports facilities, tennis, croquet lawns, swimming pools, chalets, lodges, and camping facilities. Good sport fishing for tigerfish, bream, yellowfish, barbel, and Hunyani salmon. Bilharzia and crocodile discourage swimming, but not water-skiing.

Sebakwe Recreational Park

Size: 26 sq kms
Province: Midlands
Districts: Kwe Kwe
Geographical location: 54kms east of Kwe Kwe in central Zimbabwe
Altitude: Undocumented
Physical features: Spectacular cliff scenery. The park includes the aritificial Great Dyke Reservoir.
Vegetation: Miombo woodland. Flora within the botanical reserves includes various acacias.
Fauna: The migratory game population includes sable antelope, impala, and greater kudu. Reservoir fish include tigerfish and tilapia.
Visitor facilities: Year-round coarse fishing on the dam is the main tourist attraction. Also yachting and game-viewing on foot.

Mzingwane Recreational Park

Size: 12 sq kms
Province: Matabeleland South
District: Mzingwane
Geographical location: 55kms south of Bulawayo off the Beitbridge road. The last few kilometres are on gravel road.
Altitude: Undocumented
Visitor facilities: None. The park's attractions are boating, fishing, and unspoiled scenery.

Other Areas

Great Zimbabwe National Monument
(see under "World Heritage Sites")

Imire Game Park

Size: 10 sq kms
Province: Mashonaland East
District: Wedza
Geographical location: 125 kms south-east from Harare
Altitude: Undocumented
Fauna: Mammal species include wildebeest, giraffe, zebra, antelope, buffalo, and elephant.
Visitor facilities: The park is privately owned and operated by Norman Travers. Visitors may stay at the Sable Lodge.

Iwabe Game Park

Size: 100 sq kms
Province: Mashonaland West
District: Kadoma
Geographical location: On the banks of the Munyati River near Kwe Kwe
Altitude: Undocumented
Fauna: Numerous species of antelope, zebra, leopard, and cheetah, including some white and black rhino.
Visitor facilities: This is a private wildlife ranch.

Mtarazi Falls

Size: 25 sq kms
Province: Manicaland
District: Nyanga
Geographical location: Within the Nyanga Mountains National Park
Altitude: Undocumented
Physical features: This is the highest waterfall in Zimbabwe, with a vertical drop of 762m in two stages over a vertical cliff into the Honde River Valley below.
Visitor facilities: None

Sengwa Wildlife Research Area

Size: 373 sq kms
Province: Masvingo
District: Chiredzi
Geographical location: South-east Zimbabwe
Altitude: Undocumented
Physical features: The area includes the Lutope River and its flood plain. There is a single rainy season from December to April, a cool dry season from May to July, and a hot dry season from August to December. Mean annual rainfall is 673mm and mean annual temperature 22.5–25°C.
Vegetation: Mopane woodland, deciduous thickets, acacia riverine communities, and river terrace grasslands
Fauna: Mammals include impala, buffalo, lion, and leopard.
Visitor facilities: None
Scientific Research: Impala ranging behaviour, elephant social structures, elephant communication, rodents, and several other projects

Animal Checklist

Mammals

INSECTIVORES
(*Insectivora*)
South African Hedgehog
Climbing Shrew
Four-Toed Elephant Shrew
Rock Elephant Shrew
Short-Snouted Elephant Shrew
Dark-Footed Forest Shrew
Greater Dwarf Shrew
Lesser Dwarf Shrew
Greater Musk Shrew
Grey-Brown Musk Shrew
Lesser Red Musk Shrew

BATS
(*Chiroptera*)
Megachiroptera
Gambian Epauletted Fruit Bat
Peter's Epauletted Fruit Bat
Wahlberg's Epauletted Fruit Bat
Bocage's Fruit Bat
Egyptian Fruit Bat
Straw-Coloured Fruit Bat

Microchiroptera
Banana Bat
Butterfly Bat
Angola Free-Tailed Bat
Ansorge's Free-Tailed Bat
Bit-Eared Free-Tailed Bat

Egyptain Free-Tailed Bat
Flat-Headed Free-Tailed Bat
Little Free-Tailed Bat
Madagascar Large Free-Tailed Bat
Midas Free-Tailed Bat
Nigerian Free-Tailed Bat
Pale Free-Tailed Bat
Spotted Free-Tailed Bat
Rufous Hairy Bat
Temminck's Hairy Bat
Welwitch's Hairy Bat
Bushveld Horseshoe Bat
Darling's Horseshoe Bat
Geoffrey's Horseshoe Bat
Hildebrandt's Horseshoe Bat
Lander's Horseshoe Bat

Peak-Saddle Horseshoe Bat
Ruppell's Horseshoe Bat
Swinny's Horseshoe Bat
Yellow House Bat
Lesser Yellow House Bat
Giant Yellow House Bat
Kuhl's Bat
Commerson's Leaf-Nosed Bat
Persian Leaf-Nosed Bat
Sundevall's Leaf-Nosed Bat
Botswana Long-Eared Fruit Bat
Greater Long-Fingered Bat
Lesser Long-Fingered Bat
Schreiber's Long-Fingered Bat

Ruppell's Bat
Rusty Bat
Schlieffen's Bat
Aloe Serotine Bat
Cape Serotine Bat
Long-Tailed Serotine Bat
Rendall's Serotine Bat
Common Slit-Faced Bat
Greater Slit-Faced Bat
Hairy Slit-Faced Bat
Large Slit-Faced Bat
Wood's Slit-Faced Bat
Egyptian Tomb Bat
Tomb Bat
Short-Eared Trident Bat
Damara Woolly Bat
Lesser Woolly Bat

BUSHBABIES, BABOONS, & MONKEYS
(*Primates*)
Lesser Bushbaby
Thick-Tailed Bushbaby
Chacma Baboon
Olive Baboon
Samango Monkey
Vervet Monkey

PANGOLINS
(*Pholidota*)
Pangolin

HARES & RABBITS
(*Lagomorpha*)
Cape Hare
Scrub Hare
Jameson's Red Rock Rabbit

RODENTS
(*Rodentia*)
Great Canerat
Lesser Canerat
Rock Dormouse
Woodland Dormouse
Bushveld Gerbil
Hairy-Footed Gerbil
Highveld Gerbil
Gorongoza Gerbil
Common Molerat
Chestnut Climbing Mouse
Grey Climbing Mouse
Nyika Climbing Mouse
Fat Mouse
Tiny Fat Mouse
Grooved-Toothed Mouse
House Mouse
Multimammate Mouse
Pigmy Mouse

Desert Pigmy Mouse
Pouched Mouse
Namaque Rock Mouse
Rudd's Mouse
Spiny Mouse
Striped Mouse
Single-Striped Mouse
Tree Mouse
Woodland Mouse
Mozambique Woodland Mouse
Porcupine
Giant Rat
House Rat
Selinda Rat
Nyika Veld Rat
Red Veld Rat
Vlei Rat
Angoni Vlei Rat
Large Vlei Rat
Water Rat
Springhaas
Common Bush Squirrel
Red Squirrel
Sun Squirrel
Tree Squirrel

CARNIVORES
(*Carnivora*)
Aardwolf
Honey Badger
Caracal
African Wild Cat
Cheetah
African Civet
Tree Civet
Wild Dog
Bat-Eared Fox
Large-Spotted Genet
Small-Spotted Genet
Brown Hyena
Spotted Hyena
Black-Backed Jackal
Side-Striped Jackal
Leopard
Lion
Banded Mongoose
Bushy-Tailed Mongoose
Dwarf Mongoose
Large Grey Mongoose
Meller's Mongoose
Selous' Mongoose
Slender Mongoose
Water Mongoose
White-Tailed Mongoose
Yellow Mongoose
Cape Clawless Otter
Striped Polecat
Serval
Striped Weasel

ANTBEARS
(*Tubulidentata*)
Antbear

ELEPHANTS
(*Proboscidea*)
African Elephant

DASSIES (HYRAX)
(*Hyracoidea*)
Rock Dassie
Yellow-Spotted Rock Dassie

ODD-TOED UNGULATES
(*Perissodactyla*)
Black Rhinoceros
White Rhinoceros
Burchell's Zebra

EVEN-TOED UNGULATES
(*Artiodactyla*)
Cape Buffalo
Bushbuck
Bushpig
Blue Duiker
Common Duiker
Eland
Gemsbok
Giraffe
Sharpe's Grysbok
Lichtenstein's Hartebeest
Red Hartebeest
Hippopotamus
Wart Hog
Impala
Klipspringer
Kudu
Nyala
Oribi
Oryx
Reedbuck
Waterbuck
Roan
Sable
Steinbok
Livingstone's Suni
Tsessebe
Blue Wildebeest

Birds

OSTRICH
(*Struthionidae*)
Ostrich

GREBES
(*Podicipedidae*)
Dabchick

Black-Necked Grebe
Great Crested Grebe

PELICANS
(*Pelecanidae*)
Pink-Backed Pelican
White Pelican

CORMORANTS
(*Phalacrocoracidae*)
Reed Cormorant
White-Breasted Cormorant

DARTERS
(*Anhingidae*)
African Darter

BITTERNS, EGRETS, & HERONS
(*Ardeidae*)
Common Bittern
Little Bittern
Black Egret
Great White Egret
Cattle Egret
Little Egret
Slaty Egret
Yellow-Billed Egret
Black-Headed Heron
Goliath Heron
Green-Backed Heron
Grey Heron
Purple Heron
Rufous-Bellied Heron
Black-Crowned Night Heron
White-Backed Night Heron
Rail Heron
Common Squacco Heron
Malagasy Squacco Heron

HAMERKOP
(*Scopidae*)
Hamerkop

STORKS
(*Ciconiidae*)
African Openbill
Abdim's Stork
Black Stork
Marabou Stork
Saddle-Billed Stork
White Stork
Woolly-Necked Stork
Yellow-Billed Stork

IBISES & SPOONBILLS
(*Plataleidae*)
Glossy Ibis

Hadeda Ibis
Sacred Ibis
African Spoonbill

FLAMINGOS
(*Phoenicopteridae*)
Greater Flamingo
Lesser Flamingo

DUCKS & GEESE
(*Anatidae*)
African Black Duck
Comb Duck
Knob-Billed Duck
Maccoa Duck
White-Faced Tree Duck
Fulvous Tree Duck
Yellow-Billed Duck
White-Backed Duck
Garganey
African Pigmy Goose
Egyptian Goose
Spurwinged Goose
Pintail
Southern Pochard
South African Shelduck
Cape Shoveller
European Shoveller
Cape Teal
Hottentot Teal
Red-Billed Teal

SECRETARY BIRD
(*Sagittariidae*)
Secretary Bird

VULTURES
(*Accipitridae*)
Cape Vulture
Egyptian Vulture
Hooded Vulture
Lappet-Faced Vulture
White-Backed Vulture
White-Headed Vulture

BIRDS OF PREY
(*Accipitridae*)
Augur Buzzard
Honey Buzzard
Lizard Buzzard
Steppe Buzzard
Bateleur Eagle
Black Eagle
Crowned Eagle
Steppe Eagle
Lesser Spotted Eagle
Long-Crested Eagle
Martial Eagle
Tawny Eagle
Wahlberg's Eagle
African Fish Eagle
African Hawk Eagle

Ayre's Hawk Eagle
Black-Breasted Snake Eagle
Brown Snake Eagle
Southern Banded Snake Eagle
Western Banded Snake Eagle
African Goshawk
Little Banded Goshawk
Dark Chanting Goshawk
Pale Chanting Goshawk
Gabar Goshawk
Gymnogene
Bat Hawk
African Cuckoo Hawk
Black Sparrow Hawk
Ovambo Sparrow Hawk
Little Sparrow Hawk
Red-Breasted Sparrow Hawk
African Marsh Harrier
Banded Harrier
Montagu's Harrier
Pallid Harrier
Black-Shouldered Kite
Yellow-Billed Kite
Palm-Nut Vulture

OSPREY
(*Pandionidae*)
Osprey

FALCONS
(*Falconidae*)
Lanner Falcon
Peregrine Falcon
Eastern Red-Footed Falcon
Western Red-Footed Falcon
Taita Falcon
African Hobby
European Hobby
Dickinson's Grey Kestrel
Greater Kestrel
Lesser Kestrel
Rock Kestrel

FRANCOLINS & QUAIL
(*Phasianidae*)
Coqui Francolin
Crested Francolin
Natal Francolin
Shelley's Francolin
Red-Billed Francolin
Red-Necked Francolin

Swainson's Francolin
African Blue Quail
Common Quail
Harlequin Quail

GUINEAFOWL
(*Numididae*)
Crested Guineafowl
Helmeted Guineafowl

BUTTONQUAILS
(*Turnicidae*)
Black-Rumped Buttonquail
Kurrichane Buttonquail

CRANES
(*Gruidae*)
Southern Crowned Crane
Wattled Crane

CRAKES, GALLINULES, & RAILS
(*Rallidae*)
Red-Knobbed Coot
Corn Crake
African Crake
Baillon's Crake
Black Crake
Spotted Crake
Striped Crake
Buff-Spotted Flufftail
Red-Chested Flufftail
Red-Tailed Flufftail
Streaky-Breasted Flufftail
Lesser Gallinule
Purple Gallinule
Common Moorhen
Lesser Moorhen
African Water Rail

FINFOOTS
(*Heliornithidae*)
African Finfoot

BUSTARDS & KORHAANS
(*Otididae*)
Denham's Bustard
Kori Bustard
Black-Bellied Korhaan
Red-Crested Korhaan

JACANAS
(*Jacanidae*)
African Jacana
Lesser Jacana

PAINTED SNIPES
(*Rostratulidae*)
Painted Snipe

PLOVERS & TURNSTONES
(*Charadriidae*)
African Wattled Plover
Blacksmith Plover
Lesser Black-Winged Plover
Caspian Plover
Crowned Plover
Chestnut-Banded Sandplover
Grey Plover
Long-Toed Plover
Ringed Plover
White-Headed Plover
Kittliz's Sandplover
Three-Banded Sandplover
White-Fronted Sandplover

SANDPIPERS & SNIPES
(*Scolopacidae*)
Greenshank
Common Redshank
Ruff
Sanderling
Common Sandpiper
Curlew Sandpiper
Green Sandpiper
Marsh Sandpiper
Wood Sandpiper
Ethiopian Snipe
Great Snipe
Little Stint
Whimbrel

AVOCETS & STILTS
(*Recurvirostridae*)
Black-Crowned Avocet
Black-Winged Stilt

DIKKOPS
(*Burhinidae*)
Spotted Dikkop
Water Dikkop

COURSERS & PRATINCOLES
(*Glareolidae*)
Bronze-Winged Courser
Temminck's Courser
Three-Banded Courser
Black-Winged Pratincole
Common Pratincole
Rock Pratincole
White-Collared Pratincole

GULLS & TERNS
(*Laridae*)
Lesser Black-Backed Gull
Grey-Headed Gull
White-Winged Black Tern
Caspian Tern
Whiskered Tern

SKIMMERS
(*Rynchopidae*)
African Skimmer

SANDGROUSE
(*Pteroclididae*)
Double-Banded Sandgrouse
Spotted Sandgrouse
Yellow-Throated Sandgrouse

DOVES & PIGEONS
(*Columbidae*)
Cinnamon Dove
African Mourning Dove
Laughing Dove
Namaqua Dove
Red-Eyed Dove
Rock Dove (Feral)
Tambourine Dove
Cape Turtle Dove
Blue-Spotted Wood Dove
Emerald-Spotted Wood Dove
Bronze-Naped Pigeon
African Green Pigeon
Rameron Pigeon
Speckled Rock Pigeon

LOVEBIRDS & PARROTS
(*Psittacidae*)
Lilian's Lovebird
Nyasa Lovebird
Brown-Headed Parrot
Brown-Necked Parrot
Meyer's Parrot

LOURIES
(*Musophagidae*)
Green Lourie
Grey Lourie
Purple-Crested Lourie

CUCKOOS, COUCALS, & TURACOS
(*Cuculidae*)
African Cuckoo

Black Cuckoo
Striped Crested Cuckoo
Didric Cuckoo
Emerald Cuckoo
European Cuckoo
Jacobin Cuckoo
Klaas's Cuckoo
Lesser Cuckoo
Barred Long-Tailed Cuckoo
Red-Chested Cuckoo
Senegal Cuckoo
Greater Spotted Cuckoo
Thick-Billed Cuckoo
Black Coucal
Burchell's Coucal
Coppery-Tailed Coucal
Green Coucal
Knysna Turaco
Violet-Crested Turaco

OWLS
(*Strigiformes*)
Tytonidae
Barn Owl
African Grass Owl

Strigidae
Barred Owlet
Cape Eagle Owl
Spotted Eagle Owl
Giant Eagle Owl
Pel's Fishing Owl
Marsh Owl
Pearl-Spotted Owlet
Scops Owl
White-Faced Owl
Wood Owl

NIGHTJARS
(*Caprimulgidae*)
European Nightjar
Fiery-Necked Nightjar
Gaboon Nightjar
Pennant-Winged Nightjar
Freckled Rock Nightjar
Rufous-Cheeked Nightjar

SWIFTS
(*Apodidae*)
Mottled Spinetail
Bat-Like Spinetail
African Black Swift
European Swift
Horus Swift
Little Swift
Mottled Swift
African Palm Swift
Scarce Swift

African White-Rumped Swift

MOUSEBIRDS
(*Coliidae*)
Speckled Mousebird
Red-Faced Mousebird

TROGONS
(*Trogonidae*)
Narina Trogon

KINGFISHERS
(*Halcyonidae*)
Brown-Hooded Kingfisher
Chestnut-Bellied Kingfisher
Giant Kingfisher
Half-Collared Kingfisher
Malachite Kingfisher
Pied Kingfisher
Pygmy Kingfisher
Senegal Kingfisher
Striped Kingfisher

BEE-EATERS
(*Meropidae*)
Southern Carmine Bee-Eater
European Bee-Eater
Little Bee-Eater
Madagascar Bee-Eater
Swallow-Tailed Bee-Eater
White-Fronted Bee-Eater

ROLLERS
(*Coraciidae*)
Cinnamon Roller
European Roller
Lilac-Breasted Roller
Purple Roller
Racket-Tailed Roller

HOOPOE
(*Upupidae*)
Hoopoe

SCIMITARBILLS & WOOD-HOOPOES
(*Phoeniculidae*)
African Scimitarbill
Red-Billed Wood-Hoopoe

HORNBILLS
(*Bucerotidae*)
Bradfield's Hornbill

Crowned Hornbill
African Grey Hornbill
Southern Ground Hornbill
Red-Billed Hornbill
Silvery-Cheeked Hornbill
Trumpeter Hornbill
Yellow-Billed Hornbill

BARBETS
(*Capitonidae*)
Black-Collared Barbet
Crested Barbet
Pied Barbet
Golden-Rumped Tinker Barbet
Yellow-Fronted Tinker Barbet
White-Eared Barbet
Whyte's Barbet

HONEYGUIDES
(*Indicatoridae*)
Brown-Backed Honeyguide
Eastern Green-Backed Honeyguide
Greater Honeyguide
Lesser Honeyguide
Scaly-Throated Honeyguide

WOODPECKERS
(*Picidae*)
Bearded Woodpecker
Bennett's Woodpecker
Cardinal Woodpecker
Golden-Tailed Woodpecker
Little Spotted Woodpecker

BROADBILLS
(*Eurylaimidae*)
African Broadbill

PITTAS
(*Pittidae*)
African Pitta

LARKS
(*Alaudidae*)
Singing Bush Lark
White-Tailed Bush Lark
Dusky Lark
Fawn-Coloured Lark
Chestnut-Backed Finch Lark
Grey-Backed Finch Lark
Flappet Lark

Red-Capped Lark
Rufous-Naped Lark
Sabota Lark

MARTINS & SWALLOWS
(*Hirundinidae*)
European House Martin
African Rock Martin
Banded Sand Martin
Brown Sand Martin
European Sand Martin
Eastern Roughwing
Blue Swallow
European Swallow
Grey-Rumped Swallow
Mosque Swallow
Pearl-Breasted Swallow
Red-Breasted Swallow
Greater Striped Swallow
Lesser Striped Swallow
White-Throated Swallow
Wire-Tailed Swallow

CUCKOO SHRIKES
(*Campephagidae*)
Eastern Black Cuckoo Shrike
White-Breasted Cuckoo Shrike

DRONGOS
(*Dicruridae*)
Fork-Tailed Drongo
Square-Tailed Drongo

ORIOLES
(*Oriolidae*)
Eastern Black-Headed Oriole
African Golden Oriole
European Golden Oriole

CROWS
(*Corvidae*)
Black Crow
Pied Crow
White-Necked Raven

TITS
(*Passeriformes*)
Paridae
Southern Black Tit
Acacia Grey Tit
Miombo Grey Tit
Northern Grey Tit
Rufous-Bellied Tit

Remizidae
Cape Penduline Tit
Grey Penduline Tit

SPOTTED CREEPER
(*Salpornithidae*)
Spotted Creeper

BABBLERS
(*Timaliidae*)
Arrow-Marked Babbler
Pied Babbler
White-Rumped Babbler

BULBULS
(*Pycnonotidae*)
Black-Eyed Bulbul
Red-Eyed Bulbul
Slender Bulbul
Sombre Bulbul
Stripe-Cheeked Bulbul
Terrestrial Bulbul
Yellow-Bellied Bulbul
Yellow-Streaked Bulbul
White-Throated Nicator
Yellow-Spotted Nicator

CHATS, ROBINS, & THRUSHES
(*Turdidae*)
Boulder Chat
Familiar Chat
Mocking Chat
White-Headed Black Chat
Common Stone Chat
Cape Robin
Heuglin's Robin
Red-Capped Robin
Eastern Bearded Scrub Robin
Sandy Scrub Robin
White-Browed Scrub Robin
Starred Robin
Swynnerton's Robin
White-Throated Robin
Thrush Nightingale
Capped Wheatear
Collared Palm Thrush
Groundscraper Thrush
Kurrichane Thrush
Miombo Rock Thrush
Olive Thrush
Orange Thrush

WARBLERS
(*Sylviidae*)
Bar-Throated Apalis
Chirinda Apalis
Black-Headed Apalis
Yellow-Breasted Apalis
Greater Black-Backed Cisticola
Lesser Black-Backed

Cisticola
Crackling Cloud Cisticola
Silent Cloud Cisticola
Croaking Cisticola
Desert Cisticola
Fan-Tailed Cisticola
Rattling Cisticola
Red-Faced Cisticola
Rock Cisticola
Short-Tailed Cisticola
Shortwing Cisticola
Singing Cisticola
Tawny-Flanked Cisticola
Tinkling Cisticola
Wailing Cisticola
Long-Billed Crombec
Red-Faced Crombec
Burnt-Necked Eremomela
Green-Capped Eremomela
Yellow-Bellied Eremomela
African Grassbird
Southern Hyliota
Black-Chested Prinia
Robert's Prinia
Broad-Tailed Warbler
Eastern Barred Bush Warbler
Desert Barred Warbler
Bleating Bush Warbler
Chestnut-Vented Warbler
Garden Warbler
Icterine Warbler
European Marsh Warbler
Moustached Warbler
Olive-Tree Warbler
Red-Winged Warbler
African Reed Warbler
Great Reed Warbler
River Warbler
Little Rush Warbler
Southern Forest Scrub Warbler
Sedge Warbler
Lesser Swamp Warbler
Willow Warbler
African Yellow Warbler
Yellow-Throated Warbler
Greater Whitethroat

FLYCATCHERS
(*Muscicapidae*)
Cape Batis
Mozambique Batis

White-Flanked Batis
Woodward's Batis
Ashy Flycatcher
Black Flycatcher
Blue-Mantled Crested Flycatcher
White-Tailed Crested Flycatcher
Dusky Flycatcher
Lead-Coloured Flycatcher
Livingstone's Flycatcher
Marico Flycatcher
Mashona Flycatcher
Mouse-Coloured Flycatcher
African Paradise Flycatcher
Spotted Flycatcher
Black-Throated Wattle-Eye

LONGCLAWS, PIPITS, & WAGTAILS
(*Motacillidae*)
Orange-Throated Longclaw
Rosy-Breasted Longclaw
Yellow-Throated Longclaw
Buffy Plain-Backed Pipit
Bushveld Pipit
Richard's Pipit
Long-Billed Pipit
Dark Plain-Backed Pipit
Large Striped Pipit
Tree Pipit
Cape Wagtail
Long-Tailed Wagtail
African Pied Wagtail
Yellow Wagtail

SHRIKES
(*Laniidae*)
Fiscal Shrike
Lesser Grey Shrike
Magpie Shrike
Red-Backed Shrike

BUSH SHRIKES
(*Malaconotidae*)
Bokmakerie
Crimson-Breasted Boubou
Southern Boubou
Tropical Boubou
Brubru
Southern Puffback
Black-Fronted Bush

Shrike
Gorgeous Bush Shrike
Grey-Headed Bush
Shrike
Olive Bush Shrike
Orange-Breasted Bush
Shrike
Black-Crowned Tchagra
Brown-Headed Tchagra
Marsh Tchagra

HELMET SHRIKES
(*Prionopidae*)
Chestnut-Fronted
Helmet Shrike
Red-Billed Helmet
Shrike
White Helmet Shrike
White-Crowned Shrike

STARLINGS
(*Sturnidae*)
Amethyst Starling
Black-Bellied Starling
Greater Blue-Eared
Glossy Starling
Lesser Blue-Eared
Glossy Starling
Long-Tailed Glossy
Starling
Red-Shouldered Glossy
Starling
African Red-Winged
Starling
Wattled Starling

OXPECKERS
(*Buphagidae*)
Red-Billed Oxpecker
Yellow-Billed Oxpecker

SUGARBIRDS
(*Promeropidae*)
Gurney's Sugarbird

SUNBIRDS
(*Nectariniidae*)
Black Sunbird
Bronze Sunbird
Collared Sunbird
Coppery Sunbird
Miombo Double-
Collared Sunbird
Yellow-Tufted
Malachite Sunbird
Marico Sunbird
Olive Sunbird
Purple-Banded Sunbird
Scarlet-Chested Sunbird
Violet-Backed Sunbird
Southern White-Bellied

Sunbird
Yellow-Bellied Sunbird

WHITE-EYES
(*Zosteropidae*)
Yellow White-Eye

SPARROWS &
WEAVERS
(*Ploceidae*)
Black-Winged Bishop
Red Bishop
Scaly-Feathered Finch
Brown-Backed Firefinch
Indigobird
Pink-Backed Firefinch
Indigobird
Red-Billed Firefinch
Indigobird
Red-Billed Quelea
Cape Sparrow
Brown-Throated
Golden Weaver
Large Golden Weaver
Greater Sparrow
Grey-Headed Sparrow
House Sparrow
Yellow-Throated
Sparrow
Black Buffalo Weaver
Cuckoo Weaver
Dark-Backed Weaver
African Masked Weaver
Cabani's Masked
Weaver
White-Browed Sparrow
Weaver
Spectacled Weaver
Spotted-Backed Weaver
Red-Headed Weaver
Red-Collared Whydah
White-Winged Whydah
Yellow-Mantled
Whydah
Yellow-Rumped
Whydah
Pin-Tailed Widow
Shaft-Tailed Widow
Long-Tailed Paradise
Widow
Broad-Tailed Paradise
Widow

WAXBILLS
(*Estrildidae*)
Nyasa Crimsonwing
Red-Faced
Crimsonwing
Cut-Throat Finch
Locust Finch
Red-Headed Finch

Brown Firefinch
Brown-Backed Firefinch
Pink-Backed Firefinch
Red-Billed Firefinch
Bronze Mannikin
Pied Mannikin
Red-Backed Mannikin
Green-Winged Pytilia
Orange-Winged Pytilia
African Quailfinch
Lesser Seedcracker
Green Twinspot
Red-Throated Twinspot
Black-Cheeked Waxbill
Southern Blue Waxbill
Common Waxbill
Black-Tailed Grey
Waxbill
Orange Waxbill
Sweet Waxbill
Violet-Eared Waxbill

BUNTINGS,
CANARIES,
& FINCHES
(*Fringillidae*)
Cabani's Yellow
Bunting
Cape Bunting
Golden-Breasted
Bunting
Lark-Like Bunting
Cinnamon-Breasted
Rock Bunting
Black-Throated Canary
Bully Canary
Cape Canary
Lemon-Breasted Canary
Yellow-Eyed Canary
Black-Eared Seed-Eater
Streaky-Headed Seed-
Eater

Reptiles

TERRAPINS
(*Pleurodira*)
Pelomedusidae
Hewitt's Terrapin
Lacepede's Terrapin
Marsh Terrapin
Okavango Terrapin
Serrated Terrapin

TORTOISES
(*Cryptodira*)
Testudinidae
Bell's Hinged Tortoise
Leopard Tortoise

LIZARDS
(*Sauria*)
Gekkonidae
Baobab Gecko
Bibron's Gecko
Cape Dwarf Gecko
Transvaal Flat Gecko
Spotted Ground Gecko
Tropical House Gecko
Tete Thick-Toed Gecko
Wahlberg's Velvety
Gecko

Agamidae
Mozambique Agama
Kirk's Rock Agama
Tropical Spiny Agama
Southern Tree Agama

Chamaeleonidae
Flap-Necked
Chameleon
Marshall's Dwarf Forest
Chameleon

Scincidae
Cregoe's Blind Skink
Golden Blind Skink
Giant Legless Skink
Percival's Legless
Skink
Gracile Limbless Skink
Arnold's Montane
Skink
Rainbow Skink
Limpopo Sand Skink
Wahlberg's Snake-Eyed
Skink
Common Striped
Skink
Variable Skink
Sundevall's Writhing
Skink

Cordylidae
Common Flat Lizard
Manica Girdled Lizard
Tropical Girdled Lizard
Warren's Girdled
Lizard
Black-Lined Plated
Lizard
Giant Plated Lizard
Imperial Plated Lizard
Tawny Plated Lizard
Yellow-Throated Plated
Lizard
Large-Scaled Snake
Lizard

Lacertidae
Black and Yellow Sand
Lizard

Cape Rough-Scaled Sand Lizard
Mozambique Rough-Scaled Sand Lizard
Blue-Tailed Scrub Lizard
Striped Scrub Lizard

Varanidae
Rock Leguaan
Water Leguaan

AMPHISBAENIANS
(*Amphisbaenia*)
Kalahari Round-Snouted Amphisbaenian
Swynnerton's Round-Snouted Amphisbaenian
Cape Wedge-Snouted Amphisbaenian
Kalahari Wedge-Snouted Amphisbaenian
Slender Wedge-Snouted Amphisbaenian
Square-Tailed Wedge-Snouted Amphisbaenian
Zambezi Wedge-Snouted Amphisbaenian

SNAKES
(*Serpentes*)
Typhlophidae
Schlegel's Blind Snake

Leptotyphlopidae
Long-Tailed Worm Snake

Boidae
African Python

Colubridae
Boomslang
Cape Centipede Eater
Gunther's Centipede Eater
Reticulated Centipede Eater
Common Egg-Eater
Eastern Egg-Eater
Common Slug-Eater
Bark Snake
Bush Snake
Rufous Beaked Snake
Gerard's Striped Burrowing Snake
Black File Snake
Cape File Snake
Montane Grass Snake
Olive Grass Snake
Three-Lined Grass Snake
Angolan Green Snake

Ornate Green Snake
South-Eastern Green Snake
Herald Snake
Common House Snake
Many-Spotted Snake
Forest Marsh Snake
Olive Marsh Snake
Mole Snake
Lined Olympic Snake
Purple-Glossed Snake
Kalahari Purple-Glossed Snake
Jalla's Sand Snake
Pigmy Sand Snake
Stripe-Bellied Sand Snake
Semi-Ornate Snake
Striped Swamp Snake
Tiger Snake
Marbled Tree Snake
Savannah Vine Snake
Brown Water Snake
Cape Wolf Snake
Dwarf Wolf Snake
Bicoloured Quill-Snout
Elongate Quill-Snout
Save Quill-Snout
Grey Shovel-Snout
Sundevall's Shovel-Snout
Two-Striped Shovel-Snout

Atractaspididae
Bibron's Stiletto Snake

Elapidae
Egyptian Cobra
Forest Cobra
Mozambique Spitting Cobra
Black Mamba
Green Mamba
Rinkals
Gunther's Garter Snake
Half-Banded Garter Snake
Sundevall's Garter Snake
Shield Snake

Viperidae
Berg Adder
Horned Adder
Rhombic Night Adder
Snouted Night Adder
Puff Adder
Gaboon Viper

CROCODILES
(*Crocodilia*)
Nile Crocodile

Wildlife Profile

Elephant, *Loxodonta africana*: Widely distributed throughout all major wildlife areas, and still survives in some communal lands.

Black rhinoceros, *Diceros bicornis*: Browser, now confined to major wildlife areas and subjected to heavy poaching pressure.

White rhinoceros, *Ceratotherium simum*: Grazer, mainly confined to smaller wildlife areas including Chivero (McIlwaine), Mutirikwi (Kyle), and Matobo Hills. Reintroduced.

Burchell's zebra, *Equus burchelli*: Common in grasslands and open savannah woodlands.

Buffalo, *Synerus caffer*: Widely distributed throughout major wildlife areas, with large concentrations in Hwange, Mana Pools, and Matusadona national parks.

Blue wildebeest, *Connochaetes taurinus*: Found in wildlife areas in the west, south, and south-east. Does not occur in the Zambezi Valley.

Lichtenstein's hartebeest, *Sigmoceros lichtensteinii*: Small population of about fifty animals in the south-east.

Red hartebeest, *Alcelaphus bucelaphus*: Confined to open grasslands and arid scrub in Hwange National Park and other wildlife areas in the north-west.

Tsessebe, *Damaliscus Lunatus*: Regenerated from relict populations in Matabeleland and now being reintroduced into many wildlife areas.

Blue duiker, *Cephalophus monticola*: Zimbabwe's smallest antelope, confined to forests of the Eastern Highlands.

Grey duiker, **Sylvicapra grimmia**: Widely distributed throughout the country.

Suni, *Neotragus moschatus*: Confined to parts of Mtoko district and the Gonarezhou National Park. Habitats include riverine thickets and dry woodlands.

Steenbok, *Raphicerus campestris*: Common in Matabeleland, the south, and the south-east, mainly on open grasslands with cover nearby.

Klipspringer, *Oreotragus oreotragus*: Widely distributed but confined to rocky habitats, to which it is uniquely adapted.

Oribi, *Ourebia ourebia*: Occurs in the Kazuma Pan, Gonarezhou National Park, and elsewhere in the south and west.

Waterbuck, *Kobus ellipsiprymnus*: Found throughout all wildlife areas.

Reedbuck, *Redunca arundinum*: Associated with reed beds, vleis, and stands of tall grass close to water throughout wildlife and farming areas.

Impala, *Aepyceros melampus*: Common and prolific throughout most of the country, especially in mopane woodlands.

Sable, *Hippotragus niger*: Widespread and fairly common in many wildlife areas.

Roan, *Hippotragus equinus*: Zimbabwe's second-largest antelope after the eland, widespread but nowhere common.

Eland, *Taurotragus oryx*: Africa's largest antelope, found throughout major wildlife areas and on many farms and ranches.

Bushbuck, *Tragelaphus scriptus*: Habitat includes riverine and other dense vegetation, usually close to water.

Kudu, *Tragelaphus strepsiceros*: Located throughout savannah woodlands in most major wildlife areas.

Giraffe, *Giraffa camelopardalis*: Endemic to several wildlife areas, especially Hwange and Gonarezhou national parks, but absent from the Zambezi Valley.

Bushpig, *Potamochoerus porcus*: Common and widespread, but nocturnal in habits.

Wart hog, *Phacochoerus aethiopicus*: Prefers open grasslands, vleis, and floodplains. Unmistakable in appearance.

Hippopotamus, *Hippopotamus amphibius*: Distributed throughout Zimbabwe's rivers, lakes, and swamps, especially in lower-lying parts of the country.

Lion, *Panthera leo*: Stable populations in most major wildlife areas, but virtually exterminated in farming and other regions.

Leopard, *Panthera pardus*: Found in wildlife and other areas, especially the Matobo Hills, but mainly nocturnal.

African wildcat, *Felis lybica*: Widespread but interbreeding with feral domestic cats in many areas.

Cheetah, *Acinonyx jubatus*: Nowhere common; existing populations are found on ranchlands where they are often shot for killing cattle.

Serval, *Felis serval*: Widespread in savannah and riverine woodlands, grasslands and vleis; solitary, nocturnal, and seldom seen.

Spotted hyena, *Crocuta crocuta*: Inhabits most major wildlife areas.

Brown hyena, *Hyaena brunnea*: Confined to the extreme western wildlife areas including Hwange National Park and Matetsi Safari Area.

Aardwolf, *Proteles cristatus*: Smaller member of the hyena family, widely distributed but nowhere common.

Clawless otter, *Aonyx capensis*: Found in most water bodies except the Zambezi and Limpopo, and has been known to raid poultry and ornamental ponds.

Honey badger, *Mellivora capensis*: Occurs widely throughout the country, raids wild beehives and is renowned for its bravery.

Black-backed jackal, *Canis mesomelas*: Can be seen in the south and west of the country, usually in more open terrain.

Side-striped jackal, *Canis adustus*: Found throughout most of the country, but prefers more heavily wooded terrain.

Wild dog, *Lycaon pictus*: Resides in several wildlife areas, but nowhere common and may be endangered.

Bat-eared fox, *Otocyon megalotis*: Largely limited to Hwange National Park but may be extending its range.

Mongooses, *Viverridae*: Ten species, of which the slender mongoose is probably the most often sighted.

Civet, *Civettictis civetta*: This mainly nocturnal species is found in all major wildlife areas and thrives in a wide range of habitats.

Lesser bushbaby, *Galago senegalensis*: Habitats include acacia, mopane, and other woodlands.

Thicktailed bushbaby, *Galago crassicaudatus*: Commonly found in well-developed woodlands and forests.

Vervet monkey, *Cercopithecus pygerythrus*: Widespread throughout much of the country.

Samango monkey, *Cercopithecus albogularis*: Confined to the Eastern Highlands.

Chacma baboon, *Papio ursinus*: Spread throughout Zimbabwe, can occupy virtually any habitat except desert.

Birdlife Profile

With over 600 species of resident and migrant birds, Zimbabwe has an abundant avifauna that attracts many visiting ornithologists. Habitats range from wetlands to montane woodlands and forests, each with its own characteristic bird communities. Robert's *Birds of Southern Africa* is one of several comprehensive reference works available from time to time in Zimbabwean book shops.

Ostrich: This largest of birds, *Struthio camelus*, is commonly found in grasslands and lightly wooded areas. Ostrich farming and ranching are becoming popular in Zimbabwe.

Pelicans: The **white pelican**, *Pelecanus onocrotalus*, and the **pink-backed pelican**, *Pelecanus rufescens*, both occur sporadically along pools and stretches of shallow water. The white pelican is more often seen in the west of the country.

Cormorants: The **reed cormorant**, *Phalacrocorax africanus*, is common throughout the country, while the **white-breasted cormorant**, *Phalacrocorax carbo*, is more often seen on the central plateau. The **African darter**, *Anhinga rufa*, is widespread.

Herons: Zimbabwe has nineteen herons. The **Goliath heron**, *Ardea goliath*, is the largest African heron and is found mainly along the major river systems. The **grey heron**, *Ardea cinerea*, is common and widespread. The **great white heron**, *Ardea alba*, is also commonplace, as is the **purple heron**, *Ardea purpurea*.

Egrets: Of Zimbabwe's five egret species the **cattle egret**, *Egretta ibis*, is the most common in Zimbabwe. The **black egret**, *Egretta ardesiaca*, is less often seen but is easily identified by the distinctive way it curves its wings over its head while fishing.

Storks: **Abdim's storks**, *Circonia abdimii*, arrive in large numbers from North Africa during the summer. The **white stork**, *Ciconia ciconia*, is also a summer visitor, while the **saddle-billed stork**, *Ephippiorhynchus senegalensis*, is present throughout the year in the lowveld and north-western Zimbabwe.

Ibises: The **sacred ibis**, *Threskiornis aethiopicus*, is common while the **glossy ibis**, *Plegadis falcinellus*, appears to be becoming more widespread. The **hadeda**, *Bostrychia hagedash*, is a pale olive bird found on lowveld rivers and the Zambezi, while the **African spoonbill**, *Platalea alba*, is sparsely distributed on pans, dams, and major rivers.

Flamingos: Both the **greater flamingo**, *Phoenicopterus ruber*, and the **lesser flamingo**, *Phoenicopterus minor*, are transient, but regular and gregarious visitors to Zimbabwe.

Geese: **Egyptian geese**, *Alopochen aegyptiacus*, are found throughout Zimbabwe, while the **spurwing goose**, *Plectropterus gambensis*, is seen on pan systems and along the larger rivers. The **white-faced tree duck**, *Dendrocygna viduata*, is widespread, while the **southern pochard**, *Netta erythrophthalma*, inhabits the permanent water sites in Mashonaland. Three teal occur in Zimbabwe, of which the **red-billed teal**, *Anas erythrorhyncha*, can be located at Zimbabwe's pans and dams.

Secretary bird: The secretary bird, *Sagittarius serpentarius*, can be seen foraging for insects, small rodents, and reptiles — including snakes — in grasslands and lightly wooded areas.

Vultures: Six species of vulture have been recorded in Zimbabwe, of which the **white-backed vulture**, *Gyps africanus*, is the most common. The **lappet-faced vulture**, *Torgos tracheliotus*, is a much larger bird. The **Cape vulture**, *Gyps coprotheres*, is declining and only one colony, near Shangani, is known to exist. The **Egyptian vulture**, *Neophron percnopterus*, has only been recorded three times in Zimbabwe.

Kites and **Buzzards**: The **black-shouldered kite**, *Elanus caeruleus*, is Zimbabwe's most widespread bird of prey. The **yellow-billed kite**, *Milvus migrans*, is also common in summer while the **black kite**, *Milvus migrans migrans*, is a Palaearctic migrant. Of the country's four buzzard species, the **lizard buzzard**, *Kaupifalco monogrammicus*, is most widespread, while the **augur buzzard**, *Buteo augur*, is found in the Eastern Highlands.

Eagles: Zimbabwe has seventeen species of eagle. The Matobo Hills has the highest concentration of **black eagles**, *Aquila verreauxii*, in Africa; the country's largest eagle is the **martial eagle**, *Polemaetus bellicosus*; and the best-known is probably the **fish eagle**, *Haliaeetus vocifer*, which thrives along Lake Kariba and major river systems.

Hawks: Four sparrowhawks and five goshawks occur in Zimbabwe. The **Ovambo sparrowhawk**, *Accipiter ovambensis*, is widespread in tall woodlands, while the **black sparrowhawk**, *Accipiter melanoleucus*, is found throughout the woodlands of central and eastern Zimbabwe. Of the goshawks, the most common is the little **banded goshawk**, *Accipiter badius*, a bluish-grey bird that is often seen near urban areas.

Harriers: The harriers, long-legged raptors with large wings and owl-like faces, are represented by four species, of which the **African marsh harrier**, *Circus ranivorus*, is the most common. The **gymnogene**, *Polyboroides radiatus*, belongs to this group and may be seen clambering about on tree trunks searching for insects and lizards.

Guineafowl: The **helmeted guineafowl**, *Numida meleagris*, is common in most wildlife areas and on farmlands; the **crested guineafowl**, *Guttera* *pucherani*, is much rarer and is usually seen in dense bush, forests, and along major river systems.

Francolins: The **coqui francolin**, *Francolinus coqui*, is a common woodland resident, while **Swainson's francolin**, *Francolinus swainsonii*, is found in many wildlife areas, the Zambezi Valley, and on the central plateau.

Quails: The **common quail**, *Coturnix coturnix*, and the **harlequin quail**, *Coturnix delegorguei*, are both fairly widespread. The **blue quail**, *Coturnix adansoni*, is an intra-African migrant whose habitat includes a small part of the central plateau.

Rails: Zimbabwe has eighteen species of rails, crakes, and gallinules. The **African rail**, *Rallus caerulescens*, occurs sparsely in marshy areas. The **black crake**, *Amaurornis flavirostris*, is often seen throughout the country near rivers and streams, similar habitats to those occupied by the purple **gallinule**, *Porphyrio porphyrio*. The **moorhen**, *Gallinula chloropus*, is the local form of a bird found on all continents.

Cranes: The **crowned crane**, *Balearica pavonina*, is a fairly common inhabitant of the central plateau and Hwange National Park, while the **wattled crane**, *Grus carunculata*, whose numbers may be declining, occurs in a limited area of the central plateau.

Bustards: The **kori bustard**, *Otis kori*, is the heaviest flying bird in the world, often weighing in at more than twenty kilos. It occurs in the west and south. The **red-crested korhaan**, *Eupodotis ruficrista*, is found throughout much of the country while the **black-bellied korhaan**, *Eupodotis melanogaster*, is located in the Zambezi Valley.

Jacanas: The **African jacana**, *Actophilornis africanus*, is sometimes called the "lily-trotter" and is frequently seen on most dams, rivers, and wetlands. The **lesser jacana**, *Micropapra capensis*, is an inconspicuous and rarely seen species.

Plovers: The **crowned plover**, *Vanellus coronatus*, lives in grasslands, burnt veld, and other open spaces. The **blacksmith plover**, *Vanellus armatus*, is also widespread and easily identified by its distinctive "klink-klink" call. Of the sixteen other plover species recorded in Zimbabwe, the **Caspian plover**, *Charadrius asiaticus*, and the **grey plover**, *Pluvialis squatarola*, are Palaearctic migrants.

Coursers: The **three-banded courser**, *Rhinoptilus cinctus*, is endemic to Zimbabwe's major river systems, while **Temminck's courser**, *Cursorius temmincki*, has a preference for burnt grasslands. The country's three pratincoles are all migrants; the **common pratincole**, *Glareola pratincola*, is often seen in the Zambezi Valley between April and September.

Gulls: Some gulls and terns are seen on Zimbabwean water bodies. The lesser **blackbacked gull**, *Larus fuscus*, and the **grey-headed gull**, *Larus cirrocephalus*, have become more common with the building of large dams. Of the five terns known to occur in the country only the **white-winged black tern**, *Chlidonias Leucopterus*, is widespread.

Sandgrouse: Four species of sandgrouse occur in Zimbabwe. The most prevalent one is the **double-banded sandgrouse**, *Pterocles bicinctus*.

Pigeons and **Doves**: The **feral pigeon**, *Columba livia*, is one of fourteen species of pigeon and dove that occur in Zimbabwe. The distinctive call of the **emerald-spotted wood dove**, *Turtur chalcospilos*, can be heard in all parts of the country. The **laughing dove**, *Streptopelia senegalensis*, is found in urban areas, and both the laughing dove and the **Cape turtle dove**, *Streptopelia capicola*, habitat the woodlands throughout the country. **Namaqua doves**, *Oena capensis*, occur in drier areas; curiously, the **speckled pigeon**, *Columba guinea*, probably Africa's most common large pigeon, is relatively rare in Zimbabwe.

Cuckoos: Cuckoos lay their eggs in other birds' nests, while coucals build their own. Most cuckoos are Palaearctic or intra-African migrants, including the **European cuckoo**, *Cuculus canorus*, an unobtrusive summer visitor that closely resembles the **African cuckoo**, *Cuculus gularis*. The **Senegal coucal**, *Centropus senegalensis*, is widespread, as is the **Burchell's coucal**, *Centropus superciliosus*, sometimes known as the "rainbird".

Parrots: Zimbabwe has three parrots and two lovebirds. Of the parrots, only the **Meyer's**, *Poicephalus meyeri*, is frequently seen. **Lilian's lovebirds**, *Agapornis lilianae*, occur along the Zambezi while the **black-cheeked lovebird**, *Agapornis migrigenis*, is now rare.

Louries: The **grey lourie** or "go-away bird", *Corythaixoides concolor*, is seen throughout Zimbabwe. The **green lourie**, *Tauraco persa*, occurs mainly in the Eastern Highlands while the **purple-crested lourie**, *Tauraco porphyreolophus*, is recurrent throughout the country.

Rollers: The **lilac-breasted roller**, *Coracias caudata*, is a common and spectacular species, often seen perching on poles or dead branches overlooking open ground. The **racket-tailed roller**, *Coracias spatulata*, is also fairly common except in the Eastern Highlands. The **European roller**, *Coracias garrulus*, visits Zimbabwe in summer and is usually seen in savannah woodlands.

Bee-eaters: Two populations of the **European bee-eater**, *Merops apiaster*, live in Zimbabwe. One is a native; the other consists of Palaearctic migrants. The **white-fronted bee-eater**, *Merops bullockoides*, the **little bee-eater**, *Merops pusillus*, and the **swallow-tailed bee-eater**, *Merops hirundineus*, are all local residents. Zimbabwe's most spectacular bee-eater, the **carmine bee-eater**, *Merops nubicoides*, is an intra-African migrant, breeding in large colonies, often beside water.

Kingfishers: The **pied kingfisher**, *Ceryle rudis*, is common to all waters, while the **giant kingfisher**, *Megaceryle maxima*, is the largest kingfisher in the world and also favours perennial water. The tiny but beautifully coloured **malachite kingfisher**, *Corythornis cristata*, is a resident fishing species, while the confusingly similar **pigmy kingfisher**, *Ceyx picta*, is an intra-African migrant found mainly in woodlands.

Hornbills: Zimbabwe has eight hornbill species, all characterised by their raucous voices and huge bills. The **grey hornbill**, *Tockus nasutus*, is found in highveld woodlands, while the **red-billed hornbill**, *Tockus erythrorhynchus*, is a common lowveld resident. The country's most distinctive species is the **ground hornbill**, *Bucorvus leadbeateri*, a large bird with a deep, booming call.

Hoopoes and **Woodhoopoes**: The **hoopoe**, *Upupa epops*, closely resembles the European species and is found throughout Zimbabwe. Both the **red-billed woodhoopoe**, *Phoeniculus purpureus*, and the **scimitar-billed woodhoopoe**, *Rhinopornastus cyanomelas*, are widespread and form small parties during the year.

Nightjars: The **fiery-necked nightjar**, *Caprimulgus pectoralis*, is common and easily identified by its call, said to resemble "Good-Lord-deliver-us". The **freckled nightjar**, *Caprimulgus tristigma*, and the **Mozambique nightjar**, *Caprimulgus fossii*, are local residents. The **European nightjar**, *Caprimulgus europaeus*, is a Palaearctic migrant present during the summer months.

Owls: Of Zimbabwe's twelve owls, the **giant eagle owl**, *Bubo lacteus*, is the largest. The **wood owl**, *Strix woodfordii*, the **marsh owl**, *Asio capensis*, and the **Scops owl**, *Otus scops*, are all moderately common. **Pel's Fishing Owl**, *Scotopelia peli*, is an unusual species found along all major river systems.

Mousebirds: The **red-faced mousebird**, *Colius indicus*, is a resident across much of the country; the **speckled mousebird**, *Colius striatus*, only occurs in the south-east, east, and north-east.

Trogons: The **Narina trogon**, *Apaloderma narina*, is found in woodlands and forests along the Zambezi and Limpopo rivers, in much of the south-east, and in parts of northern Matabeleland.

Barbets: Zimbabwe's most common and widespread barbets are the **black-collared barbet**, *Lybius torquata*, the **pied barbet**, *Lybius leucomelas*, and the **crested barbet**, *Trachyphonus vaillantii*. The latter is often seen in parks and gardens and has a call said to resemble an alarm clock with the bell removed.

Honeyguides: The **greater honeyguide**, *Indicator indicator*, and the **lesser honeyguide**, *Indicator minor*, are both widely distributed throughout Zimbabwe. Four other species occur, of which the **brown-backed honeyguide**, *Prodotiscus regulus*, though uncommon, is the most widespread.

Woodpeckers: Zimbabwe's most common and widespread woodpecker is the **cardinal woodpecker**, *Dendropicos fuscescens*. The **bearded woodpecker**, *Thripias namaquus*, the **Bennett's woodpecker**, *Campethera bennetti*, and the **golden-tailed woodpecker**, *Campethera abingoni*, are also located throughout Zimbabwe.

Swifts: Of the country's ten swift species, the **European swift**, *Apus apus*, is a common Palaearctic migrant present in summer. The **palm swift**, *Cypsiurus parvus*, glues its nest to the underside of palm fronds and is a prevalent resident. Several other species are intra-African migrants.

Passerines: This group is represented by a great variety of families and species, including **starlings**, **sunbirds**, **weavers**, **whydahs**, and **finches**. Several species of weaver occur within the country and build distinctive nests in a variety of shapes and designs.

Shrikes: Zimbabwe has five shrikes, fifteen bush shrikes, and four helmet shrikes. The **fiscal shrike**, *Lanius collaris*, is wide ranging. The **tropical boubou shrike**, *Laniarius aethiopicus*, has a preference for riverine woodlands but is also often seen in urban gardens. The **white helmet shrike**, *Prionops plumata*, is a resident of the country's woodlands.

Oxpeckers: Both the **red-billed oxpecker**, *Buphagus erythrorhynchus*, and the **yellow-billed oxpecker**, *Buphagus africanus*, occur in Zimbabwe. Though sometimes seen together, the red-billed oxpecker is the more far-reaching of the two species.

Plant Profile (by family)

Acanthacea (barleria; 158 species)
A prolific and varied family that contains herbs, shrubs, some trees, and woody climbers. Many species have conspicuous flowers and some are used as garden shrubs or perennials.

Agavaceae (sisal & bowstring hemp; 10 species)
The 2 genera found in Zimbabwe are *Sansevieria* and *Dracaena*. The former is found mainly in arid areas, while the latter is often a forest genus.

Amaranthaceae (pigweed & amaranth; 47 species)
Most members of this family are herbs; some are shrubs or climbers. Some species were introduced from America and can be troublesome on croplands.

Amaryllidaceae (vlei lily & daffodil; 23 species)
This family contains 9 species of vlei lily, with showy pink and white flowers that appear in December. The veld fan or windball is also a member of this family and is often widespread in woodlands and grasslands.

Anacardiaceae (mango & marula; 32 species)
The best-known member of this family is the marula, *Sclerocarya birrea*, which is widespread at medium to low altitudes and has a fruit that is much sought after by both people and wildlife.

Anonnaceae (custard apple; 14 species)
The custard apple family includes trees, shrubs, and lianas. Many species have edible fruit, often growing in colourful clusters that may be eaten by monkeys and other wildlife.

Apiaceae (carrot & parsnip; 35 species)
Many members of this family are hollow-stemmed herbs with distinctive fruits. The family also includes the carrot, coriander, fennel, dill, and parsley.

Apocynaceae (oleander; 33 species)
The wild rubber tree, *Diplorhynchus condylocarpon*, is one of the few species that can grow on the serpentine soils of the Great Dyke. Several ornamental members of the family, including frangipani and the Madagascar periwinkle, are grown in gardens. The beautiful Save star, *Adenium obesum*, is a member of this family.

Arecaceae (palm; 4 species)
The raphia palm, *Raphia farinifera*, is confined to 2 specially established botanical sanctuaries at the foot of the Great Dyke. Another member of the family, the ilala palm, is widespread at lower altitudes.

Asclepiadaceae (milkwood & stapeliad; 143 species)
Perennial herbs and erect or climbing shrubs form the majority of this large family. Of Zimbabwe's 30 stapeliads, the best-known is *Huernia hislopi*, which occurs on granite hills and kopjes.

Asteraceae (sunflower; 377 species)
This large family includes sunflowers, ragworts, marigolds, African and Barberton daisies, and chamomiles as well as lettuce and chicory. Many species have been introduced from various parts of the world.

Bignoniaceae (sausage-tree; 12 species)
The best-known member of this family is the sausage-tree, *Kigelia africana*, which is found at lower altitudes and grows large, distinctive, sausage-shaped fruits. Most other members are lianas, adapted to climbing in forests.

Bombaceae (baobab; 1 species)
The baobab is an unmistakable feature of Zimbabwe's lower-lying areas. It stores water in its thick trunk. The flowers — which last less than a day — are pollinated by bats. Baobabs provide a range of useful products including water, bark, and seeds rich in tartaric acid.

Boraginaceae (borage; 29 species)
Besides borage, which is often grown in gardens, this family includes the Cordia genus of which *Cordia abyssinica*, with its conspicuous white flowers, is the most spectacular and best known.

Brassicaceae (cabbage; 22 species)
Most species, such as rape, cabbage, kale, kohlrabi, brussel sprouts, and cauliflower, are introduced. However, several indigenous species related to the watercress can be found near water.

Cannabaceae (hemp & dagga; 1 species)
The cannabis subspecies, *Cannabis sativa indica*, is sometimes grown illegally among maize crops or in bush clearings.

Capparaceae (caper; 37 species)
The family includes trees, shrubs, and herbs. Capers themselves, *Capparis spinosa*, were introduced from the Mediterranean, but some indigenous species scramble into the crowns of low-altitude trees.

Celastraceae (catha; 32 species)
This family consists largely of trees and shrubs. The 2 largest Zimbabwean genera are *Maytenus* and *Hippocratea*; the confetti tree, *Maytenus senegalensis*, grows to 8 metres (27 feet) and has sweetly scented cream flowers.

Clusiacea (St John's Wort & mangosteen; 11 species)
The African mangosteen, *Garcinia livingstonei*, is a common sight beside low-lying rivers; but it is an Asian species, *Garcinia mangostana*, that bears the sought-after mangosteen fruit.

Combretaceae (combretum; 35 species)
Many *Combretum* and *Terminalia* species occur in Zimbabwe that are ecologically important. The so-called "jesse bush" of lower-lying areas is composed largely of *Combretum* species, while the flame-bush, *Combretum microphyllum*, flowers spectacularly in August and September.

Commelinaceae (commelina & spiderwort; 37 species)
This family is often distinguished by its jointed, succulent stems with alternate leaves. Zimbabwe's most important genus is *Commelina*, with blue, yellow, or apricot flowers. One species, *Commelina benghalensis*, is often a troublesome intruder in agricultural lands.

Convolvulaceae (morning-glory; 86 species)
Ipomoea, Zimbabwe's most common genus, is composed mainly of succulents with purple or white flowers. The tubers of some species are eaten raw or cooked, and one species, the Save morning-glory, *Ipomoea plebia*, has become a problem in irrigated lands in the south-east.

Cornaceae (dogwood & assegai tree; 2 species)
The assegai tree, *Curtisia dentata*, occurs in the Nyanga area. Another forest tree, *Afrocrania volkensee*, is found in the eastern border area.

Crassulaceae (crassula & kalanchoe; 31 species)
All members of this family are succulents. Zimbabwe has 14 *Crassula* and 13 *Kalanchoe* species, the latter bearing showy red or yellow flowers.

Ebenaceae (ebony; 18 species)
Several *Diaspyros* and *Euclea* species occur in Zimbabwe; however, none produce timber of economic significance, although the wood is sometimes used for furniture or carvings. *Diaspyros mespiliformis* is sometimes seen overhanging lowveld pans.

Fabaceae (pea & bean; 591 species)
This is Zimbabwe's largest family of flowering plants. It includes such apparently diverse species as the highveld msasa and mnondo; the mopanes of the lowveld; all the *Acacias*; the Zimbabwe teak; and many others. The major subfamilies are the *Caesalpinoideae* (80 species); the *Mimosoideae* (68 species); and the *Faboideae*.

Flacourtiaceae (flacourtia; 20 species)
1 species, *Oncoba spinosa*, has large, scented fruit used by traditional dancers to make ankle rattlers. Another, *Bivinia jalbertii*, is specially protected because of its rarity.

Gesneriaceae (African violet; 9 species)
Streptocarpus is the only genus of this family that occurs naturally in Zimbabwe. The most spectacular is *Streptocarpus eylesii*, found on rock faces and stream banks in granite areas.

Malvaceae (cotton & hibiscus; 86 species)
Cotton grown in Zimbabwe comes from cultures of the American species, *Gossypium hirsutum*. Indigenous members of the family include okra, which is cooked and eaten as a vegetable, and the *Hibiscus* genus, represented by 40 species, of which some are commonly used as garden shrubs or hedge plants.

Melastomataceae (dissotis & tibouchina; 12 species)
This family includes several rare or endemic species. *Pseudobeckia swynnertonii* is endemic to the Chimanimani Mountains, while *Memecylon sansibaricum* is a rare tree found in the eastern border forests.

Moraceae (fig & mulberry; 31 species)
Figs — genus Ficus — of several species are widespread and common. The strangler fig, *Ficus thonningi*, often begins as an epiphyte and then destroys its host. The mulberry is cultivated in many Zimbabwean gardens.

Ochnaceae (ochna; 23 species)
Members of this family occur widely in diverse habitats and include *Ochna pulchra*, a graceful woodland tree with peeling bark that reveals a creamy-white under-bark.

Polygalaceae (milkwort; 31 species)
28 milkworts of the genus *Polygala* occur in Zimbabwe, and were so named because cows that ate the plant were said to increase their milk yield. One member of the family, *Carpolobia conradsiana*, is only found in the Gonarezhou National Park.

Polygonaceae (rhubarb & buckwheat; 23 species)
All Zimbabwean members of this family are berberidaceous. Ten species of *Polygonum*, which usually have pink or white flowers, occur along stream banks and in other moist habitats.

Proteaceae (protea; 13 species)
Zimbabwe has eight *Protea* species, of which three are endemic to the Chimanimani and Nyanga mountains. An outlying population of *Protea dracomontana*, found in South Africa's Drakensberg Mountains, occurs on the summit of Mount Inyangani.

Ranunculaceae (buttercup; 10 species)
This family includes the genus *Clematis*, or old man's beard, of which five species are found in Zimbabwe. Two buttercup species are also found in Zimbabwe: the common *Ranunculus multifidus* and the rare *Ranunculus mergeri*.

Rhamnaceae (buffalo thorn; 16 species)
The buffalo thorn, *Ziziphus mucronata*, is common in open woodlands and often grows on termite mounds. One naturalised member of this genus, *Ziziphus mauritania*, occurs in the Zambezi Valley and is prized for its edible fruit.

Simbaroubaceae (kirkia; 1 species)
Zimbabwe's only species, *Kirkia acuminata*, is a graceful tree characteristic of steep, rocky slopes. Its leaves turn a spectacular red or yellow at the beginning of the dry season.

Sterculiaceae (cocoa; 29 species)
Many exotics from this family are grown in Zimbabwe. Indigenous species include *Dombeya burgessiae*, often grown as an ornamental shrub, and

the widespread *Dombeya rotundifolia*, which is covered with white flowers in spring.

Thymelaeaceae (daphne & dias; 12 species)
Zimbabwe's largest genus, *Gnidia*, has six indigenous species. *Gnidia kraussiana*, which flowers in the wake of grass fires, is the most familiar. One species, *Dias cotinifolea*, occurs on forest edges in the eastern districts but is often cultivated as an ornamental shrub.

Tiliaceae (jute; 47 species)
The genus Corchorus, from which jute is made, is represented by twelve species in Zimbabwe. *Corchorus kirkii* is a shrub found among granite boulders, while *Corchorus olitorius* is grown as a relish and for its fibre.

Turneraceae (pimpernel; 8 species)
All the Zimbabwean members of this family are perennial herbs or annuals. One perennial, *Piriqueta capensis*, has a single golden flower and is only found in the Beitbridge area. The most common perennial is the Zimbabwe pimpernel, *Tricliceras longipedunculatum*. It is strongly cyanogenic.

Vitaceae (grape; 44 species)
Members of this family are perennial herbs, climbing shrubs and, occasionally, trees. The wing grape, *Vitis Vinifera*, originated in Asia and is widely grown in Zimbabwe. None of the wild genera produce particularly palatable fruit.

Demographic Profile

The population of Zimbabwe is estimated at 10.5 million (1990). With an annual birth rate of 3.75 per cent, life expectancy averages fifty-seven years (compared to forty-five in 1960).

During the sixties the white minority equalled more than a quarter of a million. But due to a steady emigration rate of approximately 17,000 people a year over the last few years, however, the population has decreased considerably to around 100,000. There is also a small Asian community.

Population density averages sixty-five people to the square kilometre, with uneven distribution. The former white areas in the highveld are not as densely populated as the communal lands. The remote northern parts of the country are the least populated.

There has been steady urban growth. Between the censuses of 1969 and 1982 the nineteen main towns nearly doubled their populations (compared to a fifty per cent increase in the country as a whole), while smaller centres such as Norton and Kariba even trebled their populations.

Harare, as the capital city, is a special case. In the period between 1969–1989, its population grew by about 345,000 (ninety per cent). Within the "Greater Harare" area the growth was even more dramatic. To cope with the rural–urban migration, a satellite municipality called Chitungwiza has developed south of the city. Today it is the third-largest urban centre in Zimbabwe. If Chitungwiza and other outlying "townships" are included as part of the capital, Harare more than doubled its population in thirteen years and accounts for fifty per cent of the total urban population.

Nearly twenty-five per cent of the population live in urban areas. Within these cities eighty per cent of the people are African and the other twenty per cent are white. Nationwide, however, seventy-five per cent of Africans live in rural areas, while eighty per cent of Europeans live in towns and cities.

In the rural areas of Zimbabwe, communal lands suffer from overpopulation and unequal distribution of sexes (seventy men to 100 women) due to the flight of male workers to the cities. There are also many more elderly dependents in the rural areas and very few individuals with higher (secondary) education. More than twenty per cent of the rural African population live on commercial farms.

Language

English is the official language of Zimbabwe. There are two main groups of Bantu speakers: the Shona and the Ndebele.

The Shona are composed of various ethnic groups that speak dialects of the same Bantu language — Shona. All of them, except the Kalanga who occupy the western tip of the country, live in the central and eastern half of Zimbabwe. The largest ethnic groups of Shona-speaking people are the Karanga, Zezuru, Manyika, Ndau, and Korekore.

The majority of the people in Matabeleland speak Sindebele, a Nguni language, and live in the south-western part of the plateau. They originated from a group that split with the Zulu due to dissension between the founder of that nation — Shaka — and Mzilikazi, one of his lieutenants. After raiding large parts of southern Africa, the Ndebele entered present Zimbabwe from the south and established a kingdom there in the 1840s.

Besides the Shona and Ndebele, whose languages are not mutually intelligible, there are a number of minor ethnic groups that speak various languages, such as the Tonga in the north-west, and the Vendao and Hlengwe along the south-western borders.

Population (1990)

10.5 million or 65 persons per sq km.
Population by ethnic grouping (1990)

Black	10,290,000
White	100,000
Coloured *	30,500
Asian	13,000
TOTAL	10,433,500

* Local term used to identify a person of both black and white descent

Population by tribal order

Shona	71%
Ndebele	16%
Other	13%

Zimbabwe Population by sex and age (1990)

	0–14	15–34	35–54	55+	Total
Males	2,457,000	1,659,000	693,000	346,500	5,155,500
Females	2,488,500	1,806,000	735,000	315,000	5,344,500

Population by province (1982)

Manicaland	1,098,836
Mashonaland Central	563,407
Mashonaland East	1,495,193
Mashonaland West	858,962
Masvingo	1,033,901
Matabeleland North	465,937
Matabeleland South	517,432
Midlands	1,091,844

Population of major urban centres (1982)

Harare	656,011
Bulawayo	413,814
Chitungwiza	172,556
Gweru	78,918
Mutare	69,621
Kwe Kwe	47,607
Kadoma	44,613
Masvingo	30,642
Zvishavane	26,758
Chinhoyi	24,322

Redcliff	22,015
Marondera	20,263
Chegutu	19,621
Bindura	18,243
Shurugwi	13,351
Kariba	12,387

Religious Affiliation

Syncretic	5,250,000(50%)
Christian	2,625,000(25%)
Indigenous Beliefs	2,520,000(24%)
Muslim	105,000(1%)

Gazetteer

(Second line indicates kilometre distance between major towns)

BANKET
Makonde District, Mashonaland West Province.
Harare 90, Bulawayo 529, Mutare 353, Gweru 268, Chinhoyi 25, Beitbridge 836, Victoria Falls 986.
Pop: 5,698. Alt: 1,295m (4,274ft). Post Office. Makonde District Hospital Tel: 2321. Police Tel: 6. Petrol: late hours. Hotel.

BEATRICE
Harare District, Mashonaland East Province.
Harare 70, Bulawayo 369, Gweru 205, Mutare (via Harare) 353, Beitbridge 510, Masvingo 222.
Pop: 1,300. Alt: 1,393m (4,597ft). Post Office. Beatrice Rural Hospital Tel: 254. Police Tel: 7. Petrol: late hours. Hotel.

BEITBRIDGE
Beitbridge District, Matabeleland South Province.
Harare 580, Bulawayo 321, Mutare 585, Gweru 471, Bindura 670, Birchenough Bridge 460, Chimanimani 566, Chinhoyi 698, Chiredzi 301, Kadoma 606, Kariba 947, Karoi 786, Kwe Kwe 534, Marondera 656, Masvingo 288, Mount Darwin 739, Mutoko 725, Nyanga 690, Plumtree 421, Rusape 677, Victoria Falls 758, Zvishavane 372.
Pop: 5,330. Alt: 456m (1,505ft). Airport. Post Office. Hospital: none. Police Tel: 5. Petrol: day and night. Hotel.

BINDURA
Bindura District, Mashonaland Central Province.
Harare 88, Bulawayo 527, Mutare 353, Gweru 363, Beitbridge 670, Birchenough Bridge 478, Chimanimani 504, Chinhoyi 204, Chiredzi 583, Kadoma 229, Kariba 453, Karoi 292, Kwe Kwe 301, Marondera 162, Masvingo 381, Mount Darwin 69, Mutoko 231, Nyanga 360, Plumtree 329, Rusape 258, Victoria Falls 964, Zvishavane 478.
Pop: 20,000. Alt: 1,113m (3,673ft). Airport. Post Office. Bindura Provincial Hospital Tel: 6555/6666. Police Tel: 323. Petrol: late hours. Hotel.

BIRCHENOUGH BRIDGE
Buhera District, Manicaland Province.
Harare 388, Bulawayo 452, Mutare 125, Gweru 355, Beitbridge 460, Bindura 478, Chimanimani 106, Chinhoyi 506, Chiredzi 199, Kadoma 490, Kariba 754, Karoi 594, Kwe Kwe 417, Marondera 507, Masvingo 172, Mount Darwin 547, Mutoko 533, Nyanga 230, Plumtree 556, Rusape 218, Victoria Falls 891, Zvishavane 269.
Alt: 455m (1,502ft). Airport. Post Office. Hospital: none. Police Tel: Cashel 18. Petrol: night and day. Hotel.

BULAWAYO
Bulawayo District, Matabeleland North Province.
Harare 439, Mutare 577, Gweru 164, Beitbridge 321, Bindura 527, Birchenough Bridge 452, Chimanimani 560, Chinhoyi 555, Chiredzi 483, Kadoma 298, Kariba 806, Karoi 643, Kwe Kwe 226, Marondera 513, Masvingo 280, Mount Darwin 596, Mutoko 582, Nyanga 682, Plumtree 100, Rusape 609, Victoria Falls 439, Zvishavane 184.
Pop: 430,000. Alt: 1,343m (4,432ft). Airport. Post Office. Bulawayo Central Hospital Tel: 72111, Mpilo Central Hospital Tel: 72011. Police Tel: 72515. Petrol: day and night. Hotel.

CASHEL
Chimanimani District, Manicaland Province.
Harare 454, Bulawayo 547, Mutare 90, Gweru 450, Chimanimani 60, Masvingo 267.
Alt: 1,190m (3,927ft). Nyanyadzi Rural Hospital Tel: 0-2011. Police Tel: 15. Petrol: none. Hotel.

CHIMANIMANI
Chimanimani District, Manicaland Province.
Harare 413, Bulawayo 560, Mutare 150, Gweru 461, Beitbridge 566, Bindura 504, Birchenough Bridge 106, Chinhoyi 532, Chiredzi 252, Kadoma 554, Kariba 779, Karoi 620, Kwe Kwe 523, Marondera 342, Masvingo 278, Mount Darwin 573, Mutoko 559, Nyanga 255, Plumtree 662, Rusape 242, Victoria Falls 997, Zvishavane 374.
Pop: 20,000. Alt: 1,586m (5,234ft). Post Office. Biriwiri Rural Hospital Tel: 3224. Police Tel: 3. Petrol: late hours. Hotel.

CHINHOYI
Makonde District, Mashonaland West Province.
Harare 115, Bulawayo 555, Mutare 381, Gweru 391, Beitbridge 698, Bindura 204, Birchenough Bridge 506, Chimanimani 532, Chiredzi 611, Kadoma 257, Kariba 249, Karoi 88, Kwe Kwe 299, Marondera 190, Masvingo 409, Mount Darwin 273, Mutoko 259, Nyanga 388, Plumtree 657, Rusape 286, Victoria Falls 992, Zvishavane 506.
Pop: 24,332. Alt: 1,143m (3,772ft). Airport. Post Office. Chinhoyi General Hospital Tel: 2305/2546/2547. Police Tel: 2445. Petrol: night and day. Hotel.

CHIPINGE
Chipinge District, Manicaland Province.
Harare 454, Bulawayo 518, Mutare 191, Gweru 421,

Birchenough Bridge 66, Chimanimani 70.
Alt: 1131m (3,732ft). Airport. Post Office. Chiping District Hospital Tel: 2901/2. Police Tel: 412. Petrol: day hours. Hotel.

CHIREDZI
Chiredzi District, Masvingo Province.
Harare 495, Bulawayo 483, Mutare 319, Gweru 385, Beitbridge 301, Bindura 583, Birchenough Bridge 199, Chimanimani 252, Chinhoyi 611, Kadoma 521, Kariba 862, Karoi 699, Kwe Kwe 447, Marondera 523, Masvingo 203, Mount Darwin 652, Mutoko 638, Nyanga 424, Plumtree 586, Rusape 416, Victoria Falls 922, Zvishavane 300.
Alt: 429m (1,416ft). Airport. Post Office. Cheredzi General Hospital Tel: 2388/2380. Police Tel: 333. Petrol: night and day. Hotel.

COLLEEN BAWN
Gwanda District, Matabeland South Province.
Harare 590, Bulawayo 145, Mutare 545, Gweru 270, Beitbridge 170, Gwanda 25, Zvishavane 151.
Alt: 844m (2,785ft). Gwanda District Hospital Tel: 224/5. Police Tel: 284. Petrol: day hours. Hotel.

DETE/GWAAI RIVER
Hwange District, Matabeleland North Province.
Harare 708, Bulawayo 269, Mutare 846, Gweru 433, Hwange 75, Victoria Falls 185.
Alt: 1,080m (3,564ft). Airport. Post Office. Hospital: none. Police Tel: 10. Petrol: night and day. Hotel.

EIFFEL FLATS
Kadoma District, Mashonaland West Province.
Harare 146, Bulawayo 303, Mutare (via Harare) 409, Gweru 139, Kadoma 5, Masvingo 323.
Alt: 1,170m (3,861ft). Airport. Post Office. Kadoma District Hospital Tel: 2382/3. Police Tel: Kadoma 2229. Petrol: late hours. Hotel: none.

FIGTREE
Matobo District, Matabeleland South Province.
Harare 479, Bulawayo 40, Mutare 617, Gweru 204, Beitbridge 361, Plumtree 60, Victoria Falls 479.
Alt: 1,382m (4,561ft). Post Office. Hospital: none. Police Tel: 6. Petrol: day hours. Hotel.

FILABUSI
Insiza District, Matabeleland South Province.
Harare (via Zvishavane) 483, Bulawayo 90, Mutare 488, Gweru 164, Beitbridge 261, Zvishavane 94.
Alt: 1,067m (3,521ft). Post Office. Insiza District Hospital Tel: 214. Police Tel: 203. Petrol: day and night. Hotel: none.

GUTU
Gutu District, Masvingo Province.
Harare 277, Bulawayo 360, Mutare 318, Gweru 172, Beitbridge 368, Chatsworth 34, Masvingo 80.
Pop: 2,500. Alt: 1,342m (4,429ft). Post Office. Hospital: none. Police Tel: Gutu 2. Petrol: day and night. Hotel: none.

GWANDA

Gwanda District, Matabeleland South Province.
Harare 529, Bulawayo 96, Mutare 570, Gweru 295,
Beitbridge 225.
Pop: 4,874. Alt: 986m (3,254ft). Airport. Post Office.
Gwanda District Hospital Tel: 224/225. Police Tel:
492. Petrol: late hours. Hotel.

GWERU

Gweru District, Midlands Province.
Harare 275, Bulawayo 164, Mutare 480, Beitbridge
471, Bindura 363, Birchenough Bridge 355,
Chimanimani 461, Chinhoyi 391, Chiredzi 385,
Kadoma 134, Kariba 642, Karoi 479, Kwe Kwe 62,
Marondera 349, Masvingo 183, Mount Darwin 432,
Mutoko 418, Nyanga 544, Plumtree 266, Rusape 445,
Victoria Falls 603, Zvishavane 119.
Pop: 80,000. Alt: 1,418m (4,679ft). Airport. Post
Office. Gweru General Hopital Tel: 51301. Police
Tel: 2121. Petrol: night and day. Hotel.

HARARE

Harare District, Mashonaland East Province.
Bulawayo 439, Mutare 263, Gweru 275, Beitbridge
580, Bindura 88, Birchenough Bridge 388,
Chimanimani 413, Chinhoyi 115, Chiredzi 495,
Kadoma 141, Kariba 366, Karoi 204, Kwe Kwe 213,
Marondera 74, Masvingo 292, Mount Darwin 156,
Mutoko 143, Nyanga 268, Plumtree 541, Rusape 170,
Victoria Falls 878, Zvishavane 389.
Pop: 720,000. Alt: 1,455m (4,802ft). Airport. Post
Office. Harare Central Hospital Tel: 64695/64671/
64601/2. Police Tel: 700101. Petrol: night and day.
Hotel.

HWANGE

Hwange District, Matabeleland North Province.
Harare 768, Bulawayo 329, Mutare 908, Gweru 493,
Victoria Falls 110.
Pop: 40,000. Alt: 1,019m (3,363ft). Airport. Post
Office. Hwange Hospital Tel: 271. Police Tel: 222.
Petrol: late hours. Hotel.

KADOMA

Kadoma District, Mashonaland West Province.
Harare 141, Bulawayo 298, Mutare 404, Gweru 134,
Beitbridge 606, Bindura 229, Birchenough Bridge
490, Chimanimani 554, Chinhoyi 257, Chiredzi 521,
Kariba 507, Karoi 345, Marondera 215, Masvingo
318, Mount Darwin 298, Mutoko 284, Nyanga 409,
Plumtree 400, Rusape 311, Victoria Falls 737,
Zvishavane 253.
Pop: 50,000. Alt: 1,163m (3,838ft). Airport. Post
Office. Kadoma General Hospital Tel: 2066. Police
Tel: 2222. Petrol: day and night. Hotel.

KARIBA

Kariba District, Mashonaland West Province.
Harare 366, Bulawayo 806, Mutare 629, Gweru 642,
Beitbridge 947, Bindura 453, Birchenough Bridge
754, Chimanimani 779, Chinhoyi 249, Chiredzi 862,
Kadoma 507, Karoi 161, Kwe Kwe 578, Marondera
439, Masvingo 659, Mount Darwin 522, Mutoko 508,
Nyanga 635, Plumtree 906, Rusape 536, Victoria
Falls 1,244, Zvishavane 755.
Pop: 15,000. Alt: 366m (1,208ft). Airport. Post Office.
Kariba District Hospital Tel: 2382. Police Tel: Kariba
444. Petrol: day and night. Hotel.

KAROI

Hurungwe District, Mashonaland West Province.
Harare 204, Bulawayo 643, Mutare 469, Gweru 479,
Beitbridge 786, Bindura 292, Birchenough Bridge
594, Chimanimani 620, Chinhoyi 88, Chiredzi 699,
Kadoma 345, Kariba 161, Kwe Kwe 417, Marondera
278, Masvingo 497, Mount Darwin 361, Mutoko 347,
Nyanga 476, Plumtree 745, Rusape 374, Victoria
Falls 1,080, Zvishavane 594.
Pop: 8,748. Alt: 1,343m (4,432ft). Airport. Post
Office. Karoi Hospital Tel: 6315. Police Tel: 233.
Petrol: day and night. Hotel.

KWE KWE

Kwe Kwe District, Midlands Province.
Harare 213, Bulawayo 226, Mutare 478, Gweru 62,
Beitbridge 534, Bindura 302, Birchenough Bridge
417, Chimanimani 523, Chinhoyi 299, Chiredzi 447,
Kadoma 72, Kariba 578, Karoi 417, Marondera 287,
Masvingo 245, Mount Darwin 370, Mutoko 356,
Nyanga 485, Plumtree 328, Rusape 383, Victoria
Falls 663, Zvishavane 183.
Pop: 60,000. Alt: 1,213m (4,003ft). Airport. Post
Office. Kwe Kwe General Hospital Tel: 2333/4/5.
Police Tel: 2221. Petrol: day and night. Hotel.

MARONDERA

Marondera District, Mashonaland East Province.
Harare 75, Bulawayo 447, Mutare 188, Gweru 283,
Rusape 95.
Pop: 23,000. Alt: 1,662m (5,485ft). Airport. Post
Office. Marondera General Hospital Tel: 3646/3065.
Police Tel: 3515. Petrol: day and night. Hotel.

MASHAVA

Masvingo District, Masvingo Province.
Harare (via Masvingo) 332, Bulawayo 241, Mutare
337, Gweru 141, Beitbridge (via Masvingo) 328,
Masvingo 40, Zvishavane 57.
Pop: 16,290. Alt: 1,098m (3,623ft). Post Office.
Nearest Hospital: Masvingo. Police Tel: 10. Petrol:
late hours. Hotel: none.

MASVINGO

Masvingo District, Masvingo Province.
Harare 292, Bulawayo 280, Mutare 297, Gweru 183,
Beitbridge 288, Bindura 381, Birchenough Bridge
172, Chimanimani 278, Chinhoyi 409, Chiredzi 203,
Kadoma 318, Kariba 659, Karoi 497, Kwe Kwe 245,
Marondera 488, Mount Darwin 450, Mutoko 436,
Nyanga 402, Plumtree 384, Rusape 389, Victoria
Falls 719, Zvishavane 97.
Pop: 32,000. Alt: 1,094m (3,610ft). Airport. Post
Office. Masvingo General Hospital Tel: 3866/3865.
Police Tel: 2222. Petrol: day and night. Hotel.

MAZOWE

Mazowe District, Mashonaland Central Province.

Harare 45, Bulawayo 484, Mutare 308, Gweru 320, Victoria Falls 923.
Alt: 1,337m (4,412ft). Hospital: none. Police Tel: 406. Petrol: day hours. Hotel.

MBALABALA

Umzingwane District, Matabeleland South Province.
Harare (via Bulawayo) 499, Bulawayo 60, Mutare 518, Gweru 194, Beitbridge 261, Filabusi 30.
Alt: 1,098m (3,623ft). Hospital: none. Police Tel: none. Petrol: day and night. Hotel.

MBERENGWA

Mberengwa District, Midlands Province.
Harare 424, Bulawayo 164, Mutare 429, Gweru 154, Beitbridge (via Mbalabala) 384, Zvishavane 35.
Pop: 1,323. Alt: 1,040m (3,432ft). Post Office. Mberengwa District Hospital Tel: (321) 8. Police Tel: 25. Petrol: day hours. Hotel.

MOUNT DARWIN

Mount Darwin District, Mashonaland Central Province.
Harare 156, Bulawayo 596, Mutare 422, Gweru 432, Beitbridge 739, Bindura 69, Birchenough Bridge 547, Chimanimani 573, Chinhoyi 273, Chiredzi 652, Kadoma 298, Kariba 522, Karoi 361, Kwe Kwe 370, Marondera 231, Masvingo 450, Mutoko 300, Nyanga 429, Plumtree 698, Rusape 327, Victoria Falls 1,033, Zvishavane 547.
Pop: 5,335. Alt: 965m (3,185ft). Post Office. Mount Darwin District Hospital Tel: 411. Police Tel: 16. Petrol: day hours. Hotel: none.

MUTARE

Mutare District, Manicaland Province.
Harare 263, Bulawayo 577, Gweru 480, Beitbridge 585, Bindura 353, Birchenough Bridge 125, Chimanimani 150, Chinhoyi 381, Chiredzi 319, Kadoma 404, Kariba 629, Karoi 469, Kwe Kwe 478, Marondera 191, Masvingo 450, Mount Darwin 422, Mutoko 408, Nyanga 105, Plumtree 681, Rusape 93, Victoria Falls 1,016, Zvishavane 394.
Pop: 70,000. Alt: 1,113m (3,673ft). Airport. Post Office. Mutare General Hospital Tel: 64321/2/3. Police Tel: 64212. Petrol: late hours. Hotel.

MUTOKO

Mutoko District, Mashonaland East Province.
Harare 143, Bulawayo 582, Mutare 408, Gweru 418, Beitbridge 725, Bindura 231, Birchenough Bridge 533, Chiredzi 638, Kadoma 284, Kariba 508, Karoi 347, Kwe Kwe 356, Marondera 217, Masvingo 436, Mount Darwin 300, Nyanga 415, Plumtree 684, Rusape 313, Victoria Falls 1,019, Zvishavane 533.
Pop: 4,829. Alt: 1,244m (4,105ft). Post Office. Mutoko District Hospital Tel: (278) 1. Police Tel: 5. Petrol: day hours. Hotel.

MVUMA

Chirumhanzu District, Midlands Province.
Harare 192, Bulawayo 249, Mutare (via Masvingo) 397, Gweru 85, Chivu 50, Masvingo 100.

Pop: 5,035. Alt: 1,380m (4,554ft). Post Office. Chirumhanza District Hospital Tel: 401. Police Tel: none. Petrol: day hours. Hotel.

NYANGA

Nyanga District, Manicaland Province.
Harare 268, Bulawayo 682, Mutare 105, Gweru 544, Beitbridge 690, Bindura 360, Birchenough Bridge 230, Chimanimani 255, Chinhoyi 388, Chiredzi 424, Kadoma 409, Kariba 635, Karoi 476, Kwe Kwe 485, Marondera 198, Masvingo 402, Mount Darwin 429, Mutoko 415, Nyanga 415, Plumtree 813, Rusape 98, Victoria Falls 1,123, Zvishavane 499.
Pop: 2,973. Alt: 1,878m (6,197ft). Post Office. Nyanga District Hospital Tel: 316. Police Tel: 212. Petrol: day hours. Hotel.

PLUMTREE

Bulalima Mangwe District, Matabeleland South Province.
Harare 541, Bulawayo 100, Mutare 681, Gweru 266, Beitbridge 421, Bindura 329, Birchenough Bridge 556, Chimanimani 662, Chinhoyi 657, Chiredzi 586, Kadoma 400, Kariba 906, Karoi 745, Kwe Kwe 328, Marondera 615, Masvingo 384, Mount Darwin 698, Mutoko 684, Nyanga 813, Rusape 711, Victoria Falls 539, Zvishavane 286.
Pop: 3,192. Alt: 1,309m (4,320ft). Post Office. Bulalima District Hospital Tel: 291/2/3. Police Tel: 14. Petrol: late hours. Hotel.

REDCLIFF

Kwe Kwe District, Midlands Province.
Harare 227, Bulawayo 216, Mutare 492, Gweru 53, Kwe Kwe 14.
Pop: 25,000. Alt: 1,213m (4,003ft). Post Office. Kwe Kwe General Hospital Tel: 2333. Police Tel: Kwe Kwe 2221. Petrol: late hours. Hotel.

RUSAPE

Makoni District, Manicaland Province.
Harare 170, Bulawayo 609, Mutare 93, Gweru 445, Beitbridge 677, Bindura 258, Birchenough Bridge 218, Chimanimani 242, Chinhoyi 286, Chiredzi 416, Kadoma 311, Kariba 536, Karoi 374, Kwe Kwe 383, Marondera 96, Masvingo 389, Mount Darwin 327, Mutoko 313, Nyanga 98, Plumtree 711, Victoria Falls 1,048, Zvishavane 486.
Pop: 8,216. Alt: 1,430m (4,719ft). Airport. Post Office. Rusape General Hospital Tel: 2363/2365. Police Tel: 251. Petrol: day and night. Hotel: none.

SHAMVA

Shamva District, Midlands Province.
Harare 80, Bulawayo 519, Mutare 343, Gweru 355, Bindura 30.
Pop: 4,617. Alt: 1,239m (4,089ft). Post Office. Shamva Rural Hospital Tel: 304. Police Tel: 10. Petrol: day hours. Hotel.

SHURUGWI

Shurugwi District, Midlands Province.
Harare 305, Bulawayo 199, Mutare 478, Gweru 35, Zvishavane 84.

Pop: 15,000. Alt: 1,420m (4,686ft). Post Office. Shurugwĭ District Hospital Tel: 6466/6477. Police Tel: 277. Petrol: late hours. Hotel.

VICTORIA FALLS

Hwange District, Matabeleland North Province.
Harare 878, Bulawayo 439, Mutare 1,016, Gweru 603, Beitbridge 758, Bindura 964, Birchenough Bridge 891, Chimanimani 997, Chinhoyi 992, Chiredzi 922, Kadoma 737, Kariba 1,244, Karoi 1,080, Kwe Kwe 663, Marondera 950, Masvingo 719, Mount Darwin 1,033, Mutoko 1,019, Nyanga 1,123, Plumtree 539, Rusape 1,048, Zvishavane 622.
Pop: 8,114. Alt: 1,061m (3,501ft). Airport. Post Office. Hospital: none. Police Tel: 206. Petrol: late hours. Hotel.

ZAKA

Ndanga District, Masvingo Province.
Harare 367, Bulawayo 355, Mutare 250, Gweru 258, Beitbridge (via Masvingo) 363, Chiredzi 115, Masvingo 75.
Alt: 774m (2554ft). Post Office. Ndanga District Hospital Tel: 2101. Police Tel: 4. Petrol: day hours. Hotel.

ZVISHAVANE

Zvishavane District, Midlands Province.
Harare 389, Bulawayo 184, Mutare 394, Gweru 119, Beitbridge 372, Bindura 478, Birchenough Bridge 184, Chimanimani 374, Chinhoyi 506, Chiredzi 300, Kadoma 253, Kariba 755, Karoi 594, Kwe Kwe 183, Marondera 464, Masvingo 97, Mount Darwin 547, Mutoko 533, Nyanga 499, Plumtree 286, Rusape 486, Victoria Falls 622.
Pop: 30,000. Alt: 915m (3,020ft). Airport. Post Office. Zvishavane District Hospital Tel: 2781. Police Tel: 2121. Petrol: late hours. Hotel.

Zimbabwean Administrative Areas

Province	District	Province	District
Manicaland	Buhera	Midlands	Mberengwa
	Chipinge		Charter
	Nyanga		Chirumhanza
	Makoni		Gokwe
	Chimanimani		Gweru
	Mutasa		Kwe Kwe
	Mutare		Shurugwi
			Zvishavane
Masvingo	Bikita		
	Chivi	Mashonaland West	Kadoma
	Chiredzi		Chegutu
	Masvingo		Kariba
	Gutu		Makonde
	Ndanga		Hurungwe
	Mwenezi		
		Mashonaland Central	Bindura
Matabeleland South	Beitbridge		Centenary
	Bulalima Mangwe		Concession
	Gwanda		Mount Darwin
	Insiza		Rushinga
	Matobo		Shamva
	Umzingwane		Guruve
Matabeleland North	Binga	Mashonaland East	Goromonzi
	Bubi		Marondera
	Lupane		Murewa
	Nkayi		Mutoko
	Nyamandhlovu		Mudzi
	Hwange		Seke
	Bulawayo		Wedza
			Harare
			Chitungwiza

National Museums and Historical Sites

The National Museums and Monuments of Zimbabwe is the corporate body entrusted with the preservation, investigation, and presentation of Zimbabwe's cultural and natural heritage. This organization has established a network of museums to collect, store, and exhibit objects of scientific and cultural value in a way that evokes the interest of both the public and the specialist researcher. To add to the cultural thrust is an active programme of locating, identifying, and preserving monuments — both man-made and natural.

Bambata Cave, Matobo Hills
Province: Matabeleland South
District: Matobo
Features: This major archaeological site in the Matobo Hills was first investigated by Neville Jones in 1918. Artefacts found here include those of middle and late Stone Age culture and early Iron Age, as well as fine rock paintings.

Chinhoyi Caves National Park, Chinhoyi
(see "National Parks")

Gold Mining Museum, Kwe Kwe
Province: Midlands
District: Kwe Kwe
Features: Opened in 1984, the Gold Mining Museum in Kwe Kwe depicts, through mining antiquities, the history of the gold-mining industry from earliest times to the present. The focal point of the museum is the Paper House, built of *papier-mâché* and wire-mesh walls. It is the only survivor of 3 such buildings erected in 1895.

Great Zimbabwe National Monument, Masvingo
(See "World Heritage Sites")

Dhlo Dhlo Ruins, Shangani
Province: Matabeleland South
District: Insiza
Features: Midway between Bulawayo and Shangani, these ruins have unearthed a silver chalice, a ring, a bell, a medallion of European origin, and two cannons.

Domboshawa Cave, Chinamora
Province: Mashonaland East
District: Chinamora
Features: The largest and most significant collection of rock paintings in the area.

Giraffe Petroglyph, Beitbridge
Province: Matabeleland South
District: Beitbridge
Features: One of the only 10 (as yet discovered) sites of Stone Age rock art. This sophisticated engraving depicts a giraffe.

Gulubhwe Cave, Matobo
Province: Matabeleland South
District: Matobo
Features: The rock painting of this site, east of the Matobo Hills National Park, include the depiction of a 4.5m serpent with small human figures placed on its back.

Heroes' Acre, Harare
Province: Mashonaland East
District: Harare
Features: Situated 5kms west of Harare, this monument stands as a memorial to the men and women who made outstanding contributions to Zimbabwe's fight for independence, as well as to those who have showed equal dedication to the independent nation.

The 40m-high monument was erected in 1987, its main feature being the bronze Statue of the Unknown Soldier, comprising three freedom fighters (two males and a female), a flag pole with Zimbabwe's national flag, and the Tomb of the Unknown Warrior.

Other memorials have been raised to Mbuya Nehanda and Sekura Kaguvi, two spirit mediums honoured for their role in the first *Chimurenga* war.

Khame Ruins, Bulawayo
(see "World Heritage Sites")

The MacGregor Geological Museum, Harare
Province: Mashonaland East
District: Harare
Features: Located in Harare, this primarily educational museum is named after Alexander MacGregor, who arrived in Zimbabwe in 1912 and produced the first account of the country's geological features. Displays there depict Zimbabwe's geology, including economic minerals.

Memorial to Mzilikazi, Mhlahlandlela
Province: Matabeleland South
District: Matobo
Features: 15kms north-east of World's View, the Ndebele leader Mzilikazi was buried under his predecessor's old *indaba* (meeting) tree.

Mutoko Ruins and Cave, Mutoko
Province: Mashonaland East
District: Mutoko
Features: These caves house rock paintings which depict shepherds with their sheep as well as bat-like and bear-like figures.

Mutare Museum, Mutare
Province: Manicaland
District: Mutare
Features: This museum houses a transport gallery featuring examples of horse-drawn carriages and early locomotives. It also serves as a graphic display of the town's own history and includes a collection of Shona artefacts.

Naletale Ruins, Shangani

Province: Matabeleland South

District: Insiza

Features: South-west of Shangani, on the Gweru–Bulawayo route, these ruins are famous for the decorative stone wall surrounding their 50m diameter. Contrasting colours set in chevron, herringbone, and cord checker patterns leave a lasting impression.

National Archives of Zimbabwe, Harare

Province: Mashonaland East

District: Harare

Features: The National Archives, storehouse of Zimbabwe's history, is situated 6kms from central Harare on the Borrowdale Road. A multi-functional institution, it is custodian of the country's national documentary heritage. Its collections include the records of central government and local authorities; the papers of private organizations and individuals who have contributed to the history and development of the country; the national reference library, which contains the most comprehensive assembly in existence of material published in or about Zimbabwe; pictorial, audiovisual, and map collections; and special deposits such as coins, medals, and postage stamps.

Its expanding Oral History programme aims to supplement information held in documentary form by recording and transcribing interviews with Zimbabweans from all walks of life.

A small but active publishing programme has resulted in a number of guides, reports, historical works, and reproductions of material from the collections, thus making them more widely available.

A permanent exhibition showing Zimbabwe's history from the earliest times is displayed in the Beit Trust Gallery, supplemented by a number of special exhibitions to mark historic events or subjects. These displays afford the viewer an insight into the wealth of material available in the archives.

Access to the facilities and collections of the National Archives is free of charge to the general public and to researchers wishing to carry out in-depth studies.

The National Art Gallery, Harare

Province: Mashonaland East

District: Harare

Features: This modern building, located near Harare Gardens in Harare, was opened by Queen Elizabeth, the Queen Mother, in 1957. The gallery hosts many annual exhibitions of painting, graphic art, sculpture, craft, and textiles, as well as films.

The National Museum, Bulawayo

Province: Matabeleland North

District: Bulawayo

Features: Located in the city's Centenary Park, this colosseum-style museum houses a mammal collection of over 75,000 species — the largest and finest such collection in southern Africa and the eighth-largest in the world — including the world's second-largest mounted animal, the "Doddieburn Elephant".

The museum also contains exhibits illustrating the history, mineral wealth, and wildlife of Zimbabwe.

Nswatungi Cave, Matobo Hills

Province: Matabeleland South

District: Matobo

Features: The beautifully painted walls of these caves, 6kms south-west of World's View, are considered to be among the most outstanding in Africa. Giraffes are depicted through fine polychrome pictures.

Nyanga Ruins, Nyanga

Province: Manicaland

District: Nyanga

Features: These ruins cover most of the present-day Nyanga District and are the largest concentration of stone ruins in the country, being attributed to the Nsenga or other non-Shona immigrants from the north.

Pomongwe Caves, Matobo Hills

Province: Matabeleland South

District: Matobo

Features: These caves were once the most easily accessible in the Matobo Hills, but in 1970 the paintings they house were mostly destroyed in an unsuccessful attempt to permanently preserve them.

The Railway Museum, Bulawayo

Province: Matabeleland North

District: Bulawayo

Features: This museum houses engines, rolling stock, and exhibits of machinery dating back to the early days of this century. Antique locomotives and the "museum on wheels" — a beautifully restored 1904 passenger coach — take the visitor back in time.

Silozwane Cave, Matobo Hills

Province: Matabeleland South

District: Matobo

Features: This important rock painting site is located on the southern edge of the Matobo Hills. The paintings feature animals and humans who were probably Bantu-speaking agriculturalists.

Somerby Cave, Somerby

Province: Mashonaland East

District: Harare

Features: These caves located east of Lake McIlwaine Recreational Park contain rock painting depictions of hippopotamuses.

World's View, Matobo Hills

Province: Matabeleland South

District: Matobo

Features: This granite kopje was chosen for its

magnificent view by Rhodes as his permanent resting place. Also buried here are L.S. Jameson, Charles Coghlan, and members of the Shangani Patrol.

The Zimbabwe Military Museum (Midlands Museum), Gweru
Province: Midlands
District: Gweru
Features: The museum serves as the national military museum and is divided into an army gallery, an air force gallery, and a military history gallery. Together they house unique collections of arms, uniforms, medals, and planes dating from the wars of liberation (1896–1980) and both world wars.

Zimbabwe Museum of Human Sciences or Queen Victoria Museum, Harare
Province: Mashonaland East
District: Harare
Features: First opened in 1964, this museum houses a library, exhibition galleries, and a model 19th-century Shona village, in addition to holding ethnographic and archaeological collections. Exhibits are divided into 2 main themes: the story of man and the story of mammals in Mashonaland. The museum also has the largest collection of eggs (16,000) and nests (100) in Africa, and a fossil collection dating back more than 200 million years.

Other National Monuments (with Districts)

Amadzimba Cave, Matobo (Archaeological)
Ancient Park (Mbagazowa), Guruve (Archaeological)
Blakiston-Routledge Memorial, Mazowe (Historical)
Bridge Paintings, Harare (Archaeological)
BSAC Lion, Government House, Bulawayo (Historical)
Bumboosie Ruins and Rock Carving, Hwange (Archaeological)
Cecil House, Harare (Historical)
Chamavara Cave, Masvingo (Archaeological)
Chibvumani Ruins, Bikita (Archaeological)
Chikupu Cave, Bindura (Archaeological)
Chiswingo Ruins, Bindura (Archaeological)
Chiwawa's Ruins, Guruve (Archaeological)
Chumnumgwa Ruins, Mberengwa (Archaeological)
Coach House and Stables, Government House, Bulawayo (Historical)
Crocodile Men Paintings, (Glen Norah) Harare (Archaeological)
Dambarare, Portuguese Trading Fair, Mazowe (Archaeological)
Diana's Vow Cave, Makoni (Archaeological)
Elephant Cave, Mtoko (Archaeological)

Filabusi Memorial, Insiza (Historical)
Fort Alderson, Mazowe (Historical)
Fort Gibbs, Gweru (Historical)
Fort Ingwenya, Bulawayo (Historical)
Fort Mazoe, Mazowe (Historical)
Fort Mhondoro, Chegutu (Historical)
Fort Rixon Memorial, Fort Rixon (Historical)
Fort Tuli, Gwanda (Historical)
Fort Umlugulu, Bulawayo (Historical)
Fossil Dinosaur, Nyamandhlovu (Geological)
Gambarimwe Cave, Mutoko (Archaeological)
Geological Unconformity, Matobo (Geological)
Grain Aims, Mzingwane (Archaeological)
Harare Toposcope, Harare (Historical)
Harleigh Farm, Rusape Cave, Makoni (Archaeological)
Hartley Hill Fortification, Chegutu (Historical)
Hillside Dams, Bulawayo (Archaeological)
Horse Trough (Victoria), Government House, Bulawayo (Historical)
Impala Dam Painting, Shurugwi (Archaeological)
John Lee's House, Bulalima-Mangwe (Historical)
Kagubi's Stronghold, Chegutu (Historical)
Kagumbudzi Ruins, Buhera (Archaeological)
Kamwahuku Fossil Forest, Hurungwe (Geological)
Khame Waterworks Stone Age Site, Bulawayo (Archaeological)
Kongesi Ruins, Filabusi (Archaeological)
Kopje House, Mutare (Historical)
Laager Site Battle, Bulawayo (Historical)
Lekker Water Ruins, Marondera (Archaeological)
Lobengula's Grave, Binga (Historical)
Old Jesuit Mission, Sauerdale, Bulawayo (Historical)
Old Mangwe Fort, Bulalima-Mangwe (Historical)
Mabokisi Fossil Forest, Guruve (Geological)
MacDougall Weir, Canals and Tunnel, Chiredzi (Historical)
Majiri Ruins, Masvingo (Archaeological)
Makaha Fort, Mutoko (Historical)
Mambo Memorial, Bubi (Historical)
Manemba Hill Cave and Paintings, Mutoko (Archaeological)
Mangwe Memorial, Bulawayo (Historical)
Markwe Cave, Marondera (Archaeological)
Matanda Chiwawa Ruin, Guruve (Archaeological)
Matobo Railway Terminus, Bulawayo (Historical)
Melsetter Falls (Bridal Veil), Melsetter (Scenic)
Memorial Cross, Mutare (Historical)
Missionary Tree, Bulawayo (Historical)
Mother Patrick and Mortuary (Pioneer Hospital), Harare (Historical)
Mtoa Ruins, Hwange (Archaeological)
Muchuchu Ruins, Buhera (Archaeological)
Mushayamombe's Kraal, Chegutu (Historical)
Musimbira Ruins, Masvingo (Archaeological)
Mutóta's Ruins, Guruve (Archaeological)
Mutowa Ruins, Buhera (Archaeological)
Nanke Cave, Matobo Hills (Archaeological)

Ntaba Za Ka Mambo Ruins, Bubi (Archaeological)
Nyahokwe Ruins, Nyanga (Archaeological)
Old Bulawayo, Matobo (Historical)
Old Foot Bridge, Bembezana River, Mazowe (Historical)
Old Fort Victoria, Masvingo (Historical)
Old Magistrate's Court, Gweru (Historical)
Old Mission Site, Inyati, Bubi (Historical)
Old Stock Exchange, Gweru (Historical)
Orbicular Granite Site, Mzingwane (Geological)
Portuguese Earthworks, Luanze, Matobo (Archaeological)
Portuguese Fort, Aggwa, Lomagundi (Historical)
Portuguese Luanzo Forts, Mutoko (Archaeological)
Regina Ruins, Insiza (Archaeological)
Rhodes' Hut, Bulawayo (Historical)
Rhodes' Summer House, Matobo (Historical)
Rhodes' Stable, Matobo (Historical)
Ruswingo we Kasekete Ruins, Guruve (Archaeological)

Selous House, Mzingwane (Historical)
Settler Tree, Mutare (Historical)
Site of Telegraph Office, Mazowe (Historical)
Site of the Battle of Bembesi, Bulawayo (Historical)
Strip Road — Melfort, Melfort (Historical)
Strip Road — Old Lundi Bridge, Masvingo (Historical)
Stromatolite Deposit, Huntsman Quarry, Bubi (Geological)
Surtic Farm Rock Paintings, Mazowe (Archaeological)
The Painted Cave on Machela Hill, Gwanda (Archaeological)
The Trek Memorial, Melsetter, Save (Historical)
Tohwechipi Grave, Buhera (Historical)
Umvutsha Kraal, Bulawayo (Historical)
Van Niekerk Ruins (Dziwa), Nyanga (Archaeological)
Zwongembe Ruins, Darwin (Archaeological)

Public Holidays

January 1	New Year's Day
March/April	Good Friday
	Easter Saturday
	Easter Sunday
	Easter Monday
April 12	Defence Forces' Day
April 18	Independence Day
April 19	Defence Forces' Day
May 1	Worker's Day
May 25	Africa Day
December 25	Christmas Day
December 26	Boxing Day

Calendar of Annual Events

Borrowdale Arts and Crafts Fair

National Theatre Festival

National Tree Planting Day — December

Zimbabwe International Trade Fair, Bulawayo — April

Harare Agricultural Show — August

Zimbabwe International Book Fair — August (every other year)

LISTINGS

Airlines

Aeroflot
Karigamombe
Centre
Samora Machel
Avenue
PO Box 6649
Harare
Tel: 731971/2
Telex: 22395

Air Botswana
Jameson Hotel
Samora Machel
Avenue
PO Box UA327
Harare
Tel: 703132

Air Malawi
Throgmorton
House
Corner Samora
Machel Avenue/
Julius Nyerere Way
PO Box 2752
Harare
Tel: 706497/708383

Air Portugal —
TAP
Prudential House
— 5th Floor
Corner Angwa
Street/Speke
Avenue
PO Box 2240
Harare
Tel: 706231/2/3/4
Airport tel: 50586

Air Zimbabwe
Harare Airport
PO Box AP1
Harare
Tel: 737011
Reservations tel:
52681
Bulawayo tel:
72051
Chiredzi tel: 2295
Gweru tel: 3670
Hwange tel: 393
Kariba tel: 2913
Masvingo tel: 2131
Victoria Falls tel:
316

British Airways
Batanai Gardens
Corner 1st Street/
Jason Moyo
Avenue
PO Box 4785
Harare
Tel: 794622/3
Airport tel: 52055
Reservations tel:
794616

Ethiopian Airlines
Cabs Centre
Jason Moyo
Avenue
Harare
Tel: 790705/
6,795215/6
Telex: 22487

Kenya Airways
Stanley House
Jason Moyo
Avenue
PO Box 2490
Harare
Tel: 792181
Telex: 22512

KLM
Harvest House
Baker Avenue
PO Box 4500
Harare
Tel: 705430/704238
Telex: 22463

Qantas
Karigamombe
Centre
Union Avenue
Harare
Tel: 795931/
794676/7
Telex: 24809
Airport tel: 732789
Reservations tel:
737011

Zambia Airways
Pearl Assurance
Building
1st Street
PO Box 4778
Harare
Tel:793235/6/7
Telex: 26497
Bulawayo tel:
64661/2

Air Charter Companies

Astra Air
Charles Prince
Airport
PO Box HG300
Highlands
Harare
Tel: 796361
Telex: 243335

Executive Air
PO Box EH96
Emerald Hill
Harare
Tel: 32959/32999/
23659
Telex: 22393

United Air Charters
PO Box AP50
Harare Airport
Harare
Tel: 731713/731715
Telex: 24132
Victoria Falls tel:
4530/4220
Kariba tel: 2321/2

Airports

Buffalo Range
Airport
PO Box 12
Chiredzi
Tel: 2444/2720

Charles Prince
Aerodrome
Mount Hamden
Harare
Manager tel:
35543/4
Manager residence
tel: 720036

Harare
International
Airport
P/Bag 6002
Harare Airport
Harare
Tel: 50422
Telex: 4738

Hwange National
Park Aerodrome
Dete
Tel: 313/314

Kariba Aerodrome
Kariba
Tel: 2912/220711

Masvingo
Aerodrome
PO Box 149
Masvingo
Tel: 2106

Victoria Falls
Airport
Victoria Falls
Tel: 4255

Foreign Diplomatic Missions

Harare

Algeria
8 Pascoe Avenue
Belgravia
PO Box 2929
Tel: 726619/
726682/726689
Telex: 24795

Angola
Doncaster House
Corner Speke
Avenue/Angwa
Street
PO Box 3590
Tel: 790675/790070

Argentina
10th Floor — Club
Chambers
Baker Avenue
PO Box 2770
Tel: 730075/730076

Australia
4th Floor —
Karigamombe
Centre
Union Avenue
Tel: 794591/
729274/7
Fax: 704644

Austria
Room 216 — New
Shell House
30 Samora Machel
Avenue
PO Box 4120
Tel: 702921/702922

Bangladesh
8 Birchenough
Road
Old Alexandra
Park
PO Box 3040
Tel: 727004/702720
Telex: 24806

Belgium
8th Floor — NCR
House
Samora Machel
Avenue
PO Box 2522
Tel: 793306/793307

Botswana
22 Phillips Avenue
Belgravia
Tel: 729551/729553
Telex: 22663

Brazil
9th Floor — Old
Mutual Centre
3rd Street/Jason
Moyo Avenue
PO Box 2530
Tel: 730775/
732727/732728
Telex: 22205

Bulgaria
15 Maasdorp
Avenue
Tel: 730509/732504

Canada
45 Baines Avenue
PO Box 1430
Tel: 733881

China
30 Baines Avenue
PO Box 4749
Tel: 724572

Cuba
5 Phillips Avenue
Belgravia
PO Box 4139
Tel: 720256/720257
Telex: 24783

Czechoslovakia
104 Vanguard
House
Corner Jason Moyo
Avenue/4th Street
PO Box HG72
Tel: 700636

Denmark
1st Floor/
UDC Centre
59 Union Avenue
PO Box 4711
Tel: 790398/9
Telex: 24677

Egypt
PO Box A433
Avondale
Tel: 303497
Telex: 24653

Ethiopia
14 Lanark Road
Belgravia
PO Box 2745
Tel: 725822/725823

Finland
3rd Floor —
Karigamombe
Centre
PO Box 5300
Tel: 707344/704499
Telex: 24813

France
Ranelagh Road
PO Box 1378
Highlands
Tel: 48096

German
Democratic
Republic
2 Ceres Road
PO Box 4540
Avondale
Tel: 302272

Germany, Federal
Republic of
14 Samora Machel
Avenue
Tel: 702368

Hungary
20 Lanark Road
Belgravia
PO Box 3594
Tel: 733528
Telex: 24237

India
12 Natal Road
PO Box 4620
Belgravia
Tel: 795955/795956

Indonesia
26 Wavell Road
Highlands
Tel: 46809

Iran
8 Allan Wilson
Avenue
Belgravia
PO Box A293
Avondale
Tel: 727348/726942

Iraq
21 Lawson Avenue
Milton Park
PO Box 3453
Tel: 725727
Telex: 24595

Italy
7 Bartholomew
Close
PO Box 1062
Greendale
Tel: 48199/47279

Japan
Karigamombe
Centre
Union Avenue
PO Box 2170
Tel: 790108

Kenya
95 Park Lane
PO Box 4069
Tel: 790847/792901

Korea
10 "50s" Flats
102 Josiah
Chinamano
Avenue
PO Box 4754
Tel: 724052/724067

Libya
124–126 Harare
Street
PO Box 4310
Tel: 728381/3

Malawi
42–44 Harare Street
PO Box 321
Tel: 705611/3
Telex: 24467

Mozambique
18 Walton Street
Tel: 883125

Netherlands
47 Enterprise Road
Highlands
Tel: 793138

Nigeria
36 Samora Machel
Avenue
PO Box 4742
Tel: 790765
Telex: 24473

Norway
92 Josiah
Chinamano
Avenue
PO Box 4276
Tel: 792419
Telex: 24550

Pakistan
11 Van Praagh
Avenue
Milton Park
PO Box 3050
Tel: 720293/794264

Peru
8th Floor Zimnat
House
Corner 3rd Street/
Baker Avenue
Tel: 736751/3

Poland
16 Cork Road
Belgravia
PO Box 3932
Tel: 732159

Portugal
10 Samora Machel
Avenue
Tel: 725107

Romania
Corner 4th Street/
Josiah Chinamano
Avenue
Tel: 700853

South Africa
(Trade Mission)
Temple Bar House
Baker Avenue
Tel: 707901
Telex: 24777

Spain
16 Phillips Avenue
Belgravia
PO Box 3300
Tel: 738681/2

Sudan
4 Pascoe Avenue
Belgravia
Tel: 725240

Sweden
Pegasus House
Samora Machel
Avenue
PO Box 4110
Tel: 790651

Switzerland
9 Lanark Road
Belgravia
PO Box 3440
Tel: 703997/8

Tanzania
23 Baines Avenue
PO Box 4841
Tel: 724173

Union Soviet
Socialist Republic
70 Fife Avenue
Tel: 720358

United Kingdom
Stanley House
Jason Moyo
Avenue
PO Box 4490
Tel: 793781/728716
Telex: 24607

United States
Arax House
172 Herbert
Chitepo Avenue
PO Box 3340
Tel: 794521
USAID tel: 720739
USIS tel: 728959

Vietnam
14 Carlisle Drive
Alexandra Park
Tel: 701118

Yugoslavia
1 Lanark Road
Belgravia
Tel: 738668/9

Zaire
Rm 412 Shell
House
Samora Machel
Avenue
Tel: 730893

Zambia
Zambia House
Union Avenue
PO Box 4698
Tel: 790851

Zimbabwe Missions Abroad

Algeria
5 Chemin des
Viellards
Bouzareh
Algiers
Tel: 178250/798517

Belgium
21–22 Avenue des
Arts
B–1040 Brussels
Tel: 2308551/
2308535/2308567

Botswana
IGI Building First
Floor
PO Box 1232
Gaborone
Tel: 4495/6/7

Canada
112 Kent Street
Place de Ville
Tower "B"
Ottawa
Ontario KIP 5P2
Tel: 2374388/
2374389

China
No 7 Dong San Jie
San Li Tun 8
Beijing PR.C
Tel: 523795/
523665/523397

Cuba
Hotel Habana
Rivera
Calle Paseoy
Malecon
Vedado
La Habana 4
Tel: 30505155

Ethiopia
PO Box 5624
Addis Ababa
Tel: 183872/183877

France
5 Rue De Tilsitt
Paris 75008
Tel: 7634831

German
Democratic
Republic
1080 Berlin
Otto Grotewohl
Strasse 3A/IV
Tel: 2202056

Germany, Federal
Republic of
Vitoriastrasse 28
5300 Bonn 2
Tel: 356071/2

India
B–1/42
Safdarjung Enclave
New Delhi 110029
Tel: 601620/68598

Japan
11–23 Minami
Ababu
2 Chome, Minatoku
Tokyo 106
Tel: 4730266/
473248

Kenya
6th Floor ICDC
Building
PO Box 30806
Nairobi
Tel: 721071/73/
76/45

Malawi
7th Floor Gemini
House
PO Box 30187
Lilongwe 3
Tel: 733997/
733458/733988

Mozambique
Caiza Postal 743
Maputo
Tel: 744201

Nigeria
6 Kasumu
Ekemonde Street
Victoria Island
PO Box 50247
Ikoyi, Lagos
Tel: 619328

Romania
52 Galati Street
Bucharest
Tel: 246695

Senegal
Post Bag 2762
KM 6 Route De
Quaskam
Dakar
Tel: 230325/222135

Sweden
Oxtoget 5
10390 Stockholm
Tel: 304355/
32595/20572

Switzerland
250 Route de
Lausanne
Chemin du Rivage
1292 Chambesy
Geneva
Tel: 320434/320119

Tanzania
Plot 439 Maliki
Road
Upanda West
PO Box 20762
Dar es Salaam
Tel: 30455/32595

Union of Soviet
Socialist Republics
Serpov Per 6
Moscow
Tel: 2484367

United Kingdom
Zimbabwe House
429 Strand
London WC2R
OSA
Tel: 8367755

United States of
America
2851 McGill
Terrace NW
Washington DC
20008
Tel: 3327100
and
19 East 47th Street
New York, NY
10017
Tel: 9805084/
9809511

Yugoslavia
No 9 Perside
Milenkovic
Senjak
Belgrade
Tel: 647047/057/
058

Zambia
4th Floor Ulenda
House
PO Box 33491
Lusaka
Tel: 219025/219026

Zimbabwe Tourist Offices

Bulawayo Publicity
Association
City Hall
Fife Street
Bulawayo
Tel: 60867

Gweru Publicity
Association
Livingstone
Avenue
PO Box 295
Gweru
Tel: 2226

Harare Publicity
Association
Corner Jason Moyo
Avenue/Second
Street
PO Box 1483
Harare
Tel: 705085/6

Kadoma Publicity
Association
PO Box 10
Kadoma
Tel: 2717

Kariba Publicity
Association
PO Box 86
Kariba
Tel: 2328

Masvingo Publicity
Association
PO Box 340
Masvingo
Tel: 2643

Mutare Publicity
Association
Market Square
Robert Mugabe
Avenue
PO Box 69
Mutare
Tel: 64711

Victoria Falls
Publicity
Association
PO Box 97
Victoria Falls
Tel: 202

Zimbabwe
Tourism
Development
Corporation
Cecil House
95 Jason Moyo
Avenue
PO Box 8052
Harare
Tel: 706511

Zimbabwe Tourist Offices Abroad

Germany
Am Hauptbahnhof
10 6000
Frankfurt am Main
Tel: 235381

South Africa
2 President Place
Jan Smuts Avenue
Rosebank
Johannesburg 2196
Tel: 7881748
and
Tower Mall Upper
Carlton Centre
Commissioner
Street
Johannesburg 2001
Tel: 211541
and
315 Smith Street
Durban Club Place
Durban 4001

United Kingdom
The Strand
London WC2R
0514
Tel: 8367755

United States of
America
35 East Wacker
Drive
Chicago, Illinois
60601
Tel: 3222601/
(800)6212381

Hotels

Harare

AMBASSADOR
HOTEL (2-stars)
88 Union Avenue
PO Box 872
Tel: 708121/9
Telex: 2654 ZW

ASTOR PRIVATE
HOTEL
190 Herbert
Chitepo Avenue
Tel: 721664/721568

BRONTE HOTEL
132 Baines Avenue
Tel: 796631/795555

COURTENEY
HOTEL (2-stars)
Corner Selous
Avenue/8th Street
PO Box 3150
Tel: 706411
Telex: 2611 ZW

THE CRESTA
JAMESON (4-stars)
Corner Samora
Machel Avenue/
Park Street
PO Box 2833
Tel: 794641
Telex: 4166 ZW

CRESTA OASIS
(3-stars)
124 Baker Avenue
PO Box 1541
Tel: 704217/790861
Telex: 2099 ZW

EARLSIDE
PRIVATE HOTEL
Corner 5th Street/
Selous Avenue
Tel: 721101

EXECUTIVE
HOTEL
Corner 4th Street/
Samora Machel
Avenue
PO Box 3509
Tel: 792803

FEATHERS
HOTEL (2-stars)
Sherwood Drive
PO Box M200
Tel: 28472

FEDERAL HOTEL
9 Harare Street
Tel: 706118

GEORGE HOTEL
(2-stars)
King George Road
PO Box A649
Avondale
Tel: 36677/8/9

HARARE
HOLIDAY INN
(4-stars)
Corner Samora
Machel Avenue/
5th Street, PO Box 7
Tel: 795611
Telex: 2076 ZW

HOTEL
ELIZABETH
Corner Robert
Mugabe Road/
Julius Nyerere Way
PO Box 3023
Tel: 708591/3

INTERNATIONAL
HOTEL
Corner Baker
Avenue/5th Street
PO Box 566
Tel: 700332
Telex: 2679 ZW

KAMBUZUMA
HOTEL
5 Jumbo Road
PO Box 21
Tel: 63776

KAMFINSA PARK
HOTEL
Arcturus Road
Greendale
Tel: 48024/5/6

KENTUCKY
AIRPORT HOTEL
(2-stars)
27 St Patrick's Road
PO Box H63
Hatfield
Tel: 50655/50109

MEIKLES HOTEL
(5-stars)
Jason Moyo
Avenue
PO Box 594
Tel: 795655
Telex: 6063
Fax: 707754

MONOMATAPA
(5-stars)
54 Park Lane
PO Box 2445
Tel: 704501
Telex: 6078

MUSHANDIRA
PAMWE HOTEL
Nyandoro Road
PO Box DH15
Highfield
Tel: 64355/6/7

NYAMUTAMBA
HOTEL
PO Box 33
Tel: 22941

PAMUZINDA
PO Box 2833
Tel: 703253

QUEENS HOTEL
Corner Robert
Mugabe Road/
Kaguvi Street
PO Box 520
Tel: 738977
Telex: 2679

RED FOX HOTEL
Greendale Avenue
PO Box HG28
Highlands
Tel: 45466

RUSSELL HOTEL
116 Baines Avenue
PO Box 8563
Tel: 791894

SELOUS HOTEL
Corner Selous
Avenue/6th Street
Tel: 727948/49/50

SEVEN MILES
HOTEL
Waterfalls Road
PO Box 4005
Tel: 67587

SHERATON
HARARE (5-stars)
Pennefather Avenue
PO Box 3033
Tel: 729711
Telex: 22622
Fax: 796678

SKYLINE HOTEL
Masvingo Road
PO Box 4150
Tel: 67588/8950213

TERRESKANE
HOTEL
102 Fife Avenue
Tel: 707031/790231

Beitbridge

BEITBRIDGE
HOTEL (2-stars)
PO Box 82
Tel: 214/413
Telex: 3227

PETER'S MOTEL
PO Box 21
Tel: 309/321
Telex: 3428

Bindura

KIMBERLEY REEF
HOTEL
PO Box 61
Tel: 6351

Binga

BINGA REST
CAMP
PO Box 9
Tel: 244

Bubi River

LION AND
ELEPHANT
MOTEL
P Bag 9035
Masvingo
Tel: 01502
(Rutenga)

Bulawayo

BANFF LODGE
HOTEL
PO Box 9123
Hillside
Tel: 43176

BULAWAYO
CLUB
Corner Milnerton/
Leopold Takawira
avenues
PO Box 588
Tel: 64869/64860

BULAWAYO
HOLIDAY INN
(3-stars)
PO Box AC 88
Tel: 72464
Telex: 3341

BULAWAYO SUN
(3-stars)
Corner Josiah
Tongogara Street/
Tenth Avenue
PO Box 654
Tel: 60101
Telex: 3242

CECIL HOTEL
49 Fife Street
PO Box 274
Tel: 60295
Telex: 3023

CRESTA
CHURCHILL
(3-stars)
Corner Matopos
Road/Moffat
Avenue
PO Box 9140
Hillside
Tel: 41016/44243
Telex: 3551

GREYS INN
(2-stars)
75 Robert Mugabe
Way
PO Box 527
Tel: 60121/2

HILLTOP MOTEL
Gwanda Road
PO Box 2137
Tel: 72493

MANOR HOTEL
100 Lobengula Street
PO Box 1035
Tel: 61001/76803

MLIBIZI RESORT
PO Box 2335
Tel: 78060

NEW PALACE
HOTEL
Jason Moyo Street
PO Box 520
Tel: 64294

NEW ROYAL
HOTEL (2-stars)
Corner 6th
Avenue/George
Silundika Street
PO Box 1199
Tel: 65764

PLAZA HOTEL
14th Avenue
PO Box 1521
Tel: 64280/1

RIO HOTEL
(2-stars)
Old Esigodini Road
PO Box 1696
Tel: 41384/41385

SELBORNE
HOTEL (2-stars)
Leopold Takawira
Avenue
PO Box 219
Tel: 65741/2/3

WAVERLEY
HOTEL
133 Lobengula
Street
PO Box RY 12
Raylton
Tel: 60033

Chegutu

CHEGUTU HOTEL
135 Queen Street
PO Box 10
Tel: 2223

Chimanimani

CHIMANIMANI
HOTEL (2-stars)
180 Memorial
Street
PO Box 5
Tel: 511

Chinhoyi

CAVES MOTEL
PO Box 230
Tel: 2340

CHINHOYI
HOTEL
Garrard Avenue
PO Box 22
Tel: 2313

ORANGE GROVE
MOTEL (2-stars)
Mugamba Way
PO Box 436
Tel: 2785/6

Chipinge

CHIPINGE HOTEL
PO Box 27
Tel: 2226

Chiredzi

PLANTERS INN
Marula Drive
PO Box 94
Tel: 2281/2230

TAMBUTI LODGE
(2-stars)
PO Box 22
Tel: 2575

Chirundu

CHIRUNDU
VALLEY MOTEL
AND RESORT
PO Box BE104
Harare
Tel: 618

Chivhu

VIC'S TAVERN
277 York Street
PO Box 12
Tel: 2764

Dete

GAME RESERVE
HOTEL
PO Box 32
Tel: 366

HWANGE SAFARI
LODGE (3-stars)
P Bag 5792
Tel: 331/3
Telex: 51602 ZW

Guruve

GURUVE HOTEL
PO Box 32, Tel: 256

Gwaai

GWAAI RIVER
HOTEL
PO Box 9
Tel: 3400
Telex: 3489

Gwanda

HARDY'S INN
Soudan Street
PO Box 73
Tel: 476

Gweru

FAIRMILE MOTEL
(3-stars)
Bulawayo Road
PO Box 1232
Tel: 4144

MIDLANDS
HOTEL (3-stars)
114 Main Street
PO Box 276
Tel: 2581
Telex: 7666

Hwange

BAOBAB HOTEL
(2-stars)
Baobab Hill
PO Box 120
Tel: 323/493

DEKA DRUM
PO Box 2
Tel: 50524

Juliasdale

BRONDESBURY
PARK (3-stars)
Nyanga Road
PO Box UA306
Tel: 241/2/3

MONTCLAIR
CASINO HOTEL
(4-stars)
PO Box 10
Tel: 231
Telex: 8036 ZW

PINE TREE INN
Susurumba Road
PO Box 1
Tel: 25916/388
Telex: 81268

Kadoma

KADOMA
RANCH MOTEL
(3-stars)
PO Box 874
Tel: 3334/2321/2/
3/4/5

SPECKS HOTEL
Union Street
PO Box 113
Tel: 3302

Kariba

BUFFALO
SAFARIS
PO Box 113
Tel: 2645

BUMI HILLS
SAFARI LODGE
(3-stars)
PO Box 41
Tel: 2353

CARIBBEA BAY
RESORT AND
CASINO (3-stars)
PO Box 120
Tel: 2453/4
Telex: 41295

CUTTY SARK
HOTEL (2-stars)
PO Box 80
Tel: 2321/2
Telex: 41298

FOTHERGILL
ISLAND
P Bag 2081
Tel: 2253

KARIBA BREEZES
HOLIDAY
RESORT
PO Box 3
Tel: 2433
Telex: 4826

LAKE VIEW INN
(2-stars)
PO Box 100
Tel: 2411
Telex: 4055

MOST HIGH
HOTEL
PO Box 88
Tel: 2964/2965

SPURWING
ISLAND
PO Box 101
Tel: 2466

TIGER BAY
PO Box 102
Tel: 2569

ZAMBESI VALLEY
HOTEL
PO Box 105
Tel: 2926

Karoi

KAROI HOTEL
(2-stars)
PO Box 51
Tel: 6317/6382

Kwe Kwe

GOLDEN MILE
MOTEL (3-stars)
PO Box 238
Tel: 3711/2/3

PHOENIX HOTEL
Mandela Way
PO Box 30
Tel: 2141

SHAMWARI
HOTEL
Robert Mugabe Way
PO Box 659
Tel: 2387

TORWOOD
HOTEL
PO Box 189
Tel: 2676

Makuti

CLOUDS END
HOTEL
PO Box 112
Karoi
Tel: 526

Marondera

MARONDERA
HOTEL
PO Box 6
Tel: 4005/6

Masvingo

CHEVRON
HOTEL (2-stars)
PO Box 245
Tel: 2054/5

FLAMBOYANT
MOTEL (2-stars)
PO Box 225
Tel: 2005/6

GLENLIVET
HOTEL
PO Box 146
Tel: 2727

GREAT
ZIMBABWE
HOTEL (3-stars)
P Bag 9082
Masvingo
Tel: 2274

MASVINGO A1
HOTEL
PO Box M45
Chikato
Tel: 2917

Mazowe

MAZOWE INN
PO Box 5
Tel: 2243

Murewa

MUREWA HOTEL
PO Box 52
Tel: 72

Mutare

CHRISTMAS PASS
HOTEL (2-stars)
PO Box 841
Tel: 63818/63883

IMPALA ARMS
HOTEL (2-stars)
Fernhill Road
PO Box 524
Tel: 60722

MANICA HOTEL
(3-stars)
PO Box 27
Tel: 64431
Telex: 81101

WHITE HORSE
INN (2-stars)
Laurenceville Road
PO Box 3193
Paulington
Tel: 60326/216612

Nyanga

NYANGA
HOLIDAY HOTEL
PO Box 19
Tel: 336

RHODES HOTEL
P Bag 8024N
Rusape
Tel: 377
Telex: 81267

TROUTBECK INN
(3-stars)
Box 1
Troutbeck
Tel: 305/6
Telex: 81277

Redcliff

HOTEL REDCLIFF
(2-stars)
PO Box 17
Tel: 62232/3
Telex: 3318

Rusape

BALFOUR HOTEL
PO Box 95
Tel: 2945

CROCODILE
MOTEL
PO Box 166
Tel: 2404

Victoria Falls

A'ZAMBEZI
RIVER LODGE
(3-stars)
PO Box 130
Tel: 4561
Telex: 51657

MAKASA SUN
CASINO HOTEL
(4-stars)
PO Box 90
Tel: 4275
Telex: 51650

RAINBOW HOTEL
PO Box 150
Tel: 4583/4/5
Telex: 51654

SPRAYVIEW
HOTEL (2-stars)
PO Box 70
Tel: 4344/5

VICTORIA FALLS
HOTEL (4-stars)
PO Box 10
Tel: 4203/4/5
Telex: 51651

Zvishivane

NILTON HOTEL
Fowler Avenue
PO Box 68
Tel: 2794

National Parks and Reserves

All bookings and enquiries should be made through:

Central Office
Travel Centre
Jason Moyo Avenue
PO Box 8151
Causeway
Monday–Friday:
07.45–16.15
Tel: 706077
or
Bulawayo Booking
Agency
104A Fife Street
PO Box 2283
Bulawayo
Tel: 63646

Parks with visitor facilities

Cecil Kop Natural
Reserve
PO Box 821
Mutare
Park tel: 64515

Charara Safari
Area
P Bag 2002
Kariba
Warden's Office:
Kariba 557
Nyanyana Camp:
Kariba 2337

Chimanimani
National Park
Private Bag 2063
Chimanimani
Park tel: 0-3322
Senior Ranger: 14
Chimanimani
Office hours
Summer: Monday–
Friday 06.00–
12.00, 14.00-
17.00
Saturdays 06.00-
12.30
Office hours
Winter: Monday–
Friday 07.00–12.00,
14.00–16.00
Saturdays
08.00–12.30

Chinhoyi Caves
Recreational Park
PO Box 193
Chinhoyi
Park tel: 2550

Chizarira National
Park
Central booking
office tel: 706077

Ewanrigg Botanical
Gardens
PO Box 8119
Causeway
Harare
Park tel: Arcturus
23720
Gate hours:
08.00–18.00 daily

Gonarezhou
National Park
P Bag 7003
Tel: Chiredzi 397
Office hours:
Monday–Friday
07.00–12.00,
14.00–16.30
Saturday
07.00–12.00
Gate hours:
06.00–18.00

Gweru Antelope
Park
89 Kopje Road
Gweru
Park tel: 2147

Hurungwe Safari
Area
(Nyamuomba)
Central booking
office tel: 706077

Hwange National
Park
P Bag DT 5776
Dete
Park tel: Dete 371
Office hours:
07.00–18.00 daily

Imire Game Park
P Bag 3750
Marondera
Park tel: 2240/2232
(Wedza)

Kazuma Pan
National Park
Warden tel:
Victoria Falls (113)
433526
Matetsi office hours:
07.00–12.30, 14.00–
16.30 weekdays
Pandamatenga
gate open until 17.00

Kyle Recreational
Park
P Bag 9136
Masvingo
Park tel: Masvingo
2913
Office hours:
07.00–18.00 daily

Lake Cunningham
Recreational Park
Central booking
office tel: 706077
Gate hours:
06.00–18.00 daily

Lake Robertson
Recreational Park
Central booking
office tel: 706077

Mana Pools
National Park
P Bag 2061
Karoi
Central booking
office tel: 706077

Matobo Hills
National Park
Private Bag K 5142
Bulawayo
Park tel: Matobo 0-
1913
Telegrams:
"Parklife"
Bulawayo
Office hours:
06.00–12.00,
14.00–18.00 daily

Matusadona
National Park
Lake Kyle
Recreational Park
Private Bag 9136
Masvingo
Park tel: 2913

Mushandike
Sanctuary
P Bag 9036
Masvingo
Park tel: Mashava
24412

Ngezi Recreational
Park
P Bag 8046
Kwe Kwe
Park tel Munyati
2405
Office hours:
07.00–12.00,
13.00–16.30 daily

Nyanga Mountains
National Park
Private Bag T7901
Mutare
Park tel: (129-8)
274 Nyanga
Office hours:
07.00–18.00 daily

Robert McIlwaine
Recreational Park
Private Bag 962
Norton
Park tel: Norton
(162) 2329
Office hours:
07.00–17.00 daily
Gate hours:
06.00–18.00 daily

Sable Park
PO Box 561
Karoi
Central booking
office tel: 706077

Sebakwe
Recreational Park
PO Box 636
Kwe Kwe
Park tel: 247615
Gate hours:
06.00–18.00 daily

Victoria Falls
Rainforest National
Park
PO Box 97
Victoria Falls
Central booking
office tel: 706077
Office hours:
06.00–18.30 daily

Vumba Botanical
Garden and
Reserve
Private Bag V7472
Mutare
Park tel: (120)
212722
Office hours:
Monday to Friday
7.00–12.00.
14.00–17.00
Saturday and
Sunday 08.00–12.00

Zambezi National
Park
Central booking
office tel: 706077

Caravan Parks and Campsites

Bulawayo Caravan
Park
PO Box 1641
Bulawayo
Tel: 75011/63851

Caribbea Bay
Caravan Park
PO Box 120
Kariba
Tel: 2453
Telex: 41291 ZW

Coronation
Caravan Park
PO Box 1583
Harare
Tel: 46282

Ferny Creek
Caravan Park
PO Box 125
Shurugwi
Tel: 220

Gwanda Caravan
and Camping Park
PO Box 70
Gwanda
Tel: 240

Gweru Caravan
Park
PO Box 599
Gweru
Tel: 2929

Hippo Creek
Caravan Park
PO Box 385
Masvingo
Tel: 206513

Karoi Caravan
Park
PO Box 225
Karoi
Tel: 409

Kwe Kwe Caravan
Park
PO Box 115
Kwe Kwe
Tel: 2301

Lake Lesapi
Caravan Park
PO Box 17
Rusape
Tel: 581

Masvingo
Municipal
Caravan and
Camping Park
The Town Clerk
PO Box 17
Masvingo
Tel: 2431/4

Mopani Bay
Caravan Park
PO Box 130
Kariba
Tel: 22313

Mushandike
Sanctuary
P Bag 9036
Masvingo
Tel: Mashava
24412

Mutare Caravan
Park
PO Box 910
Mutare
Tel: 64412

Nyanyana Caravan
Park
Kariba
Contact central
booking office at:
706077

Victoria Falls Rest
and Caravan Park
PO Box 41
Victoria Falls
Tel: 4210

Zvishavane
Caravan Park
PO Box 5
Zvishavane
Contact central
booking office at:
706077

Resorts

Bulawayo

Zambezi Resort
PO Box 8156
Tel: 69433/62441

Harare

Admiral's Cabin
PO Box 139
Norton
Tel: 2642673

Hwange

Deka Drum
Fishing Resort
PO Box 2
Tel: 50524

Msuna-By-The-Lake
PO Box 66
Tel: 50526

Kariba

Tiger Bay Fishing
Resort
PO Box 102
Tel: 569

Masvingo

Kyle View Holiday
Resort
P Bag 9055
Tel: 223822

Mtilikwe Lake
Shore Cottages
PO Box 518
Tel: 2924/2925

Victoria Falls

Spencer's Creek
Crocodile Ranch
PO Box 18
Tel: 567

Victoria Falls Craft
Village
PO Box 49
Tel: 309

Matetsi Wildlife
Resort
PO Box 160
Victoria Falls
Tel: 33521

Vumba

Cotswold Heights
Chalets
PO Box 3101
Mutare
Tel: 2127/2123

Rio de Medaos do
Ouro Cottage
PO Box 719
Mutare
Tel: 60722/2947/
2910

Business
Associations

Harare

Agricultural
Chemicals
Industry
Association

Agricultural
Society
of Zimbabwe
Tel: 705641

Architect's Council
256 Samora
Machel Avenue
East
Tel: 735440

Association of
Women's Clubs
PO Box 339
Tel: 726910

Automobile
Association
of Zimbabwe
7th Floor Fanum
House
Samora Machel
Avenue
PO Box 585
Tel: 707021

Central African
Textiles
Manufacturers
Association

Confederation of
Zimbabwean
Industries
PO Box ST 183
Tel: 702871

Executive
Association
PO Box 8350
Causeway

Federation of
Civil Engineering
Contractors
PO Box 1502
Tel: 720379

Footwear
Manufacturers and
Tanners
Association

Institute of
Administrative
Accountants
PO Box 4469
Tel: 790382

Institute of
Chartered
Secretaries and
Administrators
in Zimbabwe
PO Box 8197
Tel: 702170

Insurance Council
of Zimbabwe
PO Box 4174
Tel: 707496

International
Labour
Organisation
PO Box 3474
Tel: 707134

International
Union for the
Conservation of
Nature and
Natural Resources
PO Box 745
Tel: 728266

Zimbabwe
Association of
Tour and Safari
Operators
PO Box A 483
Avondale

Zimbabwe
Chemical Plastics
and Allied
Workers Union
PO Box 4810
Tel: 796533

Zimbabwe
Congress of Trade
Tel: 793092

Zimbabwe Council
for Tourism
PO Box 724 A

Zimbabwe Council
on Alcohol and
Drug Abuse
Tel: 707990

Zimbabwe Motor
Industry
Workers Union
Tel: 703359

Zimbabwe
National
Chamber of
Commerce
PO Box 1934
Tel: 708611

Zimbabwe
National
Farmers Union
PO Box 3755
Tel: 704763

Zimbabwe
National
Traditional Healers
Association
PO Box 1116
Tel: 790257

Zimbabwe Nurses
Association
PO Box 2610
Tel: 700479

Zimbabwe Professional Hunters and Guides Association
PO Box UA 191
Tel: 730771

Zimbabwe Society of Bank Officials
PO Box 966
Tel: 723104

Zimbabwe Textile Workers Union
PO Box UA 245
Tel: 705329

Zimbabwe Tobacco Industrial Workers Union
Tel: 702339

Clubs

Banket

Banket Sports Club
PO Box 132
Tel: 2215

Bindura

Bindura Country Club
PO Box 21
Tel: 6307

Bulawayo

Bulawayo Bowling Club
Tel: 61157

Bulawayo Bridge Club
Tel: 41412

Bulawayo City Bowling Club
Tel: 69109

Bulawayo Club
PO Box 588
Tel: 64868

Bulawayo Country Club
PO Box 9007
Tel: 49677

Bulawayo Flying Club
PO Box 1739
Tel: 72313

Bulawayo Golf Club
Park Road
PO Box 754
Tel: 61428

Bulawayo Health Studio
Tel: 65989

Bulawayo Hunt Club
Tel: 60030

Bulawayo Municipal Sports Club
Tel: 68992

Bulawayo Sports Club
Tel: 62710

Bulawayo Tattersalls Club
Tel: 61900

Matabeleland Moth Club
33 Wilson Street
PO Box 611
Tel: 62779

Callies Football Club
Grey Street
Tel: 63830

Hartsfield Rugby Club
Grey Street East
Tel: 71588

Lions Club of Bulawayo
Tel: 68255

Matabeleland Turf Club
Ascot Race Course
Tel: 70174

Queens Sports Club
Fife Street
1st Avenue
Tel: 63642

Chinhoyi

Chinhoyi Country Club
PO Box 66
Tel: 2383

Chiredzi

Hippo Valley Country Club
PO Box 1
Tel: 2381

Mkwasine Country Club
P Bag 7012
Tel: 2811

Glendale

Glendale Country Club
PO Box 127
Tel: 416

Gweru

Bata Club
PO Box 496
Tel: 3376

Gweru Boat Club
Tel: 457519

Gweru Bowling Club
Tel: 2339

Gweru Bridge Club
Tel: 4541

Gweru Golf Club
Lundi
Tel: 3493

Gweru Kennel Club
Tel: 2754

Gweru Show Society
Tel: 3230

Gweru Sports and Social Club
PO Box 599
Tel: 2929

Harare

Alexandra Sports Club
Tel: 791126

Alliance Française
Tel: 720777

C.Z.I. Club
109 Rotten Row
PO Box 3794
Tel: 702430

Chapman Golf Club
PO Box HG 153
Tel: 736949

Dante Alighieri Society
Tel: 304437

German Shepherd Dog Club
Tel: 700007

German Society
Tel: 796381

Greendale Club
2 Grove Road
Tel: 44287

Harare Bowling Association
PO Box 8479
Tel: 791127

Harare Bridge Club
Tel: 23994

Harare Callies Sports Club
PO Box 3323
Tel: 722217

Harare Club
PO Box 57
Tel: 739733

Harare Country Club
PO Box HG 159
Tel: 732128

Harare Gymnastics Club
Tel: 735344

Harare Prison Club
P Bag 7718
Causeway
Tel: 706501

Harare South Country Club
PO Box W194
Waterfalls
Tel: 67584

Harare Sports Club
PO Box 1104
Tel: 791151

Italian Club
Tel: 302610

Lions Club of Harare
Tel: 735811

Mashonaland Flying Club
Charles Prince Airport
PO Box 343
Tel: 32922

Mashonaland Moth Club
PO Box CR18
Tel: 720835

Mashonaland Turf Club
Borrowdale Park
Tel: 728771

New Club
PO Box 2475
Tel: 722210

Old Georgians Sports Club
The Chase
Mount Pleasant
PO Box MP 108
Tel: 33168

Old Hararians Sports Club
PO Box 1220
Tel: 791166

Portuguese Association
PO Box 2260
Tel: 43210

Raylton Club
Corner 5th Street/Gordon Avenue
PO Box 667
Harare
Tel: 792233

Rotary International
PO Box 2330
Tel: 702095

Round Table
PO Box 2969
Tel: 720764

Royal Harare Golf Club
Tel: 702920

Zimbabwe Football Association
Tel: 791275

Zimbabwe Kennel Club
Tel: 727854

Zimbabwe Muslim Youth Organization
Tel: 730952

Zimbabwe Union of Musicians
Tel: 52845

Zimbabwe Volleyball Association
PO Box M85
Tel: 39283

Zimbabwe Women's Bureau
Tel: 734205

Zimbank Sports Club
PO Box BW470
Tel: 882588

Kadoma

Kadoma Golf Club
PO Box 311
Tel: 3623

Kariba

Kariba Country Club
PO Box 31
Tel: 2283

Karoi

Karoi Country Club
PO Box 19
Tel: 62001

Mkwasine

Mkwasine Country Club
P Bag 7012
Chiredzi
Tel: 2811
Telex: 9481

Mutare

Cortauld Players
PO Box 533
Tel: 63647

Legion Club
8 Victory Avenue
Tel: 61964

Moth Memorial Centre
PO Box 611
Tel: 63333

Mutare Club
Tel: 62540

Mutare Sports Club
Park Road
PO Box 36
Tel: 61862

Portuguese Recreation Club
Tel: 61518

Round Table
Tel: 60477

Umtali Golf Club
Tel: 60112

Mvurwi

Mvurwi Country Club
PO Box 32
Tel: 226522

Triangle

Lions Club
Tel: 6348

Triangle Country Club
Tel: 6492

Travel, Tour, and Safari Agents

Harare

Abercrombie and Kent
PO Box 2997
Tel: 702390
Telex: 2480

African Escapes (photographic safaris)
PO Box 3065
Tel: 39633

Astra Holdings
PO Box HG 300
Highlands
Tel: 796361
Telex: 24335

Bangala Ranch (ranch hunting)
8 Lamorby Close
Highlands
Tel: 45429

Budget Tours
PO Box UA282
Tel: 790360/720426

Carolina Wilderness
PO Box W83
Waterfalls
Tel: 29565

Centrust Travel
PO Box 1593
Tel: 704313/7
Telex: 26304

Chimanimani Africa Tours
PO Box 4479
Tel: 68451/2
Telex: 26304

Denda Safaris (big game)
20 Phillips Avenue
Belgravia
Tel: 727197

Elephant Hills Safaris (plains game)
PO Box 6638
Tel: 55-247619

Ferry Tours
PO Box UA176
Tel: 42990

Flip Nicholson Safaris (photographic)
PO Box 1380
Tel: 738-442

Gamebirds Unlimited (outfitters, gun dogs, etc.)
PO Box 3188
Tel: 780855

Garth Thompson Safari Consultants (booking agent, walking and river safaris)
PO Box 5826
Tel: 795202

Geoff Cox Adventure Centre
PO Box A456
Avondale
Tel: 35692

Goliath Safaris (canoeing safaris/ wilderness trails)
Suite 336
Bronte Hotel
Tel: 708843

Ingwe Safaris (ranch hunting)
PO Box 1870
Tel: 44910

International Tour Centre
PO Box 4275
Tel: 792575/792585

Jet Tours
PO Box 3622
Tel: 793081/2/3
Telex: 24242

Kariba Cruises
PO Box A 88
Telex: 22114

Kariba Yachts
6 Fairfield Road
Hatfield
Tel: (14) 50305

Kuvhima Safaris (ranch hunting)
7 Cinnamon Close
Chisipite
Tel: 44839

Landela Safaris (plains game)
PO Box 66293
Tel: 702634

Lowveld Safaris (ranch hunting)
PO Box 8408
Causeway
Tel: 47920

Mana Pools Wildlife Safaris
Monomatapa Hotel
Tel:795202/795287

Manica Travel Services
Jason Moyo Avenue
PO Box 3141
Tel: 703421/ 708441/708625
Telex: 24316
Fax: 736003
Bulawayo tel: 62521
Gweru tel: 3316
Hwange tel: 418
Mutare tel: 64112

Msena Ranch Safaris (plains game)
PO Box A 100
Avondale
Tel: 39275/722173

Muvimi Safaris (short ranch safaris)
PO Box 2233
Tel: 34933

National Safaris (big game)
PO Box UA 191
Union Avenue
Tel: 730771

Pamuzinda (safari hotel and conference)
PO Box 2833
Tel: 703253

Peter Garvin Safaris (river and photographic safaris)
PO Box UA 93
Union Avenue
Tel: 302781/2

Phileas Fogg Travel
PO Box 5454
Tel: 704141/2/3/4
Telex: 26448

PM Safaris (ranch hunt)
PO Box A583
Avondale
Tel: 302233

Rail Safaris
PO Box 4070
Telex: 22068

Ross Travel (PVT)
PO Box 3153
Tel: 705969/705970
Telex: 22036

Ross Travel
PO Box 5405
Tel: 795386
Telex: 26336

Safari Consultants
PO Box 5826
Tel: 795202
Telex: 26330

364

Safari Interlink
PO Box 5920
Tel: 720527/722872
Telex: 22171

Safari Operators'
Association
Union Avenue
PO Box UA 191
Tel: 730771

Safari Par
Excellence
PO Box CH69
Chisipite
Tel: 44045/6

Savanna Wildlife
(plains game)
PO Box 1830
Tel: 706661

Shearwater
Adventures
(river safaris)
PO Box 3961
Tel: 735712

Tara Consultants
PO Box A 632
Avondale
Tel: (14) 303182

Touch The Wild
Safaris
PO Box 735
Tel: 45400/48347
Telex: 24614

Trackers Safaris
(game viewing)
PO Box EH 9
Emerald Hill
Tel: 39886

Travel Tourist
Safaris
(big game)
PO Box HG 470
Tel: 44990

United Touring
Company
PO Box 2914
Tel: 793701
Telex: 22173

Van Der Riet
Safaris
(big game)
PO Box UA 191
Union Avenue
Tel: 730771

Victoria Falls
Hunters
(big game)
PO Box 1
Mufakose
Tel: 68311

Welcombe Travel
PO Box 166
Tel: 708067/8/9
Telex: 26438

Wild Africa Safaris
(booking agent)
PO Box 2937
Tel: 68666/69514

Zambezi Safaris
(big game)
PO Box 2554
Tel: 703094

Zambezi Trails
PO Box 825
Tel: 723719/705040
Telex: 26063

Zimtours
PO Box 8052
Causeway
Tel: (14) 793666

Zindele Safaris
(ranch hunting)
PO Box 232A
Tel: 175-8-25825

Banket

Track-A-Hunt
Safaris
(ranch hunting)
PO Box 91
Tel: 3212

Beitbridge

Savannah Safaris
(plains game)
PO Box 166
Tel: 302
Fax: 263-86

Sentinel Limpopo
(plains game)
PO Box 36
Tel: 43521

Bindura

Dombawera Game
Trails
(photographic
safaris)
PO Box 205
Tel: 171-6312151

Bulawayo

Bar G Ranching
and Safaris
(plains game and
ranch hunting)
7 Whitman Road
Tel: 42952

Black Rhino Safaris
(photographic and
water safaris)
PO Box FM 89
Famona
Tel: 41662

Bon Voyage Travel
PO Box 2193
Tel: 74061/2/3
Telex: 33197

Chimwara Ranch
Company
(ranch hunting)
PO Box 180
Tel: 42626

Henderson & Sons
(ranching company)
PO Box 2217
Tel: 68669

HHK Safaris
(plains game)
35 Kirklands Road
Greenhill
Tel: 30663

Inhlaba Safaris
(plains game and
ranch hunting)
PO Box 1472
Tel: 68739

Into Africa
(plain games)
PO Box 2284
Tel: 41725

Ivory Safaris
(photographic safaris)
PO Box 9127
Hillside
Tel: 61709

Lennox Kruger
(ranch hunting)
PO Box FM 264
Famona
Tel: 77540

Leopard Ridge
Hunting Company
(ranch hunting)
PO Box 1348
Tel: 49266/43109

Mitchell Cotts
Travel
PO Box 1883
Tel: 68631/2/3
Telex: 33028

Ngamo Safaris
(big game)
PO Box 467
Tel: 61495

Royal Travel
PO Box 1166
Tel: 69521/2/3

Safari Trackers
(plains game)
1 Hoopoe Hollow
Burnside
Tel: 43207

SM Lurie and
Company
PO Box 8399
Telex: 70975

Sunrise Safaris
(fishing safaris)
PO Box 485
Tel: 67551/2

Sunshine Tours
PO Box 447
Tel: 67791/77540
Telex: 3304

Thunghata Safaris
Group
(ranch hunting)
PO Box 1348
Tel: 43109

Western Safaris
(big game)
PO Box 8488
Tel: 76111/48739

Centenary

Zimbots
Photographic
Safaris
P Bag 9022
Tel: 02440

Chinhoyi

Eden Safaris
(ranch hunting)
PO Box 232
Tel: 279323

Norzim Bush Trek
P Bag 7520
Tel: 269321

Orion Hunters
(ranch hunting)
PO Box 444
Tel: 167-269523

Chiredzi

Binga Wildlife
Safaris
(ranch hunting)
PO Box 129
Tel: 2786

Chipimbi Safaris
(plains game)
PO Box 16
Tel: 251922

Chiredzi Wildlife
Investment
(big game)
PO Box 241
Tel: 2913

Hippo Valley
Safaris
(big game)
PO Box 1
Tel: 2381/2712

Humani Safaris
(ranch hunting)
P Bag 7020
Tel: 2623

Lone Star Safaris
(big game)
P Bag 7004
Tel: 236925/236916

Mokambi Wildlife
PO Box 129
Tel: 2876
Telex: 92327 ZW

Mungwezi Ranch
(plains game and
walking safaris)
PO Box 297
Tel: 2640/2865

Nyayasha Ranch
(plains game)
PO Box 177
Tel: 2557

Dete

Horse Safaris
(horseback safaris)
PO Box 43
Tel: 255

Touch The Wild
P Bag 5779
Tel: 2105
Telex: 51604

Gwaai

Deonsteffen Safaris
(big game)
PO Box 22
Tel: 2104

Gwaai Valley
Safaris
(ranch hunting)
PO Box 17
Tel: (Dete) 2304

Gweru

National Travel
PO Box 1016
Tel: 4477/2315

Hwange

G Rabinovitch
Safaris
(big game)
PO Box 216
Tel: 55521

Hwange Safari
P Bag 5792
Dete
Tel: 331/332

Rosslyn Safaris
(big game)
PO Box 5934
Tel: 70223

Kadoma

Assegai Safaris
(ranch hunting)
PO Box 348
Tel: 3222

Madoda Ranch
Safaris
(plains game)
PO Box 286
Tel: 31363

Sable Home Safaris
(plains game and
ranch hunting)
PO Box 130
Tel: 31413

Zim Ranch Safaris
(plains game and
ranch hunting)
PO Box 238
Tel: 31414

Kariba

Abercrombie and
Kent
Tel: 2321

Astra Wildlife
(big game)
PO Box 55
Tel: 22512

Buffalo Safaris
(photographic
safaris and
hunting)
PO Box 113
Tel: 2827/2645
Telex: 33028

Chipembere Safaris
(formerly Salvari)
(canoeing and
photo trails)
PO Box 9
Tel: 2839

Chris Worden
Safaris
(backpacking)
PO Box 221
Tel: 2433

Dziva
PO Box 1
Tel: (161) 2697

Fothergill Island &
Chikwenya
(backpacking,
game viewing,
river safaris)
PO Box 2081
Tel: 2253

Lake Safaris
PO Box 34
Tel: 2752

Mana Pools Safari
Private Bag 2081
Tel: 2253

Safari Services
Kariba
PO Box 3
Tel: 2433

Sanyati Safaris
(lodges and river
safaris)
PO Box 2008
Tel: (Harare)
795655

Spurwing Island
PO Box 101
Tel: 2466

United Touring
Company
Tel: 2662

Zambezi
Spectacular
(river safaris —
luxury)
P Bag 2016
Tel: 728763-4

Karoi

Call of Africa
PO Box 371
Telex: 41296

Ruwanzi Ranch
(plains game)
PO Box 452
Tel: 635216

Kwe Kwe

Chinyika Ranch
Safaris
(ranch hunting)
PO Box 232
Tel: 247520

Circle G Ranch
(ranchers)
PO Box 7
Tel: 247521

Ingwalati Safaris
(ranch hunting)
PO Box 418
Tel: 36892

Iwaba Safaris
(big game)
PO Box 5
Tel: 247723

Kavisa Safaris
(plains game)
PO Box 220
Tel: 2475-22

Munyati Ranch
(ranch hunting)
PO Box 520
Tel: 247525

Sebakwe Safaris
(plains game and
ranch hunting)
PO Box 44
Tel: 247825

Twin Spring Ranch
(ranch hunting)
PO Box 23
Tel: 155-247512

Va Doma Safaris
(big game)
PO Box 296
Tel: 38764

Mhangura

Sable Safaris
(ranch hunting)
PO Box 153
Tel: 57916

Zambezi Hippo
Trails
(river safaris and
Lake Kariba)
PO Box 47

Mvuma

African Antelope
Safaris
(plains game)
PO Box 42
Tel: 2106

Mwenezi

Alko Ranching
(ranch hunting)
PO Box 9
Tel: 03703

Edenvale Safaris
(plains game)
PO Box 6

Nuanetsi Hunter
(plains game)
PO Box 2006
Tel: 6

Nyamandhlovu

Fountain Hunting
(ranch hunting)
PO Box 20
Tel: 220

Matabele Hunters
(ranch hunting)
PO Box 4
Tel: 23629

Mziki Safaris
(ranch hunting)
PO Box 12
Tel: 187-23624

Ruwa

Zambezi Hunters
(big game)
PO Box 139
Tel: 2567

Shamva

Chipoli Safaris
PO Box 1800
Tel: 303
Telex: 400049

Hippo Pools Camp
(safari camp and
game viewing)
PO Box 90
Tel: 0-1123

Umfurudzi Bush
Camps
PO Box 90
Tel: 31/51

Triangle

Buffalo Range
Safaris
(big game)
PO Buffalo Range
Tel: 6361

HHK Safaris
(plains game)
PO Box 22
Tel: 6423

Lowveld Hunters
(big game)
PO Box 36
Tel: 627917

Turk Mine

Kudu Safaris
(ranch hunting)
PO Box 29
Tel: 0-1912

Victoria Falls

Backpackers Africa
PO Box 125
Telex: 51662 ZW

Gametrackers
PO Box 133
Tel: 4381

Guyu Safaris
(big game)
PO Box 179
Tel: 424513/517

Jed Robinson
Safaris
(backpacking)
PO Box 145
Tel: 113-4486

Kalambeza Safaris
(backpacking)
PO Box 121
Tel: 4480

Matetsi Wildlife
and Safaris
(big game)
PO Box 160
Tel: 4557

Mwari Komborera
PO Box 130
Telex: 3676

Nkwazi Safaris
(big game)
PO Box 45
Tel: 4236

Safari Travel
Agency
PO Box 185
Tel: (113) 4571/
4344

Trophy Hunters
Africa
(big game)
PO Box 147
Tel: (113) 433519

Westwood Game
Lodge
PO Box 132
Tel: (113) 4614

Westwood Safaris
(big game)
PO Box 21
Tel: (113) 4469/
4315

Woodland Safaris
(big game)
P Bag 5916
Tel: 426513

Zambezi Safaris
PO Box 159
Tel: 4219
Telex: 51662 ZW

Zambezi
Wilderness Safaris
PO Box 18
Telex: 3765

Wedza

Imire Game Park
P Bag 3570
Marondera
Tel: 2202

West Nicholson

Darcal Wildlife
Safaris
(plains game)
PO Box 22
Tel: (116) 5202/6

Mashura Ranch
(ranch hunting)
PO Box 14
Tel: 4201

Nyedzi Nyedzi
(ranch hunting)
PO Box 15
Tel: 5605

Tshabezi Ranching
Safaris (ranch hunting)
PO Box 35
Tel: 116-318

Car Rental

Harare

Avis
Samora Machel
Avenue
Reservations tel:
720351/704191
Airport tel: 50121
Telex: 26056

Europcar/Echo
Samora Machel
Avenue
Reservations tel:
702221/2/3
Telex: 24641

Hertz
Park Street
Reservations tel:
793701
Telex: 26158
Airport tel: 50320
Meikles Hotel
Tel: 793701/707721
Monomatapa Hotel
Tel: 793701/704501

Truck & Hire Car
Corner Jason Moyo
Avenue/
Chinhoyi Street
Tel: 700441/2

Bulawayo

Avis
Corner 10th
Avenue/
Robert Mugabe Way
Reservations tel:
68571
Airport tel: 26657

Europcar/Echo
Car Hire
Fife Street
Reservations tel:
67925
Bulawayo Sun
Hotel tel: 74157

Hertz
Corner George
Silundika Street/
14th Avenue
Reservations tel:
74701/61402
Telex: 3384
Airport tel: 27177

Chiredzi

Hertz
c/o Lowveld Travel
Reservations tel: 2295

Kariba

Avis
Oasis Service Station
Tel: 2555

Hertz
Lake View Inn: 2662
Cutty Sark Hotel
Tel: 2321
Caribbea Bay Hotel
Tel: 2454

Masvingo

Hertz
c/o Travel World
Allan Wilson Street
Tel: 2131/2104

Mutare

Europcar/Echo
Crawford Road
Tel: 62367

Hertz
c/o Mutare
Publicity Bureau
Tel: 64711

Victoria Falls

Hertz
Livingstone Way
Reservations tel:
4267/8
Telex: 51649
Airport tel: 32522

Boat Charter

Kariba

Anchorage Marina
PO Box 61
Tel: 254

Blue Water Charters
PO Box 78
Tel: 2971/2

Chessa
c/o PO Box X774
Harare
Tel: 46684/64032

Kariba Breezes
Marina
PO Box 15
Tel: 475

Kariba Ferries
PO Box 70
Tel: 460

Kariba Marine
Charters
c/o PO Box CH 169
Chisipite
Harare

Kariba Yacht
Safaris
Cutty Sark
Hotel Kariba

Mutepatepa
PO Box 78
Tel: 535

Sea Quest
PO Box 36
Tel: 474

Zambezi Charters
Tel: 2553

Bus Companies

Harare

Dumbwize Bus
Service
PO Box 56
Highfield
Tel: 67487

Express
Motorways
PO Box ST102
Southerton
Tel: 63505/6/7

Harare Omnibus
Company
PO Box 3298
Tel: 702121

Zimbabwe Express
Motorways
PO Box ST131
Southerton
Tel: 707288

Bulawayo

Ajay Motorways
PO Box 8215
Belmont
Tel: 74003

Alick Stuarts
Transport Services
PO Box 1779
Tel: 67291

Hall and Company
PO Box 8322
Tel: 65956

Zimbabwe Omnibus
Company
PO Box 1779
Tel: 67291

Zimbabwe Omnibus
and Touring Company
PO Box 1779
Tel: 67291

Rusape

Blue Bird Buses
PO Box 48
Tel: 454

Taxis

Harare

A1 Taxi Service
Mutare Road
Tel: 706996/722221

Cream Line Taxis
Mutare Road
Tel: 703333/727111

Taxi
5 Samora Machel
Avenue
Tel: 707707

Hospitals

Harare

Avenues Clinic
Mazowe Street
Tel: 732055

Gelfand Clinic
Josiah Chinamand
Avenue
Tel: 792244

Harare Central
Hospital
Lobengula Road
PO Box ST 14
Tel: 64695/
64690/64671

Maternity (Mbuya
Nehanda Hospital)
Mazowe Street
PO Box 8036
Causeway
Tel: 705941

Montagu Clinic
5th Street
Tel: 700216

Parirenyatwa
Hospital
Mazowe Street
PO Box 8036
Causeway
Tel: 794411

Sekuru Kaguvi
Hospital
Milton Avenue
PO Box 8036
Causeway
Tel: 726121

Other Areas

Bindura Provincial
Hospital
PO Box 260
Bindura
Tel: 6870/6878/
6666/6267/6291

Bulawayo Central
Hospital
PO Box 958
Bulawayo
Tel: 72111

Bulawayo Mater
Dei Hospital
bulawayo
Tel: 68711

Chinhoyi General
Hospital
PO Box 17
Chinhoyi
Tel: 2305/2546/
2547

Chiredzi General
Hospital
PO Box 142
Chiredzi
Tel: 2388/2380

Chitungwiza
General Hospital
PO Box 8204
Causeway
Tel: 24002

Chivhu General
Hospital
PO Box 94
Chivhu
Tel: 2644/2351

Gweru General
Hospital
Shurugwi Road
PO Box 135
Gweru
Tel: 51301

Kadoma General
Hospital
PO Box 540
Kadoma
Tel: 2066/2104

Karoi General
Hospital
PO Box 57
Karoi
Tel: 6315

Kwe Kwe General
Hospital
PO Box 391
Kwe Kwe
Tel: 2333

Makonde District
Hospital
Makonde
Tel: 2321

Marondera General
Hospital
PO Box 20
Marondera
Tel: 3646/3065

Masvingo General
Hospital
PO Box 114
Masvingo
Tel: 3866/3865/
3864/3863

Mpilo Central
Hospital
Mzilikazi Township
PO Box 2096
Bulawayo
Tel: 72011

Mutare General
Hospital
PO Box 30
Mutare
Tel: 64321

Rusape General
Hospital
PO Box 10
Rusape
Tel: 2363/2365/
2369

Banks

Harare

Bank of Credit and
Commerce
60 Union Avenue
PO Box 3313
Tel: 729372/
794695/9
Telex: 24245/
22009 BCC

Barclays Bank
Head Office
Barclays House
Corner Jason Moyo
Avenue/First
Street
PO Box 1279
Tel: 729811/2/3

Grindlays Bank
Head Office
Ottoman House
59 Samora Machel
Avenue
PO Box 300
Tel: 795871

Reserve Bank of
Zimbabwe
Samora Machel
Avenue
PO Box 1283
Tel: 790731/
729071/739701/
796251

Standard
Chartered Trust
Head Office
Corner Second
Street/Baker
Avenue
PO Box 373
Tel: 708231/2/3

Zimbank
Head Office
Zimbank House
Corner First Street/
Speke Avenue
PO Box 3198
Tel: 726105/6

Bulawayo

Bank of Credit and
Commerce
PO Box 81a
Main Street
Tel: 76201/2/3
Telex: 3452 BBC

Barclays Bank
PO Box 702
Corner Main
Street/ 8th Avenue
Tel: 67811/2/3

Grindlays Bank
PO Box 1778
Corner Main
Street/8th Avenue
Tel: 69712

Reserve Bank of
Zimbabwe
Corner Leopold
Takawira Avenue/
Jason Moyo Street
PO Box 399
Tel: 72141/2/3
Standard
Chartered Bank
PO Box 587
84 Fife Street
Tel: 76211/2/3

Zimbank
PO Box 849
Corner Fife Street/
10th Avenue
Tel: 68751/2/3

Victoria Falls

Barclays Bank
PO Box 26
Tel: (4) 272

Standard
Chartered Bank
PO Box 8
Tel: (4) 248

Zimbank
PO Box 100
Tel: (4) 541

Credit Card
Offices

American Express
c/o Manica Travel
Jason Moyo Avenue
PO Box 3141
Harare

Tel: 703421/
708441/708625
Telex: 3141
Bulawayo tel:
62521
Gweru tel: 3316
Hwange tel: 418
Mutare tel: 64112

Barclay Card
Corner Robert
Mugabe Road/
Inez Terrace
PO Box 1279
Harare
Tel: 706471

Casinos

Caribbea Bay
Resort & Casino
Box 120
Kariba
Tel: 253/4
Telex: 41295

Makasa Sun
PO Box 90
Victoria Falls
Tel: (4) 275
Telex: 51650

Montclair
PO Box 10
Nyanga
Tel: 231
Telex: 81272

Cinemas

Harare

Elite 100
Avondale
Shopping Centre
Tel: 39995

Kine 1 & 2
Cinemas
Tel: 724515

Kine 300/400
Cinemas
Tel: 791122

Mabelreign Drive-In
Tel: 36659

Mini Cine
22 Baker Avenue
Tel: 705657

New Liberty Cinema
50 Cameron Street
Tel: 792112

Seven Arts
Avondale
Shopping Centre
Tel: 302772

Vistarama
Avondale
Shopping Centre
Tel: 39995

Bulawayo

Vistarama
Fife Street
Tel: 67473

Marondera

Sundowner
Cinema
2nd Street
Tel: 3888

Theatres

Bulawayo Theatre
PO Box 731
Bulawayo
Tel: 65393

Reps Theatre
2nd Street
extension
Harare
Tel: 36706

Seven Arts
Avondale
Shopping Centre
Harare
Tel: 302772

Art Galleries

Bulawayo Art
Gallery
Grey Street
PO Box 1993
Bulawayo
Tel: 70721
Hours:
Tuesday–Sunday
09.00–17.00
Saturdays
09.00–13.00

Genesis Galleries
24 Gordon Avenue
Harare
Tel: 702469

Mzilikazi Art and
Craft Centre
Taylor Avenue
Bulawayo
Tel: 67245
Monday–Friday
10.00–12.30

National Gallery of
Zimbabwe
Julius Nyerere
Way/Park Lane
Causeway
Harare
Tel: 704666/7/8

Libraries and Museums

Harare

Beit Trust Gallery
(National Archives)
Borrowdale Road
Gun Hill
Causeway
Tel: 792741/2/3

CAPS
Pharmaceutical
Museum
Manchester Road
Tel: 63581/2/3

Harare City
Library (Queen
Victoria Memorial
Library)
Corner Jason Moyo
Avenue/Rotten
Row
Tel: 704921
Mount Pleasant
Branch tel: 35781
Greendale Branch
tel: 44392
Highland Branch
tel: 47711
Hatfield Branch tel:
52201
Mabelreign Branch
tel: 39907

MacGregor Geo-
logical Museum
(Department of
Geological Survey)
Corner Selous
Avenue/5th Street
Tel: 790701/2/3

National Archives
Borrowdale Road
Gun Hill
Causeway
Tel: 792741

National Art
Gallery
Harare Gardens

University of
Zimbabwe Library
PO Box MP167
Tel: 303225

Zimbabwe
Museum of Human
Sciences or Queen
Victoria Museum
Civic Centre
Rotten Row
Causeway
Tel: 704831/2
724915

Bulawayo

Bulawayo Public
Library
Corner 12th Avenue/
South Park
Tel: 69827

The Natural
History Museum of
Zimbabwe
Centenary Park
Selborne Avenue
PO Box 240
Tel: 60045/6/7

Railway Museum
Raylton

Mutare

Mutare Museum
Kopjr House
Victoria Avenue
PO Box 920
Tel: 63630

Turner Memorial
Library
Queensway
Tel: 63412

Utopia House
11 Rhodes Drive
Tel: 61100

Gweru

Gweru Memorial
Library
54 8th Street
Tel: 2628

The Zimbabwe
Military Museum
or Midlands
Museum
PO Box 1300
Tel: 2816

Masvingo

Great Zimbabwe
P Bag 9158
Tel: 24635/246325

Masvingo Museum
P Bag 9158
Tel: 2080

Other Areas

Gold Mining Museum
Globe and Phoenix
Mine
PO Box 687
Kwe Kwe
Tel: 2211/2212

Murray
MacDougall
Museum
Triangle
Tel: 6234

Media

Television/Radio

Zimbabwe
Broadcasting
Corporation
PO Box HG 444
Highlands
Tel: 793070/
728631/729661
Telex: 24175/24223

Newspapers

Manica Post
PO Box 960
Mutare
Tel: 61212
Telex: 22274

Sunday Mail
PO Box 396
Harare
Tel: 795771
Telex: 22274

Sunday News
PO Box 585
Bulawayo
Tel: 65471
Telex: 33481

The Chronicle
PO Box 585
Bulawayo
Tel: 65471
Telex: 33481

The Herald
PO Box 396
Harare
Tel: 795771
Telex: 22274

International News Services

Agence France
Press
3rd Floor
Robinson House
Union Avenue
Harare
Tel: 793269

Associated Press
PO Box 785
Harare
Tel: 706622/
706633/720925
Telex: 24676

BBC
PO Box 2023
Harare
Tel: 739833
Telex: 22073

ITN
PO Box UA 65
Harare
Tel: 725565
Telex: 24339

Reuters
4th Floor
Monomatopa Hotel
Harare
Tel: 730953/730954

Visnews
351 Gora Crescent
Harare
Tel: 703621 ext 206
Telex: 22613

WTN
PO Box 484
Borrowdale
Tel: 882211/882466
Telex: 24072

Bibliography

A Concise Encyclopedia of Zimbabwe (1988), edited by Denis Berens, published by Mambo Press, Gweru.

A Handbook to the Victoria Falls Region (1985), by D. Phillipson, published by Longman, Harare.

The African Voice in Southern Rhodesia (1970), by T.O. Ranger, published by East African Publishing House, Nairobi.

Avondale to Zimbabwe (1978), compiled and published by R. Cherer Smith, Borrowdale.

Birds of Africa (1980), by John Karmali, published by Westland Sundries, Nairobi.

The Bundu Book of Birds, Insects, and Snakes (1987), published by Longman for the Standing Conference of National Voluntary Youth Organisations, Harare.

The Bundu Book of Trees, Flowers, and Grasses (1988), published by Longman for the Standing Conference of National Voluntary Youth Organisations, Harare.

Bundu Series — Birds of the Highveld (1987), by Peter Ginn, published by Longman, Harare.

Bundu Series — Wild Mammals (1988), by Dale Kenmuir and Russell Williams, published by Longman, Harare.

Cecil Rhodes and His Time (1984), by Apollon Davidson, published by Progress Publishers, Moscow.

Common Trees of the Highveld (1973), by Drummond and Coates Palgrave, published by Longman, Harare.

Dzimbahwe — Life and Politics in the Golden Age 1100 — 1500AD (1983), by Ken Mufuka, published by Harare Publishing House, Harare.

Encyclopedia of Mammals (1975), by Maurice and Robert Burton, published by BPC Publishing, London.

The Fishes of Zimbabwe (1988), by Graham Bell-Cross and John L. Minshull, published by the National Museums and Monuments of Zimbabwe, Bulawayo.

History of Southern Africa (1988), by Kevin Shillington, published by Longman, Harare.

Journey Through Zimbabwe (1990), by Mohamed Amin, Duncan Willetts, and Brian Tetley; published by Camerapix Publishers Ltd., Nairobi.

Mosi-oa-Tunya: A Handbook to the Victoria Falls Region (1986), edited by D.W. Phillipson, published by Longman, Harare.

The Nature of Zimbabwe — A Guide to Conservation and Development (1988), edited and published by the International Union for Conservation of Nature and Natural Resources (IUCN), Harare.

The Rhobank Businessman's Guide to Rhodesia, compiled by the Economics Department, Rhodesian Banking Corporation Ltd., published by Rhobank, Harare.

Rhodesia — Little White Island (1972), by John Parker, published by Pitman Publishing, Nairobi.

Rhodesia: South Africa's Sixth Province (1974), by John Sprack, published by International Defence and Aid Fund.

Rhodesia — White Racism and Imperial Response (1975), by Martin Loney, published by Penguin, London.

Selous Scouts Top Secret War — The Rhodesian War (1982), by Lt. Col. Ron Reid Daly as told to Peter Stiff, published by Galago, London.

Some Common Trees and Shrubs of Zimbabwe Rhodesia (1979), by Graham Guy and Peter Guy, published by the National Museums and Monuments of Zimbabwe Rhodesia, Harare.

The Struggle for Zimbabwe (1981), by D. Martin and P. Johnson, published by Faber & Faber, London.

Wankie Birds (1974), by Peter Steyn, published by Longman Rhodesia, Harare.

Zimbabwe Tragedy (1975), by Enoch Dumbotshena, published by East African Publishing House, Nairobi.

FAX. 734125

263 · 786648
786656
H. 465126